African Spirituality, Politics, and Knowledge Systems

Bloomsbury Studies in Black Religion and Cultures

Series Editors: Anthony B. Pinn and Monica R. Miller

Bloomsbury Studies in Black Religion and Cultures advances innovative scholarship that reimagines and animates the global study of black religions, culture, and identity across space and time. The series publishes scholarship that addresses the mutually constitutive nature of race and religion and the social, cultural, intellectual, and material effects of religio-racial formations and identities. The series welcomes projects that address and foreground the intersectional and constitutive nature of black religions and cultures and privileges work that is inter/transdisciplinary and methodologically intersectional in nature.

Black Transhuman Liberation Theology
Philip Butler

Innovation and Competition in Zimbabwean Pentecostalism
Edited by Ezra Chitando

Forthcoming books in this series:

Black Gospel Music in Britain
Dulcie A. Dixon McKenzie

Decolonizing Contemporary Gospel Music
Robert Beckford

New Black Godz
Monica Miller

African Spirituality, Politics, and Knowledge Systems

Sacred Words and Holy Realms

Toyin Falola

BLOOMSBURY ACADEMIC
LONDON • NEW YORK • OXFORD • NEW DELHI • SYDNEY

BLOOMSBURY ACADEMIC
Bloomsbury Publishing Plc
50 Bedford Square, London, WC1B 3DP, UK
1385 Broadway, New York, NY 10018, USA
29 Earlsfort Terrace, Dublin 2, Ireland

BLOOMSBURY, BLOOMSBURY ACADEMIC and the Diana logo are trademarks
of BloomsburyPublishing Plc

First published in Great Britain 2022
This paperback edition published 2023

Series design: Maria Rajka
Cover image © Toyin Falola

A catalogue record for this book is available from the British Library.

Library of Congress Control Number: 2021950368

ISBN: HB: 978-1-3502-7194-4
PB: 978-1-3502-7198-2
ePDF: 978-1-3502-7195-1
eBook: 978-1-3502-7196-8

Series: Bloomsbury Studies in Black Religion and Cultures

Typeset by Deanta Global Publishing Services, Chennai, India

To find out more about our authors and books visit www.bloomsbury.com and
sign up for our newsletters

To: Bishop Hassan Mathew Kukah

Contents

Preface

The power contained in our everyday speech is enormous, and this informs the translated Yoruba saying that "words are like an egg; once broken, they cannot be taken or put back." The power of words, when spoken, is such that they cannot be retrieved. They can only either be disputed, denied, or affirmed, still using words. Besides the power in the directness of "words" as starters and movers of actions, events, and even history, words influence the vast populace. Words can be secular, ritual, and religious, yet they embody great power and influence, compelling action and reaction in whatever form they originate.

Historically, remarkable leadership or, put differently, the ability of leadership to draw a huge following has often been ascribed to the powers contained in speech, which influences listeners and readers and ignites movements. For instance, Adolf Hitler was known for great evil, just as he was for his oratory. This is such that, despite his beer hall *putsch* of 1923, he moved the Germans by appealing to their sentiments—their grouse of the First World War. Many American presidents—Woodrow Wilson, Abraham Lincoln, and Barack Obama, to name a few—are renowned for their oratorical prowess in massively influencing Americans toward a course of action and consolidating support for their projects.

At the workplace, during wartimes and in family units, mosques, churches, and ritual spaces, words are often used to motivate the human race and engineer a stimulated reaction. Words are themselves sacred in that they are powerful and possess the natural ability to influence many people. The focus here is on sacred words, spoken and written, as they affect religious practices, religious actions, and knowledge grounded in religious beliefs.

This book is about religious leadership and the interaction with texts and practices that express religious beliefs, their consequences, and the knowledge therein. "Sacred words" are used to describe holy texts, as in divination, the Bible, and the Quran, and they connect those texts to the clerics who use them. Clerics occupy leadership positions in religious institutions, be they herbalists or diviners, pastors or Imams. These texts (written or oral) provide the repository of knowledge that empowers the clerics. They interpret those texts using words that connect to emotions, spirituality, belief systems, and politics (influence). In combination, the words and the clerics become powerful agents who shape societies and create intellectual relevance.

So, why "sacred words"? I found my ontological narrative allusion in multiple traditions, dating back to when I was in elementary school. As I reported in my memoir, *A Mouth Sweeter Than Salt*, we used words to seek girls' consent to say "Yes" to our desire as children. We used words in combination with "magic" to command our brains to remember facts. We used words to hurt people, to conjure, to cast spells. The adults used invocation for the rain to either fall or stop, and in witchcraft, words are manipulated through incantations, thereby giving the witches the power to drink the blood of their victims. Clerics can fall on written texts to perform miracles.

What I experienced was universal in terms of the import. For instance, I am reminded of a story in the J. K. Rowling's *Harry Potter* series. A major character, Ronald Weasley, was scared to participate in a tournament, believing he was not good enough. But his friend, Harry Potter, made him believe he had added a "lucky potion" that, according to their teacher, would bring luck and excellent performance to whoever drank it. Weasley, of course, performed admirably, but Potter had not actually used the potion as Weasley thought; the secret to his outstanding performance was his belief in the potion as potent, based on the "sacred words" of the teacher.

The "sacred" adjective attached to "words" here derives from the authority and the belief system around it. These sacred words are mostly found in religious contexts and their belief system. These religions and beliefs in the supernatural or beyond the physical explanation of happenings have formed a knowledge system through which Africans (in this scope) have been influenced. The sacred words, informed by a guiding belief system, influence their followers and engineer practices—both of which are the focus of this book. Sacred words, and the belief in their supreme influence, compel actions and inform practices in Africa. In this manuscript, I link sacred words and the faith they communicate to a set of interlocking variables:

1. The larger context of religion, using the three major religious traditions in Africa (African Traditional Religion, Islam, and Christianity).
2. The faith that the religions espouse, that is, the power contained and influence derived from these beliefs which rub on the minds and inform the actions and practices of their adherents.
3. The religious leaders interpret the faith and the words, as in Babalawo (*Ifa* diviners) and clerics in Islam and Christianity.
4. The key ideas in the words they choose and utilize and how they formed a continuous knowledge system still in use in underlying practices today.
5. The impact of sacred words and faith on their followers: a) the politics of managing society and people; and b) knowledge systems.

Thus, besides the introduction, which extensively dwells on the "sacred words," the chapters in this book, as accordingly categorized, will focus on the narratives and practices which are subjects of the "sacred words" (carefully expatiated upon in the introduction) while fulfilling the aforementioned variables. Put differently, I will be using the introduction to serve as the foundation from which each chapter derives its narratives. Thus, my introduction will carry all the burden of the sacred words so that the chapters can enjoy the specificity of the practices, knowledge systems, and power they contain. The connection between the title and the chapters could be found first in this preface, then fully elaborated in the introduction, "Sacred Words," and finally inferred and harmonized in the conclusion. The purpose of this is to make each chapter

Preface

a stand-alone analysis, completely independent of the others or the title. It enables each chapter to be subject to the interpretative pedagogy of a reader/teacher. This is why the style of writing in each chapter is different but is linked to the contemporary moment as much as possible to make the lessons from each as elaborately broad and deductible as it can get.

Acknowledgments

Hardly is any work produced without the active or passive support of certain excellent persons within one's close quarters. To this end, I want to acknowledge the many insightful contributions of my good friends, Drs Bola Dauda, Michael Afolayan, Samuel Oloruntoba, Samson Ijaola, Nimi Wariboko, and Martins Isaac Olusanya. I appreciate their meticulousness, sustained interest, and perceptive comments, which helped shape the thought process that informed this book and made it easier to understand and eliminate ambiguous interpretations. I cannot appreciate your efforts enough for this project. Over the years, I have met and spoken to many herbalists, diviners, pastors, church founders and leaders, Imams, and spiritual leaders; their interactions with me have made this book possible.

Toyin Falola
Austin, January 2021.

Notes on Sources

This body of work was made possible by interviews with practitioners, Arabic and Ajami sources, and published works. The notes privileged published works, and the contents distilled the information from various sources, including private testimonies of those who interacted with healers, experienced hallucinations, witchcraft, and other mysteries of life. This book investigates, narrates, and expounds on the knowledge production of the three major religions in Africa while drawing specifics mainly from the Africanized variants of the religions.

The investigation was necessary to relate and situate gathered thoughts within the cosmologies of the African indigenous system. This is especially the case with African Traditional Religions, where resources beyond library research were needed. To this end, it became imperative to reach out to practitioners to ask deep and insightful questions, especially bordering on the validity of some conflicting facts gathered from different sources. This was done through face-to-face conversations and, more recently, by telephone calls, recognizing the age of the media and remaining productive within the restrictions of COVID-19 for an onsite study. Indeed, relative to the quality of projected findings, the data were rich, given the wealth of knowledge gained via online interviews.

Also worthy of mention are the Arabic and Ajami sources obtained and used, especially for the discourse on Islam. Some of these Arabic texts, although translated, were obtained through personal contacts with many people from their libraries and research institutes. Clarifications were also sought from clerics. This was most necessary, as religious beliefs and interpretations are always very sensitive matters to practitioners—reasons for religious clashes and causes of skirmishes in the continent.

Lastly, published works such as books, articles, and journals were also used for this study, while the knowledge drawn from them served equally as the foundation to introduce the idea that informed this book.

Introduction

Sacred Words

The wound inflicted by the tongue does not heal but that inflicted by the knife heals.
—Kalabari Proverb

Every day, we express realities—mindfully or carelessly—through words, and, as represented previously, it comes in the dual forms of written and spoken words. Many times, words are spoken to create an effect and written to inspire belief in the minds of the reader or listener in the circumstance of the former. This effect of words on the receiver could range from being simple things like being pleased, hurt, or carrying out an action to more difficult things like conforming to a lifestyle, adhering to a belief, executing an action, initiating a movement because of the word that has been received.

Regardless of whether they are spoken or written, words influence actions, affect beliefs, entertain audiences, motivate a group at work, and boost morale during warfare or trying times. Besides the first two, words have been depicted in their secular prowess. However, their usage and associated power are not confined to the world of men outside religion and belief system, but even more at a critical evaluation, words carry heavier weight at the instance of spiritual inclinations. This is either as inspired by the spirit(s), holy books, or as interpreted from it by clerics. Even more, the belief system informed by these wordings is such that they empower clerics and confer on them the authority to make pronouncements, both positive and negative, within and, for some, beyond the dictates of the holy books. Put differently, the firm belief of people in their clerics, who are deemed the custodians of the power contained in the holy books, also confer on these clerics the authority to as well do without it and make pronouncements based on their personal belief, which would still influence their vast followers.

For context on the secular impact, power, and influence of secular words, I have made some ontological allusion to the work of J. K. Rowling (Harry Potter), national and global leaders such as Nnamdi Azikiwe (first president of Nigeria), Obafemi Awolowo (first premier of Western Region, Nigeria), Winston Churchill, Woodrow Wilson, Barack Obama, and Abraham Lincoln, all exceptionally great orators who pulled large followings with the power of their speeches.[1] The power of their oratory and the influence it wielded was such that Idaho State University in the US offers a class called "The Rhetoric of Hitler and Churchill," which was taught by Professor Bruce Loebs for over forty years.[2] Loebs credits Hitler's oratory prowess and success to the charisma he exhibited as a leader, which eventually endeared him to people. The power of his oratory convinced people he had the right answers to the global depression that ravaged Germany.

A famous analogy of the written word with enormous impact is Thomas Paine's "Common Sense." The impact and influence it had on the American people during the American War of Independence (1776–83) is such that America's independence is hardly discussed without a mention of the book, an American bestseller until 2006.[3] The power of the written word in the book was more about the persuasiveness, the emotions it provoked in the Americans, and the need for that all-important struggle to reclaim their lands and power from the British colonialists. It gingered up and provoked a mass response from the Americans, and, with morale at a very high level, they won the decisive victory.

The previous story elucidates the power and influence of words in the secular space. Think of, like I did, the influence of words deemed sacred by adherents who are guided by these words in both written and spoken form—religious adherents. These thoughts of the power residing in holy words or, if you choose, sacred words, informed my exploration into the profundity of their use and how they influence the everyday life and belief of Africans.

A close examination of most religious settings in Africa shows a predominant pattern. All of the faithful conform to a written set of rules—laws that many of them refer to as commandments or invocations of good or evil, as well as spoken words given by their clerics. They hold on to these commandments, invocations, and words, and gradually, they begin to model their lifestyle after these commands. In the holy books of many of these religions are written commands and laid-down structures to which they must adhere as the faithful of that religion. Outside the written word in their holy books are the spoken words from the religious clerics too. Even when these clerics make utterances outside of the holy book, adherents consider them sacred (like the Hadith and Mishnah, perhaps Kebra Nagast of Ethiopia). And their words still have a great influence on the believers and their lifestyle, who trust the clerics' words, teachings, and instructions, which are considered sacred because the clerics are believed to be custodians of the power of God and mediums to the supernatural.

It is this thought process that has informed the proper scrutiny of how sacred words from the three most recognized religions in Africa embody power, form a knowledge system, influence the masses, and compel obedience. In turn, this translates into everyday African practices, (in)actions, movements, and belief from their point of contact to the contemporary and from a historical perspective, deploying analytical and narrative tools.

"Sacred" as a term generally refers to any object, art, text, or even actions "considered to be holy and deserving of respect, especially because of a connection with a god."[4] Therefore, sacred words could refer to words spoken or written and dedicated to religious activities and beliefs. From this, one can derive that almost all organized religions are founded on sacred words. Sacred words can be written under the inspiration of the Holy Spirit, as in the case of the Christian Bible—or revealed by prophets, as in Islam. Aside from the Christian faith, sacred words emerge from texts such as the Torah, which is associated with Judaism. The Torah constitutes the initial five books of the Hebrew Bible or the Five Books of Moses. The Torah is either written on scrolls or published and used for prayers.[5] In Islam, the Quran is a sacred text believed to be the Word of God revealed to the Prophet Muhammad, by the Archangel Gabriel, and preserved in the Arabic language.[6]

Unlike the previously mentioned texts, the Hindu sacred texts began in oral form, which demonstrates that not all sacred words are written, and as in the case of literature, they are either presented in oral or written form.[7] African Traditional Religions share this similarity. The sacred texts in African Traditional Religions are largely oral and passed from generation to generation through folklore. Although African Traditional Religions largely make use of orality, they also have an extensive body of written texts in the Ifa divination and others.[8] This goes further to show sacred texts are not necessarily written. It is pertinent at this point to further expound on the previous concepts individually, starting with the African Traditional Religions, for a robust comprehension. Sacred texts could also arise from borrowings from non-sacred texts. Once the borrowings are included in a sacred text, that which was not sacred becomes sacred. The Bible borrows stories from ancient Middle Eastern sources, like the Epic of Gilgamesh or Paul from Greek poetry.[9]

African Traditional Religions

In African Traditional Religions, the word "sacred" has a more impressive yet daunting effect on worshipers/believers as well as residents of the community. Sacred in many cultures and traditions is often associated with objects and places, just as much as words; it is not uncommon to come across sacred streams, lands, trees, places, and even persons. It is often expected that sacred objects, places, or persons be treated with reverence and religious veneration. Oftentimes, a trivialization or disrespect to their sacred nature is often fraught with ugly consequences, some of which are administered by worshipers and adherents or even the deities themselves.

Although Ndemanu opines that African Traditional Religions do not have "sacred texts with prescribed doctrines,"[10] this does not translate to the absence of sacred words in African religious traditions. Just as in Greek and Roman religions, orality plays a crucial role in the communication of sacred laws, performance of rituals, and other religious activities.[11] This clarification is necessary given that it might be inferred that sacred words, as operative in this chapter, have their bases in religious traditions and are, therefore, solely derived from the Bible, which is the Christians' sacred text. However, this is not the case as sacred words are those words or liturgical speeches associated with "a god, text, or prophet."[12] Words could also be sacred because they are linked to a community's ultimate concern. Things or words could be sacred in the sense of Peter Berger's "sacred canopy."[13]

In the context of African religious traditions, sacred words are solemn utterances with generative capacities and spiritual or supernatural affiliations. This could include chants, incantations, curses or blessings, markings and art forms with interpretative possibilities, songs, and other spoken or even written religious words, which could be declarations or admonitions believed to be efficacious. Having noted that, just as in the Christian traditions, the creative possibilities of these solemn utterances cannot be overemphasized. They are usually spoken to engender or catalyze possibilities and existences. In the examination of uttered chants as a form of meditative prayer in most traditional religious activities, there is a need to explore the regenerative power of those uttered chants. Those monotonous yet rhythmic recitations tend to possess immense power and enough spiritual energy to invoke cataclysmic or regenerative occurrences.

As earlier noted, curses and blessings are utterances that can equally be viewed as sacred words. They strictly involve the use of words, although some other actions can be categorized as such.[14] According to Frankfurter, curses and blessings are efficacious, liturgical speeches that are reflections of two areas of a single religion. He goes further to specifically state that: "Their linguistic mechanics are essentially the same; and those empowered to do the one tend to be the same as those empowered to do the other."[15] In the context of African Traditional Religions, curses are much more than spoken invectives as they are known to be in present times. In religious contexts, they are rather speeches imbued with spiritual potency. Frankfurter captures the cultural and religious dynamics of curses when he writes:

> But in ancient cultures the curse was a much more loaded form of speech; and while expressive insults and other displays of verbal acumen could also be quite popular, cultures regarded certain verbal declarations—or verbal declaratives uttered under certain conditions—as singularly potent, whether in a protective sense ("Begone, go to Hell, you son of the Devil!") or in a socially disruptive sense ("Let your cows give nothing but poison from this day forward!"), which might bring harsh punishment on the speaker.[16]

Frankfurter illustrates the energy and power in these utterances, aside from the spiritual constitution of the curse that mandates its occurrence; linguistically, such utterances combine a group of powerful words that portend evil. While exploring the many implications of various mystical activities, Hachalinga describes curses as the "most feared manifestations of the use of mystical power."[17] This further strengthens the notion of the primacy and power of the spoken word. The efficacies of the spoken word and the power laden in the words of an elder in cultural contexts, and the chief priest in religious contexts, have long existed in the African consciousness.[18] Hachalinga corroborates this notion when he states that, "In many African communities, the fear of curses and cursing is real."[19]

As independent speeches, curses possess the capability to elicit responses of fear, anxiety, and even repulsion from the recipient; however, the weight of these utterances is better understood in consideration of the speaker. Just as in the spiritual leaders in African Traditional Religions—the Ifa, high priestesses, or priests—are often believed to be empowered to either bless or curse. Coming from the lips of the spiritual leader or older relative who, by virtue of their seniority, is imbued with the power to bless and curse, the efficacy and generative power of the sacred utterances are not in doubt. However, following Hachalinga's ethnographic reports, some spoken curses are often believed not to have any effects; factors like proximity and relationship often come into play. Citing Godfrey and Monica Wilson, Hachalinga states that:

supernatural sanctions were believed to be effective only against kinsmen, neighbors, and those with whom man [or woman] was in personal contact. No one feared witch-craft from outside the chiefdom. Historically, also, it was those who were near who were feared.[20]

Hachalinga's statement implies that the effectuality of sacred words is often moored to particular performative contexts. Therefore, in the context of African religious traditions, just as it applies to Christianity, for the utterances to have the desired effect, mutual belief has to be operative. The fear of curses and other powerful utterances primarily emanates from belief in the efficacy of the utterances. The experiences of Africans with their religious and cultural traditions instill within them the consciousness of the existence of their own personal spiritual body, which magnifies the potency of sacred words in invoking or summoning influence in their everyday lives. This belief system is often supported and sustained with personal narratives of varied encounters. These tales help to consolidate notions of the existence of the spirit realm as well as that of persons gifted to summon and interact with it. Considering performative contexts sustained by mutual belief, it is hardly surprising that adherents of scientific interpretations and postulations of earthly existence do not consider or regard the supernatural or spiritual and would most likely not be fazed by such utterances.

Asides from curses, there are many other sacred utterances that operate within the African traditional religious milieu. Incantations and chants can essentially be viewed as a string of recited formulaic words that are spoken to trigger particular effects. Incantations, as observed by Oriloye, do not characterize an exclusive religion but rather constitute a crucial aspect of many global religious practices, including those found in Africa.[21] They have further been described as a combination of special words from one or more languages, sometimes unintelligible to the untrained ear, either uttered or sung to stimulate extraordinary actions.[22] Individuals recite incantations in the hope of accomplishing a specific agenda. In specific traditional religious contexts, they are sacred recitations reserved for a select group of spiritualists who are believed to commune with the ancestors/spirits and who also possess spiritual capabilities to stimulate supernatural occurrences.

These formulaic recitations with poetic properties are applied in varied situations, some of which include cases of traditional medicinal practices, cleansing rituals, exorcism, invocation, spiritual inquiries, and appeasing the ancestors. According to Mbiti, the incantatory chants among the Banyankore people of Uganda are used to drive away intrusive spirits.[23] Having noted that, the following excerpt is an example of a typical incantatory chant from the Banyankore people aimed at driving away spirits. When translated to English, it reads as follows:

Come and go with yours—
This is your goat—
This is your road—
Go and don't return.[24]

Aside from the cases involving the expulsion of unwanted spirits, chants and incantations are often applied in traditional medicinal practices. Although techniques ascribed to traditional medicine in Africa tend to differ from place to place, incantations seem to be an enduring feature in their various practices. Traditional medicine in Africa, although a specialized area and practice that requires specific skills in the use of herbs and roots, also works hand in hand with religious practices in Africa. According to Omonzejele, the use of herbs in traditional medical practices is accompanied and supplemented with incantations that serve the purposes of repelling the forces of evil while also communing with the potent forces resident within the herbs.[25] In this situation, incantations have become sacred words of communication between the healer and his/her medical resources (plants and herbs). It is also used to commune with the forces that be. Oftentimes in order to identify the cause and implication of the ailment, the healer communes with spiritual beings through incantatory chants, which helps to establish the right ambience for their revelations and directions.

The revelatory incantations or chants tend to precede most healing sessions. This further accentuates the potency and power of sacred incantations in warding off evil and sanctifying the environment for a successful healing exercise. However, aside from the spiritual interactions in the process, the chants and incantations are said to be soothing, often bringing much-needed relief to patients. Ganyi and Ogar further consolidate this notion by noting that although most medical practitioners use various curative agents, such as herbs, in the medical practice, they continue to place emphasis on the power and potency of the word. In explicit terms, they denote that, "The traditional medicine man depends much on the fluency and strength of the word which solicits faith and belief in its potency."[26] Following an ethnographic account of a healing incident documented by Thompson of the Azande people in Southwest Sudan, what follows is the centric and crucial position of sacred incantatory speeches in curing ailments and enabling the afflicted to regain absolute control of their health:

> The little medicine man and his two assistants shouted incantations and danced wildly around the sick man lying on a grass mat in an open space . . . he proceeded to attend the patient. He diagnosed the case immediately, explaining to his assistants that the illness was a mind troubled by the evil spirits of ancestors who had returned to torment the patient. But the incantations had lulled the patient and frightened away the evil spirits. He soon went to sleep. The Azande (commonly called Yom-Yom) tribe of southwest Sudan still treat their patients in this manner. Bone throwing is practiced by witch doctors among the Bantu tribes of South Africa. The bones, instructed with the proper magic words, are supposed to possess the supernatural power of indicating the source of evil upon which the diagnosis is established.[27]

This account depicts a healing session that combines the various expressions and uses of incantatory chants in traditional medical practices.

In addition, in African Traditional Religions, the act of blessing a person is also accompanied by various rituals performed by ritual specialists. In many cultures of the world, including African cultures, older members of society are culturally imbued with unction to bless the younger generation, usually with sacred declarations. The same applies to the chief priest and other traditional religious leaders. The pronouncement of specialized positive words often targeting specific areas of a person's life or need qualifies as blessings among various cultures in African society. A young man whose elderly relative or acquaintance says the following, "may strangers not reap all you have sown," will consider it a blessing that speaks to his lack of children and subtly gestures at the cultural repudiation of the notion of strangers possessing or profiting from the hard work of others due to lack of rightful heirs. Primarily, those words are aimed at attracting the blessing of children, who will reap what their father has sown. This statement contains generative powers to bring into existence offspring that will rightfully possess and inherit the hard work of their parents.

Moreover, in various traditional settings throughout the continent, the power and unction to bless is not solely reserved for the persons receiving the blessing. By virtue of individual power and the strength of one's àṣẹ or *chi*, as believed in the Yoruba and Igbo cultures of Western Africa, powerful and effective utterances often proceed from the lips of persons who are neither old nor possess any spiritual position. Among the Yoruba, the concept of the àṣẹ provides a compact explanation to this presumption, while certain Christian beliefs and scriptural verses reaffirm its validity. Omari-Obayemi defines the àṣẹ as "creative energy, the ability to bring things into existence or to make something happen."[28] He further opines that the àṣẹ is often associated with deities, which suggests that the àṣẹ involves "spiritual activation or manipulation."[29]

The àṣẹ (amen) is a form of power that is said to reside in all persons, objects, and even chants and incantations. In other words, it is the matter that defines and establishes the creative energy a person or thing possesses. In the Christian context, the Scripture affirms that "Death and life are in the power of the tongue."[30] The reference to the tongue reveals that the Scripture gestures at every person, since the tongue is clearly the point of utterance, which every human possesses. If that is the case, one might wonder why it seems that every living individual or object does not exhibit, control, or manipulate spiritual forces.[31] The answer lies within Omari-Obayemi's adjoining statement that "many objects or [persons] possess more ase than others."[32] The àṣẹ is a form of power that is embodied naturally by all persons. It could either be positive or negative. For those with substantial amounts of this creative energy, their proclamations in the form of blessings or curses are believed to have a higher propensity, if not certainty, for fulfillment.

Furthermore, in African Traditional Religions, sacred words are incantations, curses, or blessings, ritual chants, markings, etc., that are uttered with reverence in connection to particular religions. However, sacred words could also just be chants and incantations to either glorify or emphasize the supremacy, power, or ability of a deity, or to heal and divine the causes of various ailments or misfortunes. They could be words or incantations to summon various spirits for specific purposes or curses aimed at impacting people negatively. A host of many other sacred utterances abound within the African religious milieu; however, the following incantatory chants recorded in Yoruba and translated to English provide paradigms for the myriad incantations and chants associated with healing in Africa. Alongside other medicinal properties, the following words were chanted by the *onisegun* (medicine man) in the case of a patient with severe headaches:

Baba ní larí (Headsplitter)
Ògúdú-èdè (Pure speech)
Ògúdú-èdè (Pure speech)
Ògúdú-èdè (Pure speech)
Bí baba ti n la 'bù la 'rí (As the splitter breaks the head)
Ògúdú-èdè, ìwọ l'òó pa á dé (You, pure speech, close it up)
Baba tí nlárí ní n la'rí lágbájá (Headsplitter is now breaking lágbájá's head)
Ògúdú-èdè wá pa á dé (Pure speech come hither to close it up)
Rééréé ni kí o ré e kúrò (Topple it with Rééréé leaves)
Àlùbọ̀sà ni kó o fi sa gbogbo ibi rẹ̀ kúrò (Use onion leaves to cure the parts that
    ail)
Sákásáká lara ọmọ ikin dá (The divination nut is ever clean and fit)
Koko ni à á bá òkúta (Rocks are ever hard and fit)
Kí ara lágbájá ó yá kíákíá (Lágbájá's body be speedily restored).[33]

Clearly, to the layman, these words are nearly unintelligible, and they know not to chant words they do not understand and that are considered to contain a lot of spiritual power. There is no doubt that this seeming obscurity alongside other ritual activities that accompany these chants add to the healing session's mystic aura. In another case of snake poisoning, the following words were uttered along with other extensive ritual activities:

Alábẹ́rẹ́ orí òpó (Needle point sharp tip of the pillar)
Ọmọ mẹ́ta nì'yáa wọn bí (Three of them their mother birthed)
Ọ̀kan bínú wọ'gbó (One went fled the bush in anger)
Ọ̀kan bínú wọ'lẹ̀ (One disappeared into the earth furious)
Ọ̀kan bínú wọ'nú (One stormed into the stomach)
Èyí t'ó bínú wọ'nú kò danú láàmú (The one that went into
the stomach did not worry the stomach)
Èyí t'ó bínú wọ'lẹ̀ kò dalẹ̀ láàmú (The one that disappeared
into the earth did not disturb the earth)
Ìwọ t'ó o bínú wọ'gbó, èèṣe to fi máa dọmọfẹ̀ láàmú (You that stormed
into the forest, how come you disturb a citizen of Ifẹ̀?)[34]

Additionally, the following example is a Fulfulde incantatory chant that equally accompanies the activities of a bone setting session:

Bismillahi Murgut, fi mata murgut
(In the name of God Murgut, from what has died murgut)
Mi itti murgut, mi wati murgut
(I have removed murgut, I have put murgut).
To manga baroji, Allah jeyi jam
(Where is the main killer, It is God that provides health/recovery).
Min jeyi 'yi' yam (Blood is mine).[35]

For purposes of love enchantments among the Fulfulde people of Northern Nigeria, the following incantatory chants are uttered on the bedside or place where the love interest is expected to lie. These chants are believed to be efficacious and known to be practiced widely among the people:

Bismillahi takkam makkam
(In the name of God, come closer, come closer to me).
Hafam nafam, huuram ba ju be
(Hold me, come to my aid, and cover me just like the jujube tree).
Taaram ba del ʃi, dakkam ba nyakkabre
(Surround me like the ebony tree).
Biilaʼam, a nyaamataa, a dawrataa a dawrintaa
(Be with me like prickly grass, my beloved you will not eat).
(You would not contact somebody for advice and nobody to contact you for an advice).
Say ko dawrumi haa abada
(You abide only with what I have decided forever).[36]

Islam

In Islamic religious healing practices, sacred words are equally deployed. The Quran is itself, among other things, considered a book of healing as reflected in this verse: "O mankind there has come unto you a guidance from your lord and a healing for the diseases in your hearts, and for those who believe in guidance and mercy."[37] Inayat submits that in the Islamic practice of spiritual healing, several verses from the Quran are believed to contain the *baraka* or spiritual powers that are adopted by Islamic healers to heal their patients. In the practice, he notes that these verses are written down on pieces of paper and tied up in plastic wrappers or leather bags and used as deliberate or improvisational charms to ward away evil spirits.[38] Inayat admits that this practice is not recognized as doctrinal among Islamic scholars but rather among spiritual leaders. Islamic scholars consider the practice a folk practice that has no scriptural backing in Islam.

In the absence of the presumed folk practice, there are various Islamic prayers that mimic the concept of chants and even incantations. The *Salat*, as noted by Inayat, is an Islamic prayer that comprises a combination of actions like "body movements, recitation of Quranic verses, and supplication" with specific time frames allocated to it.[39] Although this activity is a prayer practice originally designed to cultivate closeness to God, it is often adapted in hopes of attaining physical, mental, and spiritual healing. In the context of this work, the recitation of Quranic verses is a conscious attunement to the generative forces replete in those sacred pronouncements. The same also applies to the *Zikr* prayer, which also involves the conscious repetition of Quranic verses or the "ninety-nine names of Allah" with the hope of engaging its healing energy in curing physical and mental illnesses.[40] Therefore, the ninety-nine names of Allah are also sacred words as much as the verses of the Quran. This underscores the potency as well as the creative and generative capacities of sacred words in various healing processes across religions and cultures.

Furthermore, the reference to generative powers brings to mind another operative sacred utterance that is believed to engender significant occurrences in people's lives. Just as curses are dependent on the speaker and their intention, the same applies to blessings. In other words, both concepts, although with different agendas, are guided by similar linguistic mechanics of evocative speech and creative energy that derive their efficacy from religious and cultural belief systems. For this connection with religious and cultural interactions and the existing expectation for them to take place, blessings are as much sacred words as curses. Frankfurter defines them as, "the ritual performance that transfers protective power, as well as the object or word that bears that power once transferred, as well as the protective power with which a subject is endowed following such an act."[41] Frankfurter's definition brings to our attention the place of ritualized performances in the act or process of blessing a person. However, it is also imperative to note that these performances and activities are consolidated by verbal utterances or sacred words.

Furthermore, in Islam, there are also existing powerful words, *duas*, that are often used in establishing dominion over illnesses, insecurity, etc. The following verses and prayers will be examined as sacred words which empower Muslim faithful in their journey through life:

"In the name of Allah with whose name there is protection against every kind of harm in the earth or in heaven, and he is all hearing and all knowing."[42]

"O Allah protect me from my front, behind me, from my right and my left, and from above me, and I seek refuge in your magnificence from being taken unaware from beneath me."[43]

These reveal the use of the name of Allah in prayer to establish dominion over forces both physical and spiritual that cause harm to humanity. Quranic verses also equip Muslims with sacred words aimed at asserting a spiritual dominance and subverting the authority of the wicked, such as in Surah At-Tauba, 51: "Never will we be struck except by what Allah has decreed for us; he is our protector. And upon Allah let the believers rely."[44] These verses (upon the belief of the practitioner) become formulaic and generative, providing the basis for many *duas* of protection and healing in the Islamic faith.

Similarly, the Quran also contains sacred verses that provide validation of the subjugation of women and the dominance of men. These following words are sacred, just as the biblical verses are, because they have been culled from the holy book. According to Surah 4:34:

Men are in charge of women, because Allah hath made one of them to excel the other, and because they spend of their property. So good women are the obedient, guarding in secret that which Allah hath guarded. As for those from whom ye fear rebellion, admonish them and banish them to beds apart, and scourge them. Then, if they obey you, seek not a way against them. Lo! Allah is ever High, Exalted, Great.[45]

Words—sacred words—carry powers that give beliefs and influence actions, practices, and movements that have turned the tide of history and so much more.

Christianity

The primacy of the Christian Bible, often referred to as the Word of God, constitutes the foundation of Pentecostal religious traditions across the globe. Christians view the Holy Bible as sacred; most of them consider it as the direct Word of God, and therefore integral and foundational to the Christian faith. Holm emphasizes this notion by acknowledging the submission of the Pentecostal Assemblies of Canada (PAOC) that the "holy men of God were moved by the Holy Spirit to write the very words of the scripture."[46] Several Christian denominations, including Pentecostal, have emerged from and with various theologies and hermeneutics of the biblical text. This underscores the generative possibilities of the Bible as a compilation of sacred words that have inspired various interpretations, hence resulting in the establishment of a variety of Christian denominations.

Sacred words in contemporary Pentecostalism are written, spoken, or institutional.[47] The Bible contains the written Word of God, which confers authority to their practices and beliefs.[48] Most Christians also believe that the words of their religious leaders are directly from God, so these words are believed to carry the same weight as the written Word of God. These written and spoken words have engendered institutional doctrines that are expressed as policies, rules, and belief systems that define Christianity. Put differently, sacred words refer to scriptural verses, inspired teachings, prophecies, creeds, etc. that accompany faith-based miracles and heady proclamations. However, to establish and examine the concern of this essay, these two inquiries are pertinent:

1. What relationship exists between sacred words and Christianity?
2. How do these words bind the preacher and the congregation?

These inquires will be addressed in various subtopics as the essay progresses, and the study will draw the bulk of its resources and information from Christianity in Africa. As will be seen in this book, Christianity in Africa is discussed under three broad chapters. For a thorough understanding of the chapters, it is expedient to first study and understand the Holy Bible—the foundation of their belief.

The Word

It is often said that the tongue can make or mar. The truth in this saying does not lie in the literal power of the tongue but in the power of the words spoken with it. Words are therefore generally considered as powerful because of the ability to either offer *kolanut* (maintain peace) or draw out a sword (start a war). Not limiting the influence of words to either black or white, they also have performative power to alter and change reality.

For instance, priests and religious clerics declare: "I now pronounce you husband and wife," which changes the reality of the couple's relationship to one bound in union.

The belief in the power of sacred words could likely account for the phenomenal growth of Christianity around the world but especially in Africa. Pentecostalism's practice of faith healing or miracles displays the generative capacity of the word that inspires an abundance of miracles that has popularized and proliferated Pentecostal churches across the continent. These extraordinary displays of miracles find impetus in the Christian Bible, further emphasizing the creative or originative powers of the word. Simply put, miracles are the creations of the Word of God. It further demonstrates the word as the first point of reference in the discourse of Pentecostal performativity. Jn 1:1 states, "In the beginning was the word and the word was with God and the word was God."[49] Deducing meaning not from the figurative representation of God as word, but in its impact, one would find the power of words in Gen. 1 where all creations were made with the declaration, "Let there be."[50] A deconstruction of the verse translates the creative potential of the word as a force similar to God. Put differently, the word is primal; it was there from the beginning of time, and humanity burst forth from it. Blofeld expands on this concept by exploring the power of words as exemplified in various etymological narratives of other religions and traditions in the following excerpt:

> To this day one may find in India those who assert that the universe sprang forth in response to the creative syllable OM and, in ancient times, there are probably many cultures in which similar beliefs held sway. Scattered through the works of the Greek Gnostics are passages which lead to that conclusion, and the liturgies of the Christian churches contain what appear to be distinct, although rather trifling, remnants of knowledge concerning the subtle qualities of sound [word]. The tumbling of the walls of Jericho has sometimes been viewed in this light and it is not rare to find people who affirm that "amen" and "alleluia" have . . . a mantric significance.[51]

Although "amen" and "alleluia" are common words among Christians around the world, they are still sacred words as the former implies compliance, agreement, or confirmation in prayers. Responding to a proclamation with "Amen" connotes finality and certitude to the words spoken. Although the latter simply means "praise be to God," it has become a meaningful word believed to establish dominion in the place of prayer and praise in the life of a Christian. Therefore, "Amen" and "Alleluia," by virtue of their connection and significance to Christianity, can be regarded as sacred words.

Reiterating the centric position of the word in discourses of creation, the Christian cosmogonic narrative of creation and earth's inception recounts that the earth is an effect or materialization of the Word of God: "Let there be light, and there was light."[52] According to Christian belief, at some point in the story of creation, the supreme God said those exact words and earth and humanity took form and shape. Words have generative powers; they also generate narratives, cultures, values, lifestyle, belief systems, and contextual miracles, as seen in the value Christians place on the spoken word as evidence of faith, when expecting a miracle. By likening the "Word" to God, it highlights the creative power and authority laden in these scriptural verses, as God is believed to be the author of creation; therefore, this surmises the integrality of the "Word" in Pentecostal worship.

Pentecostals—a branch of the Christian faith—as noted by Constantineanu and Cobie, believe in the sole authority of God and hold the Bible as "God's self-revelation to humanity."[53] The authority of their profession of faith is derived solely from the Bible in the case of many, while some others had personal experiences that influenced their belief system. Nell opines that there is often a contention of the emphasis and importance of the Word and the Holy Spirit in Pentecostal religious tradition. However, he concludes that a non-subversive spirit-word relationship exists as integral to Pentecostal theology.[54] Further emphasizing the dynamics of this relationship, he notes:

> Scripture provides the means to test and direct the daily specific guidance that the church and individuals purport to experience from the Spirit and provides boundaries. New experiences become the occasion for finding new insights from Scripture and familiar Scriptures would take on new meaning. However, it is imperative that all beliefs, affections, and practices should be tested to the Word continuously.[55]

The Catholic Church—another branch of Christianity—with its tradition of reverend fathers and confessions, chaplets, and rosaries is the quintessence of the aforementioned interventionist religious practices that seem to take the place and agency of the Scriptures/Word in orthodox Christianity. The bishops and reverends in mission churches, although centered around the Eucharist, are also representational of the word, as they offer blessings and listen to confessions, but punishment and forgiveness are at their own discretion. However, in Pentecostal traditions, there is an emphasis on a personal relationship with God, and confession of sins is encouraged to be rendered directly to God through prayer.[56] This Christian liturgical emphasis is derived from the supposition of direct access to God and his words through the Bible. Therefore, there is a belief in the individualistic priesthood of every "saved" person as inferred from 1 Pet. 2:9 which says: "But you are a chosen race, a royal priesthood, a holy nation, a people for his own possession, that you may proclaim the excellencies of him who called you out of darkness into the marvelous light."[57] Holm goes ahead to assert that Christians exhibit a radical appropriation of the priesthood of all its members.[58] Priesthood in this context is an allusion to the directness of the priest-God relationship as implied in this verse and various other verses in the Bible.

This is not to say that the word does not play an active role in Christianity but rather that the word's interaction within Christianity is indirect and mediational. According to Boylston, "the sacred hierarchy of deacons, priests, monks, saints, angels, and Mary herself mediate between God and the laity."[59] While these religious figures act as mediating factors between the people and God, the word takes a formulaic status, providing the basis for various creeds and benedictions regularly recited in mission churches. For instance, the Nicene Creed recited in orthodox mission churches is a derivation from the Bible often recited to the point that it reflects the people's faith and beliefs. It is used to instill hope and cause healing to ailing bodies. Those words recited have transcended the realm of everyday words to attain a level of sacredness that imbues in them creative and transformative powers.

However, given the methodization of Christianity, there is an impersonality ascribed to those words, while the rote memorization and recitation of creeds carved out from the Bible verses and teachings give an impression of distance from the word. This has led to an eventual monotony, which, among other things, has contributed to the exponential drift of the orthodox congregation toward Christianity in Africa and across the globe. This parallel exploration of the primacy and expressive use of the word in both Christian traditions illustrates the differing dispositions and opinions of both traditions toward the meaning and use of sacred words in daily and religious activities. Moreover, following the notion of individualistic priesthood as perceived to exist in Christian traditions, I am led to explore the position, role, and influence of Christian pastors in relation to the use of sacred words in their various churches.

Preachers, Sacred Words, and Empowerment

In light of the doctrine of individual priesthood among Christians, one could marvel at the amount of power, authority, and influence most Christian pastors wield. It is common knowledge that religious leaders are often assumed to possess spiritual powers and authority, as Iwuchukwu rightfully puts it; they are often believed to be "the exclusive repositories and conveyors of truth and right doctrine."[60] Generally speaking, Christians almost have an absolute faith and trust in their preachers, which explains the influence of these preachers on their congregations and the authority and weight of the sacred words they proclaim. It appears to be that although Pentecostal Christians have abandoned ceremonial robes, confessions, and priests in orthodox churches, they have willfully created new priestly overlords in less austere clothing with more progressive teachings. However, this is in contradiction to the principle of individual priesthood they proclaim, where the minister or preacher is considered a servant of God among many.[61] A question that cannot be ignored is: if equal authority is biblically granted to the congregation, why then does the preacher have such influence on his congregation? The answer is simply the following: faith and consistency.

Faith, in this context, refers to the "belief in the doctrines of a particular religion based on spiritual conviction rather than proof."[62] This applies to various doctrines and beliefs, but ultimately, faith is cultivated from shared ideologies, conceptions, and belief systems. One must establish a common reference line in order to enable an ideology to inspire faith. For instance, people who are groomed in hyper-spiritualized environments such as Africa experience various doctrines of spirit possession, exorcism, demonic attacks, etc. that engender a familiarity that elicits their continued faith in preachers that preach or perform miracles against these occurrences. Corroborating this belief is Zalanga, who notes the areas of convergence between the Christian religious beliefs and traditional African worldviews. One can infer that the notion of an enchanted world operating within the Pentecostal faith could easily appeal to the African, whose worldview is equally as enchanted. According to Zalanga:

> Pentecostals in Africa believe in what Weber called the enchanted world, where physical objects and animals are infused with powerful spirits, as are ancestral spirits, which together with subordinate deities govern the affairs of the world under a Supreme Being or creator. This way of thinking, which is also quintessential to African Traditional Religions, is essential to understanding African Pentecostalism.[63]

With an emphasis on earthly and spiritual dominion where the believer is entitled to a supernatural advantage bestowed on him by the mere act of faith, regular fasting, and fervent prayers, it is no wonder the preacher, whose belief and prayer life is theoretically more in-depth than many members of the congregation, is believed to possess the power to establish dominion over evil forces, as well as the keys to financial and material blessings through knowledge and understanding of the "spiritual realm which supersedes natural laws."[64] That being said, the reason for their influence on the lay congregation is not far-fetched and also accounts for the weight of their proclamation of sacred words. However, to examine the influence of Pentecostal preachers also requires exploration of the various incredulous narratives of abuse of power by these preachers—which is also gradually becoming a phenomenon in African states. It quickly brings to mind the extraordinary stories of church members donating more than they can afford in hopes of a multiple spiritual replenishment, drinking chemicals because their preachers requested them to do so, rejecting partners and choosing the one selected by their preachers, and many narratives of sexual abuse, among others.

As incredulous as the situation looks, it is rather a symptom of a larger issue, which is the human propensity to deify people and objects in connection with their inherent need for direction and leadership. This corresponds with anthropological categorizations of hierarchy and power in various human communities. Ultimately, the human with the best skill set, talent, or gift that appears uncommon to the rest of the group is most likely to attain a position of leadership in his/her community with the endorsement of the group. As Radcliff Brown cited in Henrich, the organization of human communities and the subject of leadership in the most basal form is influenced by many factors, which includes the following specifics:

> Besides the respect for seniority, there is another significant factor in the regulation of social life, namely the respect for certain personal qualities. These qualities are skill in hunting and warfare, generosity and kindness, and freedom from bad temper. A man possessing them inevitably acquires a position of influence in the community. His opinion on any subject carries more weight than that of another.[65]

That said, the Christian preacher with an allure of spiritual familiarity becomes a symbol of hope and proximity to a higher power that encourages and engenders faith in the people. Furthermore, to sustain the people's faith and trust in the preacher, among many things, the preacher's craft requires consistency. He or she has to live up to the expectation of their members; therefore, they need to be consistent in their religious "performance," which is neither an accusation nor an indictment of the Christian faith. It is rather a recognition that every human being is constantly performing to uphold the vision of themselves. Our self-identity is typically linked to what we do and who we believe we are. Self-performativity is a crucial requirement for human interaction and existence.

For the preacher, consistency is achieved through rigorous examination and study of the word and doctrines of Christianity—and also being a source of divine power, miracles, and capacity to see behind the veil that covers phenomenal reality. The study and mastery of the Word of God without these other things would not confer authority on him or her. That is, the Pentecostal preacher constantly needs to be ahead of their congregation; they have to exhibit a level of uncommon discernment of spiritual issues so as to constantly capture and captivate the audience. The preacher is aware of this and is constantly reading and internalizing the scriptures, and with the help of the Holy Spirit, he/she is unlocking the secret codes and meanings inherent therein.

However, dubious persons tend to take advantage of the position and status of the preacher in the Christian society, as well as the human tendency to fundamentalism and blind faith to extort or harm unsuspecting individuals. Iwuchukwu, in his exploration of the interaction of Pentecostalism, politics, and religious fundamentalism in Africa, reemphasizes this claim by noting that "Pentecostal ministers have harnessed the gullibility of the people's belief in their spiritual abilities and their oratory skills for political gain and absolute political control."[66] However, this study does not concern itself with the authenticity or phoniness of the craft; it is rather concerned with factors that stimulate and sustain people's spiritual dependence on religious figures and the attendant weightiness of the preacher's proclamation of sacred words as against the non-preacher.

Beyond the faith/spiritual scene, there are exclusive professional rights and privileges open to professionals of different fields. In other words, being versed in a particular area of study or occupation in society affords one societal respect and even reverence with regard to their expertise. That being said, Achebe, Gordimer, or Soyinka's suggestion on literature will more likely be considered or regarded than that of Pastor Enoch Adeboye's (the general overseer of the Redeemed Christian Church of God). This also applies to spiritual matters; Pst. Adeboye's proclamations or sacred words will certainly have more impact on the receiver than that of any of the aforementioned writers. This emphasizes the place of professional authority.

Also, aside from the professional privilege enjoyed by the preacher, the weight of his words is also determined by an implicit contract between the preacher and the congregation. Given the premium placed on belief in Christendom, a performative context has to be in place for those words to have effect. This is to say that the rhetorical power of sacred words is stimulated by the context of mutual belief between the preacher and the congregation. This mutual belief facilitates this contract, suggesting that Adeboye's proclamations and sacred declarations might have very little or no effect in a Muslim environment. This performative context sustained by mutual understanding and belief is also what controls the interaction between the writer and his audience.

Curses and blessings are believed to be powerful words of analogous degrees of impact, although on opposite sides of the same religion. They are also sacred words known to be efficacious and their efficacy is derived from "a god, a text or prophet."[67] Frankfurter, while taking into cognizance the energy of the words viewed as curses, defines a curse as "a ritual performance that transfers subversive power to some object, or the subversive power that plagues one following such a performance (as in 'her curse still rests on me')."[68] It is often believed that the words uttered have a tendency to prevail, although it might depend on the authority of the speaker. Most cultures around the world consider parents or priests, regardless of religion, to be the ultimate repositories of the vibrant energy of spoken sacred words.

Put differently, their words when spoken, depending on intent, have the capability of making or marring a person's life, hence, the operative existence of filial piety. The Christian Bible corroborates this assumption with various references to biblical parents blessing their children,[69] as well as the earlier cited Scripture that says: "the power of life and death lies in the tongue." The tongue in this context is a metaphor for words. However, the assumption of proclivity toward fulfillment is not limited to the maliciousness of spoken curses, the creative and transformative energy of words extends to blessings—words spoken to nourish, protect, liberate, and heal. In many religious traditions of the world, there is a strong awareness and consciousness of the potency of sacred words, which includes curses or blessings.

Among African Pentecostal Christians, this consciousness is palpable, hence the existing belief in the preacher's wherewithal to bless or curse; it also accounts for the people's reaction to the sacred proclamations of the preacher. When the preacher says to the congregation, "it shall be well with you," it is a sacred declaration, a blessing culled or derived from Isa. 3:10: "Say to the righteous that it shall be well with them, for they shall eat the fruits of their doings." This biblical injunction serves as the basis for the sacred proclamation, and even trite responses of Christian religious leaders come with a caveat of righteousness. In other words, the blessing of wellness is reserved only for the righteous. This justifies the following submission by Motyer:

> The word of God's grace and the word of God's wrath are the same word: the word, which promises life, is but a savor of death and judgment to the rebel, and therefore a curse. When God's curse falls on his disobedient people, it is not the abrogation but the implementation of the covenant.[70]

The preacher's authority to curse and bless is substantiated by biblical anecdotes and verses. In some instances, Jesus both blessed and cursed, as in the case of the unproductive fig tree in Mk 11:20-25 that withered following the impact of the word of Jesus. In response to the incredulous outbursts of the disciples of Jesus at the sight of this withered fig tree, Jesus went ahead to state that: "I tell you the truth, if anyone says to this mountain, 'Go, throw yourself into the sea' and does not doubt in his heart but believes that what he says will happen, it will be done for him."[71] This, among others, demonstrates the efficacy and potency of spoken words while simultaneously justifying the Christian's reverence for the preacher who assumes the position of a leader and, therefore, by virtue of leadership is given the prerogative to bless and curse.

Sacred words are also further used to establish dominion over the spiritual powers that exist or even the socioeconomic, security, and environmental challenges of daily life. For instance, the following verse culled from Ps. 23 provides the basis for most Christian declarations and assertions with reference to protection from harm and poverty:

> The Lord is my shepherd; I shall not want. He maketh me to lie down in green pastures; he leadeth me beside the still waters. He restoreth my soul; he leadeth me in the path of righteousness for his name sake. Yea, though I walk through the valley of the shadow of death, I will fear no evil: for though art with me; thy rod and thy staff they comfort me. Thou prepareth a table before me in the presence of my enemies: thou anointest my hair with oil my cup runneth over. Surely goodness and mercy shall follow me all the days of my life; and I shall dwell in the house of the Lord forever.[72]

This Psalm reflects Christian beliefs and the basis of their assertions in the face of bad economic conditions, troubling societal/global situations, risk, and insecurity, among others. These verses are mostly memorized and recited by Christians in the face of the issues listed, while also serving as a formula to various prayers and assertions made by Christians. By virtue of the inspiration of the Holy Spirit as believed by Christians, all Scripture is sacred, hence the notion and belief in biblical inerrancy. The use of these verses/words is usually preceded with statements like, "The Word of the Lord says . . ." or "According to the Bible, . . ." which draw attention to the significance and the need to reverence words that come from God and words that speak about God.[73] Therefore, when the preacher says to the congregation, "The Lord is your shepherd, you shall not want," especially in times of economic recession and hardship, this proclamation will resonate more with the congregation that is most likely battling with a bourgeoning fear of lack and want. The preacher's words become assertive responses to the economic situation, and since they are derived from the Holy Book, they engender faith and hope in the imminence of God's provision.

This hope and faith derived from the word is substantiated by more scriptural verses, which places emphasis on the sanctification of the word and draws further attention to the imminence of God's promises and the Christian assertions. It gestures at the significance of the word spoken by God and written in the Holy Book. For instance, Isa. 55:10-11, provided in the next sentence, emphasizes the potency of the Word of God as is written in the scriptures. The personal reference to God with the pronoun "I" in the following verse accentuates the exactitude of his promise, which further sanctifies those words:

> For as the rain cometh down, and the snow from the heaven, and returneth not thither, but watereth the earth, and maketh it bring forth and bud, and that it may give seed to the sower, and bread to the eater: so shall my word be that goeth forth out of my mouth: it shall not return unto me void, but it shall accomplish that which I please, and it shall prosper in the thing whereunto I sent it.[74]

This verse, therefore, becomes the umbrella verse that gives impetus to the Christian reverence of scriptural verses and their undying expectation of scriptural fulfillment.

For instance, since the Bible says in Exod. 23:26 that, "There shall nothing cast their young nor be barren, in thy land: the number of thy days I will fulfill" which is often abbreviated to just, "none shall be barren in the land,"[75] this verse has come to be the sacred word used to speak against barrenness in both its literal and metaphorical meanings. It is often used as a word of response to the likelihood of barrenness in any area of the believer's life. Additionally, it has inspired many declarations and proclamations of fruitfulness in the life of the Christian. For women in need of children, those words and Scripture become sacred words that propel and energize their faith and hope in the miracle of birth and fruitfulness. The pastor's faith teachings to the woman in need of children find impetus in that scriptural verse.

Christian sermons and banners are often embellished with sacred words as operationalized in this work and derived from the scriptures. Therefore, it is not uncommon to come across proclamations and sermon themes such as "It is your time to shine," a statement that primarily originated from Isa. 60:1-4, which implies an awakening to a magnificent brilliance that is believed to apply to the overall life and experience of the receiver. Depending on the area of the receiver's deficiency, this proclamation uttered by a preacher is seen as a spiritual stimulant that catalyzes any or all of the receiver's finances, health, security, and much more.

There is a myriad of other proclamations derived from the scriptures that are intended to establish dominion, which are identified in this study as sacred words. These proclamations, as believed by Christians, are potent words with creative capacities to speak things into existence. When people are commanded to "die by fire," as is normally heard among worshipers at the Mountain of Fire and Miracle Ministries, such emphatic declarations are sacred pronouncements aimed at ending the life of any force or power impacting one's existence negatively. The statement is today a trite pronouncement among members of the church and has become an evocative proclamation of one's spiritual authority to end the existence of entities that threaten their own.

Although this introduction has succeeded in linking these religious verses, known as sacred words, to a performative knowledge system and power, it is expedient to know it is only a foundation for the chapters in this book. Put differently, to borrow the word "Forerunner," as used by the Bible to depict John the Baptist, the introduction serves to prepare the way for all of the chapters, each of which deployed narrative and analytical means to espouse how these sacred words link and translate to generation and maintenance of religio-political power or produce religious leaders who interpret these sacred words and translate them into positive actions and practices. Most importantly, riding on the back of these introductions, the chapters focus on the knowledge system engendered or derived from the sacred words which inform, enhance, and advance the actions and practices of their adherents in Africa.

Part One

Indigenous Systems

Diviners and Indigenous Knowledge

Introduction

In a fast-growing world of innovations, technological advancements, and scientific discoveries, knowledge is primary. As naturally curious creatures, humans search for knowledge in different places, and each day comes with a new addition to their knowledge base, through which they impact the world in different ways. Knowledge is desired by many for a variety of reasons, including the ability to impact lives and change the course of events, such as determining the right action in a crucial moment. Knowledge is often bequeathed with the seat of power, as Sir Francis Bacon rightly observes: "*Scientia potentia est*" (knowledge is power). To say that may not be too presumptuous, considering the wealth of knowledge that can be channeled to greater courses for humanity's sake. Humans are classified scientifically as "homo sapiens," which literally translates as "humans with knowledge," distinguishing them from other organisms. The quest for knowledge is encoded in the genetic makeup of humans, so much that they may go to any length to acquire it. That insatiable hunger and zeal for knowledge have had a significant impact on different aspects of the world.

Among the rest of the world, Africans have contributed and are still contributing a great number of their resources to the production of knowledge, maintenance, and growth of the different systems of the world. Scientists, physicians, astronauts, engineers, and many others have been praised for their inventions and innovative ideas of knowledge. Many of them have even been recognized with prizes and awards for their works and contributions to human knowledge. However, diviners have received little or no recognition for the generation, that is origination and possession of ideas and knowledge, and most of the time they are not perceived as experts or even worthy of study because their works and expertise are not categorized as "professional" and do not fit in with Western concepts of knowledge and innovation.

This chapter attempts to examine diviners as experts in their fields and also as a critical cohort of authorities deserving of extensive study alongside professional recognition for their contributions toward humanity and the possession and generation of ideas of knowledge in the African space. Knowledge is constantly changing and being modified to suit situations affecting humankind, and so the possession of a certain kind of wisdom in any area establishes a niche area of expertise in the field, especially if the field is vibrant and not redundant. This chapter will examine diviners, especially the Babalawo (Ifa priests), and ideas of knowledge they generate and possess.

Likewise, the power and influence that emanates from this knowledge will also be examined. It is imperative to understand the different interpretations of knowledge and ideas, which will be explored in this chapter, and the different conceptual interpretations of knowledge. Who are diviners and how are they identified as custodians of knowledge? The categorization of some people as diviners and the origin of divination is important to this study as a vantage point to begin understanding the contributions to the world of knowledge that diviners generate and possess.

Knowledge may be an abstract concept, but its referent denotes a powerful subject despite its elusive conceptual meaning. An attempt to define the term "knowledge" is relatively due to the varied subjects that claim to espouse this term. Knowledge is drawn from both simple and complex phenomena. The concept of knowledge in the humanities is relational and contextual because of the fluidity and broad scope of the concept. In this chapter, the knowledge indigenous to the African space is what will be contextualized. Knowledge is often captured as facts, information, truths, understanding of theories of existence acquired through the study of different aspects of the world. It is synonymous with the claim of "knowing"—the data gathered from beliefs, philosophies, traditions, practices, and institutions that generate and/or deploy knowledge. African indigenous knowledge is the system/body of ideas, theories, facts, data, episteme, etc., which has contributed to the growth, sustenance, and development of the African space over time. This Afrocentric knowledge deals with worldviews, thought systems, practices, and philosophies that support the African way of life.

This chapter will delve into the ideas of knowledge that diviners, especially the Babalawo of Yorùbá descent, possess and generate. In the course of detangling the generation of ideas of knowledge, it will attempt to capture the unique types of ideas about knowledge found among the diviners of Africa. The emphasis on the type of knowledge is to delimit the scope of the chapter to capture the ideas of knowledge in the Yorùbá cosmology, which is extracted from the culture and traditions, especially those that directly impact the practice of divination and diviners' knowledge claim. This chapter will attempt to extrapolate how these ideas of knowledge are produced, how diviners generate these ideas of knowledge, what methods or ways are employed in the acquisition of knowledge, and the nature of these ideas of knowledge and their basis.

The chapter will then proceed to highlight and discuss how diviners are trained, the process of educating the diviners with the necessary skills to be successful in the profession. In this section, the chapter will investigate and highlight the process of grooming the diviner, which includes the apprenticeship selection, years of training, skills homed in on during the training process, etc. Because the diviner is an appendage to the practice of *Ifa* divination, the chapter will briefly discuss the origin of divination and the connection with the diviner's possession of ideas of knowledge.

The chapter will discuss areas that diviners have distinguished their possession of ideas of knowledge and how they dispense them. Diviners have been categorized and/or perceived as local practitioners and charlatans who do not possess scientific knowledge or have Western knowledge through formal education. However, the possession or lack of Western education makes little or no difference to the divination outcome and the knowledge gleaned from a consultation. Diviners' ideas of knowledge encompass a different discipline than modern/Western terms and concepts. Some of these ideas may intersect with different disciplines that are crucial to human life and quality of living.

Diviners and Divination

Divination is an important part of the diviner's profession; in fact, it is the act of divining that makes the diviner an expert in his field and in the generation of ideas of knowledge. It is imperative to discuss rather briefly the term divination before proceeding to the ideas that diviners possess. According to Ozioma and Chinwe:

> Divination means consulting the spirit world. It is a method by which information concerning an individual or circumstance of illness is obtained through the use of randomly arranged symbols in order to gain healing knowledge. It is also viewed as a way to access information that is normally beyond the reach of the rational mind. It is a transpersonal technique in which diviners base their knowledge on communication with the spiritual forces, such as the ancestors, spirits, and deities. It is, therefore, an integral part of an African traditional way of diagnosing diseases.[1]

Divination has been perceived as one of the methods diviners use to diagnose their patients/clients. Diviners, through divination, have a greater chance of knowing the nature of the ailment and the cause of the affliction. Divination may be carried out with divination chains, nuts, beads, cowries, shells, etc. Bascom notes that the Babalawo are herbalists as much as they can also be regarded, in some sense, as diviners— although divining is their primary function. Clients may come to them for medicine without having a divination, and they pay extra for its preparation.[2] The Babalawo possess knowledge of herbs and plants as well as medicine as enunciated in Bascom's description of the diviner. The diviner may divine in some cases and may not need to in others which require his physical or non-spiritual aid.

The word "diviner" comes from the broader term or concept of "divination," which is an act of geomancy. Diviners in Nigeria, especially in the Southwest part of Nigeria, are known as the Babalawo (who are male diviners) and Iyanifa (for the women diviners) in Yorùbá. The act of divination makes one a diviner, although without human effort and presence, the act is not achievable. Divination has been compared to a multitude of things, especially in the fields of computers and philosophy, because of the similarities that scholars have established among them. Alamu et al. capture the basic information represented in divination as "the act of seeking after knowledge of future or hidden things by inadequate means which is usually supplemented by some power which is represented all through history as coming from gods."[3] This definition captures that the retention of knowledge embedded in divination which is carried out by diviners is a method of uncovering hidden knowledge. Diviners are part of the structure of the social institutions in many African societies because of their claim of knowledge and the deployment of these ideas of knowledge in the communities.

In Nigeria, the Babalawo are known to be diviners through the manipulation of the divination beads or chains.

The diviner is the heart of the divination because he is the medium between the deities and the human who has come to seek the help of the supernatural beings. The diviner becomes the mouthpiece for the deity while consulting the divinities on behalf of the person(s). When Ifa reveals the message/solution to the inquirer's problem, the diviner explains it in a plain and simplified version for easy comprehension. The diviner becomes indispensable to the act of recovering, investigating, and acquiring knowledge through divination or otherwise. Peek writes:

> A divination system is a standardized process deriving from a learned discipline based on an extensive body of knowledge. This knowledge may or may not be literally expressed during the interpretation of the oracular message. The diviner may utilize a fixed corpus, such as the Yorùbá Ifa Odu verses, or a more diffuse body of esoteric knowledge. Divining processes are diverse, but all follow set routines by which otherwise inaccessible information is obtained.[4]

Peek extracts the diviner's duty and function in the attempt to draw out the definition of divination as a synchronized method of knowledge production drawn out from the ingenuity of the diviner's ability to configure and/or manipulate the text or employ his training to generate hidden texts and information. Divination gives the diviner an edge to synthesize ideas gathered from years of study, wisdom inherent in the society's thought system, and metaphysical data received through geomancy. Divination serves as a compass to the right direction and navigation system to get to the destination at the appropriately designated time. The diviner becomes more attuned to his knowledge base through the assistance of divination.

The Grooming of the Diviner

The ideas of knowledge possessed by diviners, especially the Babalawo, are generated from their study, training, and practice of the knowledge implicit in the exploration of their primary text, that is, the Ifa Corpus. Peek and other scholars of African divination systems recognize different types of diviners and their divination systems in Africa; however, the emphasis of this study is based on the ideas of knowledge possessed by the Babalawo in southwestern Nigeria. Diviners are trained to acquire knowledge through thorough investigation, a good memory for retaining and recollecting data, processing of information, and interpretation skills honed through careful training. Diviners go through a long period of formal or informal training under the tutelage of an experienced diviner. Peek, alongside other scholars like Abimbola and Bascom, avers that Yorùbá diviners are trained for at least ten years in the branches of knowledge on which Ifa divination is based.[5]

After the successful completion of their training, these trainees are presented to the cult of diviners for the initiation process, which is sometimes followed by a ceremonial outing and introduction into the profession. Learning and training, rather than ending after the initiation ceremony, continues throughout the diviner's lifetime because of the extensive and inexhaustible nature of knowledge in this profession. Peek's study on diviners avers that many of these diviners continue learning and refining their skills throughout their lives, sharing their expertise, and studying with more renowned diviners.[6] Falokun Fatumbi further said that in Ode Remo, a Yorùbá town, training to become a diviner begins when a child is seven years old and lasts ten to fifteen years. "The education involves memorization of 256 verses of oral scripture including the prayers, invocations, songs, dances and herbal medicine associated with each verse."[7]

Diviners can be male or female, as studies on diviners in Africa, especially in Yorùbá culture, have shown. The Babalawo or Mamalawo are specialists trained to generate ideas of knowledge from the Ifa Corpus. The services of diviners were extensive in the preliterate era in many African societies—unlike the present time when Western ideologies have pushed these Afrocentric knowledge base and epistemologies to the back burner.

The Role of the Diviner

Zuess explains:

> The greatest authority is given to diviners who have traveled into far-off cultures to learn wisdom; unlike local oracles, these practitioners make use of complex methods requiring long training. Theirs is an international science. These specialists may well be an important vehicle for cultural contact and innovation, though their role in cultural change has been generally ignored.[8]

Diviners hold important, if not invaluable, positions in the acquisition of knowledge in African societies. However, the training of these professionals has to be looked at to know how ideas of wisdom are being dispensed and how they generate meanings and knowledge from their study of Ifa or other texts. The esoteric nature of the Ifa cult and the diviners' profession hinges on the African traditional belief system, religion, and belief in the existence of supernatural beings. In describing the role of the diviner in the generation of ideas of knowledge, Peek magnifies the functionality of the diviners to include their interpretive ability among other capabilities of diviners, such as:

> Sometimes the diviner's body becomes the vehicle of communication through spirit possession. Some diviners operate self-explanatory mechanisms that reveal answers; other systems require the diviner to interpret cryptic metaphoric messages. The final diagnosis and plan for action are rendered collectively by the diviner and the clients(s).[9]

Diviners hold important positions as a repository of ideas of knowledge which Peek recognizes and affirms in his work, along with the claim that the diviner in other cultures is central to the expression and enactment of his or her cultural truths as they are reviewed in the context of contemporary realities. Diviners have been classified as mere performers, which was denounced by Peek when he described the Western conceptualization of these professionals. The European tradition often portrays the diviner as a charismatic charlatan who cleverly manipulates others with his mystical knowledge and power and is given inappropriate attention and valued by gullible and anxious people. But the opposite is the case, as African cultures regard diviners to be men and women of remarkable wisdom and high integrity.[10] Diviners and their profession are dignified priests whose ingenuous duties are carried out with so much aplomb that their presence evokes calm and serenity because of the assurance that their office and profession exude.

Diviners: The Connection to Ifa

Diviners in southwestern Nigeria, especially the Yorùbá region, known as "Babalawo"— that is, "father of secrets"—are trained in the act of divination and consultation based on the worship of Ifa. Okewande avers that "Ifá is believed to be the foundation of Yorùbá culture. This means every aspect of Yorùbá life, including religion, philosophy, science, ideology, and so on, has one link or another with Ifá."[11] Going by this assertion, it is reasonable to agree that diviners are the custodians of Ifa and its large literary corpus which makes them grandmasters and professionals in many areas of Yorùbá cosmology since Ifa is the repository of the ideas of knowledge. In light of this assertion about Ifa, Okewande affirms that scholars have defined Ifa "in different ways that establish the inexplicable and unlimited divergent scope of its knowledge, wisdom and values. Indeed, it is regarded as the bedrock of other aspects of Yorùbá life."[12] Taking a cue from the claim of this scholar, Ifa is the basis of the knowledge system of the diviner, referred to as the Babalawo, and it suffices to say that the knowledge generated by these diviners is drawn from their training and practice of Ifa. Before delving into the ideas of knowledge possessed by diviners, it is important to connect Ifa, the diviners, and the importance of the craft to the possession of knowledge by the practitioners.

Adeeko tries to account for the existence of diviners in the naming of *Odu* as names of diviners that have existed before in the Ifa Corpus. In the Ifa Corpus, the Odu Ifa signatures represent some of the names of the first diviners as elucidated by Adeeko, while in some verses, the diviner who performs the divination is named.

> The story of the original diviners is not a simple one. According to Abímbọ́lá, the named diviners led the first consultation session recounted in the story. He also adds that the names are either fragments of praise epithets (oríkì) or pseudonyms (1977:19). The names, as such, historicize the narratives and make them accounts of something that actually happened. It is not hard to disagree with Abímbọ́lá: if the priests existed in time and place, succeeding diviners who acknowledge their predecessors' activities do not seem interested in identifying them as historical figures.[13]

Ifa, the religion and system of geomancy, makes the diviner also known as "the Ifa priest," a functional sociocultural agent of religious, social, and cultural experts who officiates in his capacity as a diviner, priest, and performer in the community. Ifa is the spine of the diviner's knowledge and craft—the diviner is grafted onto the root of the Ifa religion and becomes the medium for personal and public self-development. Ifa represents the possibility of multidimensional roles that the diviner can occupy in society.

The Origin of Ifa Divination

According to Odularu, Ifa divination is limitless. It includes Yorùbá oral tradition, which is the main reservoir of authentic traditional Yorùbá culture. Another semantic aspect of Ifa divination is in its reliability as a means of revealing the underlying meanings and answers to mysterious earthly issues, occurrences, and situations. Ifa divination helps in the quest to understand environmental and sociopolitical issues and to resolve them. "Ifa divination has grown so important that almost all Yorùbá traditional political institutions and social systems, namely chieftaincy, naming, wedding, ageing, ceremonial, festivals, etc. have traces of the Ifa divinatory system."[14]

Ifa represents so many ideas, such as the name of one of the Yorùbá divinities, the system of divination, the religion, the words of the deity, etc. However, Ifa is all of these and more because of the controversies about its origin in the oral tradition. Falokun opines that "the verses of Ifa are like folder files in a computer, separated by specific topics. In the course of a day, when you encounter a problem, you recall the verse associated with the best possible solution and immediately have access to a wealth of information to guide you toward the resolution of conflict."[15]

Demystifying the origin of Ifa is not the scope of this chapter; however, it will discuss briefly some of the stories/myths about its origin. Adegboyega claims:

Some myths state that Ifa came from a deity who descended from heaven with some others. On the other hand, there are oral traditions, which identify its originator as an exceptionally wise man whose fame brought several disciples and apprentices from far and near. Ifa chose only 16 of them and their names coincided with the elder 16 Odu Ifa (the 16 corpuses). The younger 240 Odu could therefore be reasonably regarded as member of later generation of disciples and apprentices trained by the first 16 and others (Oluwole, 1996:3). To the fist (sic) view, Ifa was recognized as the first point of call when the divinities first came to the world. To the other, Ifa himself was said to have eight children all of whom later became diviners.[16]

These claims about the existence of and origin of Ifa[17] clearly indicate that Ifa points to the establishment of diviners as carriers of knowledge to be passed on through the act of divination. As one of the plethora of Yorùbá deities, Ifa is credited with the gift of wisdom and knowledge unmatched by any other divinity that is consulted by other deities and humans. And so begins the act of divination and the training of diviners who will bear the torch of knowledge and generate ideas of knowledge from the Ifa texts. The epistemological foundation of diviners is premised on the ideas of wisdom gathered from the study of Ifa. To generate these epistemes, it is necessary to establish the knowledge system in Ifa. For Opasola, epistemology is the study of human knowledge, its nature, origin, extent, limitations, justification, dependability, or certainty.[18] Knowledge itself, which is the base of epistemology, has components that establish its reliability.

These components are beliefs gathered from experience and observations of events, truth established from facts, and justification of these data. Beliefs are generated from customs and traditions of a community and the culture, which means that beliefs as fragments of knowledge are grafted from cultural materials, traditions, and customs of a society. The conception of the world, understanding of its phenomena, and the intervention of the supernatural are the main embodiments of the epistemic foundation of African knowledge. That being established, Ifa—an oracle of the ancient Yorùbá religion and practice in the Yorùbá community—proves the existence of African knowledge and the claim of diviners to be specialists and repositories of these ideas of knowledge. Odularu also opines:

> The definition of Ifa can be found in the Yorùbá belief that Ifa divination is capable of fulfillment for them, through its chief priest or diviner, *Babalawo*—father of secrecy or secrets and custodian of the Ifa divinatory system. *Babalawo* is held in high esteem by the Yorùbá and is well versed in the oral tradition of the Ifa oracle which was bequeathed to him by Orunmila, the originator of Ifa divination.[19]

Diviners and Ideas of (Yorùbá) Philosophy

Recognizing the import of Yorùbá ideas of knowledge, Adegboyega writes:

> Philosophy can be conceived as a search for answers to wide ranging questions about the nature of the universe, the nature of human being, the purpose of life, the character of good life, and the contemplation about an ideal society. This conception of philosophy may not receive universal acceptance, as every definition of philosophy is apt to be personal.[20]

African knowledge is extensive and broad and has been receiving considerable research, part of which is African philosophy. Because African philosophy is expansive, this chapter will limit its scope to the Yorùbá philosophy—cultural and traditional knowledge—which diviners possess and generate. The desire and curiosity to understand the cosmological makeup of one's immediate community and the world is what spurs humans to seek knowledge and understanding of concepts, such as the philosophical explanations of phenomena around humans. In every known culture, there exist cultural and philosophical explanations to events and natural/biological happenings that are codified in certain texts and folklore.

In the case of Yorùbá philosophy, diviners have extensive grasp of the ideas of knowledge surrounding the existence and principles of society's configurations.

Adegboyega tries to account for the materials pertaining to philosophy, as she says that a general consensus on the focus of philosophy is far from sight; however, events, interactions, and activities are some of the data used in generating philosophy about a certain community at a particular time. The foregoing captures that philosophy is concerned with human activity and the world's configuration and the interaction of entities, that is, humans, and the world.

One of the ideas of knowledge that diviners possess and generate is philosophical ideas on various matters and concepts about the environment. The possession of these philosophical ideas has created spaces for interaction with the cosmos and the manipulation of its resources to help humanity thrive. Philosophy, as a field of study, is pruned from existing knowledge and ideas on different concepts in many cultures of the world. Diviners generate and possess philosophies about the world order, especially of their immediate cosmos, which, in this case, is centered on the Yorùbá world. Africans are philosophical people and philosophize about their existence and space(s) through the knowledge passed on from one generation to the next through the oral tradition. Oral tradition is a fragment of African oral literature, which is one of the resources of philosophies in Africa. The African Traditional Religion is another important source of African philosophies that are strongly established on the religious beliefs of the African people.

The existence of African thoughts and philosophies originate from African oral tradition and orality. Adegboyega draws from one of the resources of Yorùbá oral tradition—proverbs—to prove the existence and origin of African philosophies. Proverbs are one of the most prominent oral resources in the Yorùbá world, as it is considered the kernel of discourses and words and is deployed to search out missing words. Proverbs are rich oral tools imbued with an extra delivery punch than mere words. Proverbs on their own are sage-philosophical sayings and statements that reveal cultural ethics and metaphysics of the cosmos observed by sages in Yorùbá societies. They elevate ordinary speeches and statements and embellish them with philosophical tones and hues to mark beliefs that have been considered truth. Adegboyega uses the Yorùbá proverbs to prove that African proverbs, specifically Yorùbá proverbs, carry as much weight as the Western ideas of philosophy.

According to Adegboyega:

In western philosophy appearance, reality, causality are fundamental metaphysical issues, this is also contained in Yorùbá proverbs. A number of Yorùbá proverbs reveal that there is no effect without a cause. This is explicated in the proverbs below:

a. *Kokoro to n jo lebaa ona, onluu re n be ninu igbo*

(The insect that is dancing near the road, its drummer is in the bush)

b. *Bi ko ba ni 'dii Obinrin ki je kumolu bi obinrin ba je Salawu, yoo sanwo ori.*

(Without any reason, a woman cannot be called Kumolu, if a woman bears Salawu, then she will pay tax).[21]

The author has used the proverb to foreground the cause-and-effect stratagem of the metaphysical branch of philosophy. This speculates that there is always a reason behind any act or event; things do not just happen out of chance, there are underlying agents that propel its existence. Hence, the kokoro (insect) that seems to be dancing, the drummer providing the beat, and rhythm are close-by. This philosophy says a lot about the Yorùbá people and their philosophy of cause-and-effect concepts. Diviners use proverbs and metaphors such as this to reveal a message to the client.

The reference to the diviner (Babalawo) and divination as an act of philosophizing illustrates the inclusion of the diviner as a philosopher who employs proverbs as a way to emphasize the meaning embedded in the cipher or message. The proverb indicates that every day comes with a different shade and turn; it is the reason the diviner must divine every day to be aware of the turn of events. The ẹsẹ̀ Ifá are riddled with proverbs and metaphoric statements, such as the one cited here, and it is the diviner's duty to employ the philosophy in the message and explain it to the client if he/she does not already get the message in the Ifa verse.

Diviners and Knowledge of Yorùbá History

Diviners have been known to possess a wealth of histories about the Yorùbá people, their forebears/ancestors, their origin and settlement, etc. These people, that is, diviners, possess knowledge of ancestral history and can tell them with finesse as performers trained to retell these histories with astounding accuracy and performative skills. Diviners/Babalawo possess and generate ideas of history and historicity from the Ifa literary corpus, which has been regarded as the largest body of work on the Yorùbá people. Peek illustrates this when he states that the history of a people can be gained from divination texts and traditions, as Abimbola demonstrates with Ifa divination verses.[22] In the Ifa divination texts, which are divided into Odu and ẹsẹ̀ Ifá, the history of the Yorùbá people is documented, and none are better equipped with this history than the diviner who has been studying the Ifa texts for several years. Diviners possess adequate knowledge of the history of the Yorùbá people and their traditions. The history of the Yorùbá can be found in the Ifa Corpus, which narrates how Oduduwa finds the ẹsẹ̀ Ifá that talks about the history of the Yorùbá people. Ilesanmi supports this assertion:

> The Babalawo make the distinction between tales/stories and history. They claim that history is factual and empirical, but tales/stories are not. What many of us may term myths today are, to the Babalawo, history, which relates events which are believed to have actually happened in the far distant past.[23]

Ilesanmi has clearly demonstrated that the diviner possesses ideas of history, myths, tales, stories, etc., which are clearly defined in the distinction of the different types of oral forms that may be confusing to differentiate and situate correctly by other people. He goes further to state that the The Babalawo would not tell tales, because tales are fiction and fiction has no historical basis in actual life. Ẹsẹ̀ Ifá are regarded by them as true stories, accounts of things that actually happened i.e.. the history of the Yorùbá community in general, and of individuals in particular which are recounted to enlighten every subsequent generation..[24]

Diviners and the Possession of Medical Knowledge

Diviners from time immemorial, as part of their profession and expertise, have practiced medicine in its simplest and broadest form. These diviners possess and generate ideas of medicine and medical knowledge from the careful observation, study, experiments, treatment, and application of herbs and plants to combat health maladies. Diviners learn as part of their training the act of medical examination and the application of these ideas to everyday healthcare challenges. The utilization of this knowledge of medicine varies in terms of disease or illness origin, treatment procedure, source of the materials for a cure, etc. Diviners claim to possess esoteric knowledge about the cosmos—especially the world they belong to and that of their immediate society.

This esoteric knowledge is premised on the indigenous knowledge they have received during their training as priests and diviners of Ifa. Before the introduction of Western education and medicine, diviners occupied the status and position of medical practitioners and consultants, as they possessed knowledge about several illnesses and diseases and the cure/treatment procedures. It is important to note that diviners occupy important positions in society and are highly respected by people in that community. Diviners and their professions are hinged on the belief in indigenous wisdom and spirituality aided by the belief in the traditional African belief system and religion. In different parts of Africa, diviners have been credited with intrinsic and extensive wisdom and ideas about the ways of their ancestors and the power they possess. From the foregoing, it is therefore evident that African indigenous knowledge has been in existence longer than any record of its use and methods.

Diviners use their knowledge and understanding of the Ifa Corpus—which became sacred words to them owing to the power contained in their resultant actions—as a guide and manual to deal with medical issues and ailments. Peek agrees that diviners' knowledge extends to the discipline of medicine because many diviners are also herbalists, and their diagnostic and treatment methods can aid the study of traditional healing systems.[25] Oyebola also notes that there are about seven traditional healers. "These are the *Babalawo*; *Onisegun (or Adahunse)*; *Alasotele (soothsayer)*; *Olorisa (or Abore)*; *Awon 'leku-leja* (traditional pharmacists); specialists comprising traditional bone-setters, traditional psychiatrists, traditional birth attendants (or midwives) and the 'Olola'; and a miscellaneous group consisting of *Afaa* (Mallams) and Aladura (spiritual healers)."[26]

The first on the list is the Babalawo (diviner) who may combine all the other classifications of traditional healers listed by the scholar. Clearly, the diviner possesses sufficient knowledge of medicine captured as "traditional" borne out of knowledge of sacred words, but this classification does not make the diviner practice less than what it is, which is the generation and practice of medicine before and during the advent of modern medicine. First of all, it is important to indicate that Babalawo (diviners) can function in all the capacities listed by Oyebola because of their experience and length of study and training. Although the origins of medical concepts, particularly those of Yorùbá diviners, may be traced back to tales and oral traditions, the novitiate experience of individuals who ultimately qualify as traditional healers today correlates to the early stages of their apprenticeship.[27] With the foregoing, diviners have sufficient grasp and knowledge of Yorùbá oral traditions and medicine to treat their patients.

The reliance and relevance of the ideas of medicine generated and possessed by diviners are widely known to include medical issues that have proven too difficult for Western medicine to combat or cure but are firmly situated in the African belief system of healing and in the diviner's ability of African methods of healthcare treatment. The diviner makes diagnoses, just like the Western doctor, and consults Ifa for clarification. Diviners diagnose, prescribe medication, and sometimes apply the treatment for these ailments and diseases. In the case of epilepsy known as "warapa," diviners diagnose with the help of Ifa divination for a proper examination and clarity while prescribing materials needed for the treatment or get them on behalf of their patients.

These diviners often have rooms or special places like clinics where they admit, treat, and care for their patients. Diviners also possess the knowledge of medical help in the treatment of several ailments and diseases, such as common cold, fever, migraine, malaria, measles, etc. They may sometimes also double as surgeons who may need to cut out affected parts of the patient to stop the spread of the disease. Diviners possess knowledge of medicine needed to treat infections that are common and sometimes rare through the application of herbs and plants that are safe for consumption or application. Oyebola, however, categorizes the Babalawo into the diviner (onifa) who, according to him, uses the divination chain (opele) and sacrifice as propitiation—with little or no knowledge about using herbs for healing—and the diviner/herbalist ("complete Babalawo"), who uses the opele in combination with other duties, such as offering sacrifice, and possesses ideas of herbal medicine. The whole categorization, he says, depends on the length of training.[28] Oyebola's division of the types of diviners seems to create a dichotomy about diviners and what they do. In this chapter, the category known as the "complete Babalawo" will be utilized to capture the concept of diviners who possess sufficient knowledge of the craft.

Diviners possess knowledge of herbal drinks for common illnesses, such as rashes, boils, pox, and convulsions, which they may prepare themselves or prescribe for the patient to purchase at the traditional pharmacist's stall where they are being sold. They possess much knowledge about which herbs are edible and those that are not. Some of the plants may include barks of trees, roots, stem, or leaves that may be cooked as food, ground to a powder for application on sores, open wounds, gashes, or rashes. The right dosage or direction of application is also determined by the diviner, who may ask the patient to use the mixture for bathing and/or drinking. Diviners are sometimes invited during difficult childbirths to divine the cause, solution, and treatment of the problem. In those cases, the diviner divines and consults Ifa, which supplies the answer and what to do in such cases if malevolent agents are involved. Oyebola points out:

It should be noted however that many "Babalawo" and "Onisegun" are also well-versed in the art of midwifery, especially in dealing with complications. For instance, in cases of retained placenta or post-partum hemorrhage, it may take the summoning of the "Babalawo" or "Onisegun" to diagnose that this particular problem is due to the "evil machinations of a witch within that house-hold or next-door," or that the problem is due to the "evil machinations of a co-wife who has visited a medicine-man or to someone with whom the laboring woman quarreled a few months previously." In such circumstances, it is only the "Babalawo" or "Onisegun" who can prescribe appropriate medicines, make sacrifices so that the evil forces will be removed and the hazard of such a complication averted. In this regard, there is an overlap in the functions of the traditional birth attendants and midwives, who are strictly specialists in their field and the "Babalawo" and "Onisegun" whose practice cover a broader scope.[29]

Diviners generate extensive and effective ideas of medicine that spill over to encompass midwifery, as they assist in times of difficult or complex cases. The intervention of malevolent agents mentioned earlier, such as witches, requires the knowledge of diviners to raise counterattack measures or invoke deities through propitiation measures, like sacrifices and offerings. The diviner is fluid in terms of functions and knowledge possession; divination gives wider access to penetrate hidden curative ideas and precautionary measures to forestall future occurrences. When diviners treat new cases they are normally unfamiliar with, they gain useful ideas of knowledge to treat future events or similar cases. The knowledge of herbs like bitter leaf (ewuro), neem leaves, papaya leaves, lemon peels, lemongrass leaves, etc. and tree barks, such as mango, cashew, etc. used for making herbal teas, mixtures, mouthwash, and bathing soaps are some of the ideas of medicine that diviners generate and possess.

It is in this regard that Ajayi et al. say:

> Sometimes, some trees are noted to possess certain supernatural powers. For instance, it is a common belief among the Yorùbá that some trees like *iroko*, *ose* (baobab tree), *araba*, *arere*, *peregun*, *and odan* manifest and possess some supernatural power. Hence such trees are deified.[30]

Oyebola adds to this widespread notion by stating that divination is often done in conjunction with other duties, particularly those of a medical or even religious kind.[31] For instance, diviners will treat piles (hemorrhoids) with homemade herbal products. According to Ozioma and Chinwe:

> A traditional healer is one who provides medical care in the community that he lives, using herbs, minerals, animal parts, incantations, and other methods, based on the cultures and beliefs of his people. He must be seen to be competent, versatile, experienced, and trusted. In other definitions, priestesses, high priests, witch doctors, diviners, midwives, seers or spiritualists, and herbalists are included.[32]

Ezekwesili and Okaka document how medical care is being dispensed in African communities and the personalities of these medical practitioners that included diviners who certainly combine divination, herbs, incantations, etc. for healing. The Babalawo's knowledge of traditional Yorùbá medicine is a culmination and combination of ideas and experience used in diagnosing, treating, and curing ailments and maladies. This knowledge is sometimes a repetition of past experience, practice, and observations passed orally from previous generations as stories, myths, or revealed through divination, etc. Of unique importance to the diviner's knowledge is the revelation or unraveling of the causative agent of the malady. In dealing with medical issues and medicines, diviners possess knowledge of the human anatomy and the material needed to cure many parts of the human body with little or no harm.

Like Ezekwesili-Ofili and Okaka state:

> Many traditional medical practitioners are good psychotherapists, proficient in faith healing (spiritual healing), therapeutic occultism, circumcision of the male and female, tribal marks, treatment of snake bites, treatment of whitlow, removal of tuberculosis, lymphadenitis in the neck, cutting the umbilical cord, piercing ear lobes, removal of the uvula, extracting a carious tooth, abdominal surgery, infections, midwifery, and so on.[33]

The Babalawo generates and possesses ideas of medicinal properties inherent in plants, herbs, vegetables, roots, fruits, leaves, barks, and stems of many indigenous plants and trees such that when dispensing information on the use and benefits of these plants and herbs, they may also inform the client about the preparation method and how it can be preserved for future use.

In the case of diarrhea, diviners may sometimes ask clients to chew leaves, such as bitter leaf (ewuro), efirin, bitter kola or kola nut for cough, which can be chewed for its antioxidant properties. Some of these herbs and plants are easily accessible for treatment as they are commonly grown around the house or in the farm/garden. Limes, lemon, and other citrus fruits may be squeezed as juice for treating the common deficiency of vitamin C in children and adults alike. Garlic, ginger, and other anti-cancerous roots may be used dried and ground, fresh to make teas for cold and flu, or cooked with food.

Diviners are known to recommend ginger to combat respiratory issues like iko ife (tuberculosis) and iko gbigbe (dry cough). Cashew stems and branches are chewed as a natural mouth-cleansing brush (orin) and to clear mouth odor. A sponge-fruit (tangiri) is commonly seen in many Yorùbá households and rooms because of the belief in its capacity to ward off illnesses and diseases. Some of these medicines, known as agbo (concoction), agunmu (powder medicine), ose abuwe (bathing soap), are some of the medicinal products that diviners make for healing purposes.

The diviner's knowledge of medicines is sometimes obtained through the belief in the plants in tandem with the culture of the Yorùbá society. Their societies' folklore about the plants and herbs is one of the sources from which diviners obtain ideas of medicine and herbs. Ezekwesili-Ofili and Okaka note:

> For example, information from folklore medicine in Nigeria has it that Rauvolfia vomitoria is used for treating hypertension and other nervous conditions while Ocimum gratissimum is used for treating diarrheal diseases. Others include Citrus

paradise seeds for resistant urinary tract infections, pure honey for chronic wound treatment, Carica papaya seeds for intestinal parasites, Garcinia kola seeds for pain and inflammation, and Aloe vera for skin diseases. The same is also true for plants from other African countries. Knowledge of most of these curative properties was accumulated over time from evidence-based observations.[34]

This information generated from folklore medicine is used by diviners to heal and assist their clients/patients to achieve good health. The Babalawo possess generous amounts of Yorùbá folklore knowledge that concern medicine and pharmacology. The forest and bushes serve as the source of some of their materials, where they harvest the needed amount, prepare them, and apply as necessary. When harvesting these herbs, they make sure that the rest of the plant, tree, herb, etc. is not damaged or killed in the process, unlike the untrained and unskilled individual who may pluck or cut without the knowledge of preserving and aiding the growth of the affected plant. The older generation and diviners who practice the oral tradition that some medicinal plants need to be cut or harvested in daylight to be effective often say it. Diviners possess this knowledge of plant effectiveness and generate knowledge with respect to the plant's medicinal properties.

Diviners' Generation of Words of Wisdom to Nobility

Besides the knowledge of divination, diviners possess knowledge on difficult or troublesome issues because they have ample resources containing an array of wisdom, in particular the large Ifa literary corpus. The literary corpus contains a large reserve of wisdom nuggets and prototypes, which the Babalawo can select from to solve a problem. Bascom notes that kings in Yorùbá societies have their personal diviners who are dedicated to the king's services only: "the sixteen Babalawos of the King of Ife, known as *Awoni* or 'secrets of the Oni' (Awo Oni), appear to be a special institution restricted to the Oni and the Kingdom of Ife. Other Yorùbá kings have their special diviners."[35] There are diviners kept exclusively by kings because of their indispensable knowledge and qualifications that are beneficial to the king, who is the principal authority in the community. Only the most highly reputable and oldest diviner is fit to become the king's diviner, as he acts as his adviser on all matters. In times of trouble, such as war, famine, pestilence, or pandemic, the diviner is consulted to divine for the city, village, or community. When the king has personal problems, the diviner is consulted to find a solution to the king's issues. Bascom affirms this:

At any time of the year, the Oni may send for the Awoni to divine for the good of the town as a whole because there has been an accident or trouble, or because of a dream or other omen. They go to a special chamber (Ile Omirin) in the palace (afin) that houses a shrine of Ifa and where Ifa is consulted and use the Oni's divining apparatus. They ask, "What must be done so that the Oni may live long, that the town may be in peace, that there will not be trouble among us Awoni, that the women of Ife may not be barren, that there may be no sickness or famine in town, and that there may be no deaths among the young people." The Oni provides whatever is prescribed as the sacrifice, which is made in the palace, with animals killed in the open court in front of the council hall.[36]

The king maximizes the diviner's role and knowledge to bring good fortune, peace, and stability to his kingdom and regime. In some cases, the diviner, or Babalawo, is responsible for some of the festivals and events in the community. Bascom notes that the king's diviners in Ifa, known as Awoni, are also responsible for the annual festivals for Ifa, which are associated with eating the first new yams (Egbodo) of the season. The first festival is Egbodo Oni, or New Yams of the King, before which the Oni and the palace retinue are not permitted to eat new yams.[37] Diviners play critical roles in this festival even more than they do in many other festivals. Indeed, the festivals are a display of the diviner's knowledge of ideas regarding the traditions of the community. It is their knowledge of these important aspects of the community's tradition that makes them the best people to carry out these events.

The Diviners and Knowledge of Psychology, Psychotherapy, and Psychiatry

To start with Oyebola:

> If traditional healers are to be integrated into the health services, those who are registered as "Babalawo" and the "Onisegun" who can divine will be more suitable for dealing with psychoneurotic problems as often seen in the Yorùbá ecological view of health and disease.[38]

Diviners develop and possess knowledge of psychology, as well as psychotherapy, psychiatry, and neurology. Diviners possess a myriad of knowledge relating to the significance of the human head, especially knowledge regarding the brain in its physical, psychological, and metaphysical conceptualizations. To generate these ideas of knowledge of psychology, they revert to their innate knowledge of the Yorùbá belief in "ori" and what the Ifa Corpus says about it. Van der Meer notes that in the Yorùbá Ifá/Òrìṣá belief system, orí is one's spiritual head and is an Òrìṣá. The word "foot" in Yorùbá is ẹsẹ̀. Orí in Yorùbá Ifá/Òrìṣá practice is also representative of one's destiny, and ẹsẹ̀ is representative of struggle. According to Ifá sacred literature, "in order for the head to get things done, it needs feet."[39]

This means in order for one to fulfill destiny, one needs to put in effort. In this case, ẹsẹ̀ is also one's foundation, which raises the question: how can one achieve their destiny without effort, struggle, or a foundation?[40] Diviners know how important the physical and the metaphysical head are and what it symbolizes to the Yorùbá people. The physical head, also known as *ori*, is the box that houses the control center of the body—the brain—because if the brain is ill or is bewitched, the rest of the body will be affected. Ori, as a concept, is an important aspect of the belief system propagated in the Ifa Corpus. Fatunmbi also describes *ori* as "the calabash that contains the head and the heart . . . Because the *ori* embraces both knowledge and wisdom, and because it is a manifestation of both thought and emotion, a better definition would be either the human soul, or the human spirit."[41]

From the metaphysical point of view, diviners mediate between the living and the ancestors as they reveal each individual's "destiny."[42] Peek has illustrated that diviners generate ideas of metaphysical knowledge of psychology through the manipulation of the divination and the configuration of the African belief system, which supports the argument in favor of destiny or fate. In this vein, Ogunleye links the knowledge repository in Ifa to explain the belief in destiny when he says:

> The relevance of Ifa divination to human affairs cannot be over-emphasized. Among the Yorùbá, Orunmila, the oracular god of divination through which Ifa is known, is regarded as the witness of destiny (Elerii Ipin). Thus, oracular consultation and Ifa divination, throughout the history of Yorùbá over the years has always been an essential part of their lives. When babies are born into this world, they immediately forget their destinies and lots in life. It is, therefore, the responsibility of their parents to consult the oracle through Ifa which will reveal the content of their destiny and what the future has in stock for them. Through Ifa divination, people are able to get firsthand information about the future occurrence that is usually hidden from ordinary eyes. Yorùbá people, therefore, display their reliance on the divine command disseminated to them through Ifa divination in every sphere of their lives.[43]

Yorùbá people consult diviners to enquire about their purpose and destiny because they believe in the revelation of destiny and fate. This is sometimes done for children to know their *akosejaye*, which means their fate and purpose on earth. Diviners, through the help of divination, gather information and knowledge about the person's destiny. Orunmila has notably been recorded in myths to be present during creation and a witness during the allocation of destiny, and so it is informative to note that diviners are consulted to enquire of Ifa what the future holds for a child or an adult and how an individual can use this information regarding their destiny to maximize their outcome. Yorùbá people believe in destiny and the finality of the outcome revealed through divination because they believe diviners hold significant knowledge on destiny. Diviners possess ideas of destiny and the means to seek out the meaning of destiny through the knowledge gained from the Ifa literary corpus.

Through divination, diviners reveal psychological information when they foretell a child's akosejaye (the child's fate). This psychological information is used in guiding the parents to raise the child in the proper way in order to foster the psychological traits to achieve his maximum potential. The Odu or Ifa signature revealed during the consultation guides the diviner to chant several Ifa verses appropriate to the client's situation as a therapeutic procedure to heal the patient. When the client recognizes the verse most suitable to their problem, there is a psychotherapeutic release that eases the client's distress and assures them of a possible solution. So, the diviner's performance of the *ęsę Ifá* avails the client/patient a psychotherapeutic release. Diviners' performances of Ifa poetry, their body language, and divination have psychotherapeutic effects on the clients. Packer and Sierra observe the following:

> Psychologists are inclined to view reasoning as a solitary and cognitive process. It can be, but reasoning can also be a social, contextualized activity. A Babalawo does not simply consult the oracle and dictate a course of action. He must reason with the client, relating what is in the signs to events in her life, to her concerns and the reasons she chose to consult him in the first place. He must justify the course of action spoken by Orula, anticipate possible objections, and provide both logical and empirical grounding for his claim about its worth. Our analysis suggests that the Babalawo is guiding his client in what amounts to a process of constitution, of self-mastery.[44]

The Babalawo is also a psychologist whose job is to psychoanalyze the client and their problem using leading questions to reveal the hidden areas underlying the cause of the problem. The Babalawo's divination reveals the necessary actions that must be followed, and the diviner begins to guide the client on their proposed method of solution. In divination, the diviner chants several ẹsẹ̀ *Ifá* that, along with being critical to the situation, match the Ifa signature. Like the psychiatrist, the Babalawo analyzes the pathological causes of mental imbalances, such as insanity (whether partial or total), determines the psychological archetypes that have been inherited by the client, and evaluates the psychodynamics of possible treatment.

Diviners possess adequate knowledge on psychiatry and psychological imbalances, such as *efori* (headache), *tulu* (migraine), psychosis, insanity, and how to treat them. This knowledge may include causes of these mental issues, curative measures, and the healing procedure, recovery mechanisms, etc. Diviners, especially the Babalawo in the Yorùbá societies, are known to possess ideas on psychiatric and psychoneurotic issues. It is not uncommon to find that diviners treat patients with psychiatric problems through divination to find the cause of the psychiatric problems and the solution. Ogunleye avers:

> It is through *Ifa*, which is the message of *Olodumare* that the solution to individual problem would be revealed. It is to be noted that regular visit to *Babalawo* (*Ifa* priest) will keep one abreast of his or her spiritual status. This priest, as a diviner, possesses exoteric knowledge through which he pries into the future and brings the message from the super sensible world for his client.[45]

Diviners and their Tools

Diviners use some equipment for their professions that distinguish them from other experts in traditional knowledge. These costumes and tools are used to differentiate diviners and signify the importance of their craft with the right assemblage. Bascom observed that the Babalawo are identified by a beaded bracelet known as *ide* (or *ide*

Ifa), which is often made of imported tan and light-green beads, known as *etutu oponyo*.[46] Just as modern/Western experts are to be garbed in their attires denoting their profession, diviners also appear in attire befitting their duties and roles in their societies. The signification of these beaded bracelets to their personality shows that the diviners' identity is grounded on the cosmological importance of their society.

Beaded bracelets in Yorùbá society are known to be the signature of nobility, chieftains, and African spiritual leaders. Bascom further clarifies:

> The babalawo are distinguished by a beaded bracelet worn on the left wrist and known as ide or the beads of Ifa (ide Ifa), which generally are of imported tan and light green beads, also known as etutu oponyo. These are called etutu opoyo in Ilesa and otutu opun in Meko, where the green beads are distinguished as dark or "black" (dudu) and·the tan ones as "red" (pupa). One verse (256-3) refers to the use of these beads by Orunmila worn around his neck, and in another (35-3) they serve to identify Hyena as a babalawo. In Ife the bracelet may also include a palm nut or a light opal-colored glass bead (emu) of European manufacture, as well as beads of other colors. The tan and green beads are worn as medicine by others, although not around the wrist, but the opal-colored bead is used only by babalawo.[47]

This proves that diviners use Orunmila's model and are properly garbed as befit their roles. Additionally, Bascom also describes the "cow-tail switch (irukere, iruke, iru) or flywhisk as another insignia of the Babalawo,"[48] which he takes with him when he goes to make divination for people. Diviners also use the iron staff (orere, osun, osu), which has many small conical bells with iron clappers connected to it that jingle when the staff touches the ground.[49] This iron staff is a representation of the diviner's authority and strength and is usually stood erect in the Ifa shrine in the diviner's house.

Bascom also noted:

> Each diviner has one stuck into the ground at his Ifa shrine, and it is said to guard him while he sleeps. It must never be allowed to fall over, lest the owner dies; and at his death it is knocked down. In Meko, it is considered as a symbol of the God of Medicine (Osanyin), who is described as the owner of herbs and leaves and is venerated by the Babalawo because they so often use leaves in preparing medicines for their clients.[50]

Diviners and Ideas on the Ecosystem and Ecology

The Babalawo possesses knowledge and ideas of the Yorùbá ecology and the ecosystem of the immediate environment from the lengthy study of and forays into the forest and observations of the interactions of humans with the ecosystem. Through the study of what is codified in the Ifa Corpus and long-term study of the flora and fauna of the Yorùbá environs, diviners develop ideas on the use of these animals and vegetations for human use. In the Ifa poetry, Eji Ogbe, the verse contrasts two related animals, aaya and edun:

> Are lo ba edun nle,
> Edun o moo sa.
> A difa fun edun ti I se omo iya aaya . . .
> Are lo ba edun nile,
> Edun o moo sa,
> Are ori igi lo ye edun.

In this *ẹsẹ Ifá*, Abimbola opines that even though aaya and edun are from the same family, they possess different characteristics and behaviors which make each unique in its own way. Although the two animals are related, they perform better in their own individual space: edun is fast when it is on the tree but when it is on plane ground its speed is nonexistent. This is why the saying that "*lagbaja ti di edun arinle*" (lagbaja has become powerless or reduced to the barest minimum) is derived from the nature of the animal in the Ifa poetry.[51] Diviners have extensive access to the Ifa poetry, which makes them knowledgeable in generating ideas about the Yorùbá flora and fauna and producing sayings, proverbs, and pieces of wisdom from nature's characteristics.

Diviners and Ideas on African Traditional Religion

Diviners in Yorùbá possess knowledge of other deities and divinities of the Yorùbá pantheon. Because of Ifa's presence beside *Olodumare* during creation, Ifa is a link between Olodumare (the Yorùbá Supreme Being) and other divinities, and he mediates between these divinities and Olodumare. Ilesanmi further supports this assertion when he states that the idea of Olodumare as a Yorùbá Supreme Deity has often been advertised by the Babalawo.[52] Diviners in the course of divination receive information on what divinity is responsible for the predicament of the client and what appropriate measures can be offered to the deity to appease him or her. Diviners possess knowledge regarding how Yorùbá divinities can be consulted and appeased for good fortune and positive results. The diviner has to have sufficient knowledge of what the divinities want and the taboos to beware of. An extensive knowledge of how the Yorùbá divinities interact with one another is perceived from the structure of the Ifa.

Because of the history contained in the Ifa Corpus, diviners possess knowledge of the Yorùbá divinities and the history of the Yorùbá pantheon. It is observed that each of the Yorùbá divinities has its own Odu, such as Ifa in Eji Ogbe or *Sango* in Okanran Meji. In Otua Meji, the history of Islam as a religion is documented while Otuurupon Meji historicizes Egungun. Diviners are armed with the Ifa Corpus, which gives them knowledge of the behavioral characteristics of these Yorùbá pantheons alongside their taboos and precautionary measures to take to avoid incurring their wrath. To elaborate the knowledge possessed by diviners through the digestion of the Ifa Corpus, Abimbola delves into the history of Sango, who is also known as Arira, the son of Oranmiyan.

Patambole okiribiti.
A dia fun Arira gagaaga,
Eyi ti i somo Oranyan lOko,
Nigba ti Sango n be laarin osiiri,
Ti Olubanbi n be laarin ota.
Nje kin lArira fi sete?
Igba ota.
Igba ota lArira fi sete
Igba ota.[15]

Diviners memorize these *ẹsẹ̀ Ifá* and are able to reproduce them when the occasion arises. This *ẹsẹ̀ Ifá* shows that Sango, a descendant of Oranmiyan, comes from the ancient town Oko. This Ifa poem reveals that at the time Sango was surrounded by adversaries, he offered a sacrifice of bullets, and afterward, he began to conquer his adversaries with bullets.[53] In Ifa poetry, Otuurupon Meji, Ifa talks about the Egungun cult:

Igbo nigboo Geegeese.
Odan ni odan Gbogbofo.
Odan Gbogbofo lEgun gbe sowo aso welewele.
A dia fun nitafa
Ti o toko la wale.
Won ni ki onitafa o rubo.
O sir u u
Igba t'o rubo tan,
O si la.
O ni bee gege.
Ni awon awo oun n senu reree pefa.
Omode yii o mawo,
Je n fawo han o.
Egberi o mawo.
Je n fawo han o.[16]

This Ifa poem discusses the Egungun cult; non-initiates and children cannot know the secret of this cult except when they are initiated into it. This *ẹsẹ̀ Ifá* describes how *Egun* dances in the two forests and groves.[54] Diviners possess knowledge of the Yorùbá traditional religions, which is why Ilesanmi opines that

some Awo, who may be described as intellectual advocates of the Ifa system, are, together with the Babalawo, theologians.[55] Theology deals with the expert interpretation of the mind of the deity, an explanation of the divine purpose for humanity. This is exactly what the Babalawo do. They always present Ifa verses as divine truths, which should not be questioned without commensurate punishment for any questioning client. They do not even make any distinction between revelation, myths, and theology. Every *ẹsẹ̀ Ifá* assumes the status of historical fact among the Yorùbá.

Diviners are experts on theology as espoused by Ilesanmi, as they deploy the ẹsẹ̀ *Ifá* and knowledge of the other Yorùbá deities to the clients in clear and succinct terms. The Babalawo, unlike other priests, develop and possess ideas about Ifa and other Yorùbá deities. They possess the history of these deities and their systems of veneration.

Diviners and Ideas of Reincarnation, Spirit Possession

Diviners have a specific view of the Yorùbá belief systems and worldview, especially with regards to reincarnation. The cultural beliefs in the (re)emergence and life after death and the existence of another world where extraterrestrial beings live are some of the ideas of Yorùbá beliefs that Babalawo possesses and generates. The Babalawo possess ideas of predestination, reincarnation, and abiku (a child born to die repeatedly) that they acquired through their years of apprenticeship and training in the Yorùbá cosmology. Reincarnation (atunwaye) is one aspect of the Yorùbá philosophy on the ancestors' and divinities' interaction and intervention in the affairs of humans and their descendants.

The Ifa Corpus dwells on this phenomenon—the re-invention and re-multiplication of their essence in human bodies and subjects. In order to understand the significance of the belief in reincarnation, one only needs to look at children with names like Babatunde (father has come again), Yewande (mother has come to me), Yetunde (mother has come again), Iyabo (mother comes), and Babajide (father rises again). Diviners who bear the name Awo or Ifa as part of their nomenclature understand the complexities of this phenomenon. The gravity to which diviners understand this complex phenomenon is represented in the names given to their children that bear a resemblance to their forebears or whose birth coincides with the demise of their grandparents.

Diviners replicate this belief of reincarnation in their names, such as *Awotunde* (the Ifa cult has come back) and *Ifatunji* (Ifa has risen). Odesanya and Akinjogbin noted that names derivative of Ifa origin can be from Ifa such as *Ifatola*; also, from the Odu as in Odugbemi; from Awo as Awolowo; or Osun (not the female river deity) in Dosunmu or Amosun, and from Ope, found in Dopemu and Opebunmi.[56] These names are mainly derived in the *esentaye*—Ifa divination for the child's purpose on earth. Children who come in the shadow of a previous ancestor are given an Ifa name to denote the child's connection to his predecessor.

In their study, Odesanya and Akinjogbin opine that Akosejaye and Esentaye are pathways to how a child gets his or her name and sometimes also resonate with reincarnation beliefs.[57] This implies that the diviner's revelation of the child's destiny (akosejaye) through divination sometimes resound the belief in reincarnation. They also observed the existence of "Igboro," which is a divination to generate names and to reveal which deceased family member is reincarnating or "returning" through the child. "Time was when Igbori served as the divinatory process from which such names as Babatunde, Yeyejide, and Iyabo could be sourced."[58] Diviners' knowledge of this system of divination and ideas of Yorùbá belief in reincarnation is employed when they are consulted.

Diviners possess and generate ideas of knowledge about the abiku phenomenon and how to help couples who are being afflicted or troubled with an abiku child. According to Odesanya and Akinjogbin, "Some spiritual mates in the spirit world are calling a child (an *abiku*) to reunite with them by dying, as he has always shuttled between births and deaths. However, because the child now no longer sees any reason to die to join his mates, he tells them to forever part ways with him."[59]

Diviners gather charms and knowledge about these kinds of children and how to properly handle these cases. Diviners are consulted to assist the parents of an abiku child to secure the child to the world of the living. The diviner may also foretell the reason behind an abiku child's power source so that he may sever the connection between the child and the other power source.

Diviners and Political Ideas of the Yorùbá Milieu

In the preliterate Yorùbá society, the system of governance and political system is the monarchical system headed by the Oba (king). In this system, the king has a court where there are other elected chiefs that assist him in governance. Diviners are indispensable in this kind of system because of their knowledge on political matters and wisdom gathered from years of experience divining and providing solutions to political problems. In this vein, Ogunleye says:

> Although the king is powerful, he still relies on the support and advice of his traditional chiefs who form the Councils of State in each Yorùbá town. Of all these chiefs, Babalawo, the chief priest in charge of Ifa divination plays prominent roles toward peaceful and smooth running of the government. In fact, most of the traditional rulers in Yorùbá land have their own Babalawo at their disposal and who could be called upon at any point in time to consult Ifa for them.[60]

The Babalawo generates ideas of political importance to traditional rulers and chiefs, sometimes from preexisting knowledge of political issues in the past. Diviners are reputable for their wisdom in several matters, especially the ones of a political nature, as they have experience in giving advice from past events and the ones in the Ifa literary corpus. In the event of political upheaval, governments, chiefs, and kings consult diviners to obtain proper information on how these political issues can be resolved. In the course of installing or choosing a traditional ruler in many Yorùbá societies, diviners are the first to be consulted and summoned to predict who the right choice for the installation is among the royal families.

Diviners and Knowledge of African Rites of Passage

Diviners possess ideas of African traditions and customs, such as rites of passage. Some of the rites of passage in the Yorùbá milieu are marriage rites, burial rites, maturity, and initiation to adulthood rites, etc. Diviners are instrumental to the society because of their in-depth knowledge of their society's traditions and customs. Diviners are consulted in determining the right partner for marriage. Ogunleye opines that it is Ifa that illuminates the major phases of life referred to as the rites of passage. According to the Yorùbá, the essence of life is in Ifa. This is primarily why the diviner is consulted to ask Ifa for proper guidance before engagement, wedding, and childbirth. As such, it is the duty of the Ifa priest to recommend the appropriate rituals for each of the stages.[61]

These rites of passage are sometimes carried out with the help of the diviner who acts as a guide during crucial events. In the betrothal or marriage rites, diviners are consulted to find out hidden information about the lady, man, or the potential spouses' family to know if there is any record of diseases, such as insanity, leprosy, epilepsy, barrenness, etc. For Packer and Sierra, in instances of illness, impotence, or unfruitfulness, a Babalawo will be contacted. Also, before childbirth and soon after, the parents of the baby will consult the Babalawo to check the child's future and find out his or her guardian spirit. If the newborn is a boy, the Babalawo decides if he should be circumcised immediately or at the age of eighteen.[62]

Some of the rites of passage require the presence of a diviner to officiate and to direct them, such as in the burial rites of a king or traditional ruler. The diviner uses his knowledge of the burial rites to usher the deceased king or noble to the great beyond. In some cases, where the king's or traditional ruler's remains are to be buried in a specific location, stipulated by tradition, the diviner takes the lead in such cases. In the coronation of a new ruler, the diviner is summoned to perform the rites (etutu) for the new ruler. Diviners in many societies still perform these sacred duties as part of their sociocultural and politico-religious functions in society.

Diviners and Ideas of Wealth Generation

Diviners possess ideas regarding the generation of wealth and how the physical and metaphysical world can be manipulated in one's favor. The Babalawo consult people who desire good fortune and who desire to be informed of the methods to employ in order to generate riches in their businesses or trades. Ogunleye enunciated:

> The scramble for materials well-being has led many to be involved in regular oracular consultations. In this modern world, people still consult *Ifa* priest for instant wealth or as a shortcut to wealth. Magical practices are still in vogue. People visit Babalawo who prepares it for protection and security. In a nutshell, people patronize *Ifa* priests for protection while on business trips, economic advantages and commercial gains.[63]

Diviners possess ideas on garnering wealth and knowledge on the methods to employ to secure wealth. These ideas may or may not involve divination as they have gathered ideas over time about wealth manipulation. Diviners may give advice on how to apply methods of increasing sales or the use of potent charms to attract customers. In terms of security measures to protect these people against malevolent forces known to humans, diviners prepare charms or amulets for protection against loss. Oladiti and Oyewale discuss and give an example, the *ẹsẹ̀ Ifá* Oworin Iwori. In the following verse, a person who visits the diviner to inquire about his fate of becoming prosperous is given a divination chanted through the verse:

Oworin Iwori A
(1) Eleyiun ti sise sise Ifa pe yio la, sugbon isee re ee se ise ikanju o.
   Nnkan ti eleyiun o ta solaje nnkan tawon eeyan o moo sun meyin,
   to won o mooju kuro nbe."
   Oworin Iwori A
(2) Awon le la laye awon bi?
   Won niki won rubo
   Won ni bi on batirubo
   Won niise tan . . .

The first example, presented above in the "Oworin Iwori A," suggests a search or inquiry into whether a person would become affluent or prosperous (name not mentioned). The Babalawo's response after the divination procedure tells the inquirer that this individual has toiled and struggled hard but has nothing to show for it. The diviner predicts that the individual will be wealthy in life; nevertheless, the source of their riches will be the consequence of selling an unusual commodity. It is clear from the above that the inquirer wants to ascertain the likelihood through which they would achieve riches. While the diviner promised them prosperity, this will only happen if they accomplish something that many other people have overlooked as a way to become rich.[64]

The two verses of Ifa poetry and many others are sources that affirm diviners' knowledge about wealth generation in the Yorùbá society. These Ifa verses aid the diviner in giving advice or in helping the client to generate wealth. This act may require diligence on the part of the client—hard work, patience, and perseverance are some of the secrets that the diviner may give to the inquirer who has come to know what measures to take to be rich. In some cases, the diviner may recommend sacrifice (ebo) to attract fortune to the client and to appease the deity in his family, like in the Ifa poetry verse, Obara Meji:

Ifa pe ire fun eleyiun. Ori ola lori e. yoo la,
Yoo si obi laye. Osun kan n be nii dile e,
 bi o ba si Osun, Ko beere nibi won gbe da Ifayii fun un:
kosi loo bo Osun ohun tori ilodo Osun nigbogbo ire ti o
nii laye Otiwa. Omo Osun ni ohun paapaa.[65]

The diviner prescribes ebo (sacrifice) to the Osun deity as a measure to usher in riches to the client in the Ifa verse. Diviners are instrumental to the accumulation of riches and fortune in the Yorùbá communities because of their possession of ideas of wealth creation and the use of Ifa divination. Diviners remain relevant in many African societies, especially in Yorùbá communities, for their knowledge and expertise in wealth management and creation from the primordial era to the present.

Diviners and Ideas of Personal Security

Diviners prepare safety measures and tools for people who consult them for many reasons. Security, as well as, protection against physical and spiritual forces is one of the diviners' specialties. Diviners possess ideas on personal protection measures during out-of-town trips, household attacks, and unforeseen assaults. These protection and security devices are made to keep people safe from physical and spiritual harm. Eva-Marita Rinne writes:

> To prevent a misfortune, people wear many kinds of charms and amulets. They may be carried visible or invisible as a necklace, or they can be worn around an arm, be hidden under clothes or kept inside a pocket. They can also be tied on the doors or doorsteps of houses, buried in the ground near a doorstep, a house, or a shop, hung from the ceiling of a house, suspended in a pot over the door, or fastened to the walls of a house. Furthermore, a charm may be something to eat such as a combination of leaves, roots, and other materials ground together, a concoction to be rubbed on the body, especially the head or the arms, a traditional medicine mixed with "native soap" to be used for washing or bathing, a silver ring with mystical signs engraved on it, or some medicine that is inserted into a necklace, a waist band or a bracelet.[66]

Diviners engage in these security measures from ideas gathered from their training and experiences. In the preparation of charms such as igbadi (waist charm) and ifunpa (charm worn on the arm), diviners combine knowledge of spiritual components and physical/natural ingredients to make these security devices for people. Just like the modern bulletproof vest, known as "ayeta," diviners also make the traditional charms that prevent bullet penetration for people who require them. Rinne further elucidates that charms are used as protective devices to prevent witches and evil spirits from entering a house or attacking a person, to prevent small-pox, to insure against accidents, such as the earlier mentioned motor car collisions, to nullify harmful attempts of enemies or sorcerers, and to keep thieves from breaking into one's house. Usually, one obtains a charm from a healer or a diviner after it has been specially prepared for the person or the family. After preparing the charm, the Babalawo usually presents an Ifa odù and asks Orunmila's aid to make it effective for the purpose that it is prepared for.[67] Diviners are similar to security experts who provide security measures for personal and communal safety.

People of different ages and status consult diviners to provide safety equipment for them. Hunters who may require this protection during their hunting expedition in the forest, where dangerous wild animals lurk and are liable to attack, may acquire Egbe, a charm known for its disappearing abilities. This charm helps them escape these animal attacks and attacks from other harmful sources. Diviners possess and generate these kinds of safe and protective gadgets. Moreover, diviners dispense incantations that also function as security measures. Diviners generate diverse incantatory verses for different purposes; these verses come in handy when evil or danger lurks. People may acquire these charms and incantatory verses for protection against known and unknown assailants.

Diviners and Ideas of Yorùbá Anthropology

The Babalawo possess ideas of Yorùbá origin, nature, and destiny of human beings in the Yorùbá cosmology. Diviners possess knowledge of the Yorùbá people and their ancestors who are reputed to have originated from Ile-Ife, from where the Yorùbá people spread to other parts of the world. The Babalawo draw from the knowledge of their forebears and teachers who impart anthropological knowledge of the Yorùbá people through stories, which are committed to memory from years of practice. Packer notes that the diviners' ability suggests that a Babalawo is skillful and responsible and has mastered a body of traditional learning as well as the practical ability to consult and make divination.[68]

Diviners are one of the most reliable sources of Yorùbá history and anthropology due to their possession of the Ifa Corpus as a guide and manual into the vastness of the Yorùbá cosmology. Van dan Meer opines that though Yorùbá Ifa/Orisa practice is grounded in myth, it also contains historical references or markers about real Yorùbá history.[69] The ẹsẹ̀ Ifá chanted by diviners are historical poetry illustrating knowledge of the origin of the people. Van der Meer also notes that these Ifa poems affirm and corroborate historical evidence from place and personal names to lists of ancient tools and implements.[70]

In accounting for the existence of the Yorùbá ancestors-cum-divinities, Van der Meer noted that Oduduwa is recognized as the ruler of the first place of settlement—Ile-Ife. He further enunciated that Oduduwa's legacy as the progenitor of the Yorùbá people is rooted in their traditional belief system. His legacy is grounded in Ilẹ́-Ifẹ̀ as well as the Ọ̀yọ́ Empire through his grandson Òrànmíyàn.[71] The anthropological manifestations of the Yorùbá divinities and ancestors and how they were transposed are codified in the Ifa Corpus, which diviners can access from their aural memorization and digestion of the texts.

Additionally, Van der Meer noted that the history and origins of the Yorùbá Ifá/Òrìṣá belief system are a complex narrative woven with myths, legends, and folktales. It has a complex philosophical and ethical epistemology that is rooted in Yorùbá cultural life and nature. It connects the natural world with the supernatural world and the benevolent forces with the malevolent forces. Nature, animals, and humans are linked and personified as one. The divinities and ancestors are placed in the forefront as having significant roles in the lives of all human beings.[72]

Peek enunciates the role of divination and diviners in the expression and articulation of African epistemology when he proposes that

> The diviner in other cultures is central to the expression and enactment of his or her cultural truths as they are reviewed in the context of contemporary realities. The situating of a divination session in time and space, the cultural artifacts utilized (objects, words, behaviors), the process of social interaction, and the

uses made of oracular knowledge all demonstrate the foundations of a people's world view and social harmony. Divination systems do not simply reflect other aspects of a culture; they are the means (as well as the premise) of knowing which underpin and validate all else. Contemporary Africans in both urban and rural environments continue to rely on divination, and diviners play a crucial role as mediators, especially for cultures in rapid transition.[73]

The diviner plays a paramount role in the spread of anthropological ideas of the Yorùbá and its benefits to the people. Some examples of anthropological ideas and knowledge possessed by diviners are where Yorùbá people originated from and how they have spread to other settlements over time. Diviners also possess ideas of the different ethnic groups of Yorùbá descent and the marks of identification that differentiate one from the other.

Conclusion

In this chapter, it was demonstrated that diviners are knowledgeable on several matters, ranging from personal security to governance, and from the sacred to the mundane. Diviners have held prominent positions in the preliterate era in many African societies, particularly in Yorùbá communities, where their ideas of knowledge on medicine, herbs, and plants are greatly appreciated and deployed to good use. Diviners employ knowledge in the oral tradition with their training as priests to become philosophers in their societies. This chapter has established in many ways that diviners do generate and possess ideas of knowledge in the field of medicine, psychology, psychiatry, African traditions and culture, traditional religion, oral narratives, and literature, etc. Diviners generate a myriad of ideas on wisdom and morality from the indigenous oral tradition, such as legends, folklore, panegyric poetry, praise poetry, etc.

Indeed, diviners are not only embodiments of knowledge or repositories of a knowledge system, they are also considered spiritual authorities. In fact, in precolonial Africa and even in traditional African settings, the knowledge possessed by them on matters of African spirituality made them forces to be reckoned with, such that their contributions to politics were translated for them in the sense that they wielded strong political power. With their knowledge and power of divination, their utterances were treated as sacred, not only by Africans but also by their rulers. This chapter evidently has proven how diviners not only come to be but also how they pass on their skills in divination to their apprentices. Indeed, more than anything, the focal point of mirroring this chapter was via the lens of the practitioner who wielded, as a result, spiritual power-cum-political influence. Surmising all, the knowledge production from divination was not only valid in the ideas and practices of spirituality but also very influential in the political space, especially during turbulent times deemed to be beyond mortal control.

Their knowledge stems from their training as young apprentices and adults who continue to seek knowledge on several matters from peers and superiors. Diviners' knowledge of the Yorùbá metaphysics, proverbs, ethics, and philosophy are numerous which is why they are revered as wise men and women who employ metaphors, proverbs, and epithets in addressing matters of high risk with diplomacy and tact. Diviners are known to be tactful and precise in the use of words and language because of the nature of their profession and the issues they handle. Like the Western idea of physician-patient confidentiality, diviners have to keep their clients' personal issues to themselves as professionals who are bound by the secrecy of the Ifa cult. It is not so surprising that the term "Babalawo" means "father of secrets," as they have been sworn to keep the secrets of the cult and that of their craft.

The roles diviners occupied in the preliterate era in many African communities appear to be gradually shifting toward extinction; the importation of foreign religions has reduced the importance of their craft, especially in the public sphere. Some Africans perceive the consultations with diviners as barbaric and primitive because of Western projections of African knowledge systems, especially of the indigenous type, which may or may not possess empirical evidence or basis. From the foregoing chapter, it is imperative to elevate the study of these experts and professionals, that is, diviners, as sources of Afrocentric knowledge that is pertinent to the resolution of African problems. The study intends to foreground and instigate research in the ideas of knowledge generated and possessed by diviners in the African space. This chapter is not exhaustive of the harvest of ideas that diviners possess and how this source of knowledge can be explored.

It cannot be overemphasized that diviners in the African space and especially in the Yorùbá milieu have untapped resources of knowledge that are yet to be fully explored by researchers in the African continent and beyond. Therefore, there is a need for more rigorous efforts to study these professionals who have received little or no extensive research to explore the ideas of knowledge they possess and generate. Diviners have proven to be indispensable in the preliterate Yorùbá societies, and are still being consulted, although to a very redundant degree, yet they possess ideas of knowledge that are yet to be fully explored and investigated like other modern professions.

2

Shamanism as a Knowledge System

Introduction

An attempt to provide an all-encompassing and definitive conceptualization of shamanism may be impossible due to the proliferation of works in anthropology, religion, sociology, and history, all of which have defined it, respectively. In Krippner's perspective, shamanism is a procedure for obtaining information by shamans.[1] He theorizes that they are the first professionals to achieve a diverse field of knowledge that includes physiotherapy, psychology, dramatics, meteorology, folklore, and performance. Wynne, who advanced it as a practice that "spans across continents and is deeply embedded in the culture of many different traditions," brought the cosmopolitanism of shamanism to the fore.[2]

However, this system of knowledge, according to Franz, has been pejoratively condensed into five aspects: "shamans as magicians or charlatans; shamans as psychologically different or distinctive subjects; shamans as universal religious practitioners; shamans as geographically defined and limited to Siberian territory; and shamanism as a regional-cultural tradition in which shamans may or may not exist."[3] However, this categorization has not diminished the potency of knowledge in shamanism.

Marovic and Machinga assert that shamanism is a system of teleporting into the spirit world to gain knowledge to heal members within the same group.[4] It is a practice and system that involves a conscious transition into a metaphysical space where communication and interaction between humans and spirits occurs. This system and practice is spread throughout different parts of the world, although Marovic and Machinga note that shamanism originated from a group of people known as the Tungus.[5] This is also affirmed by Bock, as he reiterates that shamanism can be traced to Siberians who perceived the shaman as a professional who possesses mystical knowledge.[6] Shamanism has been linked to a number of communities in the primeval period who used this system to gain knowledge to benefit society, as this knowledge is of utmost authenticity; hence they depended on it for survival.

Shamanism is more than just a practice—referring to it as such reduces it to a primitive activity. It is an organized system of operation whereby religious, secular, spiritual, and psychological wisdom is obtained for the stability of the community. Put differently, it is a whole body of knowledge that includes interactive alternation between the physical and non-physical realm seeking specific answers. In the primordial era and even in present time, the activities of indigenous healers, herbalists, religious heads, etc., are under the purview and jurisdiction of a shaman. This then connotes that shamanism encompasses various aspects and fields of indigenous and modern knowledge.

Shamanism is a system that is practiced in several places in the world and is known by different names and titles. In Southern Africa, where it is a common traditional practice, shamans who are also versed in healing are called by different appellations.[7] Whether they are given different nomenclatures in different places does not change the basic and fundamental aspect and essence of their knowledge export; the production of indigenous and contemporary wisdom that connects the past, present, and future. Shamanism is an important institution in society as the belief, practices, and rituals as well as the experts who uphold this belief and carry out the practices are sources of information which contributes to the body of knowledge on the cosmology of their community.

This made Bock suggest that shamans occupy positions of power as leaders who commune with spirits and influence the actions of their adherents or clients as a result.[8] It is illuminating that Bock argues that a delineation of shamanism is yet to be conceived; rather it is a notion in pejorative terms for indigenous practices that involve mysticism, spirits, and magic.[9] Some of the activities shamans carry out include rites, ceremonies, initiation, healing, etc., which percolate into different aspects of religion, beliefs, customs, traditions, and culture on an individual level. Yang offers yet another definition of shamanism "as a religious culture that revolves around certain gifted and respected holy men and women who have rare abilities to communicate with or be possessed by gods, spirits, or ancestors and to go into trance or ecstatic states, or to travel to other worlds, whether Heaven above or the Underworld below."[10]

Yang's perception not only established that shamanism is a religious culture and a medium for obtaining knowledge but also deliberately demystified the gender of the expert—in this case, as both male and female. Shamanism is a system of knowing where the distinction between men and women who possess power and knowledge is leveled. To have a substantial grasp of this notion, Eliade perceives shamanism to be relative to spirit possession, one that emerged from the phenomenon of trance.[11]

From the above, it can be surmised that shamanism operates using various mediums, such as trance and possession, as systems of altered consciousness from the physical to mystic worlds. This knowledge involves the interaction between non-ordinary forces and human beings to achieve a synthesis of body, mind, and soul. Eliade further asserts, "Ecstasy is the characteristic feature of shamanism which sets it apart from other forms of spiritual systems."[12] This discussion of shamanism as a knowledge system would introduce us to what shamans do and how knowledge is acquired.

Shamans and Knowledge

Before discussing the roles of shamans and their function in the community, it is imperative to know who they are. Singh defines shamans as "practitioners who enter a trance to provide services."[13] Singh's depiction of shamans as people who offer labor or a commodity through trance is inadequate and reductive, as a shaman occupies a distinguished profession and possesses a huge corpus of information. Their role is more than to provide "services," and it is in this vein that Krippner's conception of the term "shaman" would be examined with a view to expand the knowledge of the activities of a shaman and the belief system that encourages their actions.

The roles of shamans are many in traditional societies, communities, and urban settings, and they occupy a special status. It is in line with this argument that Krippner opines that "the term shaman is a social construct that describes a person who attends to the psychological and spiritual needs of a community."[14] Although they perform the roles mentioned above, their work exceeds the psychological and spiritual realm to include physical, medical, cultural, religious, and social needs. A shaman can be a male or female practitioner who has the ability and access to obtain a broad spectrum of knowledge on diverse issues that people can seek out for personal consultation. They perform different functions and their roles differ from one society to another, depending on the shaman's area of specialization. Krippner briefly analyzes a shaman's function as thus:

> A recent cross-cultural study of shamanism focused upon magico-religious practitioners, individuals who occupy a socially recognized role which has as its basis an interaction with the non-ordinary, nonconsensual dimensions of existence. This interaction involves special knowledge of spirit entities and how to relate to them, as well as special powers that allow these practitioners to influence the course of nature or human affairs in ways not ordinarily possible.[15]

One can thus posit that shamans also possess magical powers and abilities to carry out unconventional acts that are typically physically impossible to achieve. The performance of magic is a special domain in shamanism that involves knowledge of the cosmos and the science of combining this wisdom to bring about an expected result. Magic and magicians employ knowledge of metaphysics with the spiritual and physical world to create extraordinary realities. Shamans may perform magic; however, not all magicians can be called shamans because of the altered state of consciousness that these professionals must fulfil. Shamans also perform religious activities such as rituals, prayers, mediation, intercession, etc.

According to Krippner, there are differences in their mode of operation when compared with specialists in the exact field where shamans also function. For instance, in his words, "shaman-healers specialize in healing practices while healers typically work without the dramatic alterations of consciousness that characterize shamans and shaman-healers."[16] This differentiation between a healer and shaman-healer denotes that shamanism is premised on the ability to go into an altered state of consciousness. The ability and control the shaman has in entering and exiting the shamanic state of consciousness is that which distinguishes shamanism from any other religious and spiritual practice.

Witzel also identifies several key roles that shamans execute in the community: "healers, fortune-tellers, political advisers; they preserve their individual tribal traditions through storytelling and singing songs,"[17] which are essential for the development of the community. Other functions include mediating, presiding over sacrifices, and functioning as priests. He further states that "a shaman also determines society's features—such as the movements of nomadic tribes. He thus acts as the transmitter of traditional tribal lore, including that about the 'origins' of the tribe or 'the shaman' as such, known only to some extent by most elders."[18] These roles not only show the functions of shamans in a society but also exemplify the indispensability of the role of shamanism and the knowledge derived from it in the society.

Scope and Structure of this Chapter

This chapter will focus on shamanism as a knowledge system by examining the forms, nature, application, and relevance of this knowledge in Africa.[19] It will also attempt to define knowledge in shamanism by way of delineating the notion of knowledge by different researchers. This conceptualization of the knowledge in shamanism will lead us to understand the characteristics of knowledge, how this knowledge is conceived, and the dimensions of its growth in Africa. While discussing its nature, this chapter will also attend to its form and types as a branch of epistemology that is broad and encompassing. The individuals as well as groups of people responsible for creating, upholding, producing, managing, disseminating, and transmitting this knowledge will be discussed.

Unlike the proliferation of extant literature on shamanism as only traditional knowledge, this study proposes that shamanism as a knowledge system is both scientific and traditional, which means shamans are both traditional and modern scientists producing indigenous and modern scientific knowledge. It is not only a knowledge system; it is one that is relevant for the development of different aspects of indigenous and modern African civilization. It is also similarly crucial to understanding extant beliefs and practices of African traditional societies. This chapter concludes that a re-evaluation and re-appropriation of this knowledge system is paramount in the search for Africanized solutions to some indigenous problems, while some of these practices could still be applied to contemporary Africa.

Shamanism as an Indigenous Knowledge System

Shamanism originated from a branch of epistemology known as indigenous knowledge—primarily from an indigenous group or community of people—which is deployed for varied and specific purposes for the growth and well-being of society. This knowledge in shamanism has been and continues to be a part of traditional society and wisdom. Shamanism is the composite deployment of religious, spiritual, indigenous, and several other forms of knowledge. Marovic and Machinga perceive it as an interconnected string of religion, culture, spirituality, and healing systems.[20] Traditional or indigenous knowledge is conceived as a system of knowledge that is developed and found among members of indigenous communities. This wisdom is theorized out of beliefs, culture, experiences, and oral tradition.

It reflects the lives and cosmology, arts and crafts, philosophy, history, and ecology of the people. Shamanism in an indigenous system of knowledge that encompasses how people understand their existence in relation to their divinities, ancestors, spirits, and gods. The language, literature, music, dance, etc. is reflected in this knowledge system. It also defines the identity of the people; the individual, and the collective consciousness of each member of the community is woven into this knowledge system.

Knowledge in Shamanism: Nature and Definition

The nature of shamanic knowledge is holistic; this wisdom encompasses all aspects of society, such as education, administration and governance, politics, entertainment, religion, marriage, family, etc. Indigenous knowledge in shamanism embraces the totality of African social existence and possesses insight into every activity as its practice permeates traditional cosmology. Intrinsically, shamanic knowledge espouses wisdom into the very core and essence of the people. This holistic nature of knowledge in shamanism secures every facet of indigenous past, present, and future: wisdom from their ancestors enhances maximum productivity of their successors, as it is a knowledge that knows the future from the past. It is also timeless. It is a system of knowledge that can be traced to the beginning of human existence and is present in many societies today.

Again, one of the characteristics of knowledge in shamanism is orality; the knowledge that originated from the indigenous people of Africa was transmitted by word of mouth from one generation of knowledge custodian to the next generation via apprenticeship. This way of acquiring information during primeval times was primarily oral, and the custodians of this knowledge taught it to neophytes who will pass it on to their succeeding generation as well. In addition, knowledge in shamanism is both esoteric and non-esoteric, as it is intelligence gathered from communication with mystic entities. Esoteric knowledge is obtained by professional custodians who have achieved the required length and experience to possess such wisdom. Non-esoteric knowledge is obtained through training, experience gathered over time, and from working through recurring issues that require basic shamanic knowledge. For example, a shaman who is also an herbalist may not necessarily require esoteric wisdom to heal common or mild health issues like constipation, dysentery, toothaches, and body pain. They can apply ointments, balm, oils, and concoctions or even massage the body.

Knowledge Producers in Shamanism

Knowledge in shamanism is essentially produced through several mediums by trained experts mostly known as shamans. This person becomes a custodian and producer of this knowledge through the engagement with extraordinary forces and ability to communicate and interpret the wisdom derived therein. Joshi speaks of the role of the shaman as a person who possesses a unique gift of reaching the mystic realm through trance. He goes further to state:

> This ability of shamans to get into trance coupled with voluntarism can be identified as the diagnostic marker of shamanism. Thus shamans are individuals who have the capacities of getting into trance at will. Here, trance is the shamanistic state of consciousness, a state wherein the shaman exhibits physical movements (shaking of body, head, hands, etc.), speech transformation and often communication with the culturally postulated divine powers. Furthermore, the trance state of the shaman is marked by sharp lucidity and spontaneous imagery.[21]

Shamans, who are professionals of indigenous wisdom, are experts in creating traditional intelligence steeped in transportation into the metaphysical world of spirits and beings to gain dimensions of knowledge that are hidden to ordinary people. Marovic and Machinga note that shamans are highly revered people with extrasensory knowledge and perception, who possess the power and ability to commune with extraordinary spiritual entities and can manipulate human activities.[22] More importantly, shamans double as healers, psychologists, psychotherapists, herbalists, pharmacists, and counselors. Their position is important, as they serve as links to ancestral bodies and divinities. Their roles and experiences help to create and maintain balance; they maintain and preserve cultural practices, beliefs, and the worship of mystical beings and spirits. One salient and important function of shamans as producers of knowledge is the purification and stability they create between the physical world and metaphysical spaces, along with their interaction between these spaces and the individual.[23]

The purpose of this section is to examine who shamans are, how they are trained, the kind of training they undergo, their duties, and their significance to this traditional knowledge dissemination. It is unclear how shamans are called to this system, whether it involves a selection process, a voluntary choice or decision, or if it is inherited. For some, the knowledge and practice may be transferred to a family member who is qualified or has been chosen for the responsibility.[24] It is no doubt a system that thrives on the transfer of mystic power and knowledge, so there is a possibility of transference of duties to another family member. Joshi examines the role of shamans in society and avers that they are people with the ability to approach mystic powers through an "altered state of consciousness."[25] The ability to alternate between two realms and convey knowledge in their physical body distinguishes these people from ordinary healers. Joshi goes further to expound on the principal utility of shamans' oeuvre when he states:

> The shamans perform multiple roles, the primary role being that of diviner, counselor and therapist. They make use of and manipulate the cultural codes, metaphors and symbols in their interaction with their clients. The diviner's role is primarily used in locating and contextualizing the problem. The shaman may "see through" or use mechanical means such as throwing of grains and looking into seeds and myriad other means in arriving at divination of the problem.[26]

The aforementioned list of indispensable functions not only shows that shamans are integral to the belief systems of their indigenous societies but that they also represent the people's culture and belief in traditional wisdom. Shamans glide through similar and sometimes dissimilar roles to acquire knowledge of different kinds and dimensions. As discussed above, the shaman is a diviner who uses geomancy training and knowledge to decipher the cause of a problem while also assuming the role of a healer to administer the knowledge obtained to address a client's issue. The change of roles from diviner, healer, counselor to that of a therapist are testament to the diversity in functions of a shaman. Interpretative skills employed during shamanistic performance attests to how shamans engage, analyze, and apply knowledge to different situations. Joshi affirms this when he opines that a diagnosis is subject to the shamans' skill in communicating and interpreting to transmit his understanding to the client in a clear and distinct format.[27]

A shaman could also be by creation, via the acceptance of the call to shamanism by inheritance, an affliction, or sudden recovery from a chronic ailment, spiritual possession or intrusion, through visions and dreams, or extraordinary ability and behaviors.[28] Krippner also corroborates this idea and further adds that while some people may enter the profession by inheritance, others may possess unusual features like an "extra digit, albinism, or an unusual birthmark; unusual actions such as seizures or else behavioral patterns culturally associated with the opposite gender, or strange experiences such as out-of-the-body sensations and vivid or lucid dreams."[29]

These various methods of responding to the call of shamanism differ from person to person and depend on their personality. These strong physical reactions to a call to shamanism may be due to the resistance encountered by spiritual forces, while other reactions may be mild if the inheritor is open to embracing the call, which manifests in their vision or dreams. Some may be receptive to the shamanic call because their forebears and ancestors may have been in the system, and they were groomed to inherit or take over such a profession. People who have disturbing experiences, such as epilepsy, fainting spells, psychotic behavior, convulsion, and other strange experiences may come to accept their responsibility when they are treated or assisted by an experienced shaman.

However, Bock notes that aside from people who are "chosen," there are also people who voluntarily choose to undergo shamanic training or serve under a professional shaman to become one. Although there is yet to be a consensus of the age range for the summons to practice shamanism, Krippner suggests that the system of practice and tradition of each society may determine the age at which people may join the craft.[30] Additionally, it may seem that when a child is chosen to take up this profession, he or she would need to get training and obtain some common knowledge about the practice. Doing so may be a rigorous process, so the child could grow into his or her understanding and take on responsibility when he or she is mature and knowledgeable enough. Regarding the process of training, Krippner observes that

> In some societies there is no formal training program, while in others the training process may last for several years. The mentors may be older shamans or even spirit entities including one's ancestors, nature spirits, and power animals who can give instructions in the neophyte's dreams.[31]

It is clear that some of these people receive their education from a renowned shaman who prepares them for the practice.[32] Whether "chosen" or a volunteer, during training, both groups are initiated into experiencing a trance, an out-of-the-body experience that is likened to a "death and rebirth."[33] This journey may be experienced throughout the course of training and after the completion of their education. Bock recognizes that there are processes that are carried out with the trainee or apprentice to help him or her achieve the ability to reach this state of ecstasy.

These processes, which include inducing pain, extreme fasting or abstinence from food and water, sonic stimulation, such as singing and drumming, and restriction of movement and isolation are methods used on the apprentice shaman to achieve the trance state. Training the neophyte may vary between different societies and cultures. However, common elements of training include "diagnosis and treatment of illnesses, contacting spirit entities from non-ordinary dimensions, supervising sacred rituals, interpreting dreams, predicting the weather, herbal knowledge, prophecy, and mastering the self-regulation of bodily functions and attentional states."[34] These skills are interwoven and require discipline for the apprentice to be successful since the profession engages with humanity and knowledge for its preservation.

Bock states that during the length of training, the apprentice is made to learn physical and metaphysical aspects of the profession, such as receiving visions, dream interpretation, consultation with spiritual entities, and drawing information from extant sociocultural resources, such as philosophies, beliefs, ritual, and rites.[35] Part of the training includes learning the lore of the shamanic profession and its application in various situations, clients, patients, and events. It is during this education that the shaman novice learns of psychological and metaphysical features of mind transformation, the mental development through interaction with mystic beings. The ability to master the alternation of consciousness from the physical to the netherworld is the ultimate achievement of shamanic practice.[36]

In a similar fashion, the ability to stand in between two realities—that is, the physical and the extraterrestrial—and to gather knowledge for the purpose of helping people marks the shaman as an important producer of indigenous knowledge. Besides mastering the entry and exit of the altered state of consciousness, there are other skills to be acquired, which include an acquisition of cultural motifs, symbols, songs and poems, body movements, chants, myths, and stories. The importance of this education sets the shaman profession and practice apart from that of other religions since shamans are able to move, dance, sing, chant, mime, and divine in synchrony and with effortless delivery. At the completion of training, the trainee is initiated into the practice fully, where he or she may decide to create a separate practice. Krippner notes that "some tribes arrange a special feast when the initiate passes a key phase of his or her training."[37]

Acquisition of Knowledge in Shamanism

As hitherto noted, knowledge is acquired in shamanism through different mediums, one of which is through apprenticeship under a practicing shaman. As with the method of acquiring knowledge in Western society through education and training, so too is the attainment of wisdom in shamanism. Some of the techniques required in the education of a shaman prepare the trainee to be able to transform into an altered state and to have effective interaction with spiritual beings. These techniques help in aligning the mind of the shaman to the mystic realm and ensure his receptiveness to knowledge released in this realm. The apparatus around the shaman includes percussive instruments (drums, gongs), attire, and the chewing of traditional plants and herbs, which serve to induce an altered state of consciousness.[38] The use of song, dance, and drums is effective in ushering the shaman into the "shamanic journey"[39] and to exit it. The purpose of the journey is to "bring back knowledge and power to heal and regenerate individuals and the community."[40] In light of this acquisition of knowledge, Walter and Fridman argue that

> So-called spirit entities need to be contacted for different purposes. If they are dissatisfied, they need to be propitiated; if a person dies without leaving a will, the deceased person's spirit needs to be contacted to determine property disposition; if a deceased person's spirit is causing trouble, the spirit needs to be appeased.[41]

It is true that the spiritual world is a procedural pathway for the acquisition of hidden information that is helpful in resolving client issues.

Forms of Knowledge

In this section, the different branches and forms of knowledge in shamanism will be explicitly listed and discussed. Here, we will take this form of knowledge from various cultural practices, beliefs, and activities in shamanism across various societies in Africa.

Knowledge of Psychotherapy in Shamanism

Psychotherapy is a field of knowledge that is covered and converged in shamanism. It is characterized by the ability to diagnose the cause of a client's affliction while also acquiring methods to solve their issue through mystic instruction. Thus, psychotherapy finds balance between the client's troubled psychological or innate state and their physical problems. Joshi confirms that shamans treat "cases of sicknesses, many of which exhibit behavioral disturbances."[42] It is a very common belief in African societies to link problems to non-physical causations and roots which create tension or manifest issues in the physical state. Apprentice-shamans have rules that they must live by; some of which include dietary restrictions, habits, hygiene, and relationships with others.[43] These restrictions and rules imposed on shamans may be due to their importance as mediums for deities and spirits, which requires them to be in a "holy" state to be able to commune with the spirit realm.

Aspects of psychotherapy include diagnosing psychological causes for a physical ailment, reconnecting the client's spiritual essence to their physical body, and balancing their physical and mental health.[44] Some of the techniques used in psychotherapy include: "waking visions, archetypal dreams, imaginal work, and body experiences."[45] When comparing Jung's theory of psychology with shamanism, Bock found similarities, such as "the healing and growth of the psyche."[46] These two fields of knowledge seek an understanding of the psychological state and mind to heal unpleasant manifestations in the physical. Another peculiarity between shamanism and the Jungian theory is "both methodologies maintain the premise of the existence of a sphere to which the psyche has access."[47]

The shaman, as a professional, approaches a client by connecting his psyche to the mystical realm, while psychologists seek to understand a patient through the unconscious pool of existence and his mind. Bock also states that "Jungian therapy and shamanism both seek a direct experience with the inner world."[48] Shamans go into a trance and enter the shamanic state of consciousness to access knowledge while psychologists explore unconscious images in a client's dreams to assess information that is needed for treatment. Both shamanism and psychology draw from a transpersonal experience to diagnose, treat, and cure their patients.

In transpersonal psychology, the tripartite divisions of the human psyche, that is, physical, psychological/mental, and emotional parts, are harmonized for whole health.[49] Bock also connects the practice of shamanism with transpersonal psychology and opines that

> Like shamanism, some transpersonal psychotherapists regard caring for the soul to be a key element in working with a client. The therapist may well integrate traditional therapeutic techniques in addition to methods resulting from spiritual disciplines. Yet, consciousness is considered not only to be the means for changing behavior and the contents of consciousness, but also the object of changes itself. As in shamanism, living in harmony with others and the environment is affirmed. The relationship of the client to society and the natural environment is considered an aspect of an individual's health and development.[50]

The work of a psychotherapist and a shaman intersect through the application of mental purgation to heal the outer physical body. In the case of shamanism, the connection of the psyche with the environment and the treatment of the soul is seen as a unified whole.

Techniques used by psychotherapists to heal include "treating physical health through bodywork movement, emotional catharsis, existential inquiry, imagery and dreamwork, meditation, deidentification exercises, confessions, and altered states of consciousness."[51] It is not presumptuous to conclude from Bock's comparison of techniques in shamanism and transpersonal psychology that shamanism as a traditional knowledge exhibits and incorporates scientific methods; the analysis of dreams as mental texts, vision interpretation, and shamanic trance states for treatment are scientific in nature. Shamanism portrays modernity as an indigenous system of knowledge that has attributes of science, such as combining, mixing, analyzing, and appropriating knowledge to existential problems.

Knowledge of Psychiatry in Shamanism

The knowledge of mental health and state are carefully studied and undertaken by shamans. In shamanism, physical and mental health are perceived as "unity," hence according to Krippner, "there is no sharp division between physical and mental illness."[52] People with mental issues, such as insanity, psychosis, schizophrenia, etc. are examined and treated by shamans due to their knowledge of the psyche and their connection to the spiritual realm. Mental illness and instability can be caused by physical, social, and psychological issues that cause an eruption, breakdown, and total loss of control of one's mental faculty.

In the event of traumatic experiences, such as rape, abuse, and accidents, shamans may treat patients by helping clients confront their nightmares and events that trigger a mental imbalance. It is not strange or uncommon to hear of malevolent forces like witches, spirits, and jinn causing some of these mental problems. In this case, the shaman treats the patient suffering from insanity through separation and forceful removal of the offensive entity. They may also tend to people with mental breakdowns to help them purge bad or evil energies by inducing the patient into a trance state where they can detach their mind from malicious manipulation.

Traditional Medicine

In many societies across the African continent, traditional knowledge of medicine is found in shamanism. This wisdom is the combination of their skill, practice, and ability to diagnose, treat, and cure different types of maladies in indigenous communities. The knowledge system in shamanism has produced a wealth of understanding to diagnose causes of symptomatic and asymptomatic health issues, offering maintenance of physical well-being, curing spiritual and physical diseases, preventing mental and psychological breakdowns, etc. There is no limit or end to acquiring information about medicine in shamanic wisdom. One of the methods that shamans use to obtain knowledge about medicine is through trance.[53] Medicinal plants, procedures, and treatments are generated by shamans for healing.

The Knowledge of Herbs and Plants

Knowledge in shamanism also extends to the use of medicinal plants and herbs for the treatment of an array of health issues. Shamans are sometimes known as "medicine wo/men," however, not all medicine men are shamans. Because of their multiple roles and functions, shamans may also possess an understanding of herbal application and use for patients with treatable health conditions. This indigenous knowledge is pivotal in the practice of shamanism, especially before the advent of modern science, hence people depended on this system for their health problems. The use of *ayurvedic* medicine to treat ailments and diseases is also found in shamanism.

The knowledge of herbs, plants, therapy, chiropractic, homeopathy, etc., is an alternative medicine that shamans have access to for the treatment of diseases. The shaman obtains knowledge of alternative medicine in healing indigenous people through the wisdom and belief in the medicinal properties of plants and herbs. Some alternative medical practices in shamanism espouse a knowledge of the body that is utilized in chiropractic healing. After diagnosing the patient, the shaman can cure the ailment by massaging joints, muscles, bones, and ligaments. This therapy may be followed by the application of a concoction and herbal ointments on the affected body part.

This knowledge is based on the belief in herbs and plants as products for physical, mental, and emotional healing. The use of shamanic healing practices (in the modern sense) has increased in the "US as almost 83 million people use one of the sixteen alternative therapies, which include relaxation techniques, herbal medicine, massage, chiropractic, spiritual healing, megavitamins, self-help groups, imagery, commercial diet, folk remedies, lifestyle diet, energy healing, homeopathy, hypnosis, biofeedback, and acupuncture."[54] The knowledge of alternative medicine is a shaman's forte, as the shaman combines knowledge of geomancy, therapy, herbs and plants, and psychology in his practice.

Herbs, roots, fiber, stem, and bark of a plant may be dried, cooked, and ground into powder for usage. The shaman may also use his knowledge of alternative medicine in making herbs into oils, ointment, or syrup for the patient. Shamanism is an indigenous knowledge system that offers a holistic healing of the body, mind, and emotions. In many indigenous communities, the reliance and complete trust in shamanism is premised on its affordability, effectiveness, and its synchronicity with people's faith. Even with the advent of Western medicine, many Africans still consult shamans for their problems because of their ability to detect and cure what modern medicine may not comprehend.

Spiritual Wisdom and Counseling

Shamans obtain life wisdom from their interaction with mystic and celestial bodies, effective in dealing with the realities of life. This wisdom is garnered from years of training, experience in solving issues, and practical application of counsel. Shamans act as advisers to people in indigenous communities. Shamanism is a traditional knowledge system that explores wisdom from ancestors, deities and celestial beings, ecology, cosmology, and philosophy of the people. Many people in indigenous communities consult shamans for counseling and guidance because they believe these people possess wisdom about challenges in life, emotional development, marital, career, and spiritual concerns. Shamans may not necessarily need to use their own intelligence as they can rely on the deities to gain counsel on certain problems. The shaman divines to get adequate clarity and guidance on how to assist clients in solving issues that are confusing to them. The counsel/advice may be in the form of proverbs directed at the philosophical issue that the client may be experiencing.

Shamans may act as a counselor to be consulted by traditional rulers and leaders in the community during a crisis. They are a source of wisdom trained at approaching issues with calm, patience, and concentration to discover the kernel of a problem in order to find a durable solution. Shamans can employ different methods and techniques in counseling their clients according to the issue presented. They listen to their clients and ask appropriate questions to get an understanding of the problem at hand, resulting in them proffering solutions. Shamanic counseling makes use of indigenous knowledge to address life challenges, and, through dialogue and questioning, shamans can find solutions to the client's issue. Shamanic counseling may be applied to cases of "trauma, abuse, addictions, anxiety, depression, obsessions, phobias, psychosis, etc."[55] These counseling sessions may reveal hereditary traits and habits that may influence the patient's issue. Spiritual guidance could be followed up with further counseling to facilitate a long-term solution and prevent a relapse.

How Knowledge is explored in the Practice, Belief, and Philosophy of Shamanism

Knowledge is explored through various beliefs, thoughts, philosophies, and practices in shamanism, some of which will be discussed further on. Witzel lists some of these beliefs as follows:

(a) All the surrounding world is animated, inhabited by the spirits who can influence man's life; (b) there are general and reciprocal interconnections in nature (humans included); (c) human beings are not superior but equal to other forms of life; (d) human society is closely connected with the cosmos; (e) it is possible for human beings to acquire some qualities of a spirit and visit the other worlds; (f) the aim of religious activity is to defend and make prosperous a small group of kinsmen.[56]

Knowledge in Shamanic Trance

In shamanism, trance is a practice that shamans enter to obtain knowledge for both the community and individual. To illustrate the function and importance of trance in shamanism, Riboli notes:

The trance is an important part of shamanism, since the shaman functions as an intermediary between the world of humans and that of the supernatural. In general, altered states of consciousness allow communication with the other, nonhuman world.[57]

Trance becomes the link that connects people in the world of the living to the non-human world. This level straddles two realities of existence that shamans can voluntarily enter for the purpose of knowledge acquisition. This shamanic trance assists the shaman's spirit in communicating with mystic entities on behalf of the client or community.

Perhaps, the most important function of shamanic trance is the connection with extraordinary bodies where visions about knowledge are shared from divinities to the shaman and then to the client.[58] There are a number of ways for the shaman to go into a trance: stimulants, such as plants with hallucinogenic properties, can be ingested; auditory stimulation by drumming, singing, and chanting; and extreme behavior like fasting, isolation and meditating. Knowledge is acquired in the trance state by the shaman through interaction with the spirits, divinities, and ancestors. Riboli agrees with this argument as she states that "shamans enter into trance on different occasions, mainly to determine the cause of an illness or some form of calamity that has befallen the whole village or a single individual and establish the cure or most appropriate solution for the latter."[59]

Trance is a powerful medium that requires the understanding of the otherworld, control of one's physical and mental state, mastery of communication, attentiveness to information, and a retentive memory for recollection. There are two types of trances: spirit possession and soul journey.[60] In the case of spirit possession, the spirit of a dead relative/ancestor can possess the shaman, thereby the shaman begins to perform like the incarnated spirit. In the latter type of trance, the shaman's spirit enters the mystic world on a journey to acquire information. Teleporting from a physical conscious state to an extraterrestrial space is one of the mediums that shamans rely on to obtain useful information to produce knowledge. Trance, otherwise known and referred to as an altered state of consciousness, is a procedure for knowledge acquisition that shamans enter for the purpose of garnering wisdom.

Hypnosis as Shamanic Knowledge Practice

In shamanism, knowledge is explored in the practice of hypnosis on patients. Hypnosis is an essential part of shamanism and requires a psychological conditioning of the patient's mind and imagination during shamanic acts.[61] Overton explores the role and function of hypnosis:

> This close relationship between shamanism and hypnosis can be clearly observed in at least two areas of the shamanic complex. First, both shamanism in its healing rituals and hypnosis in its therapeutic encounter rely essentially on the skillful manipulation of the patient's imagination in order to achieve the desired therapeutic benefits.[62]

Hypnosis is a technique and practice which shamans employ on patients with specific health issues. The experience of an altered state of consciousness which the shaman goes through to acquire information and knowledge shares similarities with hypnosis.[63]

Rituals and Sacrifice in Shamanism
as a Medium of Knowledge

In the practice of shamanism, ritual is one important aspect and practice that produces knowledge in many indigenous communities. It is practiced in different societies with various systems and reasons. In the performance of shamanic ritual, different aspects of it, such as singing, dancing, chanting, etc. embody a belief in sacrifices, ritual, rites, initiation, incantation, and possession. During a ritual, the shaman invokes mystic forces and brings them to the awareness of their presence. Maskarinec asserts that "every shamanic healing ritual concludes with either a sacrifice, usually a blood offering, demanded by the familiar spirits with which shamans work or, minimally, a temporary substitute postponing that offering."[64] Ritual and sacrifices have an important significance in shamanism; they serve as links and stabilizers of the relationship between humans and their ancestors and deities and keeps channels of communication alive. Items for ritual and sacrifice differ from one culture or community to another and may bear a symbolic meaning to the deity and ancestor that the offerings are presented to.

In essence, the practice of ritual and sacrifice in shamanism served to provide offerings to mystic spirits in exchange for knowledge. Ancestors depended on human relationships in ritual and sacrifice, and humans also depend on extraterrestrial entities for information and, consequently, survival, as knowledge is essential for survival. Materials for ritual and sacrifice may include animals such as pigeons, pigs, sheep, goats, ram, chicken, food items, oils, etc. Each of these items is significant to the ritual and sacrifice to spiritual forces, as they may represent the continuation of life in an exchange of animal life for human life, a renewal of covenants/promises, and the strengthening of relationships. Sacrifices and rituals are also techniques of invoking spirits to assist during a shamanic performance. Schiller concludes, "Useful information about social, political, and economic conditions in contexts where shamanism is practiced may be gleaned by understanding the nature of the offerings presented."[65] Furthermore, ritual and sacrifice provide non-verbal communication between humans and spirits. It is a dual communication channel for the reception of knowledge.

Philosophy of Shamanism

In African communities where shamanism is practiced, there are many ideologies and philosophies that produce knowledge. One of these philosophies in shamanism is that the world is made up of three layers: the earth, the firmament/heaven and the extraterrestrial where the shaman can traverse.[66] This cosmology supports the distillation of power and knowledge in other non-human realms and the belief that when the shaman approaches either of these realms, they can connect to information available there. These three levels of the world are interconnected, and it is the role of the shaman to mediate between these levels of reality. Indigenous people believe in this worldview; hence, the status and function of shamanism is highly revered and appreciated as a medium to acquiring knowledge. This belief enables an effective flow of power and knowledge insofar that when wisdom bestowed from divine entities is applied, a solution is sure to occur. Human beings occupy earth and, after their demise, are transformed into spirits as ancestors to aid their descendants.

Deities and ancestors occupy the extraterrestrial level and are also powerful enough to assist humans, while heaven accommodates the high God or Supreme Being who is sovereign over other levels of the universe. Indeed, in the extraterrestrial level, spirits may be helpful or manipulative and are usually consulted for assistance.[67] However, these spirits can manipulate human affairs on earth; they can also be sought out for information about certain issues, such as the future, career path, marriage choice, and decisions about life. Communication can occur here with a deceased relative, ancestor, or soul. This is why Bock opines that "an individual in many shamanic societies is found to have two or more souls . . . one soul was found to live in the chest cavity and die when the physical body died, and the other was theorized to reside in the head, to be immortal, and survive death."[68]

The belief that a dual human soul can be found in the extraterrestrial space is strongly circulated among indigenous practitioners and believers in shamanism. This duality of soul accounts for how the shaman can move between realms, such as when he goes into trance.[69] This notion of multiple souls is connected to the idea that when there is a loss of one of these souls, it can affect the physical frame/body and so may result in illness, disease, and death. This philosophy provides knowledge regarding how the soul affects physical health along with the souls of shamans who enter a shamanic state to acquire information. It is a system of knowledge that emphasizes the plurality of souls and its ability to live on in the extraterrestrial space of existence.

The Belief in Spirit Possession/Intrusion

Spirit intrusion is when a human body is forcefully invaded and occupied by a spirit or maleficent entity. This notion is propagated in shamanic practices as the condition whereby an individual is taken over by an external force, usually known as a spirit, which causes the possessed person to exhibit unusual behavior, such as rapid speech, incoherent mumbling, extraordinary strength and power, strange illness, etc. This phenomenon of spirit intrusion can either be caused by a familiar spirit or a strange entity with an intension to cause harm to its host. The shaman determines if the spirit is good for the host, and, if it is not, the spirit has to be expelled and disconnected from the body of the possessed. This unwanted harmful spirit is exiled by the shaman by going into a trance state to exorcise the evil spirit.[70] Eliminating the intrusive entity involves a separation either by invoking the spirit to come out or by appealing to it to peacefully exit the individual. The spirit may speak through the host to demand propitiation like sacrifice to be offered before it exits the patient.

In shamanic trance, the shaman could be exposed to being possessed by a spirit when in the mystic realm. Spirit intrusion during a shamanic practice may be induced by burning incense, percussive instruments, and performing rites and rituals. Spirit possession and intrusion are referred to as "mediumship," whereby the shaman is taken over to receive and transmit knowledge.[71] However, there is a difference between spirit intrusion and the shamanic state; the former is usually involuntary and requires the effort of professional assistance while the latter is entered at will and requires a conscious effort to enter and exit the mystic space.

Divination as Knowledge

Shamanism, as discussed previously, is a synchronized system of employing diverse techniques for the purpose of acquiring wisdom for the good of the community. There are different kinds of geomancy that exist across the African continent and the universe. This system has knowledge at its core and works by using divining beads or chains, trays or cloth, bones, etc. to inquire from deities wisdom that is unknown to humans. Divination in shamanism is used for diagnosis, inquiry, prescription, healing, and other existential purposes. The shaman is also a diviner who consults deities, ancestors, spirits, and gods for knowledge about a particular issue, which requires divine intervention.

When a shaman divines, they receive clarity about a problem that includes, among others, causes of the problem, effect, solution or remedy, the ritual or sacrifice to offer, instruction on how to carry out the propitiation sacrifice, etc. In some cases, the shaman uses a divining bead by throwing it on a tray or cloth to seek wisdom from the otherworld to understand the client's issue. They may then proceed by chanting incantations or divination poems to draw illustration from a previous incident like the present one. When the shaman tosses the divining chain, they move it around a couple of times and read the sign and shapes of the bones and beads to unravel the mystery.

During a consultation, the shaman operates with the knowledge of divination to perform rites and rituals for the client's benefit. Divination is a knowledge system that shamans are trained for that enables them to receive sufficient information on their shamanic practice. In divination, knowledge is provided through communication with signs and symbols displayed on divining bones or beads which are then analyzed, demystified, and appropriated to the client's problem. Divination, according to Winkelman, "is concerned with the acquisition of information."[72] This information is 'divinely' acquired, which makes it a system of knowing that is extraordinary. When discussing the importance of divination, Winkelman explains:

> Divination mirrors the functions of shamanism: diagnosis of causes of diseases; prognosis regarding the patient's recovery; determination of the interests and intents of spiritual forces; location of animals for hunting; learning about the condition of separated family members; planning the future movement of the group or its enemies; determination of the intentions and whereabouts of others; and prophecy.[73]

Beside the aforementioned functions of divination as knowledge in shamanism, it has been earlier mentioned that the community is stabilized by its performance. The stability of the community is drawn from divination's use of cultural ethos, myths, customs, traditions, and cosmology for such social functions as predicting the future of a child, choosing and coronation of a traditional ruler, affirmation of decision, etc. Indeed, knowledge in divination is representative of a society, educating the community about customs and culture, and regulating the actions of the people.[74]

Psychology in Shamanism

The practice of shamanism unveils and unpacks knowledge of psychology as a medium of understanding the covert action behind an occurrence or a situation. Shamans who double as psychologists possess esoteric and non-esoteric knowledge of the African people through an intrinsic wisdom of bridging two spaces—the physical and the metaphysical. This knowledge is used to determine, diagnose, treat, manage, and cure psychological problems. Through mystical science, the shaman examines the patient who may or may not be aware of having psychological issues requiring help from a shaman. The shaman is able to diagnose this ailment through consultation with mystical forces, which would then lead to the discovery of the cause or agent of the aliment.

The shaman's psychoanalytical knowledge includes inducing the patient to see visions and dreams as part of his inner turbulence manifesting itself in his actions and decisions. The repressed inner turbulence erupts into physical and behavioral actions, such as dissociative personality, confusion, identity disorder, and identity crisis. The shaman knows that for every physical disturbance, there is an underlying psychological imbalance or problem. Therefore, they would ask questions, compare images and information about the patient's dreams to heal or treat the condition. In some cases, shamans may take time to study the patient's behavior and interaction with people to determine the innate turbulence.

Knowledge in Shamanic Songs

Music is one of the oldest means of preserving knowledge systems of indigenous people who produce different kinds of wisdom. Shamans use performance and music to gain insight that is hidden to ordinary people. Music and songs are powerful tools of knowledge and can encode spiritual and esoteric understanding of different kinds. Songs are employed as mnemonic devices and a medium to guide shamans into the right mood and mindset for knowledge to be received. It is also a code that shamans use to pass their intention and inquiries to mystic forces. Songs played during a shamanic experience is both a source of knowledge and medium for encoding and relating knowledge.

With new discoveries in indigenous traditions and knowledge, shamanism has been the focus of much research, especially in terms of its function and nature of producing knowledge that were useful in the preliterate and modern periods. Songs are a lucid and lyrical tool for passing messages to people who may or may not understand the culture or language in which the song is written to a larger audience across the world without knowledge of its origin. Songs are, therefore, used in shamanic practices to elucidate and encode knowledge.

The place and importance of music in shamanism is essential, as it is a channel of interaction between and among forces involved, that is, the shaman and mystical entities.[75] This argument is valid because rituals are accompanied by songs or music to open the communication and transposition of knowledge resources through sonic or lyrical tools. Walker further elucidates that songs or music are "power and knowledge that is accessed by the shaman from the spirit world."[76] The rhythm, tone, and lyrics of the song radiate mystic knowledge and power; the shaman rides on the musical stimulation while the spirits also respond to its call. Beyond the accentuation of music as a powerful epistemic tool for interaction, shamanic songs also possess the unique quality of stimulating, stabilizing, and producing knowledge in shamanism. For reference, songs can arouse the shaman to be receptive toward knowledge from metaphysical bodies. So, music and songs become conductors for the transfer of indigenous knowledge in shamanism. The extent to which songs and music are knowledge in shamanism is diverse and will be explored in the rest of this chapter. This is why Walker opines that

> In shamanic ritual, music articulates the integration of mind/body/spirit/emotion in the cosmology of Indigenous peoples, their relationship with the land as the source of life and culture, the subtle connections between this physical world and the spirit world within the Indigenous world view, and the dynamic nature of traditional knowledge.[77]

This conceptualization of songs in shamanism as knowledge, signifies the bridge and links that songs possess in shamanic practices, such as the ability of songs to alter the mood during a ritual. Music is the wisdom of combining different layers of consciousness and existence to produce a meaningful experience. Indigenous people, especially of African descent, have been known to use songs and music to discuss their beliefs, faith, religion, and most importantly, indigenous knowledge. With this understanding, it is important to observe that songs are, and make accessible, indigenous wisdom in shamanism. Songs in any kind of religion and culture are powerful and play a pivotal role in the dissemination of the community's ethos.

They represent an indigenous and modern system of codifying knowledge, particularly among indigenous societies. Chants and songs used by acolytes and shamans are wisdom that is embedded in incantatory poems and songs, as they communicate present issues to spirits and beings and may receive validation or solutions to these problems through lyrical codes. Shamanic songs take wisdom from a basic level to be encoded in notes and sounds that invoke spirits to release knowledge to the shaman. These songs are not just ordinary ones that are composed in the community.

Instead, they are extremely sensitive codes used to invoke the spirits. Songs in African societies perform a myriad of functions ranging from educating the younger generation to disseminating ideologies, celebrating ideas, people, events, art, to psychotherapeutic purposes of lulling babies, pacifying aggrieved persons, and healing people with different psychological issues. In the case of shamanism, songs are codes of knowledge themselves to both shamans and spirits. Esoteric knowledge and information are codified in shamanic songs that serve as an accompaniment during shamanic rites and rituals, as they encourage an appropriate ambience whereby transfer of information and wisdom can thrive.

Aural knowledge in shamanic songs, poems, and incantations contain healing properties. Songs are vital aspects in shamanic practices to release energy to connect both physical and extraterrestrial spaces. Songs have healing effects on people suffering from psychological imbalance by calming their troubled minds and psyche. The mind is reconnected to its peaceful state through humming, singing, and miming. Songs have soothing and therapeutic functions in serving as a balm on ruffled nerves. They may be used on patients with neurological problems to lull them to sleep. They can be also be used on people with a sleeping disorder to help them relax and possibly fall asleep. If a patient is plagued by a malevolent spirit, shamanic songs are sung to exorcise the spirit out of its host.

Shamanic Knowledge in Drums and Drumming

Drums and drumming are also important components of shamanism that possess symbolic knowledge and information. Walker explores the role of both when she enthused that:

> The shaman's voice, the drum and other percussive sounds produced by metal pieces attached to the shaman's dress, bells or rattles—all these combine with the movement of the shaman's body and the tassels and fringe on the shaman's dress to produce a rhythmic sound bridge that facilitates travel to the other world in search of knowledge that will benefit people in this world.[78]

The performance and language of drums in shamanism releases veiled codes that encapsulate information for the shaman and the client. Drums and drumming in the African milieu have a language that can be encrypted and decoded by professionals to convey information that does not require verbal expression. The argument points to the use of drums and drumming as systems of knowledge that shamans engage with during their performance to facilitate the procurement of epistemic material. To further ground her argument, Walker states that the "sound bridge is a conduit for the transmission of knowledge, power, inspiration, awareness, or intent between worlds or consciousnesses."[79] Drumming is more than just an instrument for knowledge; it is encrypted information, as it has a system and pattern for encoding and decoding information.

Dreams and Visions as Knowledge in Shamanism

Dream interpretation is another technique in shamanic practice for obtaining knowledge from the extraterrestrial world. Shamans receive knowledge through visions and dreams that, when interpreted, reveal information about the subject. They encode knowledge that is subject to interpretation by shamans who explore hidden meanings that are beneficial to the dreamer or person who the dream is directed at. The function of dreams and visions is to pass along information to people when verbal expression may not be necessary. Dreams and visions are pictorial knowledge that may be in chronological or non-linear order and could sometimes be confusing to whom the dream is revealed, hence requiring the service of a shaman to elucidate and give meaning to the images. Krippner considers knowledge derived from dreams and visions as vital sources regarding one's physical and mental state.[80] The symbols and metaphors that are represented in dreams and visions are unraveled to express hidden codes of knowledge beneficial for the improvement of the client's situation.

Dreams and visions are a part of the shaman's experience and technique for acquiring knowledge before and during his call to the profession. They are ways for shamans to communicate and gather wisdom for their patient or client. Dreams act as communication channels that shamans receive during a brief or deep sleep. In this sleep state, they remain conscious enough to receive flashes or sudden images that are different from what they perceive in everyday sight. Degarrod explains that

> Shamanic discourses about dreams and visions in many societies are valued not only for their different healing, religious, or political meanings but also for their aesthetic value, as these narratives are not transmitted only by the shamans themselves but also by other narrators.[81]

Dreams and visions exhibit symbols and signs that are coded with information for the dreamer or for the community. They act as metaphors that need to be examined, analyzed, and interpreted to determine their meaning and to appropriate them in the community or to the targeted individual. Some symbols in dreams, like rain or animals, may be subjected to different interpretative techniques.

Degarrod notes that there are two methods of interpretation: the "metaphoric" and "literal" techniques.[82] Both techniques require knowledge; whether it is the interpretation of dreams and visions through the metaphoric lens, which applies a system of symbolic representation of images as meanings, or the direct and literal interpretation that lacks a deeper connotation, dreams and visions are a knowledge system in shamanism. They are used to diagnose and heal sick clients. This is expressly explored by Degarrod as he avers that

> Dreams are a frequent means of diagnosing what it is that is ailing a sick person. If the source is a malevolent being or a human person wishing the victim ill (as in sorcery), then the dream can reveal the identity of such a being or person. Furthermore, the dream can be used to identify the nature of the medicines to be employed with the sick person. These medicines are usually plants. The kind of plant, its location, and time to be picked can be provided to a shaman or healer by dreams.[83]

Dreams and visions are important aspects of knowledge because of their invaluable function in shamanism and to the shaman. They are mediums of summoning an individual into the craft and a technique of receiving knowledge.

Magic as Knowledge in Shamanism

Magic is an aspect of the knowledge base—carefully examined in the succeeding chapter—which shamans explore in their craft to gain wisdom and diverse mystic messages. While training a shaman, Krippner noted that

> Magical performance of one sort or another is learned including sleight of hand, taking advantage of synchronous events, or the utilization of what Westerners call "parapsychological phenomena," including extrasensory perception and psychokinesis.[84]

The performance of magic is both a skill and knowledge that shamans acquire during their education that is deployed to create a desired dramatic effect for their client. Magic and magical performance in shamanism is a display of knowledge inherent in the practice. Shamans demonstrate their knowledge of magic by changing form from a human to an animal and vice versa, jumping into fire without being hurt or scalded, disappearance acts, etc. that are performed through magical power.

This magical power gives the shaman an ability to transform and take on extraordinary actions that are impossible to carry out with human ability alone and helps them perform acts on their patients and clients. Some of these actions include the removal of offensive objects in their bodies, instant healing, exorcism, etc. Magic can be demonstrated in the use of charms and amulets; during an attack the shaman can conjure a magical safety measure to escape such an assault.

People also consult a shaman's use of magic for protection, safety, revenge, wealth, security, etc. Magic is the science of creating an extraordinary reality out of an ordinary one. Magic in shamanism is the combination of knowledge of the culture's cosmology, power, metaphysics, and authority to cause an unusual event. Shamanism is a system of knowing and using the magical power of plants, incantatory poems, and metaphysical manipulation of spiritual energy and resources. There is a strong belief in magic and magical power in communities where shamanism is practiced.

Knowledge of Healing in Shamanism

The healing addition to shamanic powers and actions have been hitherto mentioned. In African indigenous communities, healing or perfect health, is conceived as the connection of the three divisions of human existence: the physical body, the psychological entity of the mind, and the spiritual component (spirit). When the physical body is ill, it means the other components are affected or have caused the physical manifestation on the body. This belief is largely supported in shamanic societies, as shamans go into trance to connect with spirits or mystic beings to gain information or through divination, which as a medium, connects to symbolic spiritual bodies of knowledge to obtain codes of information, such as a cure for ailments and diseases. This worldview is what makes shamanism different from Western medicine or allopathic healing. In shamanism, the shaman connects the patient's belief to the root cause of physical and spiritual illness and draws necessary solutions from their communication with celestial beings. Vuckovic et al., reiterates that during the treatment, shamans need to establish between two factors:

> Two principal types of spiritual factors can contribute to or bring about illness: (1) loss of a spiritual energy that is important to the patient's well-being (personal soul loss and guardian spirit loss are chief among these) and (2) presence of a spirit or energetic force that is detrimental to the patient's well-being (e.g., spirit intrusions, involuntary possessions).[85]

This diagnosis is important to the treatment and healing of a patient's health issue as it will help the shaman reconnect the client to his spiritual wellness and achieve perfect synthesis of the physical, spiritual, and psychological makeup. Their connection with mystic beings through trance, otherwise known as "shamanic state of consciousness,"[86] produces knowledge that is not accessible or attainable in the human conscious form. Healing starts from the inside out through this connection with spiritual forces. These professionals obtain timeless knowledge by penetrating the mystic space and reality to commune with powerful spirits.[87] Knowledge of healing in shamanism is acquired through entering the shamanic state, which is achieved through trance and stimulation by singing, drumming, and dancing. Schneider et al., opine that

> Shamanic healing is interactive. It enables individuals to regain their "power" and participate in their own healing if they choose to do so. Thus, treatment may involve helping the patient to integrate the effects of shamanic healing through changes in behavior, diet, or lifestyle, engaging in counseling, or incorporating ritual or spiritual practice (e.g., learning to journey for themselves) into their life.[88]

This participatory process makes shamanism a system of knowledge that implements the patient's will and input in achieving their own healing through singing, dancing, and willfully entering a trance, thereby making the patient susceptible to connecting to mystic healing powers. Some of the illnesses are "soul loss," "power loss," "spiritual intrusion," and "dispirited or low energy."[89] These illnesses are treated with the knowledge of shamanic healing through its connection with the patient's belief in shamanism, participation in ritual, song, and dance. Healing in shamanism is not an isolated event, but a connection of faith and trust in the system.

Knowledge of Surgery

In societies where shamanic practices are found, shamans are consulted to carry out rites of passage. Their knowledge of the community's tradition, culture, norms, and shamanic wisdom is sought out for activities and rites such as circumcision, coming of age, adulthood, and death and burial rites. In the case of accidents, complications during childbirth, circumcision, disease and illness, shamans may be summoned as traditional surgeons to operate on the patient. In the case of circumcision, the shaman performs this rite whether as a man or woman on babies or adolescent boys or girls depending on the custom of the community. In the event of affliction of boils or other growth on the body, the shaman may be beckoned to decipher the cause and then perform surgery on the patient.

In shamanic surgery, a constellation of knowledge is displayed in the treatment of patients with broken and mangled body parts such as hands, fingers, legs, bones, etc. Their knowledge of human anatomy and divination, which reveals how the procedure will be carried out, is manifested in shamanic surgery. During circumcision, the shaman knows how and what part of the genital is to be cut and how it is carefully treated to avoid infection from setting in. The shaman operates on their patient with instruments that may consist of different sizes of knives and scissors. This is also accompanied with herbal products to sterilize equipment as they may be used on multiple children. Herbs may be administered to the child or body part to reduce pain and suffering during the surgery. Rituals or rites may be carried out prior to the circumcision to ensure a successful surgery and healing process.

This knowledge of shamanic surgery may be simple and complex in that there are cases when the shaman may sever and cauterize parts of the patient that may be infected with disease or infection. The amputation of the infected part is carried out by using native anesthesia to prevent excruciating pain, sometimes due to the length and severity of the surgery. The shaman may require the assistance of other shamans, men, or women. After the surgery, the shaman continues to treat the patient's wound until he or she fully recovers. Other types of surgeries that shamans perform are the removal of excess limbs, teeth, fingers, etc. Shamanism is a knowledge system which holds duality of modern and indigenous scientific wisdom in the treatment and operation of diseases.

Knowledge of Art in Shamanism

Art, drawings, engravings, sketches, and paintings from the Paleolithic Age have shown that shamans and shamanism contributed their knowledge to arts and creative designs. Hoppal theorizes that "based on the material of rock art of different territories, establishing contacts between the drawings, engravings or paintings, and the magico-religious beliefs"[90] express the practice of shamanism and ritual. The connection between art and shamanism is drawn from an array of artistic engravings, drawings, and paintings found on rocks and caves in primeval societies. Hoppal, in establishing the connection between shamanism and art, opines that

What seems to be certain, at least in Siberia, the locus classicus of shamanism, is that a theoretical possibility exists finding the first expressions of shamanistic rituals and symbols on the rocks of Central and North Asia. Moreover, Siberian rock art could be seen as the earliest documents available to us on the prehistory of Eurasian shamanism, or to use a more precise expression, these data could shed light on the religious belief complexes from which the Siberian shamanism emerged and started to develop.[91]

Hoppal's summation on shamanism expressed through artistic images on rocks and caves illustrate that shamans also developed a method of documenting their art, existence, and knowledge through these drawings and paintings.

Relying on the example of Siberian rock art to draw conclusions about the beginning of shamanism leads to an oversight, as these drawings of rituals and shamanistic practice are representations of an indigenous artistic knowledge in shamanism. In determining the existence of shamanism, Hoppal uses figures of human-like paintings on the caves as signs that confirm his argument that shamanism had existed for a longer time than the general consensus. Like the hieroglyphs of Egypt, art on caves and rocks depicting shamanistic practices represent a writing system and artistic knowledge of shamanism in the Paleolithic Era. Shamanism displays an advance knowledge system even in traditional communities to show its potential of expanding knowledge in the modern age.

Hoppal affirms concerning shamanism and rock art that figures on the rock have similarities with images on the Siberian shaman's dress.[92] These drawings reveal shamanistic practices and knowledge, which are signs of a system of knowing. This system is expressed in the use of art in paintings, engravings, drawings, and patterns on rocks, caves, houses, and dresses in communities where shamanistic practices are performed. It is in this light that Hoppal asserts that "a more constructive point for departure would be to regard the rock carvings sites as something more than just a collection of pictures."[93]

These images are more than just art. They are signs and symbols of shamanism through their representation of this ancient knowledge system. The paintings demonstrate the act of ritual, sacrifice, ancestor worship, and veneration. Shamanism uses art to express knowledge through communication of belief in ritual. Sacrifice and rites engraved on rocks show how they interact and worship their divinities.

Knowledge of the Future

One of the major attributes of shamanism is the ability to gain information about the future. This knowledge is hardly a common wisdom easily accessible by people, especially when there is a need to channel resources and strength to prepare for it. Shamanism unravels the mystery of the future by bringing the past, the present, and the future into perspective. Shamans use divination out of many methods to obtain insight into a specific future occurrence for clients who seek elucidation. Shamanism employs more than a single technique in garnering knowledge about the future, as shamans can enter a trance state.

They may also receive visions and dreams that are subject to interpretation and analysis to draw out conclusive evidence about the future. In some African communities where shamanic practices are performed, indigenous people often seek the help of a shaman to see what the future holds for them or to inquire on behalf of their wards and children. Sometimes, indigenous people want to know if a business venture, profession, union, or partnership would be profitable, peaceful, rewarding or otherwise; hence a visit to the shaman becomes an option.

Clairvoyance as Knowledge in Shamanism

Clairvoyance is a system and technique in shamanism that produces knowledge of communication with the dead. The perception and communication with metaphysical entities is a system of knowing that shamans possess. When shamans are consulted to unravel the source of a problem, it is common practice for them to commune with the ancestors of the client, as they possess knowledge about the living and are believed to keep watch over their descendants. This extrasensory perception enables the shaman to make an extensive investigation about a specific issue by communicating with these bodies.

Shamans are also considered professionals who possess the ability to hear voices as "voices are always an expression of beings, ancestors, spirits, elementals, angels, etc. Therefore, shamans seek to relate and engage with ancestors of spirits as whole beings."[94] Dead relatives can be contacted in shamanism based on the knowledge that shamans can converse, summon, and see these mystic beings. The information they receive through their conversation with such "beings" are then analyzed to decipher the cause and solution to the issue that required communication with a deceased relative.

Clairvoyance is not only a technique in shamanism; it is a system of knowing the past, the present, and the unknown future. In communities where shamanism is practiced, indigenous people believe in this knowledge of gaining wisdom from their dead ancestors to have a better grasp of how to navigate their lives. The shaman may hear the ancestor's voice and enlighten the client, or the ancestor may speak through the shaman by possessing him or her. Clairvoyance in shamanism produces knowledge from the otherworld that is then applied to situations in the world of the living. Lambrecht provides an illustration of how knowledge is obtained:

In the South African context, shamans hear their ancestors in their head or from the outside, as well as offer their bodies to the ancestors so that they can use the shaman as an instrument, a voice to communicate with the community or the client. (. . .) It is however worth mentioning that the voices of the ancestors are heard during divination, are expressed through the shaman's body whilst dancing, and are seen and heard in dreams or visions.[95]

Hence, it is safe to conclude from the above that the shamanic system keeps the line of communication open between two or more levels of existence for the purpose of producing knowledge. This knowledge is not the only byproduct of clairvoyance in shamanism, as functional relationship and communication is also achieved. Shamans are also conceived as professionals who have mastered spirit possession as they can control their communication with them and also appropriate information obtained accordingly.[96]

Some of the knowledge obtained through clairvoyance and listening to spirit voices in shamanism include the cause of illness, guidance on medicinal concoctions, healing regimen, etc., all of which are essential to the growth and stability of the community and people.

Knowledge of the Weather

Another specialty of shamans is their ability and knowledge of the weather. In traditional society, shamans are a common source of information and knowledge about the weather and how it can be directed to favor the people. In some societies, they are reputed to have the knowledge of rainmaking or the ability to stop and redirect it to other places. Knowledge of the weather is grounded in shamanism because this information can serve indigenous farmers for the good of their land and crops. This knowledge can be acquired in shamanism by divining or by studying the clouds. Predictions and sayings made by shamans are taken seriously by the locals who have faith in the system as a reliable and authentic source of information. Because shamans can see visions, study the clouds and atmosphere, gauge the movement of the wind, learn about the position of the moon and sun, and notice changes in the atmosphere, they can predict rainfall, drought, famine, and other seasonal events.

Sociopolitical and Cultural Knowledge

Despite all that has been said about shamanism, it does not function as an isolated system; it incorporates society's social, political, and cultural characteristics. The shaman is an expert at sociocultural and political issues and events and can be consulted for adequate knowledge on matters that affect the community. In some indigenous communities, shamans also act as advisers to the traditional ruler or leader on all matters because of their extensive knowledge on several subjects. They act as a repository of cultural and political insight since they can acquire wisdom that is not easily accessible to the public. During times of crisis, the shaman may intervene to avert such pandemics or inquire about why such calamities occur. When the shaman makes the inquiry, he or she may prescribe a ritual to be carried out on behalf of the entire community. They also counsel traditional heads and leaders on matters of national importance.

It is always essential for the shaman to have a mastery in the mythology of their culture in order to impart knowledge of customs and traditions onto the next generation.[97] This is also supported by Yang that shamans serve as cultural specialists when she states that, "in the Han Dynasty, shamans continue to be used in the court as ritual specialists, diviners, and healers in the state religion."[98] The extent of functions and roles of shamans is wide and extensive because of the array of wisdom in their profession. In some communities, shamans are usually consulted before the installation of traditional chiefs, rulers, and leaders to seek the consent of the gods and to ascertain the legitimacy of chosen candidates. Shamans serve as custodians of the community's customs and traditions because shamanism is a constellation of cultural ethos, cosmology, religion, and traditions.

Knowledge of Performance in Shamanism

Relevance of the shamanism knowledge system in Africa is found in its peculiar nature and performances that can be studied. Shamans can be viewed as artists for the various ways they carry out shamanic practices that exhibit features and aspects of performance. The method of beating drums and its cadence, the humming and singing, the swaying and movements of the body to the music can be studied as elements of knowledge and meaning in shamanism. The types of drums, the rhythm, number of beats, and significance of the drums ushering the shaman into an altered state of consciousness are features of knowledge that need to be explored to generate meaning. Part of this significance is due to the role they play in healing and treatment during a shamanic ritual.

Kister, in the appraisal of shamanistic ritual as performance, opines that "its mimetic activity, feats of wonder, music, and dance make the gods directly present before our eyes. It brings to the stage the inherently dramatic encounter between human beings and the gods and spirits that constitutes the core belief of a shamanist community."[99]

The performance brings to the fore the elements of knowledge as drama; the shaman is the artist who uses his skill to maximize the display of wisdom. The shaman is seen as an artist onstage who demonstrates power and healing using his physical ability.[100] Every aspect of shamanism can be studied as performance: the dance, chants, rites and ritual, and the participants are elements of drama. Each part of the shamanic practice, ritual, trance, and healing present a dramatic performance. Sometimes it is theatrical as the shaman performs magic before an audience that is amazed by the display of supernatural power.

The shamanic ritual is an assemblage of performance in that the shaman wears his costume. The trance is an impersonation of the spirit. He or she dances, sways, jumps, and moves to the drumming and song in a manner that conveys meaning. The conversation between the shaman (artist) and client (audience) is a dialogue. Sometimes there is a dramatic monologue as the shaman converses with the spirit. In cases where the shaman converses with a deceased ancestor or relative, the shaman takes on the demeanor and behavior of the dead, which becomes dramatic as he or she speaks in that manner accordingly.

Relevance of Shamanism-Derived Knowledge for Africa

In Africa, shamanism-derived knowledge is relevant for the future, its growth, and advancement. This knowledge needs to be identified, documented, and codified for research purposes. To advance this knowledge, shamanic practices in different regions of the continent should be carefully studied to ascertain similarities or variants in states or communities where shamanism is practiced. Knowledge of this kind is relevant to African science and technology, medicine, literature, education, religion, and economy.

Research on African Variants of Shamanic Knowledge

Since there are various societies outside of Africa where shamanism is practiced, a comparison and scholarly research on African shamanic practice can be carried out. This research will investigate and explore varied aspects of shamanic knowledge, philosophy, practices, and systems in different regions of the continent. In this exploration, the knowledge derived from each region can be codified and documented to shed light on similarities and dissimilarities in practices, philosophies, beliefs, costume, and performances. The shamanic-derived knowledge can be documented and codified to be taught in shamanic schools and establishments for the preservation of this system. Knowledge especially of this kind needs to be preserved from extinction for future generations to build and improve upon. The creation of a database for shamanic-derived wisdom is necessary for the growth of the African continent. Several aspects of this practice need to be codified and documented for reference and research to ensure that this knowledge is enhanced and promoted.

Knowledge Applied to Sociopolitical Issues in Africa

Knowledge derived from shamanism can be applied to indigenous issues and problems facing the African continent. The wisdom in shamanism can be documented as a philosophy and belief of the African people in books and other formats for distribution to the different parts of the world. Africa is experiencing many sociopolitical challenges that can be solved using shamanism-derived knowledge. African shamanic philosophy, epistemology, and cosmology gathered from esoteric and non-esoteric wisdom can be theorized for common African sociopolitical issues. Literature on African shamanism-derived knowledge could yield philosophies, beliefs, customs, and practices that are relevant to Africa and its people today. The dependence on Western knowledge to solve African issues will be substituted for African solutions and methods.

Development of the African Economy

Knowledge derived from shamanic practices in Africa can encourage an upward surge in the continent's economy. The production of shamanism-derived knowledge in literature of all kinds would boost the economy. This economy development can be achieved through the cultivation, storage, and dissemination of shamanic knowledge. Information about clairvoyance, divination, astrology, meteorology, ecology, etc. should be codified to avoid theft and misappropriation. The wealth of knowledge in African shamanism will increase the production of resources that will generate foreign benefits, grants, loans, and support from various internal and external organizations. The planting, grooming, processing, and sale of roots, plants, herbs, and materials to pharmaceutical companies will boost the economy of the African states. The amount spent on Western drugs can be used to develop other sectors or African traditional medicine to facilitate expansion and growth in the economy.

African Shamanic Literature

The production and interdisciplinary collaboration of knowledge in shamanism and performance, art and photography, technology, computers, language and literary studies, and a host of many others could be carried out. This work in interdisciplinary research would enhance the production and multiplication of works on African knowledge. The production of shamanic arts, films, photography, proverbs, folklore, myths, etc., are examples that speak to the relevance of shamanic-derived knowledge in African literature and education. This relevance becomes diversified and dynamic when new knowledge is produced through the study of African shamanism and other African fields of epistemology. In literary studies, aspects of literariness can be studied in shamanic folklore, stories, myths, proverbs, and metaphoric use of language. The extent and scope of relevance of shamanism-derived knowledge is extensive beyond the scope of this chapter.

Establishment of African Medicine

Knowledge of herbs and plants derived from shamanism can be improved and developed alongside Western medicine. The progress of shamanic medicine will lead to the development and growth of alternative medicine in Africa. Diverse vegetation, trees, plants, and herbs that are medicinal and used for the treatment of different ailments can be cultivated, preserved, processed, and stored. Improvement of alternative medicine will reduce the dependence on Western medicine and thereby enhance the development of Africa. This shamanic-derived knowledge could help the creation and establishment of the practice of medicine using African shamanic techniques and science. This knowledge could be taught in schools and tertiary institutions as a professional and academic field of knowledge. Healing, treatment, and preservation of lives through shamanic-derived knowledge in Africa will not only produce experts in this field, but it will also open avenues for collaboration between Western and African medicine.

Again, shamanism-derived knowledge in Africa will enable the sustainability of African shamanism as a field of epistemology. The extinction and loss of knowledge peculiar to the African milieu will be preserved, archived, and promoted. The appreciation and establishment of this African knowledge will encourage Africa's youth to study and use this wisdom. This knowledge is relevant to the cultural, political, religious, and educational systems. The promotion and participation in African cultural practices, spiritual and religious teachings, political ideology, and literature in shamanism will enhance the stabilization and continuity of the continent's future.

Conclusion

This chapter examines shamanism as a system of knowledge and belief that indigenous people of Africa consult to solve their problems. It further explores some conceptualization of this notion to know and acquire information that is not accessible by ordinary human intelligence. In the discussion of shamanism as a way of obtaining wisdom, the research conducted also explored how knowledge is acquired and who the producers are. The shaman is recognized as the producer of knowledge because he or she becomes the principal link to mystical beings. The role and function of shamans as mediators, healers, herbalists, psychologists, magicians, and performers are illustrated and discussed. The shaman is imbued with knowledge through training and through experience gathered during his call to the profession.

More importantly, while this chapter contrasts from the previous one on the subject of study—shamanism art and practices, unlike "diviners" in the previous chapter—it also addresses how knowledge production enables practitioners to wield both spiritual and political power. I elected to use shamanism practices to explore knowledge production in this chapter. This already suggests that whether it is divination/shamanism or diviners/shamans, the results are nearly the same, only subject to the level of their acceptability in specific African communities. In African communities where the practice was prevalent and widely acceptable, shamans were often consulted by African rulers when evil looms—for luck. In addition, given the belief of their ability to communicate with the world beyond, they were always afforded a seat during critical decision-making councils, and their warnings were often not to be trifled with. In fact, their abilities to conjure spirits, commune, etc. already apportion to them great power, fear, and a modicum of political control.

Further, a discussion of its definition along with the nature and form of knowledge in shamanism is then explored by examining its oral nature of transmission and dissemination from information custodians down to generations of apprentices and descendants. This exploration of the nature of shamanism as a knowledge system leads to the forms of knowledge in the shamanic practice. Shamanism is illustrated through divination, a system of geomancy that diviners who are also shamans employ to seek out answers to various problems. Other forms of knowledge in shamanism are obtained through trance—also known as the shamanic state or altered state of consciousness—shamanic songs, drumming, hypnosis, etc. The scope of knowledge in shamanism is extensive, and this chapter has only scratched the surface.

In conclusion, shamanism is a knowledge system for acquiring information on various aspects of the indigenous African Traditional Religion, cosmology, ecology, beliefs, traditions, and customs. This system of knowledge is both traditional and modern in practice.

3

Magic and Witchcraft

Introduction

The etymology of the word *magic* derives from the Greek word *Magike*, which refers to the art and craft of ancient times and was categorized into different forms. In ancient Greek, *goetia* signified charms, sorcery or the invocation of demons while *theourgia* referred to high and benevolent magic connected to the supernatural realm.[1] African scholars have also defined magic within cognizance of the African context. According to Ki-Zerbo, magic may be understood to describe the management of forces, which is a neutral activity that is not ethically weighed. The expression of magic, by the magician's will, is assumed to have a positive or negative (evil) outcome.[2]

In the same vein as in ancient Greece, magic in Africa has shared a close relationship with other practices, such as medicine, witchcraft, rituals, and divination. Indeed, as mentioned in the preceding chapter, it also shares close affinities with shamanism, although not to be re-examined in this chapter. However, ancient African culture was in the habit of discerning the difference between magic and these concepts and the desire to separate them was born out of a need to appreciate magic wholesomely. This is what this chapter sets out to further amplify with sight on its knowledge system, including the varying forms and nature in which this knowledge can be seen. For instance, Bonmgba finds witchcraft and oracles among the Azande responsible for the devaluation of magic and prevented its study from becoming a definite concept.[3]

Despite the categorization, however, the concept of magic, witchcraft, rituals, religion, and related practices have to be studied together to fully understand their epistemology and evolution over the years. Although there is an abundance of literature on magic, much of it, specifically on African magic, fixates on a defective narrative of reducing it to a tool for injury, darkness, and destruction. The focus is oft engrossed on negative aspects in dark Eurocentric stereotypes of the African continent. Although several anthropological studies have been carried out in Africa to explain African worldviews and beliefs, especially in relation to the African epistemology of magic, many of them sadly end at theoretical discussions or are subservient to Eurocentric historical descriptions that already exist.

In these Eurocentric narratives, magic is often reduced to mere tricks—creative displays aimed at deceiving its audience and, in worst cases, for extortion. Magicians are seen as those who play on people's intelligence to create illusions. This is better depicted in the popular maxim "the more you look, the less you see." Consequently, the persistence of this wrongly conceived belief has impeded the proper understanding of the knowledge system in magic and how there stemmed a strong belief system which explains the existence of practitioners and adherents. It also erodes the impact of magic and its contributions toward what could be regarded as "African science."

Regardless of these misconceptions, however, studies show that magic has been a serious practice in Africa before contact with Western explorers and subsequent colonizers. Its forms range from sympathetic to contagious and can be housed under craft tradition rather than theoretical and scholarly tradition. Put differently, it is an art considered as part of the African culture and not as a strange concept. According to Emedolu, "Much as there are so many misinterpretations and misunderstandings of magic, we do not just wish, at least, to see magic from the anthropological threshold of the distinctive mentality of 'primitive.'"[4] This explains that magic, in its original sense, is not primitive and distant. It is a culture—one that, in fact, continues to evolve as a knowledge system that influences its practice.

To properly understand magic in Africa, it is of utmost importance to consider traditional religious practices across African societies, all of which inform the basic African thought processes and beliefs. This will invariably involve the concept of witchcraft, which has been reduced to a naïve analysis and, according to Emedolu, is but a special grade of magic. An understanding of all these will put in better perspective the discourse of magic and also provide clarity on discussing its place in African science to eliminate the cankerworm of Western negativity toward the practice of magic holistically. This will be made possible by examining the epistemology of magical practices in Africa and its relation with Western science.

Conceptualizing Magic in Africa and Deconstructing the Misconceptions

The question of if magic and other practices, such as witchcraft, rituals etc., exist in Africa is no longer up for debate. However, the point of divergence begins when the purpose and knowledge of these practices is up for determination and is misconstrued. Several literary texts try to argue that there is no causal link between African magic and the evolution of science in Africa. This argument extends to the fact that while the witchcraft phenomenon might have existed in Europe, it was around during the medieval era—essentially, in the past. These arguments largely insinuate that science has had no link with such mystical practices as magic and witchcraft. However, this wrong conception of African magic and associated practice fails, as it could not explain the continued belief and adherence in the practice in Africa. Not only that, it is one of the strong bases for the absurdly primitive aspersion cast on Africa as a continent of the ignorant.

However, when viewed through the lens of history, will this stand the test of objective cross-examination that takes in the African perspective, understanding, and interpretation of this phenomenon? While this chapter seeks to further the discussion from the religious influence perspective of magical practices in Africa, it will explore the pathway of comparison with science to assert the existence of African magic first, then by that, show how it influences beliefs and practices in Africa.

In European tradition itself, magic was regarded as the "matrix of a truly scientific experimentation."[5] This was equally affirmed by John Henry in *Magic and Origins of Modern Science*:

> Without the tradition of European magic, science and scientific medicine could hardly have developed as successfully as they have . . . so history reveals that modern science was able to make such rapid gains in the 17th century only by plundering natural magic.[6]

Not only did the Henry's statement assert that magic indeed existed in Europe, its historical significance could further be seen, as it is credited with setting the pace for the progression of science. Put differently, it can be logically inferred that magic provided a leeway for modern empirical science like an active forerunner. It was not until later that the two concepts—magic and science—became distinct within the realms of modernity. The logic behind this deliberate distinction, according to Emedolu, is that "while science gradually increased, magic rapidly decreased until interest in it faded in the wake of the 19th century."[7]

This created a lacuna between the blend of science and magic. Paul Feyerabend precisely describes this by explaining that science employs ideological ways to draw from other forms of life, particularly through witchcraft and other types of magic, using them to increase itself.[8] By so doing, other forms of life, such as magic, gradually became redundant. All of this shows that there is no separation in the origin of science from magic. The evolution of the two are intertwined and would be understood by anyone who appreciates history well enough. There is no doubt that magic and witchcraft have played a significant role in the development of science and technology, dating back to ancient Egypt. To appreciate this, a careful look at this history linking Africa is in order.

Marin Bernal, a leading Egyptologist, discussed how much modern European science is indebted to African antiquity. He describes the sixteenth century Hermetic doctor, Paracelsus (1439–1541) thus:

> He [Paracelsus] was only near the beginning of a tradition which continued up to and included Newton, in which scientists justified turning to experiment as a way to retrieve the wisdom of Egypt and the orient which the Greeks and Romans had failed to preserve.[9]

[Sacred] texts from the Egyptian doctor contained what was referred to by Bernal as *prisca theologia* and *prisca sapiential*,[10] which are predominantly religious thoughts, magic, and general wisdom on reality. Thus, it can be said that much of the text was about magic. As argued by Emedolu, "A few happy Renaissance thinkers of Europe were so fascinated by some of these legendary and important texts and made some incursions into them. In this manner modern Western science was able to make its mark from the debris of African science of antiquity,"[11] which, of course, involved magic and other forms of mystical practices.

Can we then say sacred texts from Egypt contribute not only to the practice of African science but also to the evolution of European science? To further buttress this, references can be made to James's statement where, when speaking in the context of Egyptian antiquity, he explains thus: "It must . . . be noted that magic was applied to religion or primitive scientific method."[12] Further corroborating this is Awolalu who posits that "it is a human art, which involves the manipulation of certain objects which are believed to have power to cause a supernatural being to produce or prevent a particular result considered not obtainable by natural means."[13]

This appears to contradict Karl Popper's widely held belief that primitive science began at the Ionian school of Philosophy in Greece rather than Egypt: "The first beginnings of the evolution of something like a scientific method may be found, approximately at the turn of the sixth and fifth centuries B.C., in ancient Greece."[14] Certainly, this is a Eurocentric view which aimed to displace Egypt as a focal point of reference in the discourse of primitive science. Reemphasizing the Egyptian origin of science, T. U. Nwala brilliantly submits that:

Alexandrian Academy [in Egypt] was the intellectual center of the world between 300 B.C. and 400 A.D. What is called Greek Science from 300 B.C. . . . was indeed Alexandrian science. The Alexandrian Academy hosted some of the most eminent philosopher-scientists who laid the foundation of modern science and philosophy.[15]

Indeed, there is more to African magic than demons and spirit entities, as often proclaimed. A case in point was when St Thomas Aquinas warned against the inordinate acquisition of the knowledge "of the future through demons";[16] for some of such truths are "above the capacity of (man's) own intelligence."[17] Magic can be harmful and otherwise and this is not unique to Africa. Across the world, the principles upon which harmful magic and other forms thereof are the same. Both are governed by very deep intuitive principles of sympathetic magic. It is this aspect of magical practices that influenced the outlook of people who believe in its existence negatively, as it instills paranoia in them, hence ensuring a cautious thread—affecting the sociocultural behavioral pattern of Africans, as in other places across the world.

According to Frazer, sympathetic magic involves two dominant principles—law of contagion and law of similarity—which characterize magical practices across the world.[18] For Nemeroff and Rozin, the law of contagion refers to the pervasive, implicit belief that "physical contact between [a source object] and [a target object] results in the transfer of some effect or quality (essence) from the source to the target."[19] Essentially, this refers to when an action on a part—such as strands of hair—can affect the whole, that is, the owner of the hair. An ontological explanation would find reference in several Nollywood movies with themes as such where items gotten from a target (for evil doing) such as a hair strand, clothing, accessory or anything the target is certain to come in contact with is used to harm them. However, the law of similarity or homeopathy believes that "things that resemble each other at a superficial level"—like a voodoo doll that resembles a person—"also share deeper properties."[20] An example is when a doll can be manipulated in such a way that anything done to it will affect the target being replicated.

The above principles guide the malicious use of magic or otherwise. Harmful magic is not peculiar to any continent. The inability to tell the difference between truly demonic magic and natural magic was prominent in Europe at one point, with white magic being so harmful that witches were burned at the stake.[21] In fact, even supposed free scientific minds met a similar fate, with Giordano Bruno burned at the stake in 1600[22] and Galileo subjected to inquisition from the 1630s until his death in 1642.[23] So when placed on critical analysis, the practice of harmful magic—either genuinely harmful or based on societal perceptions—is a problem that pertained to the practice of magic across the world and is not restricted to an African peculiarity. Once this is settled, arguing for the place of magical beliefs in signaling innovation and science in Africa and other parts of the world becomes more feasible.

Moreover, magic has served a similar purpose as technology has done in modern times by providing ease in life and access to opportunities they otherwise would not have. Regarding this, Uduagwu discussed a concept among the Igbo people of Nigeria that very well sounds like teleporting. He explains thus:

> Among the Igbo, magicians perform some of their arts to give the illusion of disappearance and re-appearance using some physical structure they built. They create the impression to make things disappear and re-appear, even though in reality, this is not the case. The architectural structures they use help them to make this illusion seem real. However, with time, advancement in method gave birth to what the Igbo call ikwu-ekiri. This is similar to the modern-day Western Science fiction ideas of tele-transportation or time travel. Ikwu-ekiri carries the same idea of disappearance and re-appearance of bodies as is magic but, in this case, it is actual rather than illusory. One can say that the elementary magical idea has sufficiently advanced into science.[24]

In view of the foregoing, the argument that some of the features of African magic and witchcraft cannot be linked to or has not influenced science becomes unsettling. In this discourse, it is important to look at Robin Horton's comparative analysis in *Patterns of Thought in Africa and the West: Chapters on Magic, Religion and Science*. In the study, he compared African magic and witchcraft with Western science and showed that African science has always been considered a crude alternative to Western science and was seldomly recognized or mentioned. The willful neglect or gross misinterpretation when mentioned seems to stem from the agelong demonic desire to downplay all that is African. James Frazer even claims that, "magic is a spurious system of natural law as well as a fallacious guide of conduct"[25] which is quite contentious. Frazer goes further to conclude that "magic is never a science," or that it is "a false science," that, "it is always an art" or "an abortive art."[26]

This dismissive attitude of African science can also be gleaned from the streamlined standards and criteria by which the West determines what constitutes knowledge. A premium is not only placed on the organization and systemization of knowledge but also their ability to demonstrate it. This demonstration—which is largely determined by the ability to show logical validation—carefully excludes African magic, which is more of an observational and experimental form of knowledge. This shows the need to adopt more peculiar standards for assessing what constitutes knowledge in Africa, so that it is not lost because it does not fit within a Western definition of the term.

Essentially, African magic and witchcraft on their own conveniently constitute a body of knowledge that does not necessarily need external validation. This truth finds reference in the Western world as well, thereby being one of the crucial indications of similitude between Western and African science. How this truth found a good landing in the West can be seen in a statement by Glanvill, the house philosopher of the Royal Society, when he regarded "witchcraft as the paradigm of experimental reasoning."[27] Safely, we can agree that the body of knowledge found in African magic is a wholesome experimental reasoning. This body of knowledge informs scientific practices by Africans and the ability of this to proffer extant healing solutions to some of the "medical" problems in the African traditional setting.

An Appraisal of Witchcraft and the African Belief System Behind the Practice

Witchcraft is another concept closely associated with or seen as another form of magic. Its long held prevalence across Africa makes it an important subject of discourse. There have been many debates around the actuality of witchcraft, that is, whether or not it truly exists. Several scholars and philosophers have argued back and forth on this matter, with European writers especially dismissive of the validity of witchcraft itself, largely because it does not conform to their logical assessment. The irony of this disbelief is seen in Western ontological adventures such as Merlin, Legend of the Seeker, among many others where wizards are depicted as possessing magical powers for good and evil.[28]

Wilson (1951) described witchcraft as a phenomenon employed to preserve social order in small-scale communities by taking advantage of the people's belief in the notion and exacting compliance from them.[29] However, some anthropologists do not believe that witchcraft itself exists but agree that belief in the concept of witchcraft is real, which explains the actions and behaviors of African followers. This must have likely inspired early anthropologists to carry out research about the concept of witchcraft in the African society.

Bongmba cites two factors that could explain why some anthropologists do not believe in witchcraft: (1) it does not fit their view of rationality,[30] and (2) it is just a "way of moralizing terminologies."[31] However, these perspectives, as expressed by different scholars, are based on ethnographic research carried out on different African populations. After evaluating all these views, Bond and Dane arrive at four conclusions: "[1] Witchcraft [beliefs] are real, [2] There are no witches, only the belief in them, [3] Witches may or may not be real, and further research may shed light on the issue, [4] For the study of witchcraft, the above positions are irrelevant."[32]

Given the extent of African belief in witchcraft, one could say it is one of the reasons the African continent has not fully embraced modernity and advancement in technology. For instance, some Africans still attribute the causes of their sicknesses and diseases to witchcraft attacks and spiritual forces and would rather seek divination for a cure than go to a hospital. The Yoruba people in the Western part of Nigeria are known to say "O ni owo aiye ninu" (literally meaning, "the 'hand of the world' is involved") when someone is sick, especially when the sickness has defied medical treatment. This expression demonstrates that they think someone with a malicious intent has chosen to hurt another. In other words, every tragedy or illness is attributed to ancestor spirits, evil magic, sorcery, or witchcraft in the African mentality.[33]

Lumwe, in *The Cosmology of Witchcraft in African Context*, shares a similar experience on HIV/AIDS:

> I still remember very well when one of my relatives contracted the HIV virus (allegedly transmitted from her husband) that led to her death. However, even after the death of her husband from the same disease, which could be viewed as proof of the virus, some still said that the cause of her death was because she was bewitched. To make matters worse, when she was ailing, I learned that she was taken to a witchdoctor for some traditional treatment by another close relative. I had to intervene and took her to the hospital for a diagnosis only for it to be confirmed that she was suffering from HIV/AIDS. This case study illustrates the fact that the belief in witchcraft often does not recognize scientific reality; hence, rendering some witchcraft accusations as a belief with no basis.[34]

This demonstrates that sometimes the belief in witchcraft blurs other perspectives and can be damaging to society and human lives. Nonetheless, this does not displace the concept of witchcraft, especially the thought process that forms its basis of existence.

Witchcraft in Africa: The World's Perspective

Without a belief system, witchcraft does not exist in Africa. Ayisi, Harries, Kirwen, and Mbiti, among other scholars who have studied African customs, religion, and philosophy, have consistently maintained that witchcraft in the African traditional setting is mainly a worldview phenomenon.[35] This worldview is the African truth; it is the lens through which Africans see the world. According to Geoffrey Parrinder, "everything in nature is living, or at least pre-living, and there is no such thing as absolutely dead matter."[36] This implies that a plethora of spirits exist in the world, demonstrating that how Africans view their immediate environment is unique to them. A majority of academics agree that there is no such thing as "dead" in the African concept, since the spiritual realm is inextricably linked to the land of the living.[37] Mbiti also argues that "the spiritual world of African peoples is very densely populated with spiritual beings, spirits, and the living-dead."[38]

The concept of causality is one of the basic principles upon which witchcraft continues to thrive. Witchcraft is predicated on the idea that when bad things happen, they must be the result of an unseen force. For Mbiti, this, "belief in the function and dangers of bad magic, sorcery, and witchcraft is deeply rooted in African life, and in spite of modern education and religions, like Christianity and Islam, it is very difficult to eradicate this belief."[39] This guiding concept continues to be critical in elucidating why disasters occur in Africa. This idea is shared by a variety of African ethnic groups, each with its own distinct manifestation.

For every practice that exists, there are certain thought processes backing them. These form the basis for the continued existence of the practice. When the question of "why" is raised, these thought processes serve as a point of reference. This same reasoning pertains to the concept of witchcraft in Africa. As Mwalwa argues: "I am convinced that witchcraft is NOT imaginary, nor unreal. It is still a strong force in Africa."[40] This comes from a place of seeking to understand why Africans believe what they believe regardless of if it goes against dismissive approaches embraced by missionaries and foreign religious institutions that came to Africa—dismissive approaches which created even more problems for them. In contemporary Africa, no particular orientation is required to believe in witchcraft. This fact has remained unaffected by the development of Western science and education. This explains why witchcraft inclinations persist even in urban areas.[41] According to Haar, "it is notoriously difficult to change people's beliefs, particularly when they are as deeply entrenched culturally as is the case with witchcraft beliefs in Africa."[42]

Scholars have further debated over the thought process that could possibly have influenced the practice of witchcraft. According to Evans-Pritchard, in his study of the Azande in Southern Sudan, witchcraft was their natural philosophy and a cultural ubiquity that showed itself throughout their life.[43] He believed that the African mindset, as shown by witchcraft among the Azande, was as logical as the European thought system and that witchcraft practice served as a unifying element for many facets of the African culture. Additionally, he said that the value of the Azande witchcraft practice is in its capacity to make sense of the uniqueness of tragedy.[44] His arguments contradicted Levy-Bruhl's assertion that Africans' mentality was mystical and pre-logical when compared with Europeans' speculative and logical mentality.[45]

In Gluckman's study on the Zulu people in South Africa, the argument he puts forward is fairly different. To make sense of the reasoning behind witchcraft practice, he claimed the belief that only Africans experienced misfortune while other continents enjoyed health and prosperity contributed to the concept of witchcraft.[46] Regarding the occurrence of misfortune, Gluckman raised two important concerns: "The first question is 'how' did it occur, and the second is 'why' it occurred at all."[47] He argued that although common sense and empirical observation showed "how" tragedy happened, witchcraft explained why certain people experienced specific disasters at particular times. This invariably leads us back to the notion that in Africa, when misfortune occurs, it is perceived as caused by unseen powers. Isak Niehaus, however, expanded on the scope of thoughts that illuminate witchcraft in Africa. Specifically, taking South Africa as a case study, he argued that the historical process of population relocation and the implementation of exploitative agricultural betterment schemes provided the social context for the conception of witchcraft.

The problem started when the intrusion of Whites altered how Africans held land. The Native Land Act of 1913 imposed a system of labor tenancy on white-owned farms. The head of the African household, or his sons, worked for the white landlord for three months each year without pay. For the rest of the year, they would cultivate their own lands and take care of their own cattle.[48] The land agents would monitor movement between different farmlands, collect taxes from the people, and order the arrest of people who moved about without getting permission from the European masters, making the situation worse for the natives.[49]

Following the start of the Second World War there was a severe food crisis in South Africa. Households were unable to harvest crops, and food supplies were inadequate owing to wartime constraints. People collapsed from hunger, and a kid was crushed to death during the scramble for food at a general dealer shop.[50] These situations created tension and resentment, as Africans were not only denied the product of their labor but also good conditions of living. Social segregation and disparity occasioned the necessity to look toward a tool to address what residents perceived as injustice. Hence, Niehaus asserts thus:

> These processes of agricultural decline formed the social context of witchcraft. My elderly informants could recall 27 cases of witchcraft accusation that occurred in Impalahoek during the 1940s and 1950s. Thirteen occurred between neighbors, 10 between relatives by marriage, and four between cognates. In all cases witchcraft was said to have been motivated by feelings of envy, greed, and resentment. The accusations articulated tensions resulting from unequal harvests, troubled relations between mothers and daughters-in-law over domestic labor, and disputes between kin over the inheritance of cattle.[51]

Clearly, from the long narrative presented, we see that several factors could be ascribed to the existence of witchcraft. From those who argue that it originally is part of the African culture to those who argue that it was formed as a response to oppression and exploitation, the fact remains that certain thought systems lie behind the notion of witchcraft. This makes its existence more understandable and shows the defect in the dismissive approaches of missionaries in Africa. This explains why, even in places where Christianity overthrew African Traditional Religion, it was not a comprehensive takeover, as residents still practiced their original beliefs in secret.

Sources of Witchcraft Powers

A witch "is believed to have an inherent power to harm other people."[52] Witches are believed to be individuals who can function in many forms, including as animals (birds and reptiles) and may hide from humans by adopting these forms. This is in contrast to a sorcerer, who uses objects and other accoutrements to do damage. As a consequence, Bellamy contends that, while sorcery is practiced consciously, witches do witchcraft subconsciously.[53] According to popular belief, witchcraft is a power unique to the spirit world and "available for use by anyone who knows how to tap it."[54] However, only a few people in the society may possess the "skills on how to tap, control, and use these forces . . . These mystical forces of the universe are neither evil nor good in themselves, they are just like other natural things at man's disposal."[55]

In Mbiti's classification of the African concept of order and power in the world, the main source of witchcraft power in Africa may be found in what he terms "mystical order."[56] He goes on to say that this witchcraft power is linked to God, which explains why it is "hidden and mysterious at the same time."[57] These powers are either used for the benefit of others or to destroy lives. Witchdoctors use their own power to help people; while witches are those who use their power to harm others. The witchdoctor is tasked with mitigating the effects of witchcraft.[58] As a result, we see that witchcraft powers in themselves are really just powers. It is the practitioner who determines the purpose that they would serve. This takes us back to the apt definition of Asare Opoku that witchcraft is "the exercise or employment of esoteric power for a definite purpose, good or evil."[59] In other words, these powers can serve both purposes in the hands of the right or wrong person.

Magical powers and witchcraft practices can be obtained in a variety of ways: Acquisition by supernatural ability, admission to membership in a witch society, inheritance from parents, and various other means.[60] Jealousy, hatred, and sheer wickedness are some of the reasons witches attack people.[61] With this knowledge, it is clear why witches are the most feared people in a society due to the potential evil they are believed to be capable of causing with the power they possess. However, since we already established that witchcraft power can fall into the hands of witches or witchdoctors, it becomes expedient to discuss cases where witchcraft has been positive. This helps to moderate the narrative that paint it only as a tool of destruction.

Positive Values of Witchcraft Powers in Africa

Notwithstanding the misconceptions it encounters, witchcraft has been employed to better the lives of the people and to solve attendant challenges. One fundamental place where this is reflected is in delivering people from sickness and healing them from disease. Lumwe discusses a practice in this regard among the *Mijikenda* people found in Kenya, stating:

> the *Mijikenda* (the people group I belong to that is found along the Kenyan coast) use a protective charm called fingo. Fingo is made from medicinal herbs and dry powered roots of trees that are then placed in a sacred pot. The pot may be buried at the center or in one corner of a homestead. The main purpose is to protect the homestead and the family members from evil men. This custom grew out of the practice of early *Mijikenda* settlers who lived in dense forests. They put fingo at the center of the homestead to protect the people against invaders. They believed that the charm made the settlement invisible to the invading enemy or could also counteract any magical powers used against them or create confusion among anyone attacking them. They further believed that the powers of the fingo could cause the invaders to expose their intensions by causing some form of insanity (field notes taken during my ethnographic study among the *Digo* people in 2009).[62]

Practices like this entrench how much regard is attached to the use of witchcraft power to protect communities not only from invaders but also from sicknesses that may be invoked by evil men. This belief is further given relevance when we consider the literary world of Africa; after all, literature found in a continent reflects the reality of its communities. In *Things Fall Apart*, written by Chinua Achebe of Nigeria, it was a witchdoctor who Okonkwo invited to deliver his daughter from Ezinma of the *Ogbanje* spirit that possessed her. This depicts the belief in the powers of witchdoctors and their importance across different communities in Africa. Witchdoctors are those with immense knowledge of spiritual matters and can communicate with the supernatural world to save rather than destroy. Describing witchdoctors, Robert Priest writes thus:

> In societies that attribute misfortune and death to human parties identified as witches or sorcerers, there is often also another category of magico-religious practitioner who acts with social approval to combat the witch or sorcerer/sorceress. Indigenous terms for this other category of magico-religious practitioner have often been translated into English as "traditional healer," "witchdoctor," "diviner," "shaman," or "medicine man." In most societies historically that had both "witch" (*mchawi*) and "witchdoctor" (*mganga*), the "witch" was thought of as acting towards anti-social ends—towards the harm of others, and the "witchdoctor" or "shaman" as acting towards pro-social ends—towards the healing of others. And, prior to the presence of Christianity, in most societies both the evil "witch" and the good "witchdoctor" were thought of as drawing from the same source(s) of power—which were neither intrinsically evil nor intrinsically good.[63]

As described by Kohnert, a classic example of witchcraft power is that of Nicephore Soglo, a former director of the World Bank. Soglo contested for the president of Benin in 1991, and toward the end of his term, he became severely sick with an ailment that Kohnert claims to have allegedly been induced by "bewitchment" by his then political opponent.[64] Despite being flown to the military hospital Val-de-Grace in Paris for treatment, his health did not improve until the intervention of a powerful *vodounon* with tremendous power. Soglo was resuscitated, and he subsequently began to recover.[65]

More so, witchcraft facilitates the protection of life and this is why people swallow charms, wear talisman, amulets, charms around their necks and genitals, among others—all of which are prepared by witchcraft power. These practices are largely seen among warriors and people who have cause to endanger their lives. Premised on the former, Bauer writes in detail:

> One of the African worldview assumptions that allow Christians to continue to seek the help of diviners and witchdoctors is the view that witchcraft powers can be used for good in society. This view suggests the possibility that positive mystical powers can continue to be helpful in protecting those who have supposedly made a total commitment to Jesus Christ. The belief causes some Christians to continue to wear charms and amulets, take medicine, or have the prescribed concoction rubbed into their bodies . . . Some also continue to keep dry bones, snakes, and birds on the rooftops of their houses, or place marks on private parts of their bodies. Such

dual allegiance among Christians is grounded in African religious thought that regards the metaphysical world as "amoral. Spiritual forces, traditionally, were seen as intrinsically neither good nor bad, although their power could be channeled for moral or immoral purposes."[66]

Lastly, witchcraft tends to bring about crime reduction in society. Even in this modern time, many of us are familiar with the notion that the gods of witchcraft dish out justice faster than the gods of Christianity or Islam. In the Yoruba culture, there exists *Ogun* the god of iron reputed to strike down a guilty person once the spirit has been invoked. This is often used among Sango believers to serve justice because of its immediacy. Regarding such a belief system, Kombo asserts:

> ordinary people do not want to attract the attention of witches by going out of the ordinary. Areas where witchcraft beliefs and practices are common do not experience high rate of crimes and immorality. Incidentally, some people including normal Christians argue that without witches, their social world would lack a social control mechanism . . . And since all people are believed to have access to witches, people do not underestimate the ability of their neighbors to revenge in case of social, political and economic misdeeds.[67]

Other Traditional Religious Practices in Africa

Traditional religious practices are replete in Africa, including rituals, miracles, and several other variations. A careful appraisal of these practices demonstrates the lifestyle of Africans and the general belief systems from which other practices stem. It is essential to discuss the origin of the belief in God in Africa before we delve in the practices that characterize the worship system of Africans. There are different views on the concept of God in Africa. Some believe that religion arose out of fear. People saw the grandeur of the cosmos, as well as the lightning, thunder, and other workings of the universe, and as a result, they formed trust in a superior deity who would protect them from these events. Although there are varying views on the origin of God, three can be said to exist:

(1) Africans began to believe in God as a result of their perception of the world. This alludes to Africans' attempts to make sense of the mysteries around them, which resulted in the development of a belief system that provided an explanation. In his book, *Introduction to African Religion*, Mbiti notes that it must have taken a long time to arrive at this position, and that "there must have been many myths and ideas which tried to explain these mysteries of the world."[68]

(2) As a consequence of seeing their own limitations, Africans began to trust in God. This point of view is based on man's limitations and unquenchable desires. As a result, Africans were compelled to admit that there must be a supreme being who

is more powerful than they are. According to Mbiti, "this idea made it logical and necessary for man to depend on the one who was more powerful than people."[69]

(3) Nature's forces also contributed to man's belief in God. As Africans became more aware of natural forces, their reverence for nature increased, as did their belief in the presence of God. Man adored nature and felt compelled to comprehend its existence. Hence, Mbiti argues that this may be the reason "that God is so much associated with the sky and the heavens."

While Africans recognize a God, they, however, also recognize several divinities in their religious ontology. These divinities have been referred to by several scholars as "gods," "demigods," etc. Mbiti explains that the term "covers personification of God's activities and manifestations, the so-called 'nature spirits,' deified heroes, and mythological figures."[70] In Africa, the idea of divinities is widely held. There are numerous similar divinities in West Africa, where the idea is well articulated. Idowu, for example, argues that there are as many as 201, 401, 600, or 1700 divinities in the Yoruba pantheon.[71] Mbiti recounts that in Edo, Nigeria, there are as many divinities as there are human wants, actions, and experiences, and the cults of these divinities are acknowledged as such. In his words, "One [divinity] is connected with wealth, human fertility, and supply of children (*Oluku*); another is iron (*Ogu*), another of medicine (*Osu*), and another of death (*Ogiuwu*)."[72] Premised on the concept of God and divinities, practices such as rituals find reference and shall now be discussed.

A ritual, like religion, is a notion that cannot be defined by consensus. It has been subjected to many interpretations by various anthropologists. As such, focusing on what a ritual does rather than what it is makes it less difficult to appreciate it as the form of religious expression that it is. African religions are characterized by harmonious relationships toward the Supreme Being or the divinities. To this end, a ritual serves as the most important tool to negotiate a responsible relationship in a human community with ancestors, gods, and other divinities. It is a tool of negotiation and communication to appease the gods and to gain insight into necessary courses of action.

In this realm of rituals, divination stands as one of the most important tools driving African religion. Divination seeks clarity and revelation through the reading of signs, objects, a random cast of cowrie shells, Kola nuts, etc. It is a practice through which random physical arrangements can be read to construe messages from the spiritual realm. Africans find the need to communicate with the spiritual world in a bid to foster a harmonious relationship between the two worlds. This also helps them make a sense of occurrences in their immediate world.

As noted in Chapter 2, one of the most prominent practices of divination in Africa is found among the people of Yoruba. It is called *Ifa*, which is practiced by Babalawo— fathers of secrets—and is classified as "wisdom, divination."[73] Babalawos are highly trained in the interpretation of random signs that evolve from the cast of kola nuts. The signs can produce 256 sets referred to as *Odu*. There are verses associated with the signs through which they are invoked. While these verses are open to interpretation, Ifa's set of Odu is closed and unchanging.[74] Aside from wisdom divination, rituals are employed to heal sick persons and to prevent affliction. In Zambia among the Ndembu people, *Isoma* is a curative ritual that is very prominent.[75] This practice is documented by Victor Turner in his book called *The Ritual Process*. Isoma refers to "slipping out of a place of tightening" and is invoked to help women solve the problem of infertility.[76]

African traditional religious practices also extend to the concept of masks and masquerades, which are very common across different cultures in Africa. This is a typical example of religious thinking manifested in ritual. Spiritual entities are said to inhabit the masks and interact with them via them. In Yoruba, once a masquerade kicks off, it becomes referred to as *ara orun*—someone of the spiritual realm. It is, however, notable that while masquerades are offshoots of rituals, the concept of masquerade attire and masks are not without reason. They are largely representations of the cosmic order. For instance, the *Sirge* mask of the Dogon of Mali, which contains a zigzag design, is said to represent the interwoven nature of the world.[77]

Essentially, what all these indicate is that practices in Africa are explainable, even though they may prove difficult to understand especially to non-Africans. There is a belief system, and this influences the actions, practices, and relations of Africans. The approach adopted, which commenced with explaining magic's relatability with science, seeks to reemphasize the need to understand the *Africanness* of these practices in a bid to fully appreciate the knowledge derived from culture.

Conclusion

Magic and witchcraft in Africa have long existed and, in fact, have not been stopped by modernization. Significantly, they are used for both good and evil, depending on who is using it. That, in itself, already explains where the power lies or where it comes from. As a result, magicians and witches and wizards were greatly feared in their respective communities. This fear translated into power for them, especially for those believed to be top-tier in the knowledge of magic and witchcraft. They were deemed as powerful not only by the communities they served, but also by traditional rulers in African societies who were happy to align with them. The Yoruba particularly refer to kings fondly as "oko awon aje," translated as "the husband of the witches." Kings always strived to not offend these people because of their spiritual powers and knowledge of happenings in the present and future.

The belief in the effectiveness of their utterances—be it curse or blessing—serves as another huge source of their political power, derived from spiritual knowledge. Indeed, even when these utterances were likely not occurring, the belief in the utterances influences Africans, especially adherents. Also, especially important is the fact of utterances—spoken words are central to invocation in magic and witchcraft as well as divination and shamanism. Indeed, it is often the belief that wrong utterances, slights, or mistakes in pronunciation, etc. could invoke the undesirable.

However, despite the importance of these powers in African society and its contribution toward African science, they seem not to fall within an acceptable European context of scientific knowledge knowing fully well that the parameters used in deciding what constitutes scientific knowledge are largely unique to the European understanding of knowledge. This thus begs the need for Africa to create its own criteria for determining what constitutes knowledge. Even in Europe, scholars admit that magic provided leeway into the science widely practiced today. It then begs the question of when magic in Africa was described only as evil and erroneously stamped as such, which rendered it unable to contribute toward what we could call African science.

The problem with the African narrative when it comes to her practices started with the writing of armchair scholars who made their submissions largely on anthropological findings of others, as opposed to experiential learning and understanding of the culture for themselves. This notion refuses to take into consideration the thought process that backs various practices in Africa and, as such, becomes very defective in dismissing these practices. This misconception persisted until indigenous African academics, such as John S. Mbiti and E. Bolaji Idowu, set out in the 1970s and 1980s to debunk some of the false assertions about African religion. There are belief systems upon which every practice is premised, and these systems are what should be studied to gain insight into the perspective of Africans. It is following this clarification that it made sense to assert the knowledge system derived from magic, first of which is the science, and then understand how it influences the belief of Africans, as well as informs their practices and actions.

However, one fundamental concern still remains: How African practices and concepts are described. There is a need to promote an Afrocentric paradigm in researching African experiences from an African viewpoint, such as looking at African history, religion, and philosophy through an African lens. This paradigm has become essential since the majority of African experiences have been documented from a Eurocentric viewpoint. As a result, the European colonizers have dictated the world's religio-politico-socio-economic trend, and numerous terminologies such as savagism, juju, fetishism, animism, magic, paganism, heathenism, and ancestral worship have developed to denigrate African spirituality. For the most part, Eurocentrism has existed as a system of ideas that puts Europe at the center, relegating all other ways of thinking to the periphery by establishing criteria in which their reality may be evaluated.[78] Thus, Eurocentric scholars are seen as agents of a basic conspiracy to deny Africans' contributions to civilization.[79] Hence, the modification of perspectives and retelling of our practice is how we truly establish the place of African magic, witchcraft powers, and other traditional practices in the evolution of science.

Part Two

Islam

Sufism as a Knowledge System

Introduction

Abu Hamid Al-Ghazal, a renowned Sufi, defined *Sufism* as "taste."[1] His explanation is both simple and profound: Sufism can be summarized as the "direct knowledge of transcendent truths, closer to an experience of the senses than to mental knowledge." Sufism aspires to be a knowledge system that is best experienced as a feeling or as an experience that is remarkably different from the general experience of acquiring knowledge.

In West Africa, Sufism is closely linked with Islamic mysticism. It remains a powerful and popular manifestation of Islam, and it "constitutes the most common institutional expression of mystical Islam in the region."[2] Sufism is more than a mystical branch of Islamic belief, and it should not be conflated with Islamic mysticism. However, from West Africa's Sahelian belt in the north to the Gulf of Guinea in the south and the shores of the Atlantic Ocean in the west to the slopes of the Mandara and Adamawa mountains in the east, a strong correlation exists between Sufism and Islamic mysticism. Scholars have traced Sufism's origins in Africa to the introduction and practice of Islam. As a system of knowledge, it permeates spiritual and non-spiritual aspects of African life.

Sufism is regarded as a philosophy for the comprehension of Islam's unknown or hidden truths. Although many scholars have challenged the idea that Sufism is Islamic mysticism, this chapter focuses on Sufism's significance as an intellectual tool for the analysis, theorization, verification, discussion, and validation of sociocultural, spiritual, secular, political, and existential issues that affect all human beings. This work examines how Sufism affects actions, beliefs, and practices in Africa.

Knowledge of the self and the surrounding environment is a perpetual goal for humanity, and Sufism is an ontological apparatus for discussing and exploring knowledge about the universe and the existence of God. The human drive to understand the self and its place in the world has fueled developmental efforts from religious dogma to philosophy and the empirical sciences. Although great strides have been made in understanding human nature, many issues remain unsolved. Islamic books, the Quran and Sunnah, serve as fundamental concepts for Sufism's epistemology. However, the knowledge of Sufism focuses not only on religious texts, but also on personal perceptions of divine touch and communication with celestial bodies. Sufism is a dynamic concept that encompasses the individual and collective spiritual experiences of Muslims.

Spirituality has been practiced for ages in all kinds of religions, claiming to answer unresolved questions. Spirituality forms an important part of most belief systems, across cultures and religions, for people who link their spirituality with their daily existence. Sufism offers a genuine platform for seeking deeper meanings, reaching into a realm of spirituality where people believe that they can find the answers they seek.

Sufism is often regarded as a science. Its understanding of the natural and spiritual worlds is founded on facts that have been analyzed and confirmed by observations and experiences. Sufi theories, doctrines, ethics, and cosmology are simultaneously empirical and spiritual.[3] Before discussing Sufism as a mystical and scientific philosophy of wisdom, a brief overview of Sufism's past will be useful to examine its meaning, characteristics, and agents of knowledge. It is also helpful to discuss Sufis as intermediaries and channels for this knowledge system. This chapter will also examine Sufism as a knowledge system and the various expressions of Sufism in West African contexts, paying special attention to the ways that Sufi teachings and doctrines influence people, the power carried by those teachings, and how Sufism approaches the concept of spirituality.

This chapter will emphasize what knowledge means for Sufism, exploring the truth and wisdom embedded in various Sufi sects and practices, especially in Africa. It will conclude by discussing the relevance that this system of knowing holds for Africa and its people.

Origin of Sufism

Islam emerged in 610 A.D., mainly among Christian and pagan Arabs, from the Prophet Muhammad's teachings, which were claimed to have been revealed by God through the Archangel Gabriel.[4] The emergence of Sufism, as a mystical practice of Islam, was influenced by interactions between Muslim and Christian cultures during Islam's formative years. Sufism primarily arose from the Islamic traditions established in the Quran. Some Islamic schools of thought regard Sufism as heresy.[5] However, the pillars of Sufism—the idea of God, the possibility of esoteric wisdom, and ways to access God by self-purification through prayer, fasting, and repentance—can all be found in the Quran and in the Prophet Muhammad's teachings.

Sufism was originally an individual pursuit. Sufis lived in seclusion and practiced self-mortification. Sufism identifies with the ideology and practice of direct communion with God; it did not become part of Islamic history until generations after the *tabi'un* (the followers or successors of the prophet's companions) and the *zahids* (the scholars and devotees who came right after).[6] The first spiritualist who identified as a Sufi was Sheik Abu Hashim Kufi.[7]

The origin of the term *Sufism* is unclear. Sufis believe that the term is derived from the Arabic word *safa*, meaning purity. Others believe that it came from the Arabic word *suf*, which means wool, referring to the appearance of mystics who renounced the physical world and wore wool clothing. There is yet the suggestion that Sufism is modified from a related Arabic word *saff*, which means line or row, describing those associates of the Prophet who occupied the first row during prayers. The word Sufi may have also originated from the word *suffah*, meaning veranda, referencing homeless companions of the Prophet who were known to reside on the porch of his mosque.[8]

Despite the unclear origins of the term, it is obvious that Sufis were direct descendants of Prophet Mohammed's close associates; almost every account points to a similar relationship. The discipline suggests a higher degree of devotion, either because of special clothing, more time spent with the Prophet, or their residence on the porch of the Prophet's mosque. These claims of extraordinary devotion could be the reasons for Sufism's associations with heightened spirituality. The origin of the name for practitioners of Islamic mysticism is itself shrouded in mystery.

Sufism's origins are linked with the origins of Islam; the Prophet Mohammed is considered to be the first Sufi of Islam. The discipline's core belief is that the divine revelations that the prophet received are of two dimensions—one of which takes the form of the Quran's written words, and the other is the divine inspiration from the Prophet's heart and mind.[9] Each dimension refers to a different form of sacred words—one written in texts, and the other written in hearts.

The rise of Sufism and Sufi spiritualists started in the tenth century, when the decline of the *Mu'tazila* and rationalist ideologies paved the way for new philosophical ideas based on Islamic theology. The rationalist Mu'tazila, heavily influenced by Greek philosophy, had used political power to promote Islamic theology based on reason and to persecute those who opposed them. Mu'tazila was accused of using reason to promote skepticism and atheism, by arguing that the Islamic philosophy of monism meant seeing God and the created world as similar. According to the orthodox elements of Islam, Mu'tazila beliefs led to heresy for not recognizing the difference between the Creator and the Created.[10]

Orthodox Muslims used sustained repression, resistance, and the aid of contemporary political authorities to decimate the Mu'tazila. The victorious traditionalists created four schools of Islamic law. The Hanafi School, very liberal, spread among the eastern Turks who later migrated to India and founded empires.[11] The birth of Sufism as a "modern spiritualistic ideology" can be directly associated with these developments.[12]

The practice of Islam has three components: *iman*, or belief in the words of Allah; *ita'ah*, obedience with the Islamic creed; and *ihsan*, the cultivation of the habits of truth and virtue.[13] Sufism places the greatest emphasis on ihsan, the practice of virtue, sincerity, and piousness. In practice, this is recognized as a level of devotion in which a Muslim is completely absorbed in the worship of Allah.

Sufism is also considered to be an extension of pre-Islamic asceticism that has incorporated Islamic doctrines. There were many ascetic groups in the Middle East prior to the advent of Islam, and these groups believed in the emancipation of the self. They considered the body a prison that is the source of life's evil and misery, and the renunciation of worldly pleasure is seen as the only way to escape. After they embraced Islam, some members of this group retained their earlier ascetic ideology and merged it with Islamic doctrine.[14] This history has led some to claim that Sufism is not a legitimate branch of Islam, existing as a blend of Islamic and non-Islamic principles.

The Sufism ideology went through a series of institutional changes around the thirteenth century, effecting organizational and doctrinal changes, introducing mystical schools, and developing techniques and practices that attempted to systemize mysticism.[15] This restructuring and institutionalization led to the growth of Sufism and the development of mystical schools where well-defined systems of spiritual exercises were practiced under the tutelage of a *shaykh* or master.

Islamic texts—the Quran and Sunnah—are foundational sources for Sufism's epistemology. However, knowledge in Sufism includes personal experiences of divine contact and communication with heavenly bodies. Sufism is considered to be a dynamic term for the personal and collective experience of spirituality in Islam; Sufis strive to attain a level of spirituality where they have the experience of seeing God. They believe that only *niyyah*, a prayer inspired by true intentions, can yield the desired result.[16] An important prayer for the Sufis was popularized by the great Andalusian Sufi, Muhyiddin Ibn 'Arabi: "Enter me, O Lord, into the deep of the Ocean of Thine Infinite Oneness."[17]

Like other Muslims, the Sufi consider the Prophet Mohammed to be the perfect embodiment of Islamic ideas and beliefs. The life of the Prophet provides an example for the Sufi to follow. Narrations of the Prophet's life are replete with tales of sincerity, selflessness, deep devotion, total submission to God's will, divine inspiration, and nearness to God. The Sufis also emphasize purification, following the words of the Quran (91:9), "He will indeed be successful who purifies his soul, and he will indeed fail who corrupts his soul."[18]

According to the teachings of the Quran, God is said to have made the human soul perfect, with an understanding of right and wrong.[19] However, humans on earth have a propensity to choose what is wrong, thereby corrupting their souls. Purification is necessary to restore the pristine nature of the soul. Sufis believe that the act of purification is pleasing to God. Early Sufis were also known for embracing poverty, believing that material possessions would distract them from focusing on God—this belief probably stems from their ascetic background.

Ways of the Path and Orders of Sufism

From the sixth to the eleventh centuries, the universal form of Sufism expanded throughout the Arab and Islamic cultures, proliferating and gaining influence. By the early eleventh century, Sufism had grown into *Sufi turuq* (orders or paths), becoming defined as a popular religious form and as a form of social expression.[20] The Sufi route has been acknowledged and modified in a number of ways, all of which are founded on the fundamental "Sufi road" or "order." These include its component aspects, instructional and moral procedures, standards for reaching and achieving goals, and the authority and influence it wields over individuals.

The historical evolution of Sufism has taken several detours, and new directions emerge when Sufism arrives in a new society or culture. In its early years, Sufism had an independent culture founded on personal spiritual experience and was dominated by an elite community of people seeking to become closer to God by severing their ties to society and the physical world. After the fifth century, this individualistic nature grew into a more mainstream social manifestation.[21]

J. Trimingham defined the *tariqa* or Sufi path as follows:

A tariqa is a practical path that guides the wayseeker by defining a manner of thought, feelings and action which will lead the wayseeker through a succession of spiritual stations or "maqamat" in integral association with psychological experiences called spiritual states or "ahwal," in order to experience the Divine Reality or Truth. At first, a tariqa simply meant a progressive method for contemplative and soul-releasing mysticism, with circles of disciples gathering around an acknowledged master of the "way," seeking training through association or companionship, but not linked to him by any initiatory tie, covenant or vow of allegiance.[22]

A Sufi tariqa is made up of an erudite scholar who has spiritual authority because of his education or the ability to logically discern what is right from an Islamic perspective, including ambitious students who desire knowledge of Sufi tariqa.[23] The students' direction is set by the order's educational and instructional methods, teachings, and worship practices, which they follow in their faith, devotion, words, and actions.

The first Sufi order that arose in a structured manner, with distinct attributes and characteristics, is believed have emerged in the sixth century or at the start of the twelfth century. This order is characterized by three distinguishing features: a founding *shaykh* who serves as a point of reference for the followers; a tariqa (or doctrine) prescribed by the founding shaykh; and special relationships that bind members of the group together.[24] The fusion of these three characteristics determines each Sufi order, *ribat*, or shaikdom, giving it distinct personality, cohesion, and power. This extends to any of its members as a feeling or emotion that provides a sense of protection, cohesiveness, and authority.

Sufi orders differ from early Sufism by assuming distinct personalities and techniques for achieving *fana* (self-annihilation) and *shudud* (the direct witnessing of God). Sufi orders are ruling, commanding, and prohibitive in nature. Its power fluctuates in response to changing social and political conditions, rising and fading in accordance with its degree of support, followers, and funding, as well as the personality and influence of its shaykh or founder. Sufism's position and subsequent advancements during the Ottoman and colonial periods were founded on the notion that Sufi leaders have paranormal abilities and were required to perform miracles in order to attain the rank of shaykh or elder.[25]

Prior to the Mongol invasion of AH 656 (AD 1258), several Sufi orders existed. Following that, they flourished and spread throughout the Islamic world during the fourteenth century. In Baghdad, "Abd al-Qadir al-Gilani was the first to advocate for and establish an order."[26] A Sufi order's characteristics and synergy are crucial in Arab and Islamic worlds, especially in areas and eras fractured by ruling families struggling for power. Religious and theological disagreements could sever ties due to cultural and power struggles occurring between ruling families, peoples, and regions, which would create a tense atmosphere. In such settings, a community where relationships are formed and based on spiritual unity was highly valued; it helped to alleviate some of the pressure imposed by external circumstances.

According to Hammer, in "Sufism for Westerners," a Sufi order will often honor its most famous founder or shaykh by taking that person's name.[27] The affiliation of these individuals with their orders help to immortalize their names. These decisions can be chosen on the basis of scholarship, commitment, hard labor, or service to the order—aspirants, pupils, disciples, and devotees make these choices independently of the founder's influence, request, or demand. The founders' philosophy and practices, as well as their knowledge, diligence, excellent manners, and moral character, have a direct effect on the order and how its rituals are conducted and how well they use the sources.

Fundamentals of Sufism

From the beginning, the Sufi philosophy has been centered around the concept of God and the forms and essence of communion with God.[28] Early Sufis understood God in strict conformity with the Quran as infinite, everlasting, unchanging, all-powerful, compassionate, and the creator and cause of all life. Sufis see the soul as a means of communicating with God. They believe that the higher soul is made up of the heart (*qalb*), spirit (*ruh*), and conscience (*sirr*), and it is produced before humans are born and before they developed the ability to know God. For many Sufis, consciousness represents the "secret shrine of God himself, wherein he knows man and man can know him."[29] Sufism also places a premium on the qalb, since it is the location of the key to spiritual awareness, a confirmation of God's declaration that, "I, who cannot fit into all the heavens and earths, fit in the heart of the sincere believer."[30]

In Sufism ideals, Prophet Muhammad holds a special role. Spiritual enlightenment, or the ascent of the higher soul to God, is said to occur as a result of a sequence of transmissions to Muhammad—communion with God is only possible through him. Sufis claim that ascension is only possible through the purification of the soul, which is the path (tariqa).[31] Sufis seek spiritual awareness and communion with God through the wisdom found in the Quran (*ilm*) and Islamic practice of Islam (*amal*). Sufi philosophy's development resulted in a paradigm change about God, from being regarded as the source of all life to being viewed as the only real existence.[32] This belief is based on Muhammad's statement that "the first thing that Allah created was my light, which originated from his light and derived from the majesty of his greatness."[33]

Sufism has too many facets to track individually. It holds significant sociopolitical implications, despite its emphasis on otherworldly sanctity. Islam's saints have served as advisers and challengers to sultans, sometimes endorsing legitimate rule and other times claiming divine authority over political leaders of the period.[34] Sufis have successfully mediated conflict in tribal cultures by standing above clan interests, and they serve as moral figures in villages and towns. Their distance from corrupt politics allows them to serve as a bridge between society and government, connecting the state to local citizens. Followers of a saint act as part of a separate domain that governmental and nongovernmental groups must negotiate with, acting to balance interests and principles within society.[35] In his book, *The Political Role of Islam*, Ngala Chome wrote:

It is also true that Sufism has been a very successful agent for Muslim society's religious revival, a subject that has yet to be thoroughly explored. This may be particularly true in largely illiterate communities, where the task of reacquainting the faithful with God's ways cannot be accomplished through the distribution of texts, but rather through saintly figures who represent godliness in their own person, in their words and deeds, for all to see, including the least educated. The role of Sufism in reinvigorating Muslim culture with Islamic ideals and the spirit of prophecy as carried by the saint is not limited to any time of Islam, but the widespread existence of the phenomenon in the eighteenth and nineteenth centuries has piqued academic interest in recent years and yielded much scholarly fruit.[36]

The Quran mentions not only prophets but also saints, who are described as God's friends or allies.[37] With Muhammad accepted as the final prophet, the issue of prophethood has largely been resolved. However, the essence and intent of sainthood remains ambiguous. If Sufism has a meaning, it must be the realization that sanctity is the culmination of the divine path begun by the Quran, placing the concept of sainthood at the core of Sufism. Sainthood encompasses various forms of holiness, as defined in *manaqib* (hagiographical literature), observed during shrine visits (*ziyarat*), and commemorated in song and processions on feast days (*mawalid*).[38] Saints have been mendicants, miracle workers, and even warriors who were commemorated for their erudition, asceticism, and expertise in counseling, mediation, and making peace.

Sufism's founders stressed that obeying God's commands was not enough—such actions can be done hypocritically, not for the sake of God, but to gain acceptance from the community.[39] Faith can easily devolve into a business transaction, expecting rewards for obeying God's orders and punishment for disobeying them. Sufism opposed hypocritical religious practices and the commercialization of religion. Under the value system of Sufism, it is important to combine adherence to Islamic standards—ritual and moral action—with an analysis of the soul.

Early Sufism blended aspects of asceticism and mysticism. Its adherents felt that a close connection with the physical world was in opposition to the spiritual aim of completely orienting oneself within the other world. As the Quran had proclaimed, the final prize to earn was the ascetic detachment from the world and its ways.[40] The universe was viewed as a threat to one's redemption, and it needed to be renounced as a source of temptation.

The Quran described humans that had been created frail, with spirits that were inclined to do evil. Mere detachment from the environment was not sufficient; it was crucial to maintain a sense of separation from oneself. This was envisioned as self-annihilation in God, starting as spiritual warfare, or jihad against evil, and ending with the soul's complete identification with God. As Heck explains:

> Only when the self is vanished and only God existed in the inner recesses of the heart could one be assured of acting without concern for oneself. Spiritual practices such as ceaseless recitation (dhikr) of the names of God as found in the Quran until they were inscribed on one's soul, training the soul—in accordance

with a canonical hadith—to concentrate only on God, to see only God at all, brought about the mystical absorption of the soul in God, communicated by ecstatic utterances as a loving intimacy with the divine, were brought about by spiritual practices.[41]

Sufism expanded beyond its ascetic origins to bring religious value to the larger world. Without Islam, its growth would not have been possible—Sufism's theology strives to reconcile Islam's values with the world's facts. The theological roots of Sufism allow it to cross potentially insurmountable differences between religious values and secular realities, Muslims and non-Muslims, and between nations and cultures that have seemingly irreconcilable political interests.

Sufi manuals from the tenth and eleventh centuries show that its adherents considered their way to be superior to legal formalities and religious claims.[42] As a living manifestation and absolute expression of Islam, Sufism was the solution for physical ailments such as heart disease and the answer to questions that no amount of religious argument or philosophical debate had been able to resolve. The mystical proof provided by Sufism and its saints was crucial for the truth of Islam, not just its moral mission.

Sufis derive reasons for the world's existence from God's urge to reveal Himself, following the Hadith: "I was a hidden treasure that longed to be known, so I created the world."[43] Sufism is rooted in the dual viewpoints of "knowledge" (*ma'rifa*) and "love" (*mahabba*). Each of these two approaches to the divine reinforce the other. Sufis use love and wisdom in tandem or separately, but many agree with the statement that they are identical. The belief is that one cannot love God without knowing him, and one cannot know God without loving him.

The Sufi method of spiritual investigation is based on inspiration and "unveiling." The messages of Ibn 'Arabi and the poetry of various Sufi masters are claimed to have been influenced by God.[44] However, there is a distinction between inspiration and revelation. Although it is believed that only prophets can receive revelation, all Sufis access the spiritual world through inspiration or unveiling. The act of unveiling is said to remove the spiritual blindness that the mortal body experiences in the material world. Geoffroy and Gaetani expound:

> Often described as a bolt of lightning that illuminates the consciousness and fixes itself upon the latter through its intense flashing and clarity, this "unveiling" leads to the vision of certainty (yaqīn) and to the direct perception ('iyān) of spiritual realities, which evaporates the doubt associated with the speculative sciences. It has its foundation particularly in Koranic verse 50:22: "You were heedless of this; now have We removed from you your veil, and piercing is your vision this day."[45]

The knowledge gained from such inspiration is not restricted to literate people; it can be accessed by almost anyone willing to receive "the knowledge that comes from God." This informs the wide acceptance of Sufism in West Africa; simple farmers and traders can learn directly from God through inspiration or unveiling, placing them on equal footing with the greatest saints. Sufi masters emphasize that sincerity and purity of intentions are much more important than literacy or status for anyone who aspires to inspiration.

Sufis pursue many objectives, based on their different spiritual experiences. Overall, its adherents are responding to the moral degradation that has afflicted humanity—and themselves—since the beginning of time.[46] Sufis believe that the only way to manifest a noble character (*khuluq*) and correct conduct (*adab*) is through devotion to the purification of the soul (*tazkiyat an-nafs*).[47] Their ideas of noble virtue or character are essentially the same as mainstream Islamic virtues, but Sufis place special emphasis on bringing those virtues to life within themselves. Some Sufis pursue a deep knowledge of God in order to worship God better. With this approach, purification is considered to be a means to an end, but not the end itself. Regardless of their aim, inspiration and unveiling are necessary for the ultimate Sufi goal of being united with God.

Sufi rites are classified as systems and as forms of knowledge.[48] The act of purification is simultaneously a system of cleansing oneself of worldly desires and a form of knowledge of oneself and of God. Another such rite is the system of recitation. The Sufi recitation of religious texts usually focuses on a particular sentence or phrase that is continuously repeated to emphasize and assimilate its truthful revelation. The recitation of repeated words and verses evokes meditation and meaning for Sufis, illuminating the recognition of wisdom and truth. Recitation and invocation are analogous to prayer, which is a Sufi rite that professes knowledge of God; the act of repetitive recitation is based on the idea that God created the world through speech, and this speech consists of sacred formulas that evoke deep knowledge.

Asceticism is another fundamental Sufi tradition, involving severe self-discipline and the avoidance of all forms of indulgence to prepare for spiritual immersion.[49] Knowledge in Sufism is attained by self-control, which makes asceticism a very important practice. Sufis strive to gain wisdom through the methodology and methods of asceticism. These practices facilitate the spiritual conversion of the body and mind, enabling an awareness of God and obedience to His will.

Sufism's asceticism has been compared to a deep cleaning of the heart in order to receive knowledge. The ascetic lifestyle of the Sufis is believed to be a way of living their essence and finding reality for the greater good of humanity.[50] This commitment to searching, disseminating, and teaching information to elucidate deeper, fundamental activities of life has resulted in strict attitudes. Sufis are distinguished by their abstention from worldly possessions and wasteful practices, making their knowledge sacrosanct and holy. As Rachida explains:

> Sufism's asceticism, which is based on three principles: life's brevity/transience, the presence of durable realms of life outside of the material world, and the withdrawal from pleasure, is thought to help people avoid being engrossed in tedious worldly living that will not bring them fulfillment. These Sufi principles are extensions of the belief that human beings have no possessions and truly own nothing. Since the goal of Sufism is self-knowledge, ascetic practices put a person's courage, intelligence, and will to the test. Empirically, one cannot fully assess awareness of one's world and self unless one denies oneself anything that one has previously enjoyed or had. [51]

Sufism has progressed through distinct phases, beginning as a solitary form and evolving into the practice and philosophy of spiritual wisdom. It eventually organized into tariqa social systems, whose saintly leaders often become focal points for massive public devotion. This transformation is evident in the prominent doctrines promoted by Sufism. [52]

Major Sufi Teachings and Doctrines

Sufi doctrine includes several points of view that relate to fundamental reality, and some may be contradictory when considered solely on the basis of their logical structure. One Sufi master may deny a doctrinal argument made by another master, even as they respect each other's authority. In the book *Al-Insan al-Kamil* (*Universal Man*), based on Ibn Arabi's teaching, Abd al-Karm al-Jl rejects Ibn Arabi's assertion that Divine Knowledge, like all science, is dependent on its object.[53] The rejection is based on the argument that such an assertion will lead anyone to believe that Divine Knowledge is conditional on that which is relative. Explaining this, Idries Shah states:

> Sufi philosophy has many divisions, with two primary domains: universal truths (al-Haqiq) and human and person phases of the path (ad-daqiq), or metaphysic and a "science of the soul," respectively. These domains are not, of course, divided into watertight compartments. Metaphysic encompasses everything, but in Sufism, it is often envisioned through the lens of spiritual realization.[54]

Apart from the domains of al-Haqiq and ad-daqiq, there are three major domains of doctrine: metaphysics, cosmology, and spiritual psychology.[55] These encompass the triad of God, the macrocosmic earth, and the microcosmic soul. Although cosmology must involve the cosmic truth of the soul in its full creation, no metaphysical psychology can separate the soul from cosmic concepts. According to the Prophet, "He who knows himself (*nafisahu*) knows his Lord," and the Sufi discipline is a path toward self-knowledge.[56] This extends to the Unique Essence, or the immutable Self (*al-huwiyah*), transcending any cosmological or psychological viewpoint. Knowledge of oneself must involve a science of the soul, on a relative level, to address one's human existence.

General requirements of inspiration (*al-wrid*) can be used to demonstrate how cosmological concepts motivate soul discrimination. Inspiration—in the sense of sudden insight elicited by spiritual practices—is not to be confused with prophetic inspiration, which can come from various places, including from an "angel" and other forces with connections to God.

Individual or collective soul impulses focus on an object of desire, while satanic influence uses the lure of passion provisionally; satanic influence seeks the implicit negation of spiritual reality, which is why the devil routs discussion by changing the "theme" every time an argument is questioned.[57] Satan argues merely to agitate man, while the rational sequence of a soul that experiences passion can channel its impulses into legitimate channels through sufficiently convincing arguments. Satanic impulses must be dismissed in their entirety.

Knowledge is the main objective of the Sufi path, and an eternal focus on God is the only condition for reaching it. It may seem unusual for Sufi scholars to discuss virtues in this context, but no mode of consciousness can be considered outside of absolute Knowledge—or outside of Truth—and no inner attitude can be considered neutral. The heart cannot receive Divine Truth when the soul holds a denialist attitude toward that Truth, whether conscious or otherwise. It is even more difficult to avoid this conflict because the soul's realm, an-nafs, is dominated by an egocentric illusion that creates a blind spot.[58]

The Sufi approach involves making the soul accessible to the infinite inflow. The soul's propensity to close in on itself can only be countered by a movement on the same plane; this movement is virtue. In its natural state, Metaphysical Truth is impersonal and motionless. Virtue makes this accessible in a "personal" mode. Some Sufis display their disdain for the world by dressing in shabby clothing, while others affirm the same inner attitude with lavish outfits. The affirmation of a Sufi's person is only a concession to the impersonal truth that they embody; modesty lies in the distinction from a glory that is not their own.[59]

Sufi virtues appear similar to religious virtue, but they differ in their contemplative nature. The virtue of gratitude is based on the recollection of benefits gained from God for most believers,[60] meaning that one believes these benefits to be truer than the suffering that was endured. This feeling supports the goal of the contemplative. Spiritual virtues act as supports for and reflections of the Divine Truth (al-aqqah) in humanity.[61] For example, sincerity (al-ikhl) and veracity (al-idq) are manifestations of the spirit's freedom from psychic impulses. Nobility (al-karam) is a human reflection of Divine Grandeur.[62] The inversion of these "positive" virtues is in the mode, not the material, meaning that they are "saturated" with modesty.

Knowledge in Sufi Doctrines

Most of the Sufi doctrinal teachings and postulations rely on knowledge as their bedrock. One such doctrine is annihilation, known in Arabic as *fana*, which is a state of "spiritual attainment."[63] Sufis aspire to achieve this state so that they can gain knowledge of God; the annihilation of self engenders the acknowledgment of God and wisdom. This is the foundation of Sufi doctrines, which is also identifiable in the phrases "There is no god but God" and "Muhammad is the Messenger of God."[64] In Sufism, annihilation seeks to expose that there is no knowledge except through the total acceptance of God as the main source of knowledge. This knowledge is bestowed on those who seek to know God and God alone. Sufism is also seen as a knowledge system that explores the personal journey of self-annihilation and the pursuit of knowledge through dedication and veneration to God.

The Sufi system of knowledge is derived from the saying that "There is no god but God." It is the foundation of the Sufi doctrine of Divine Unity, known as *tawhid*.[65] Ogunnaike explains how it is perceived and explored as knowledge in Sufism:

The first stage corresponds to the verse, Lā ilāha illā Huwa, "There is no god but He" (2:255), in which God is described by the distant third person pronoun. At this level, God is out there somewhere, and we believe there's only one of Him, but that's about as deep as it goes. This is called the shell of tawḥīd. However, as the Sufi novice progresses, he or she reaches the stage of Lā ilāha illā Anta, "There is no God but You" (21: 87). At this level of tawḥīd, the Sufi stands before God as he does in the ritual prayer, where he or she says to Him, "You alone do we worship, on You alone we rely" (1:1). But in this stage, the Sufi addresses God like this all the time, not only in prayer. He relies only on God, and when he speaks, he speaks only to God, and when he listens, he hears only God. This is the kernel of tawḥīd. Then, if he continues, he or she arrives at annihilation in God and there is only Lā ilāha illā Anā, "there is no God but I" (21:27).[66]

Sufis are driven to pursue an understanding of God's reality, knowledge, and will because of this doctrine showing that God is one. The doctrine is a metaphor for the understanding that God is wisdom, and wisdom is God. It invariably explains that "God is life and everything is God," also known as the "Oneness of Being" or "Unity of Nature," stating that human existence depends on God, and that nothing can exist without God. Human beings are a manifestation of God's creation, and all that exists is God.

As a system of knowing, Sufism can also provide sensory or rational knowledge[67] that is significant for Africa and its people. It explores mystical knowledge expressed through sensory and extrasensory methods. The interpretation of this wisdom transcends the physical to accommodate the transcendental. Sufism is important in education because it impacts understanding that is not limited by logical or empirical science.

Deductively, education or educational frameworks infused with Sufi methods for acquiring knowledge are thought to promote intellect, sensitivity, and commitment to an achievement of extensive, broad-spectrum knowledge—this is an alternative to streamlined, Western, or cult-oriented approaches to knowledge. As a philosophy of knowledge, Sufism may be contextualized in the African educational system, which results in an inclusive and universal approach to the pursuit of knowledge in Africa.

Sufism has remained relevant as a knowledge system in Africa for many reasons. It has been noted that "Sufi mysticism has always played a major role in African countries, and the particular qualities of the performative side of Sufi organizations have had a significant impact on social and political history of the continent."[68] As a system of knowing, it has influenced the production of sociopolitical knowledge in Africa. In discussing the relevance of knowledge for Africa and its people, Sufism presents a dynamic platform for resistance against colonial imperialism.

Sufism not only provides a dynamic platform for emancipation, but signifies a viable and indigenous epistemology; it enables Africa and its people to develop a system of governance that meets their distinct physical, social, political, and spiritual needs. The aim of Sufism is the pursuit of God's knowledge. Purification and the avoidance of self-gratification are important virtues for peaceful coexistence with people of different faiths and orientations. These aspects of Sufism make it relevant for the promotion of peace, political stability, tolerance, and independence from imperialists who would control knowledge and power. Woodward, et al. explain how Sufism has been instrumental for physical and mental emancipation:

> Ethical Sufism dates to the first centuries of the Islamic era. It began as a moral protest against political triumphalism, rigid legalism and ritualistic piety in the early periods of Islamic history. Its most basic themes are renunciation of individual will and everything other than God.[69]

Sufism is relevant in Africa's political climate when one considers the regions that are engulfed in conflict. Sufi doctrine espouses love, tolerance, peace, flexibility, and emotional intelligence. These important qualities facilitate independence, sovereignty, and unity among different communities.

Economic (and Health) Viability of Sufism

Sufism's relevance as a knowledge system for Africa can be seen in its economic potential. Knowledge can generate economic growth for the African continent; the theorization of knowledge emanating from African Sufi masters and Sufi orders can be patented and documented for further research, ultimately delivering economic independence. The development of theories, schools of thought, ethics, codes, and symbols should be recorded to prevent data loss, knowledge theft, and misappropriation.

Sufism, as a knowledge system like Ifa, has received wide acclaim as Islamic mysticism. The development of its theory of meaning, ethics, and philosophy can enrich other fields of knowledge in Africa, such as psychology, psychoanalysis, mental health, and social theory. This would create diverse avenues for economic growth and the expansion of knowledge. Beyond its primary domain as a religion, Sufism can be applied as a system of knowing for medical or psychological issues through its practices and used as an alternative indigenous system of diagnosis, treatment, and recovery for some medical issues.

Sufism's knowledge can demystify health issues for Africans who believe that their problems have spiritual dimensions, because "spirituality is accepted as one of the defining determinants of health, and it no more remains a sole preserve of religion and mysticism."[70] This knowledge should be studied as psychotherapeutic treatment for some mental disorders and illnesses. The need to combine modern healthcare techniques with African medicine and Sufi knowledge is paramount to the development of an indigenous African healthcare system. The development and codification of Sufi knowledge, beliefs, and practices for healthcare professionals can grow African knowledge in the field of mental health.

Mental health, psychology, clinical sciences, psychotherapy, and medicine in Africa can be enhanced by Sufism—this system of knowing has similarities to African traditional medicine, especially the belief in spiritual healing. Interpretations of mystic experiences, such as visions, dreams, and trances, are relevant as psychic experiences for diagnosing, treating, and managing psychological issues, which is relevant for establishing a reliable and efficient healthcare system in Africa. The parallel development of African medicine and Sufi medicine will encourage the proliferation of knowledge in and about Africa.

Sufi Interpretation of Quranic and Islamic Concepts

Sufism's doctrine is essentially an esoteric commentary on the Quran that reflects the inner nature of Islam. The Prophet Mohammed provided ways to understand Quranic exegesis in preaching and teaching that are authenticated by concordance.[71] The Prophet's words that are central to Sufism were enunciated not as a lawgiver but as a contemplative saint. These statements were addressed to companions who were to become the first set of Sufi masters. There are also "holy utterances" (*hadith qudsiyah*), in which God speaks directly to the Prophet in the first person. Although these have the same level of inspiration as the Quran, they are not the same "objective" style of revelation. Primarily, they set out truths intended for contemplation rather than for the entire religious group. This forms the basis of the Sufi interpretation of the Quran.

The Prophet stated that each part of the Quran contains several meanings.[72] This feature is shared by all revealed texts; the process of revelation resembles divine manifestation in that it involves several stages. The symbolic nature of the described objects, and the multiple meanings of the words, are used to interpret the Quran's "inner" meanings. Every early language, including Arabic, Hebrew, and Sanskrit, has a synthetic character. These verbal phrases imply all forms of a concept from the concrete to the universal.[73] Abdul Hamid El-Zein adds:

> It could be said that traditional Quran epistemology takes the expressions in their direct meanings, while Sufi exegesis uncovers their transposed meanings, or that while exotericism understands them conventionally, Sufi interpretation conceives their direct, original, and spiritually essential character. When the Quran states, for example, that whoever follows God's guidance will be directed "for himself" (linafisihi) and that whoever refuses to follow God's guidance will be ignorant "on himself" (ala nafisihi), the exoteric understanding is limited to the concept of recompense and punishment.[74]

Philosophical commentary on the Quran initially appears to be objectively superior to the text itself; the Quran's language is religious in nature, making it connected to human emotionality and imaginative cultural relativism, and the commentary explicitly states universal truths. However, exegesis suffers from the drawbacks of abstract language. The sacred text benefits from the concrete symbol, or the synthetic existence of a single, concise form encompassing a wide range of meanings.

Sufi commentators recognize that the holy text not only fulfills a practical need to communicate to the hearts of people but also relates to the Divine Manifestation process as the Spirit loves to clothe Itself in basic and tangible forms.

The Sufism Idea of Creation

The idea of creation that is shared by all three monotheistic religions seems to contradict the idea of the essential unity of all beings. Creation, it is argued, tends to deny the pre-existence of the Divine Essence. However, these two notions become more compatible when we consider that the metaphysical meaning of the "nothingness" (*udum*) from which the Creator "draws" may only be the "nothingness" of "nonexistence," that is, of the main state's non-manifestation. The possibilities inherent within the Divine Essence are indistinguishable until they are manifested in the world.[75] These possibilities are not even "existing" (*mawjud*) because life implies a starting condition and the existence of a virtual distinction between "knower" and "known." The act of "creating," in the Arabic sense of the word "khalaqa" is equivalent to "assigning to each thing its proper amount." This refers to the Divine Intellect's first determination (*taayyun*) that measures possibilities when translated into metaphysical order. "Creation" logically precedes the "production to existence" (*ijad*) of these same possibilities, according to this interpretation of khalq.[76]

From these perspectives, the universe is God's manifestation of Himself. The sacred saying (ḥadīth qudsī) asserts, "I was a hidden treasure; I wished to be known (or, to know) and I created the world."[77] This perspective demonstrates how the Sufis equate the world with a set of mirrors for self-contemplation as an extension of God.[78] Being affirms the essence, while the main possibilities are reducible to being through a sort of negation; they are merely constraints, to the degree that they can logically be distinguished from Being. "All possibilities (*mumkinat*) are principally reducible to nonexistence (udum), and there is no Being (or Existence) other than the Being of God, may He be exalted, (revealing Himself) in the 'forms' of the states which result from possibilities as they are in themselves in their essential determinations," writes Ibn Arabi in his *Fusus al Hikam*, as quoted by Burckhardt.[79]

Indoctrination in Sufism

A Sufi is a person seeking wisdom or gnosis, choosing to forgo worldly pleasures in exchange for a modest and subdued communion and fellowship with Allah; learning is their sole motive. The pursuit of a relationship with and knowledge of the Supreme Being is prioritized over every other material possession. Sufis are religious people who practice absolute ingratiation through a minimalist lifestyle, living in accordance with the holy teachings and edicts of the Quran. In Sufism, the mystic must aspire to live a life that is worthy of the pursuit of wisdom.[80]

Sufis are regarded as people who live by the teachings of the Prophet and who follow his lifestyle. They are recognized for their in-depth knowledge of the Quran and the wisdom of God (Allah). Sufi training used to follow a master-apprentice structure until their educational system evolved into Sufi orders, also known as *tariqas*.[81] The tariqa centers on a Sufi master or saint whose acolytes codify the teaching and training for others to follow. This system of training simplifies the transfer of knowledge, ensuring that the complexity of teaching is minimized through preexisting structures and ways of living. An order is led by a shaykh, or a spiritual instructor, who is responsible for the training and initiation of novices through designated methods of knowledge acquisition. The shaykh has also followed this process, creating a chain of mystic knowledge transfer that connects to the original source—the Prophet Muhammad.[82] This sequence of knowledge transmission, referred to as *silsilah*, upholds the Sufi order.

The importance of knowledge for humanity and Sufism can be seen in the beliefs of Sufis and aspects of their craft as skilled handlers of knowledge. "The sign of a sincere Sufi is that he feels poor when he has money, modest when he has strength, and secret when he has fame," Shahida says.[83] The emphasis on modesty in material wealth and character is what marks a Sufi adept as someone who deserves the title of mystic king.

Sufi characteristics should be commensurate with their spiritual intellect and status as leaders. Absolute obedience, restraint, abstinence from pleasures, and deep devotion to the pursuit of knowledge are some of the virtues attributed to Sufis. Shahida also lists Sufi ethical tenets that include submission to the master and God, devotion to God's worship, repentance, and fear of God.[84] These characteristics are essentially aspects of God's nature that Sufis can imitate.

Sufis can only hold their titles after receiving proper education in a school or institution that teaches self-control, meditation, modesty, and spiritual ascension in the pursuit of knowledge. This usually entails studying with an instructor and a group of Sufi seekers who adhere to a Sufi order's traditions.[85] Their knowledge requires a proper forum for debate and instruction for achieving absolute dependency and contact with the Divine Being.

Various chants may accompany Sufi litanies. The shaykh will recommend seclusion from various distractions to teach novices the act of meditation and spiritual ascension. During these retreats, apprentices are taught to recite verses for a set amount of time to accomplish the goal of seclusion.[86] In Sufism, wisdom is generated in seclusion, especially when it comes to invocation. After apprentices have completed schooling, they are initiated into the order or tariqa under which they had trained.

Initiation is the final stage before an apprentice becomes an adept, entering the Sufi order for the attainment of spiritual wisdom. It has been described as the "transmission of divine power" that a senior colleague or shaykh confers to a trainee in the Sufi art.[87] Each Sufi order develops its own ritual or rite for initiation; it may involve taking vows or receiving a mantle.

Sufism and Politics

Governments, pundits, and many Sufis have promoted Sufism as a pacifistic, apolitical alternative to Islamic fundamentalism and violent extremism. There is a long Sufi tradition of avoiding politics and finding peace, and today's Islamic radicals are aggressively anti-Sufi.[88] However, broad claims regarding an apolitical Sufi existence ignore their centuries of political involvement. Sufi figures have been uniquely influential mobilizers of social and political forces in many parts of the world, due to their established cultural position. Local rulers and colonial officials have often regarded Sufi leaders as either their most powerful allies or their greatest foes.

Sufi adherents link their spiritual practice to ideals for social and political reform. Examples can be found in colonial and postcolonial North and West Africa, and some contemporary Islamist reform movements began from Sufi roots. Sufi leaders were seen as the main obstacle to French and British attempts to divide and conquer North and West Africa.[89] Sufi leaders had a unique ability to unite fractious communities because of their ability to transcend tribal and ethnic identities.

Sufis have also participated in overt Islamic reform campaigns, including those that have ostensibly been opposed to widespread Sufi practices. Many Islamist movements were formed by Sufis, or they adopted Sufi traditions and ideas, even though many of the present-day members have moved away from Sufism toward literalist piety and political activism. The Society of Muslim Brothers and the Deobandi educational movement are two such movements.[90]

Sufi networks have always been transnational. The development of air travel, global culture, the internet, and smartphones have allowed them to become even more so. Sufism's social roles, modes of organization, and dissemination have evolved in ways that are unconnected to its decline or resurgence in the global era. Some countries may have seen Sufism lose its once-unquestioned position as Islam's theological component, but many Sufi movements and societies have thrived by embracing reforms.

Women have taken on more visible positions as leaders and followers in many Sufi orders around the world, and this has increased since the late twentieth century. Examples of outstanding premodern Sufi women include Rabia al-Adawiyya, the prolific Damascene poet and author Aisha al-Ba'uniyya (d. 1517), and Uthman dan Fodio's daughter, the Northern Nigerian writer and leader of women, Nana Asma'u (d. 1864).[91] However, many women have more recently begun to behave more freely as Sufi leaders, leading other women or combined groups of men and women.

Another recent trend is the acceptance, adaptation, and appropriation of Sufism in various contexts outside of Muslim cultures practicing *tasawwuf*—this frequently involves erasing or weakening Sufism's historical links to Islam.[92] Sufi thought, practice, and culture have been independently incorporated into non-Muslim, Western circles since the early twentieth century. It has sometimes been portrayed as a type of Eastern wisdom, transcending any specific religion. Western practitioners of Sufism developed "Traditionalist" or "Perennialist" thinking, asserting that all religions, despite their external differences, share a single esoteric reality. Yalda notes:

> Sufism possesses elements of performance which can be explored as a means of modern method to the study of religious activities as domains of performance. Several peculiar practices in Sufism that can be studied for their peculiar orality, literariness and performance are the mystical experiences that Sufis experience during their rituals, ceremonies, festivals and traditions. Such practices of trance in Sufism can be studied as performance as it involves other elements of dancing, singing, drumming, music, chanting, etc. Sufism as a system of knowing possess dramatic elements of performance such as in the chanting of litanies repeatedly, believed to be invocation of God or mystic spirits.[93]

These dramatic monologues are meant to transform the chanting person through mystic intervention. The body's movements, responding to the rhythmic recitation of litanies, are mnemonic techniques that assist the Sufi chanter in entering a trance. The introduction of Sufism into different African regions has added elements to African performance that draw from Sufi origins. A comparative analytical study of African performance and Sufi performance has been under-explored. According to Shai's description:

> The associations dance, move and sing, and by dancing they induce trance and possession. This possession or trance is close though not identical to the form of worship in the Swahili spirit associations, the chamas, and known all over the coast. The chamas are highly institutionalized and use certain kinds of possession crafts, often spoken of as witchcraft.[94]

This observation suggests that elements of performance in African communities could influence Sufi performances, creating a dynamic form of performance and knowledge. Sufism's relevance as a system of knowledge would be reflected in the study of Sufi performance elements that have impacted African performance, recognizing that its study and performance in Africa have influenced the production of Sufi music, dance, and performances. It is an opportunity to fuse different fields of knowledge.

African music and the musical instruments that accompany the dancing and singing of Sufi songs is important for pursuing the trance state. The agencies of different types of African drums, and the tempo at which they are beaten, can be studied to determine how they induce trances. Every aspect of performance in Sufism rituals is essential for the experience of ecstasy. The *dhikr* of Sufism is one of the practices and performances that is used and adapted in secular domains, enhancing "increased public use of Sufi trance music at festivals and tourist events."[95]

One example is "the performance of the maulidi at popular festivals in Zanzibar," which demonstrates how traditions can transform and relax their strict requirements to accommodate other social functions and religious purposes.[96] In Africa, Sufi performance has involved the recognition and promotion of African art, artists, and knowledge. It also has made its own contributions to African art, and the region's economic strength could be increased through the study, research, and promotion of this unique cultural form.

Sufism and African Culture

As a knowledge system, Sufism's diverse history and activity in different regions of the continent have made it relevant to the production of African epistemology and cultural ethos. In this age of globalization, knowledge shapes culture and often recreates sub-cultures within existing cultures. Sufism has had contact with different aspects of life across Africa, including culture, tradition, marriage, education, religion, and politics. This is exemplified in Sufism's cultural impact in Ilorin, a city in Nigeria's Kwara State. Sufi teaching guides people on their behavior, thoughts, and relations with one another in society.[97] Sufism's dynamic knowledge has been infused into their day-to-day activities, seen in their religion and acts of worship.

Solagberu has explored Sufism's impact on the establishment of religious groups and organizations, known as "alasalatu groups (people seeking Allah's blessing for Prophet Muhammad)" in Ilorin.[98] He observed:

In these groups and organizations, Sufi traditions of reciting litanies and prayers are structured into the order of worship. These organizations grew from the mentorship and followership influence of the Sufi teachers and masters in the region. The spread of these religious groups across the nation is tailored after different Sufi orders in the country. The adoption of some Sufi rites such as prayers of forgiveness; prayers on the Prophet; remembrance of God and chanting of the religious scripts and verses for some specific numbers are also influences of Sufism on the people and their acts of veneration.[99]

Sufism has been influential for wedding ceremonies in Ilorin. These events reflect local customs, and observers have identified Sufi practices, such as the participation of the bride, bridegroom, and their families in performing the Maghrib prayer and recitation of some "Islamic poetry."[100] These poems "reflect a principle within the Sufi thought which is known as *Zhud* (the abandoning of worldly desire)."[101]

Sufism has also influenced the naming of children among the Ilorin people, who commonly choose the names of Sufi masters. Sufi themes have been identified in Ilorin folk music. Local poems illustrate the Sufi doctrine of intercession by invoking the names of Sufis in the community; naming children after Sufi adepts seeks God's blessing in the hopes that the Sufi essence will be bestowed upon them.[102]

The Sufi knowledge system is relevant for developing a social theory to study its history and influences across African customs, traditions, culture, religions, and societies that engage in similar practices of Sufism. The study of African adaptations of Sufi knowledge, in different cultural contexts, can be developed and applied in social and cultural theories to solve sociocultural problems in the African milieu. In folklore and music, Sufism has created a sub-genre of music that integrates aspects of spirituality, secularism, entertainment, education, and culture—it has created a multidimensional epistemic theory on the discourse of music, performance, culture, and religion. The study of Sufism and African culture presents an exciting field of knowledge that allows African folklore, tradition, customs, and Sufi practices to be examined. Adequate facilities and resources should be dedicated to establishing this field of inquiry.

Sufism's relevance in Africa is also evident in its linguistic forays and the variations in different African languages and written works. Sufi dictions and definitions have been acculturated into African languages to mix language codes; Sufi words and African languages interact to create new vocabularies. Language is a dynamic phenomenon, and forces, such as globalization, migration, and acculturation, have accelerated its use, development, and spread.

Sufi words and sayings have appeared in other languages, such as Hausa, where they undergo modification, transformation, and adaptation. Words and phrases with

Sufi origins are present in African words and meanings, including *madrasa* for school and *alfa* for teacher. In the field of semantics, Sufi signs and symbols can be studied in African languages, where they can be analyzed and interpreted using semiotics. Diverse theories of meanings, such as semiotics, can be applied to interpretations of Sufi sayings, producing African epistemology on the subject of Sufism. As a knowledge system, Sufism has been relevant for the development of African orthographies, languages, and phonology. The proliferation of Sufi words and sayings in African languages can be studied to trace the history and dynamism of the African writing system and its orthography.

Sufism in West Africa

In the West African context, Sufism is referred to as "Islamic mysticism."[103] The most important Sufi orders in West Africa are the Qadiriyya, named after Abd al-Qadir al-Jilani (d. 1166 in Baghdad); the Tijaniyya, founded by Ahmad al-Tijani (d. 1815 CE in Fez, Morocco); and the Muridiyya, established in the late nineteenth century by the Senegalese Shaykh Amadou Bamba (d. 1927).[104]

Colonial administrators created the foundational documentation of Sufism in West Africa. Their vast corpus of writings was intended to help French, British, and a few Portuguese colonial governments managing African Muslim subjects. The alleged fusion of "traditional" African religion and some Sufi beliefs and practices was generally referred to as "African Islam." French writers saw this form of Islam as less of a threat to their colonial project than "Arab" Islam, which they felt was "xenophobic."[105] These colonial views contributed to the debasement of Sufism as a legitimate form of Islam, but they also encouraged the spread of Sufism across West Africa, especially as anti-colonial resistance movements developed.

Sufism arrived in West Africa in the eighteenth century, although earlier evidence of Sufi practices has been identified in parts of the Western and Central Sahara, most notably in Timbuktu and the A'r Mountains of modern-day Niger.[106] However, Sufism seems to have been a matter of personal devotion in many cases—it is unclear how strongly this early Sufi influence contributed to the gradual Islamization of West Africa. Sufi groups developed into formidable forces through a combination of social, economic, and political influence, rather than Sufism's influence as a mystical religion.

Sidi al-Mukhtar al-Kunti (1729–1811) and 'Uthman dan Fodio (1754–1817) were two of the most famous West African Sufi practitioners around the turn of the eighteenth century.[107] Although they were both accomplished Qadiriyya Sufi shaykhs, their legacies are very different. Dan Fodio, a Fulani by birth, is best known for his jihad against local Hausa leaders in regions that are now known as the south of Niger and northern Nigeria. Muslims in Niger and Nigeria continue to commemorate Dan Fodio's triumphant jihad that founded an Islamic state, and many regard him as the "renewer" (*mujaddid*) of Islam during his time.

The creation of religious communities based on a common Sufi identity is directly linked to Sidi al-Mukhtar al-Kunti. He belonged to the Kunta, a Western Saharan race of Arab origin that arrived in the area in the sixteenth century. Sidi al-Mukhtar's experience debunks the widely held belief that Sufism in West Africa is primarily ethical, rather than metaphysical. Sidi al-Mukhtar placed great value on spiritual experiences and acted as a guide for followers who wanted to travel the Sufi path.[108]

Movements led by these great Sufis contributed significantly to the spread of Islam in many parts of West Africa, but West Africans only started to embrace Islamic values and practices on a larger scale after European colonial rule. Islam made its greatest strides in Africa between the 1880s and the 1930s, which alarmed officials in European colonial governments. Their policies had unwittingly aided the spread of Islam, instead of suppressing it.[109]

Sufism's interactions with other types of spirituality led to the emergence of new Sufi practices in West Africa, in a process that is similar to the way that other manifestations of Sufism shifted after travel to new regions. New styles of Sufi leadership emerged in urban Mali, for example, transcending the organizational structure of Sufi orders to carve out a niche in a growing religious marketplace.[110] Despite the complexity and diversity of Sufi experiences in West Africa, Western political analysts have repeatedly described West African Sufis as "good" Muslims, seen as potential allies in the "War on Terror" following the extremist attacks of September 11, 2001.

Tijaniyyah Sufism in West Africa

Most of the philosophy and theology of Ahmad al-Tijani's Sufism came from Muhyi al-din ibn al-Arabi (1165–1240), who was the greatest mystic to emerge from medieval Muslim Spain. Ibn al-Arabi was a significant influence on later generations of Muslim mystics.[111] Three elements of his Sufism, which are also found in Tijani thinking, flow from one to the other like water cascading down an incline. Seesemann highlights these elements as follows:

> The first element is the veneration of Muhammad—akin to the pre-existent Word in John's Gospel—al-haqiqatal-muhammadiyyah (the heart of Muhammad), as the fountainhead from which all created things originate. The second element focuses on Muhammad's veneration, as prescribed for the entire Tijaniyyah by the saintly influence of 'Ahmad al-Tijani, who claimed the title of qutb al-aqtāb (the supreme pole of sainthood) or khatm al-awl jyli' (the seal of the saints). This recognizes the overflowing source of all human closeness, both to God and to Muhammad, not only for his own generation but for all genealogy. The third element is attachment to and respect for a mystical propagandist (muqaddam) in the Tijaniyyah, channeling the spiritual benefits derived from Ahmad al-Tijani, the Prophet Muhammad, and God, to the individual member.[112]

The seemingly exaggerated statements made during the special supererogation prayers of Ahmad al-Tijani and his followers have set them apart from other Sufis and Muslims since the beginning of the Tijaniyyah. Membership in multiple mystical orders was popular in late-eighteenth-century northwestern Africa, and Ahmad al-Tijani himself had belonged to four separate Sufi orders, including the Qadiriyyah and the

Khalwatiyyah, but he eventually forbade such pluralism and eclecticism among his followers.[113]

Sufism and Psychiatry

Spiritual or psychic phenomena occur in cultures and religions all over the world. Despite the lack of specific research on Sufism, surveys have found that 20–45 percent of all people claim to have had psychic encounters. Specific occurrences vary based on time, gender, faith, and other factors.[114] Despite the differences in behaviors, values, and societies where they occur, these interactions share many characteristics. Psychic encounters can occur in the realms of thought, perception, or feeling (a dynamic perceptual experience), and they all share similar characteristics. These experiences are immediate, typically fleeting, ineffable, unanalyzable, and they involve intimate association with a specific other self that transcends time, space, and individuality. According to Sufi accounts, these encounters are felt as a deep sense of bliss.[115]

Psychic experiences have previously been associated with divine experiences, demonic possession, heresy, and even insanity. Over time, various interpretations have been affected by the claimant's gender, social status, the nature of the interactions in relation to established political and religious norms, and other factors. Events have been interpreted to support or refute specific political viewpoints or to justify claims of insanity. Mansur al Hallaj and Bayazid Bastami are two well-known Sufis who claimed to have had intense mystical experiences.[116] Both left conflicting legacies, regarded as great Sufis who were also sentenced to death for heresy.

Sufis believe that psychic experiences are sources of absolute wisdom, because they go beyond the ordinary (*marifa* or *gnosis*).[117] The possibility of such interactions yielding valid information has been challenged from metaphysical and scientific viewpoints. Kant dismissed the idea of ultimate wisdom as something beyond the scope of human experience, and therefore unreasonable.[118] Sufi thinkers have proposed that such experiences might be an extension of ordinary human experiences. For example, Fakhruddin Iraqi, a foremost Sufi philosopher, considered that it was possible for these experiences to occur in different orders of time and space due to shifts in human consciousness.[119] The subjective essence of psychic experiences, which opposes the classically objective nature of science, has been the greatest impediment to the study of these experiences.

As a phenomenon, Sufi illusions can be similar to psychotic hallucinations or delusions. Based on this resemblance, the spiritual essence of these encounters and the knowledge that they yield have been questioned. Some proposals assert that insanity is the source of all paranormal encounters and religious beliefs, implying that all psychotic phenomena are abnormal. Hallucinations and delusions are fairly common in the general population and during seemingly innocuous spiritual encounters.[120] However, others have stated that not all psychotic phenomena are pathological, suggesting that the term "abnormal" should be redefined.

Sufism, like other manifestations of faith, has re-emerged in Oriental and Western cultures. Sufi traditions are becoming an increasingly important part of belief systems for a growing number of people, within and beyond the Muslim world. However, the dramatic rise in mental-health-related issues in recent years has meant that an increasing number of people require mental-health services.[121] When people of the Sufi faith encounter these service providers, it raises concerns on several levels. Sufi values and traditions are ingrained in the belief systems of most Muslims, especially for a growing number of people in Africa. Sufism has made important contributions to the interpretation of revelation—the root of religious knowledge in Islam and other Semitic religions—and it has had a profound impact on the mental health of its adherents and practitioners.

Conclusion

Sufism is a knowledge system that offers a dynamic way of obtaining a personal and direct experience with wisdom. It originated with Islamic mysticism; the Quran and hadith are the common sources of its knowledge. This chapter has explored Sufism as a spiritual and rational system of knowing that Sufis claim to obtain through meditating on religious scripts and verses. Sufis repeatedly chant verses and phrases that invoke metaphysical elements, which they have been admonished to do as an act of veneration.

The Sufi system of knowing seeks to explain the conception and structure of the cosmos as revealed in the philosophies and metaphysics of knowledge in Islamic texts. Sufism seeks to prove the knowledge that God exists as Light reflected on all other creations. Scholars of Sufism have elevated mystical knowledge to the point where they have rendered it in opposition to logic.

This chapter elaborates on knowledge production in Sufism and how it influences a large population of Muslim believers. The knowledge derived from Sufism was power in itself, which is evident in its millions of adherents around the world. Sufism was able to penetrate Africa and gather an enormous following of believers who accepted ideas that were written, and later preached and interpreted, which will be examined in the following chapters. Written spiritual knowledge was translated into influence and political power in the hands of people who assumed leadership positions to lead people along a path that they believed to be true and right.

This chapter focuses on Sufism's religious practices. Its various activities translated into power wielded by individuals who could heal, guide, and influence large masses of people. They were believed to be capable of cursing or blessing people. Their knowledge of mystical occurrences also made the astute practitioners-cum-Sufi leaders into a point of contact with the mystical world, offering solutions to problems that were considered to be beyond mortal eyes; they were often consulted for their wisdom. This knowledge informed the beliefs and actions of Sufi adherents.

This chapter argues that Sufism, as a knowledge system, is both mystical/spiritual and empirical. Empiricism deals with the verification of knowledge through observation and tests. Knowledge in Sufism is logical and uses human faculties to acquire wisdom, but this way of knowing transcends rationality. It offers a validation of rational and empirical knowledge regarding the physical world. The domain of Sufism's knowledge system is multidimensional and dialectical, combining physical and rational faculties to gain extrasensory knowledge.

Sufism is relevant as a knowledge system because of its interdisciplinary approach to science, philosophy, religion, ethics, psychology, sociology, and other fields of inquiry. Sufism holds the potential to produce knowledge in and about Africa because of its influence in different regions of the continent.

Political and Intellectual Thoughts of Usman Dan Fodio

Introduction

The previous chapters have examined the knowledge system evolving around the origin of practices and beliefs. In this chapter, and the succeeding one, there will be the exception of examining the beliefs and practices through the lenses of leadership and power. Put differently, the focus here will be on how religious leaders in Islam espouse this knowledge system interpreted from the holy Quran and how they (differently) interpret its sayings to provoke movements in Africa with distinguished ideology, belief, and, consequently, actions. This chapter commences with the intellectualism, teachings, beliefs, actions, and movements engendered by Usman Dan Fodio.

Dan Fodio's political and intellectual thought in Islam found justification and foundation from the intellectual and political movements-cum-jihads in the days of the Prophet Mohammed as well as the sociopolitical environment of the northern part of Nigeria. There has been a rise in interest in the study of Islamic political and intellectual thoughts in recent times. Scholars have taken up the challenge of exploring its content, context, and meaning, as well as its significance within Islam and to humanity in general.[1] Through influential philosophers, concepts, and religious movements across the Islamic world, Islamic political and intellectual thought has impacted religious, secular, and academic communities. Given this intellectual and practical significance, the need to fully comprehend the dynamics and development of Islamic political and intellectual thought is necessary, especially because of the tension generated across the globe—particularly in the Islamic world—over what should be the descriptions of the makeup and virtues of an ideal society.

This chapter seeks to examine the role and impact of this political and intellectual thought in regions of western Africa occupied by Muslims. Although there were several Islamic movements that took place in precolonial West Africa, the Usman Dan Fodio jihad was exceptional for establishing a vast Islamic state in the region that lasted for a century. Dan Fodio, like leaders of other Islamic movements, raised critical issues with regard to religion, politics, justice, education, women, economy, and society which shaped the development of Hausaland in the nineteenth century. Growing discontent in the political leadership in Hausaland was a contributory factor to the Dan Fodio jihad, as it served as an invitation for the intelligentsia of the time to question the basis of the philosophy governing the operations of Habe rulers in the region.

The history of the political and intellectual thought in Islamic Hausaland is associated with the intellectual works of Shaykh Usman Dan Fodio as well as his jihad campaign's onslaught in the region. The Islamic religion provided the momentum for further engagement between the *umma* (Islamic faithful), the jihadists, and Habe rulers who exist as political, social and economic entities required to function appropriately in the Islamic-dominated Hausaland.[2] Hence, it is appropriate that this piece locate the foundation of Shaykh Usman Dan Fodio's knowledge system within the context of Islam.

The evolution of political and intellectual thought in Islam begins with the activities of the Prophet Mohammed while in Mecca and Medina. Though undeveloped,[3] the impact of the activities of the Prophet laid the foundation for the development of political and intellectual thought across the Islamic world. The Islamic world has enjoyed a considerable flow of knowledge, producing scholars who broadly expanded the frontiers of Islamic knowledge. This culture of knowledge production also gave birth to reformists that transformed the sociopolitical, economic, and religious landscape of different Muslim territories at various times across the world. The intellectual works produced in the Islamic world and the nature of contact Muslims had with the outside world led to the growth and expansion of Islam and its knowledge throughout Africa and elsewhere. The spread of Islamic literature and political reforms, whether violent or peaceful, also contributed to the spread of revolutionary ideas across Islamic territories, facilitated by trade across West Africa and Hausaland in particular.

The Wangarawa traders, well-known merchants in the trans-Saharan trade, were the principal actors in the introduction of Islam and Islamic literature[4] in Hausaland. As trade merchants, the Wangarawa came into contact with different cultures in North Africa, Sahel, and the Sahara. In North Africa, where Islam was already established, they obtained scholarly works and other valuable items of trade. In West Africa, their contact with Hausaland resulted in the importation of Islamic texts, which they carried along with them to Borno and other parts of the West African Sahel region. It is imperative to state that the contact Hausaland had with the Wangarawa did not significantly change many aspects of the culture and traditions of the Hausa people: the political, social, and economic structures of the Hausa people continued to be based on the preexisting principles of the culture of the people and not on the teachings of Islam. Although Islam was established in Hausaland, a substantial population of the people and their aristocrats remained nonbelievers, or as commonly called, pagans.[5]

In terms of intellectual composition, the Hausa community was divided into two traditions. The first specialized in preaching using the local language because of their poor command of the Arabic language. Also, their relationship with Islamic texts was restricted to research on theological issues and the status of sinners. They were politically famed for recruiting runaway slaves into Islam and forming radical Islamic communities. The second tradition had a vast engagement with classical Arabic language; while some served primarily as teachers, others were preachers. Scholars from this tradition specialized in Islamic jurisprudence (*fiqh*) and legal studies, which required studying a wide range of books and international sophistication and was also important for merchants and *qadis* who mediated trade disputes.

Students of the second tradition had a good appreciation of the functions of Islamic governance, especially in judging when governments operated according to Islamic teachings and when they went against Islamic laws. This tradition exhibited revolutionary tendencies. This intellectual tradition accounts for the immediate origin of Shaykh Usman Dan Fodio's revolutionary approach.[6] Dan Fodio used his literary works, written in Arabic, to reform *ulama*, and he preached to people during his Friday sermons, gave speeches on different subjects, and taught the fundamental teachings of Islam. Dan Fodio broadly placed the people of Hausaland into three categories: those who believed in Islam; idolators who believed in the animistic worship of stones, trees, and other parts of the natural world; and those who combine Islam alongside other forms of pagan worship.[7]

This understanding and sorting defined the kind of message that was passed across to each group, whether related to politics, religion, society, or even the jihad that was being carried out at that time. For Dan Fodio, the need to continually persuade the *umma* (community) toward the right path to Islam was the primary aim to be achieved first. However, the education of the people was an essential part of the change that he was trying to propagate in society. Thus, fiqh, which was previously the exclusive reserve of the preachers (*ulama*), was first presented to the people to learn and practice. Dan Fodio had a deep knowledge of Islamic science and Arabic literature, as his first occupation was as a dedicated writer until the jihad started. Through his writings, as the leader of the jihad, he was able to guide the jihadists on different issues throughout the region.

The ideals of the jihad were intellectual and academic because much of what was put into practice were things being taught in Islamic schools, and Dan Fodio's ideas were largely drawn from his formal education.[8] The political movement was supported with scholarly writings that vehemently justified the need for jihad. For example, Dan Fodio detailed charges brought against the Habe rulers about their deviations from Islam, which are contained in *Kitab Al-Farq* and *Wathiqat al–ikhwaan*.[9] These texts condemned the venal Habe *ulama'u*, while *Ihya-us–Sunnah Nur-al Bab* and *Bayan al bid'ah al shaydaniyya*[10] discussed the need for Islamic reform in the territory, and *Tamyiz ahl-Sunnah* was written to charge Muslims to unite.

Many other literary works written by the jihadist, such as *Masail Muhimma, Bayan Wujub al Hijrah alal-Ibad, Ta'alim al-Ikhwan, Tanbih alIkhwan, Amr bil-Maaruf,* and *Wathiqat ahl-Sudan*, were made available for the education of the umma and in preparation for the impending reformation. There are more than 100 recorded texts credited to Shaykh Dan Fodio from both before and after the jihad,[11] but this chapter shall focus on those that deal with knowledge production and belief as manifested in religion, politics, women, education, law, and jurisprudence.

People, Politics, and the Economy of Hausaland Before the Jihad

The Hausa live in present northern Nigeria, northwestern Niger, Ghana, Chad, and other parts of the West African region of the Sahel. Prior to the jihad of Usman Dan

Fodio, the Hausa people consisted of powerful but disunited kingdoms that had great influence over the sub-Saharan trade routes with vast commercial centers of trade such as Kano.[12] Before the introduction of Islam, Hausaland had evolved a complex political system that centralized power and control under the *Sarakuna* (ruling aristocracies). Dynastic and institutional changes occurred between the ninth and eleventh centuries, producing a political culture that was known as the *Sarauta* (chieftaincy) system and subsequently saw the emergence of the seven Hausa city-states (Hausa Bakwai): Biram, Daura, Gobir, Kano, Katsina, Zazzau, and Rano.[13]

These states were not formally unified, and although they were torn apart in fratricidal wars politically, they grew robustly economically, independently, and cooperatively where need be. Biram, for instance, was the city-states' first seat of government administration, while Gobir supplied the soldiers

> Kano and Rano grew cotton and produced textiles. They were also known for their valuable and beautiful indigo dye, which they used both for art and for dying their textiles. They traded these with the other Hausa states, such as Zaria, which provided slaves and grain. Katsina and Daura had direct access to the trans-Saharan caravans and so traded the products produced in Hausaland for foreign goods, such as salt. Islam was to become an important part of Hausa culture. The religion seems to have first appeared in the region around the eleventh century, brought by merchants and pilgrims, but conversion was slow. Kings and rulers were attracted to the new religion, perhaps for the prestige it granted them in the eyes of other great Islamic states. The common people only gradually adopted Islam, and generally practiced it along with ancient Hausa religious customs. Still, Arabic script was eventually adopted for writing the Hausa language. Muhammad al-Maghili, an Islamic scholar and missionary, is credited with converting the Hausa to Islam at the end of the fifteenth century. It was probably around this time that Islam became firmly integrated into Hausa society, though polytheism would be common in the region until the nineteenth century.[14]

Syncretism in this context, the practice of Islam and the use of mystical powers embedded in the traditional religion provided a dual opportunity of political control for the rulers to exert political power on their subjects (who are now either Muslims or pagans). The adoption of Arabic as the language of religious exercise in the state was also an opportunity to expand Hausaland's regional and international relations as well as trade and commerce with the broader Islamic world. Despite this acceptance of Islam, traditional Hausa rulers did not see the need to disengage from the traditional belief systems and worked to ensure the preservation and sustenance of the traditional religion, something they held dear as part of their indigenous customs and tradition. The unholy relationship between the new religion and the old religion continued, though strange to one another; they only co-existed for a time.

Growing Islamic education led to an increase in the population of Muslim ulama and new converts who became the educated elite who then disapproved of the states' meddlesomeness and un-Islamic venal activities.[15] For example, one of the corrupt practices that the pre-jihad government was known for, was the sale of justice to the highest bidder. According to Dan Fodio, "if you have an adversary (in law) and he proceeds you to them, and gives them some money, then your word will not be accepted by them, even though they know for a certainty of your truthfulness, unless you give them more than your adversary gave."[16]

With Dan Fodio's exposure of injustice and his revivalist attempts through teaching and preaching, Islam grew and became very strong while new centers of Islamic education were established across Hausaland, becoming renowned for the promotion of Islamic ideals while also exposing the social, political, religious, and economic ills in the Hausa society. The culture of Muslim teachers and students moving from one place to another for religious education and trading activities helped to develop many communities in Hausaland and built a sense of identity. Already immersed in venal activities, the Hausa rulers could not tame the growing Muslim population who had grown into consciousness and were ready to change their fortunes. It was this condition that gave birth to revolutionary ideas and the reformers, such as Dan Fodio.

The Birth of a Revolutionary: Islam and the Education of Usman Dan Fodio

Usman Dan Fodio belonged to a family from the Fulani ethnic group that migrated from the Futa Toro region of present-day Senegal and settled in the Nigerian area. Born in Marata in December 1754,[17] Dan Fodio lived in Gobir until 1802 when his reformist ideas against the city's leader, the Sarkin Gobir, compelled him to lead his followers out of Gobir to Degel. He was educated under his parents according to the traditional Fulani system of education, where children were first taught societal norms and values from their parents before learning from other forces of socialization. He was further educated in an Islamic school where he learned how to read and write in Arabic and to memorize and translate the Quran and other Arabic manuscripts.

Dan Fodio's education was significantly shaped through the influence of Jibril Umar, who was his teacher. Jibril Umar went on tour twice to Makkah and Madinah, Islam's holy lands. At that time, Madinah was the epicenter for Islam's illustrious scholars and the core of the drive for Muslim students to return to Islam's original sources, the Quran and the Sunnah.[18] As part of his education, Dan Fodio gained knowledge of Hadith and Islamic jurisprudence, grammar, and arithmetic. He also received extensive Shari'a knowledge from his tutors, Shaykh Abd al-Rahman b. Hammadah, his maternal uncle; Usman Binduri; Muhammad Sambo; Muhammad b. Rajab; and Jibril b. Umar. Although it is unknown whether Dan Fodio ever visited Hijaz, the majority of his professors were Madinah-trained, and several were Al-Sindi pupils.[19]

At the age of twenty, Dan Fodio started his career as an itinerant teacher, educating people on the appropriate practice of Islam. Subsequently, the focus of his teaching and writing steadily metamorphosed from religious matters to social and political issues regarding fiqh. Fiqh is the Arabic word for "rules of God," and it relates to how people are obligated to follow the laws. This includes respecting what is *wajib* (obligatory), *mahzur* (forbidden), *mandub* (recommended), *makruh* (disapproved), or merely *mubah* (permitted);[20] the abuse of Sufism; the sacrosanctity of a singular Islamic school of jurisprudence as the basis for the interpretation of justice in the society; ignorance of the truth and law of Islam; and the general exploitation of the *talakawa* (masses). Dan Fodio's teachings and preaching were intended to educate his followers as a first step toward preparing his followers for the revolution that followed, beginning the religious obligation of teaching and preaching in his hometown, Degel, in 1774 by performing several itinerant missions there accompanied by his brother Abdullahi.

Dan Fodio also moved, in the company of his followers, to the east and west, Kebbi being his first point of call. Though Degel was his station, he and his group expanded their religious activities to other neighboring communities, where they preached and taught religious messages of liberation. His intellectual exposition on fiqh and Hadith were essentially to educate his students and the public on the distinction between the un-Islamic practices that were prevalent in the Hausa state and their implication on Islam as a way of life. Dan Fodio concentrated on the religious enterprise of educating and training his people according to Islamic teaching and the *sunnah* of the Prophet Mohammed (S.A.W.).

It was stated that, "the imparting of the idea of *tajdid* (revolution), in his students and involving them in the process of tajdid as a necessary part of education was, perhaps, Shehu Usman's greatest contribution in Hausaland."[21] Worried over misinterpretation and misrepresentation of Islamic ideals in the society, he warned the umma that any ruling in fiqh that was opposed to the Quran, sunnah, or *ijmā'* must be rejected. To clarify this position, Dan Fodio authored *wathiqat al-Ikhwan* so that the umma would be educated appropriately on the subject matter of fiqh and the Quran. His intellectual training was anchored on the spiritual development of the students and the umma and this was the subject of his work *Umdat alUbbad*.[22] The *tasawwuf* (theology) was recommended for internal purification and spiritual training. According to Abdullahi, who was the Shehu's brother, the Shehu urged the people to reawaken the faith, Islam, and good deeds and give up contrary practices.[23]

While Dan Fodio was attempting to prepare the people, he met stiff opposition from the ulama, who opposed his views on jihad and decided to pitch their tent with the rulers to preserve the status quo because their power and authority in the courts of the aristocracy and among citizens was fast declining. Dan Fodio called this category of scholars "*'ulama al-Suu*," evil scholars whose sole interest was maintaining the existing power structures.[24] When it became clear that the political authority of the Hausa rulers was diminishing and Shehu commanded a significant number of loyalists, some Hausa rulers, such as Sarki Bawa, decided to offer him "peace overtures backed by offers of gold," but Dan Fodio "instead asked [the Sarki Bawa] to free the prisoners and not to overburden the subjects with taxes."[25] There were five specific demands that Dan Fodio made to Sarki Bawa of Magami in 1788–89:

1. To allow him to call people to God in their land.
2. Not to stop anybody who intend to respond to his call.
3. To treat anyone with a turban respectfully.
4. To free all the political prisoners.
5. Not to burden the subjects with taxes.[26]

According to Masri, "these demands clearly had 'political' as well as religious implications, and Bawa, having acceded to all his requests"[27] knew that, sooner rather than later, his territory would come under the leadership of Dan Fodio. Both knew that the community had become dominated by a religio-political movement that favored Dan Fodio.[28] With this success in 1793, Dan Fodio wrote his masterpiece, *Ihya' al-sunna* ("The Revival of the Prophetic Practice and Obliteration of False Innovation"), a guide to usher in ideal Islamic practices significantly different from the offensive practices of the past that has to do with the practice of syncretism.

The instigators of the Sokoto jihad framed their work as an intellectual movement and their goals as re-orienting society to become Islamic. The war was not to produce a secular society. Smith stated:

> All ideals are intellectual but the ideals of the Sokoto jihad were also academic . . . in the sense of educational, having to do with what is taught in schools, in academies . . . the Mujahidun in Sokoto drew their ideas from scholarly literatures, from a tradition of learning. They were primarily students and teachers, not politicians or warriors.[29]

Islam provided the ideological support for the development of the revolutionary ideas that Dan Fodio espoused as an intellectual and political reformer.

A Gifted Revolutionary: The Intellectual Writings of Usman Dan Fodio

Dan Fodio's work of preaching, teaching men and women, and writing on different subjects differentiated him from some of his contemporaries and marked him as a distinguished scholar. His methodology and use of sources were consistent and systematic, allowing the authorship of his works to be ascertained with a considerable degree of certainty by its general characteristics.[30] Dan Fodio was vast in knowledge and his multilingual ability allowed him to navigate easily across diverse cultures, enabling him to pull followers widely. One of the powerful tools he used was the large number of poems he wrote, composed in Hausa, Fulfulde Arabic, and Ajami (a local Arabic vernacular). The poems were recited by his followers and cherished by many because of their injunctions pulled from the Quran, Hadith tradition, and Ijma (consensus).[31]

Shaykh Usman Dan Fodio wrote more than 100 books containing his thoughts on culture, government, the economy, and society though there is a list of 115 known works[32] including chapters or chapters of collected volumes. Other works appear to be repetitive; for example, Suleiman noted that Dan Fodio's work, "*Bayan al-Bid`ah al-Shaytaniyah* is largely identical with the bid`ah section of his work, *Ihya' al-Sunnah wa Ikhmad al-Bid`ah*"[33] and is also "reminiscent of al- Ghazali's '*Ihya ulum al-din*' upon which he draws extensively."[34] *Ihya' al-Sunnah wa Ikhmad al-Bid`ah* underscores "the need for adherence to Sunnah and avoidance of the *bid`ah* (pagan innovation), and the nature and requirements of faith (*iman*)." Apart from these topics, the book focuses largely on jurisprudential matters.

Dan Fodio's Contribution to *Fiqh* (Jurisprudence)

One of Dan Fodio's greatest contribution was in the area of Islamic jurisprudence. His views on different schools of law (*madhahib*) were broad and not restrictive, as will be examined later. Although his exposition on many issues of Islamic importance was in consonance with the Quran and Hadith, some of his interpretations were based on the Maliki rite and others were taken from other schools, such as the Hanbali. Dan Fodio maintained that it was not ideal to follow any one rite, as it would be an aberration for the people to act in accordance with the Hadith to which a particular rite did not give weight.[35] He believed that the different schools of Islamic jurisprudence available to Muslims ensured that people had an array of choices to find what suited them most, without necessarily confining them to a particular legal dogma.

He particularly preferred to use different injunctions from many schools in order to contextually clarify issues where there were competing theories, though contended that jurists must base their judgments using a dominant school. According to El-Masri, Dan Fodio's view on Islamic jurisprudence was a significant step toward the liberalization of Islamic law, as independent thinking around Islamic jurisprudence by Muslim jurists had, after the tenth century depended on findings from leaders of the Islamic school of law. It thus demonstrates the reason he established the Sokoto Caliphate and how he was able to consolidate it through his knowledge of Islamic laws, leading him to establish the Shari'a as the foundation of practical law and to guide the process of building Daral-Islam. He hated pre-jihad customs, especially the payment of taxes such as the cattle tax; therefore, he abolished the old practices and replaced them by approving Muslim taxes and made the *zakat* (tithe) the most important. To prevent corruption and be able to exercise maximum administrative control, "the Shehu kept his state officials to a minimum: a vizier, a judge, a chief of police, and a land-tax official."[36]

In Dan Fodio's theory of a state, justice, more than any other virtue in governance is emphasized rather than having multiple paraphernalia of government without justice. Dan Fodio's conception of a prosperous state is hinged on the principles of justice, which was why he preached often that one of the swiftest ways to destroy a kingdom is to give preferential treatment to people within a state against their fellow statesmen. Much as he was concerned with the issues of religious incorrectness and revivalism, he maintained that a state can survive unbelief but not injustice.[37]

Islam provided the foundation for the development of sound scholarship to Dan Fodio; the commitment of his teachers and their submission to Islam and dedication to learning were essential to the overall principles and practice of the scholarship that he was known for. Dan Fodio wrote twenty-one pieces on fiqh.[38] He enjoins the faithful to enforce the precepts of fiqh,[39] which are: *wajib* (obligatory), *mahzur* (forbidden), *mandub* (recommended), *makruh* (disapproved) and *mubah* (permitted). Fiqh was important as tasawwuf because tasawwuf was an important source of Shari'a law.[40]

As a religious scholar, he reproduced works on fiqh and tasawwuf for his followers to read in order to understand the inconsistencies of the Habe system of governance, which was supposed to function based on Islamic jurisprudence but instead featured a prevalence of un-Islamic practice. As hitherto iterated, Dan Fodio's writings were highly influenced by the venal practices in Hausaland, thus his contributions were principally directed toward bringing to the fore the ills inherent in the society and advocating solutions to correct these ills in line with Islamic injunctions. For example, the fiftieth chapter of *Bayan Wujub Al-hijra Ala 'L-Ibad* is focused "on the law concerning the possessions of missing persons and their wives' Idda; and the law concerning the washing of martyrs, shrouding them, and praying for them." While referring to Ibn Juzaya's *qawanin*, Dan Fodio maintains that there are four cases relevant to wives of lost husbands who are:

1. lost in a Muslim territory,
2. in the enemy territory,
3. fighting in the enemy territory and
4. lost while the Muslims are engaged in civil strife.

For the person lost in a Muslim territory, if his wife raises her case before the *qadi*, she will be asked to provide concrete evidence of her husband's absence. "The *qadi* will seek information about him, and if he is alive, he will be required to either return or divorce her" and if he refuses, she will be divorced from him. If there is no information about him in response to inquiries by the qadi, "she is given four years, if the husband is free and two years if the husband is a slave . . . but in case of death, she must observe *Idda*, after which she can marry."[41] On matters concerning washing and shrouding martyrs, it is stated that, "if a martyr died in the jihad battled field, he is neither washed nor shrouded nor prayed for. But if he is killed wrongfully elsewhere or is taken alive from the battlefield when his wounds were not fatal, then he later dies, he is washed and prayed over, according to the accepted opinion, following al-shafi'i."[42] Dan Fodio compared different viewpoints of Arab scholars who had expounded on issues of martyrs, their deaths, and how they could be prepared before burial, observing that "whoever that is killed in the field during the battle against [rebellious] Muslims is washed and prayed over. But if the martyr is in the state of major ritual impurity, there is a dispute as to whether he should be washed or not."[43]

A different contribution discusses the "obligation of appointing an imam and the obligation of obedience to him and the unlawfulness of rebelling against him and deposing him for any reason short of unbelief," illustrating—as part of his responsibility to build and sustain the newly created state—Dan Fodio's works that were relevant to organizing the society as well as its survival.[44] He was guided by the provisions of the Quran and his experiences under the defunct Hausa state and belief that they had governed their subjects unjustly, although guided by sound principles of the rule of law.

Following the tradition of the Prophet, Dan Fodio stated that the appointment of an imam was essential to safeguarding the interests of the people and the development of the society, especially in accordance with the dictates and provisions of Islamic law. The followers were enjoined not to remain obedient to illegitimate constituted authority, especially imams, caliphs, and vicegerents, though he cautioned that there should not be more than one imam in a place. Revolting to depose an imam may scatter the *umma*, but it was allowable to depose one whenever they exhibited unbelieving practices.[45] Throughout, Dan Fodio offered a political philosophy with a marked element of dissimilarity between what was practiced during the Hausa rule and the new Caliphate.

Women and Education

One of the political and intellectual reforms of Shaykh Usman Dan Fodio was on women and education. He challenged the ill treatment of women and their position in the society where their education was neglected, leaving women deprived of their rights to inheritance from their deceased parents, children, and husbands. Under the rule of the Habe aristocracy, whatever was left behind by a deceased individual was taken over by the most senior male member of the family, and women were excluded. Women were subjected to slavery in their matrimonial homes, and the need to be modest in appearance was an enforced norm. Stripping nursing mothers and washing them in the open, as well as indecent dressing and half-naked appearances were common by both men and women.[46]

Further, Dan Fodio was opposed to the idea of the ulama restricting the acquisition of education to male students alone without extending these opportunities to women. To him, the education of both men and women was an essential part of the development of the society, so women should be educated equally to their male counterparts and a woman should be allowed to go out in search of knowledge whenever her husband could not teach her—implying that the education of a woman was one of the sole responsibilities of a man. To demonstrate his passion for the education of all, Dan Fodio was committed to teaching and preaching to congregations made up of both men and women. In one of his religious gatherings, he was confronted by a scholar, Al-Mustapha Gwoni, who challenged Dan Fodio for accommodating men and women together for the purpose of religious activities, even though there was considerable space between the two genders. Dan Fodio asked his brother Abdullahi to respond to Al-Mustapha's charges, who wrote:

O you who have come to guide us aright. We have heard what you said. Listen to what we say . . . Indeed, devils, if they come to our gathering, spread evil speech, exceeding all bounds! We have not had promiscuous intercourse with women, how should that be! We have warned (others against this); on the contrary, I said we agreed. That it was thus. But I do not agree that their being left alone to go free in ignorance is good, for the committing of the lesser evil has been made obligatory. Ignorance pardons, even though it were disobedience. We found the people of this country drowning in ignorance; shall we prevent them from understanding religion?"[47]

Abdullahi's statement reveals the danger in neglecting women from being educated and allowing them to wallow in ignorance. In practice, childless women, and those who could not bear children as a result of menopause, were abandoned or divorced. According to Boyd and Last, "it seems that in the urban milieu, in marked contrast to the agricultural and pastoral economies of the countryside, women's reproductive capacity was far more valuable than women's labor, and, in consequence a kind of serial polygyny, in which post-menopausal women, particularly if childless, were discarded and divorced, had become the norm even among the relatively wealthy class of scholar-merchants."[48] In contrast, Dan Fodio upheld the belief that these women should be educated so that once they were beyond childbearing, they could be teachers for Islamic learning in their household rather than being rejected as though they were not useful. The pursuit for education of women was personal to Dan Fodio, as one who came from a culture and tradition of learning, and he ensured that his daughter Asma'u was educated.

In his book *Kitab Nar ul-Albab* (The Book of the Light of the Intellectuals), Dan Fodio, observing the inhuman treatment meted out to women who went without education or guidance, wrote:

This is a chapter regarding the affairs that have caused a general calamity in these lands, I mean Hausaland, which are increasing, and are a general crisis in other lands also. Among them is what many of the Ulama of this land are doing by leaving their wives, daughters, and slaves neglected like animals, without teaching them what Allah has required of them in their ablution, prayers, fasting, and other areas. And they have not taught them what has been made permissible for them in questions such as business transactions and what is similar. This is a major error and a prohibited innovation. They have dealt with them like a dish which they use until it is broken and then throw it into the garbage or some unclean place, how strange it is that they leave their wives, daughters, and slaves in the darkness of ignorance and teach their students morning and evening! This is nothing but their own error for they teach their students *riya* (showing off) and vanity. This is a grave mistake for the education of wives, daughters, and slaves is compulsory while the teaching of students is optional.[49]

Dan Fodio's brazen attack on the Hausa community's treatment of the status of women signaled the need for change to empower women's education as compulsory. To ensure that women's opportunity to be educated is achieved, Dan Fodio set aside special days for women to learn and to ask questions regarding their problems. He was fiercely devoted to the issue, criticizing men and inciting women in one of his statements:

O Muslim women do not listen to the words of the lost, misguiders who deceive you by ordering you to obey your husbands without ordering you to obey Allah and His Messenger (May the Peace and Blessings of Allah be upon him). They say that the happiness of a woman lies in the obedience to her husband. This is nothing but the fulfilment of their desires and objectives by requiring what neither Allah nor His Messenger have made compulsory on you in the first place like cooking, washing clothes, and other things that are nothing but what they want. At the same time, they are not requiring of you that which Allah and His Messenger oblige for you in obedience to Allah and His Messenger.[50]

Dan Fodio challenged the denigrating status of women, their responsibilities, and the supposed responsibilities of men toward them in a professed Islamic society. His viewpoint on women centered on education as essential to human capital development in a society. Discrimination bordering on denying the provision of the requirements for the development of women was frowned at by Dan Fodio, as he maintained that it was bad to allow women to be mired in ignorance. Beyond the education of women, Dan Fodio encouraged them to be involved in economic activities that would empower them financially, though he admonished them to be obedient to their husbands, who he believed were the basis of their happiness.

Abdullah Hakim Quick maintained that, while Dan Fodio's encouragement of women's scholarship and participation in business aimed at "changing the quality of the relationship between men and women, [it] should not be interpreted as a type of revolutionary women's liberation in the Western sense of the word. The Shehu (Dan Fodio) was very careful to temper most of his treatises on this topic with a reminder that the woman should be basically obedient to her husband."[51] His revolutionary statements were aimed at changing the status of women in the Hausa African society, seeing the development of a scholarship that critiqued this status was necessary because of the greed, paganism, and violation of the standards of Islamic law that demanded women's education and development. Women's thirst for education was sparked by Dan Fodio's research during and after the revolutionary wars; thus, education was particularly encouraged for both women and children in the post-revolutionary Caliphate. In some Fulani houses, primary education was left in the hands of aged women. The legacy of Dan Fodio's quest for women's education was maintained and carried on by his daughter, Nana Asma'u, who translated his works into Hausa when the use of Fulfulde declined in the Caliphate. On a personal level, she took up the responsibility of teaching women in the house where she was married to Gidado. Other women that emerged out of the movement for women's education included Fatima, Maryamu, Hafsa, Safiya, and their cousin Aisha among many others. Importantly, Dan Fodio's political and religious reform movement was not only aimed at eradicating the religious and social corruption of the various rulers in Hausaland, which he saw as betraying the fundamentals of Islamic teachings, but also at establishing an egalitarian society based on the principle of justice and equality.

Economy and Society

The sociopolitical reforms of Dan Fodio span across many structures. The ideas of the Shehu's proposals for the entire structure of social relations of production were aimed at fairness, to build a just society on the principles of equality and prosperity for all. He did not formulate modern economic concepts; instead, his ideas on the economy were influenced by the Quran and works of earlier scholars, such as Ibn Khaldun and Ibn Taymiyyah. Their theories guided his understanding on distinguishing between what was economically just and unjust in the society in which he found himself. He was not oblivious of the interplay between the market forces of demand and supply, and, with this, he was able to postulate economic practice on the principle of fairness.

To ensure fairness in economic activities, Dan Fodio insisted that rulers should appoint *muhtasib* (supervisors), whose sole responsibility was to supervise activities among people in markets and safeguard the interest of the buyer and seller. In *Bayan al-bid'a alshaytaniyya*, Dan Fodio warned against ignorant people buying and selling because they did not know what is permissible and forbidden. As a principle aimed toward encouraging economic prosperity, he maintained that governments must ensure that those appointed to regulate its activities are those who are considered just, trustworthy, honest, and steadfast.[52] He was mindful that the preexisting system suffered from entrenched corruption and unjust practices that were not promoting equality, justice, and the economic development of the people.

His approach to economic matters was anchored on the principle of fairness while safeguarding against anything that could usher back the wrongs of the past. Toward this aim, Dan Fodio posited that a state treasury (*bayt al-mal*) should be established for rulers to use in solving matters of state, funded through *khums* (one-fifth of booties), *kharaj* (land taxes), *jizya* (poll taxes), *fay* (proceeds of conquered lands given to all Muslims), *ushr* (tithes), the wealth of deceased people without heirs, and lost properties whose owners were not known, but not through the *jangali* (cattle taxes), *kudin gari* (fines levied on town people), *kudin salla* (taxes levied on people during salla), sequestrating the wealth of people who faced undue banishment, the forceful collection of money from butchers, the seizure of cotton in the markets, or taking bribes and delivering justice based on the highest bidder.[53]

Overall, he was against the use of high taxation for funding the state treasury because the lower taxes provided greater incentives for economic prosperity and participation of citizens in the economic activities of the state and proposed that people should be taxed according to their source of income. The state Dan Fodio established had no written constitution but was guided by Islamic principles of administration drawn from the provisions of the Quran. He forbade laziness among his followers, encouraging them to acquire a trade in order to make a livelihood since it was deemed inappropriate to consume food that had not been obtained by one's own labor. Sultan Muhammad Bello argues thus in *Usul al-Siyasat*:

> For this purpose, he (ruler, governor/president) shall foster the artisans, and be concerned with tradesmen who are indispensable to the people. They include farmers, smiths, tailors, dyers, physicians, grocers, butchers, carpenters, and all sort of trades, contribute to (stabilize) the proper order of the world. The ruler must set up these tradesmen in every village and locality. He should urge his subjects to produce foodstuff and store it for future use. He must keep villages and countryside peopled, construct fortresses, bridges, maintain markets, roads, and

realize for them all what are of public interest so that the proper order of this world may be maintained.[54]

He also discouraged rulers from taking gifts from their subjects. In *Bayan Wujub Al-hijra ala 'l-ibad*, Dan Fodio stated:

> As to law concerning gifts offered to them, there is a prophetic tradition in Bukhari's Sahih that the prophet appointed a man called Ibn al-Lutbiyya as governor. When the man returned to the prophet, he said "O Messenger of God, this is for you and this was given to me as present." The Prophet said angrily, "Why should a man whom we employ to perform a task for us say, 'This is for you and this was given to me as a present?'" Why should he not have stayed in the house of his father and mother to see if a present were sent to him there.[55]

The act of receiving gratification was abhorred by Dan Fodio because leaders could be induced to corruption through it and the powerful positions which they occupied could be made less respectable. He emphasized the need to avoid amassing wealth through fraudulent means, such as governors receiving bribes and other methods which gave them riches which they did not have before ascending to a position of jurisprudence. Surplus wealth had to be deposited in state treasury, referring to Maliki's describing of how Umar b. al-Khattab confiscated half of his governors' possessions when it became apparent that they owned more after gaining their office than what they previously had.[56] He stated that:

> O my Brother, I warn you against amassing wealth to exceed others, you should stick to what is sufficient of the permissible things and then consume it with the intention of serving (Allah) . . . The Companions of the Prophet Muhammad used to inherit legal wealth and then leave it in fear that it would corrupt their hearts.
>
> O my Brother, if the collection of wealth for the purpose of philanthropic deeds had been better than forsaking that wealth, nobody would have surpassed Muhammad (the Prophet) in this virtue.[57]

The Shehu quoted Juz'ai and explained how the state treasury (*baytul mal*) should be spent, writing that:

> The practice of just imams concerning fay and khums is to begin by securing the dangerous places and frontier posts, by preparing armaments and by paying soldiers. If anything is left then it should go to the judges, state officials, for the building of mosques and bridges and then it should be divided among the poor. If any still remains, the imam has the option of either giving it to the rich or keeping it (in the baytul mal) to deal with disasters which may occur to Islam.[58]

Another issue that caught Dan Fodio's interest was land management. As a major method of production, he was worried about how it could influence wealth creation and distribution. He was inclined to accept Islamic jurisprudence's customary rules, which divided lands into two categories–usable, inhabited, and dead land, and unoccupied, uncultivated land. These divisions were also based on whether the lands were seized by force, by peace treaty, or by the owner's conversion to Islam, with each kind having its own set of distribution, allocation, grants, endowment, and enclosure regulations. For example, the rulers were allowed to grant cultivable land, or, where there was immovable property of unbelievers not captured by force, to persons either permanently or temporarily, while land which was taken by force was owned collectively by all Muslims and could only be allocated temporarily to individuals. Conversely, lands taken through peace treaties could not be allocated by the ruler, as it remained the property of its owners and an imam was not obliged to grant lands which belonged to people who embraced Islam while it was in their possession.[59] As in other aspects of religion and life, Dan Fodio envisioned the need to correct economic corruption widespread in the society by presenting the tenets of Islamic teaching on it and using them to describe how the state could thereby function appropriately.

While this method of surplus appropriation was feudal, the society's economic boundaries underwent significant modifications. Markets and free business flourished, aided by policies that set prices, weights, and measures under the supervision of a *muhtasib* (supervisor). In the north, urbanization developed rapidly and several new towns arose, including Yola, Bauchi, Bida, Gombe, Kontagora, Keffi, and Nasarawa.[60]

On the whole, Dan Fodio's economic ideas contributed to the prosperity of the Caliphate, though there were other factors supporting the economic growth in Sokoto Caliphate including its size and existing markets structures. For instance, Agadez, Katsina, and Kano were important commercial centers in Hausaland before the jihad.[61] The Caliphate had enormous economic advantages because both long-distance traders as well as local producers supplied them with some of their trading goods, with its large size ensuring good supply of different raw materials at competitive prices and guaranteeing a very large internal market. External markets were also easily controlled by the Caliphate, while the quality of labor featured diverse skills and technological resources which were highly advantageous.

Politics and Society

Dan Fodio's political contributions were based on the essence of justice and understanding of Shari'a as the foundation of good governance and justice administration in an Islamic state. He was not oblivious that circumstances could influence people to resort to *Siyasat* (politics) in solving some judicial problems, anathematizing in *Kitab Al-Farq* some of the sharp political and injudicious practices that were common among the Habe rulers. Dan Fodio's understanding of the nature of the society he wanted to build and the nature of the people within it made it important to him that the modus operandi be laid down properly before the jihad started. A cursory look at Dan Fodio's religious revivalism reveals a fusion between the individual, society, religion, and the state. Since man is said to be political by nature,

Dan Fodio could not evade this attribute despite his intentions to religiously revive Islam in Hausaland.

The relationship between Dan Fodio and Islam was so relevant and powerful that one can describe his political ideas as inspirations derived from the body of laws revealed divinely by God. The 1804 jihad, though founded on Islamic ideals, is difficult to divorce from the social and political inclinations of the population and the need to change Hausaland's trajectory that was arising from the decay in the system sustaining the political and social structure of relations in the Hausa society. Specifically, Dan Fodio's political ideas were derived from the Islamic sources of law including the Hadith and Sunna. These combine to form the Shari'a, and, thus, the Islamic idea of a state, and its paraphernalia of governance, is guided by the provisions of Shari'a law.

While this is important for the genesis of the ideas that formed Dan Fodio's political thought, there were also works by his predecessors, such as Ibn Khaldun, Ibn Taymiyya, Al-Ghazali, and Al-maghili whose works on Islam, politics, and society greatly influenced him. The religio-political changes aspired for by Dan Fodio were the emancipation of the Muslims and the establishment of an Islamic state based on the Islamic principles of Shari'a, but this could not be achieved without the development of a concrete political manifesto that appealed to the conscience of the people. Dan Fodio realized that the handicapped nature of the people's development of theory and practices necessary for change, so he began to preach, teach, and write relevant works that were circulated among the people.

The earlier works by Dan Fodio mentioned elsewhere in this chapter are relevant to his views on the idea of politics and society. His *Masa'il Muhimma yahtaju ila marifatiha bad d al-Talaba* ("Important Questions that Some of the Students Need to be Aware Of"),[62] *Watiqat Ahl al-Sudan*, and most importantly *Bayan Wujub Al-hijra ala'l-ibad* depict Dan Fodio's approach to politics and the survival of Islamic state. For example, *On the Principles of the Emirate*, the eighth chapter in *Bayan Wujub Al-hijra Alal-Ibad*, Dan Fodio mentioned five basic principles of leadership under which an emirate must function. He first drew attention to people who have too much desire to rule, suggesting such people should be avoided because of the model of Joseph not claiming kingship by seeking to be put in charge of the storehouses of the land.[63]

Instead, the good works of men should demonstrate them worthy to occupy positions of authority not because they desired it but because the society found them noble, humble, and always valuable to the state. Therefore, it was necessary to allow for a democratic process in the selection of an imam and Islamic scholars, who should represent the people as the commanders of the faithful. Another characteristic of an appropriate imam is that he had to be a virtuous man of sound mind, qualified to give independent judgment, courageous, and not afraid of facing the enemy or enforcing the prescribed penalties.[64] The second principle was to ensure that leaders consulted as wide as possible before taking any decision. Dan Fodio was concerned with wrong decisions that could negatively impact the lives of the citizens governed by the king. This knowledge is often beneficial for decision-making, especially when consultations are made with wise counsel. He understood that the state was not a private enterprise and should be governed carefully and according to the dictates of Islam.

Dan Fodio maintained that, "One of the worse qualities of a king is to be opinionated and to neglect consultation."[65] Referring to the Quran, Dan Fodio maintained that leaders must avoid harsh measures, embodied in the third principle, justice, and the fourth, charity. Dan Fodio stated that the state must ensure justice in the discharge of their duties, so knowledgeable religious leaders had to be companions of the Sultan so that he could be guided toward ensuring justice in the administration of the state. As for charity, Dan Fodio argued that leaders must understand that not all those who are governed prosper through justice, some also needed charity. Following these principles, he divided the people into three groups based on the ways which they should be treated, writing that "the old one should be treated as a father, the middle ones should be treated as a brother, while the young one be treated as sons."

Pre-jihad Hausa states had a monarchical government, which Dan Fodio argued should be based on the principles of Shari'a and popular consultation, with officers elected into office based on their qualities and qualifications rather than aspire to them while keeping their virtues hidden from the public. Dan Fodio educated the inhabitants of Kitab al- Farq as part of his political and intellectual activities:

> One of the ways of their government (in Hausaland) is succession to the emirate by hereditary right (monarchy) and by force (military take-over) to the exclusion of consultation. And one of the ways of their government is the building of their sovereignty upon three things: the people's person, their honor, and their possessions; and whomsoever they wish to kill or exile or violate his honor or devour his wealth they do so in pursuit of their lusts, without any right in the law—Shari'a.[66]

With the establishment of the Caliphate, there was the need to establish a system to administrate the justice they had been advocating for, particularly imperative because Gobir's injustices and other un-Islamic practices had been heavily criticized by Dan Fodio. With the power shift to him and his men, he was required to bring his rule into force as well as uphold the principles of justice among his subjects. Another issue was that the supporters of the jihad held a range of different motivations to participate in the movement, so the new society had to determine the nature of the political arrangement that would foster peace and unity among the people of the newly founded state and the system of administration of justice and other related operations necessary to strengthen the paraphernalia of governance. Ensuring and maintaining social stability in the new community had to be committed to, and to this end, Dan Fodio warned that:

> One of the swiftest ways of destroying a kingdom is to give preference to one particular tribe over another, or to show favor to one group of people rather than another, and draw near those who should be kept away and keep away those who should be drawn near.[67]

Dan Fodio noted that no form of discrimination should be tolerated, lest it leads to chaos that could cause the collapse of the state. He argued that, "A kingdom can endure with unbelief but it cannot endure with injustice."[68]

One of the distinguishing characteristics of the political philosophy of Dan Fodio was the insistence that government should be based on Islamic concepts of justice to all and consultation with the populace. The latter practice gave room for equal participation by all citizens of the state as a fundamental human right. Politically, the consultation was necessary for the survival of the emirates and broadened in many dimensions with the establishment of the Caliphate, and Sokoto was often consulted to clarify issues of religious and administrative importance, helping preserve and legitimize the authority of the Caliphate.

The establishment of the emirates expanded the caliphate's political authority over areas that were hitherto not part of the revolutionary movement but sought the military and political power of the Caliphate. The establishment of the Caliphate created a large centralized political and administrative structure, where dependent emirates paid tribute to Sokoto. According to Njuema, tributes from Yola were particularly considerably paid with items such as salt, livestock, native cotton, glass, beads, ivory, and labor,[69] but the tributes were not limited to Adamawa alone as other emirates did the same. The tributes were necessary, demonstrating the emirates' loyalty and commitment to the Caliph and the Caliphate as a whole and, in return, the Caliphate provided needed protection and mediated in disputes over succession.

Because the movement was predicated on its scholarship, its followers were already aware of Dan Fodio's earlier warning on the need to be loyal and committed to their leaders, so long as they remained believers. The jihad indeed ushered in an intellectual epoch-making era in Hausaland and Western Sudan in general. Throughout its stages, it was supported through intellectual discourses anchored on Islamic knowledge that helped establish the structure and ethos of the Caliphate, smoothly fulfilling the intentions of Dan Fodio and his comrades. The production of knowledge through text, teaching, and preaching, especially on different issues of sociopolitical and economic knowledge, conscientized the people toward the need for change in the Hausa-led political system.

Conclusion

Dan Fodio's contributions to the historiography of African political and intellectual thought were not limited to issues of jurisprudence, women's education, economics, and politics alone but also extended to other endeavors. The entirety of what culminated in his preaching, teaching, and writing of relevant and selected texts; the conduct of the jihad he led, and its success in the establishment of a centralized political system with emirates within its sphere of influence; were anchored in religious principles about government and politics. Unlike in Western political thought, where there is a distinction between the spiritual and physical, ecclesiastical and civil, and religious and secular,[70] Dan Fodio forged a form of political thought that did not try to separate itself from the cultural values of Islam.

The result could not be better seen than in the socioeconomic, religious, and political configuration of northern Nigeria. There is indeed no better proof of how the Islamic knowledge influenced and made Dan Fodio, such that he influenced a revolution that completely turned around the dynamics of the Nigerian geo-political configuration. The Sokoto Caliphate—created as a result—functioned as a religious and political headquarter/hub of power. Till date, emirs, regarded as religious leaders, equally wield political powers. Indeed, it was Dan Fodio's understanding and teaching, which of course birthed the jihad revolution, that, to make desired changes, one must actually aim for and seize political power, where enforcement lies. Not only that, Dan Fodio's approach validates the instrumentalization of the jihad for religious and political purposes.

As seen in many of his works, Dan Fodio dealt not only with matters of government, politics, and the state, but also addressed issues of acceptable personal behavior and the ethical responsibilities of both the ruler and the ruled before God. This gives us the impetus to discuss Dan Fodio's political and intellectual thoughts from the perspective of the nexus between religion and politics. It was on the basis of the foundation of Islam and its political craft that Dan Fodio was able to exploit the religious and political leadership deficit of the Habe rulers to aid to the establishment of Caliphate. The development of his religious scholarship and Dan Fodio's tenacity to revive Islam served as the entry point for changing the fortunes of the Hausa state. He contributed significantly to strengthening Islam through Islamic education while broadening the horizon of the people toward the tenets of Islam through the production of a great deal of writing on different Islamic religious issues. For example, the sixty-three chapters of his work *Bayan Wujub Al-hijra Ala 'L-Ibad*, dealt with wide-ranging issues of religious importance, such as the conduct of jihad, the appointment of imams, the distribution of booty, and issues of Islamic law among many other topics, significantly transforming Islam in Hausaland.

The nineteenth-century social, political, and religious movement marked a turning point in the political and intellectual thought and history of West Africa. Islam became the medium through which the machinery of state operated and the dominant civilization through a system for the documentation and development of Islamic education. Because of the historical antecedents of people within the Sokoto areas, the emergence of Dan Fodio and his political and intellectual thoughts, bound with and derived from Islam, developed into a valid alternative for the oppressed people Hausaland. With the revival of Islam and founding of a new state, the people underwent a radical change in lifestyle as a people.

Dan Fodio's thoughts provide us with an understanding of the influence of religion on individual and state ideologies. His methodology in the craft of developing and transforming his society was essentially based on training people by example and not by theory, but his ability to combine theory and practice made him an exceptional leader and secure his place in the history of West Africa. His preaching and teachings transformed scholarship and religious enterprise into political action and successfully established a state in accordance with Islamic teachings.

Shaykh Amadou Bamba and
the Muridiyya Sufi Order

Introduction

This chapter furthers the discussion on knowledge systems as professed through leadership and power. While this was examined through the work and life of Usman Dan Fodio in the previous chapter, this chapter will examine how the life and works of Amadou Bamba derived from the Quran to profess a belief system that influenced his adherents. Indeed, the West African region contributed to the development and spread of Islamic literatures within Africa. Although Islam in Africa predates the nineteenth century, Islam's influence was overshadowed by the many religious and political figures that emerged in the nineteenth century with different social and political ideologies and movements that drove the economic, social, and political ideals of many African societies. In some climes, the ideologies culminated in violent and nonviolent movements. Groups' decisions to approach ideological shifts in a violent or nonviolent approach were influenced by a few factors, such as the declining popularity of existing social systems, the inferiority of current systems, or their social systems were threatened by external forces—predominantly from European forces.

Prominent figures who emerged in several movements that aimed to seize control of their communities' futures included Shaykh Amadou Bamba (1853–1927), Shehu Uthman Dan Fodio (1754–1817), and Sekou Toure (1922–1984), just to mention a few. Not only did their contributions help to mobilize people from different ideological backgrounds, but additionally, some of these individuals engaged in the production of literature addressing a large array of different subjects. They were also committed to developing theories that reflected real life practice, some of which are still evident in present-day Africa. Today, the manuscripts left by the nineteenth century generation of scholars are great sources of knowledge of the past and inspiration to many societies and communities of their followers. The contributions of these individuals to knowledge have also helped in understanding the trajectory of events in the activities of people in the region. While there are a multitude of individuals who contributed to the preservation of knowledge, this chapter will focus on the contributions of Amadou Bamba, a Senegalese Islamic scholar, in the formation and transformation of the Muridiyya Sufi order in Senegal.[1]

Shaykh Amadou Bamba (1853–1927) is addressed in a variety of ways in both the literature and his community. Aḥmad ibn Muhammad ibn Habib Allah[2] is also known as Khadimu r-Rasul, or "Servant of the Prophet." In the Wolof language, he is known as Serin Touba, which means "Holy Man of Touba." Amadou Bamba was born in the Mbacke village in the Kingdom of Baol in West Central Senegal. His father, Momar Anta Sali, was a marabout from one of the oldest Muslim brotherhoods in Senegal—the Qadiriyya Sufi brotherhood. Amadou Bamba was a spiritual leader who produced literary works on different subjects.

Bamba is known for his emphasis on work, a virtue that is instilled in his disciples who are generally known for their industriousness. He started his career as a teacher in his father's school, where he was formerly a student. While his father initially appointed him as an assistant teacher, Bamba soon demonstrated his intelligence and ability to impact knowledge in the school. This ability gave him respect over his peers. He won the trust and confidence of his father who later assigned him a teaching role, among other responsibilities in the school. He proceeded to teach at the school until the death of his father in 1883. The death of his father marked a turning point in his religious activities, especially with the initiation of the new method of spiritual education that led to the formation of the Muridiyya Sufi order. Thereafter, Bamba instituted a new technique that focused around *khidma* (service) to promote spiritual education.

By the nineteenth century, Islamic scholars in the region, particularly among the Wolof, had become critical of the continuing decay of Islamic education. They were perturbed by the nature of Quranic education—which ought to place much emphasis on scholastic activities characterized by memorization of the Quran—but rather represented an utter disconnection from the praxis of wisdom and the promotion of wealth and prestige to the detriment of religion. Trivializing Islamic scholarship, drums were sometimes rolled out during scholarly encounters, a practice that reduced serious religious activities to mere religious jamborees. Such reductionism was seen as a betrayal of the value system that produced the *ulama*, as they promoted such unhealthy practices among the Wolof instead of imparting knowledge for the glorification of God and for the common good of the society.

Unhealthy competition became the order of the day; corruption became rife in the educational system; and the preachers became weak and uncritical of the aristocracy who allowed the *ceddo*, a value that caused a decline in their character.[3] *Wann* and *lawaan*[4] was admitted as a practice where scholars opposed each other in a show that depicted one's intellectual ability in the mastery of the Quran. Additionally, this apparent decay in the Wolof society coincided with the activities of French colonial enterprises in Senegal. O'Brien argued that "[t]he Mouride movement originated . . . as a response to French imperialism, which (in its direct and indirect effects) created the social environment in which the brotherhood took root and grew."[5]

However, the emergence of Bamba—the "renewer" (*Mujaddid* in Arabic) of Islam— gave hope to the Senegalese society. It is imperative to note that Bamba emerged in between two devastating historical periods in Senegal's history. First, his emergence came at the conclusion of the trans-Atlantic slave trade, followed by the beginning of French colonial conquest and domination of the African peoples and cultures. At the imposition of French colonial domination, the colonialists envisaged the need to invalidate African and Muslim value systems and to replace them with those of France. This was eventually "partially" achieved through the introduction of the French colonial educational system, which undermined Quranic schools in Senegal. Furthermore, the French, in order to fully achieve this, employed a strategy in which the Senegalese who adopted the French (Western) culture were promoted and given equal rights and citizenship to Frenchmen.

Conversely, those who resisted colonial powers were defeated in the ensuing war of resistance, while those who submitted to colonial power became auxiliaries of the French. The people's sources of power and economy were destroyed. Through this, the French ensured that the Senegalese became solely dependent on the French colonial apparatus for their authority. The Wolof communities were balkanized into smaller units, and their rulers became powerless adjuncts of the French government. Following the end of the Wolof leaders' authority, their whole religious and social structure became fragmented and dislocated.[6] Thus, this situation, combined with internal dynamics, especially compromised by Muslim teachers in Quranic education, contributed to the sociopolitical and economic degeneration of Senegalese society. Violent opposition to the French colonial enterprise increased significantly in some parts of the country. Ma Ba Daiakhou and Dammel Lat Dior gained prominence due to their violent resistance against the French.

However, rather than resort to a violent approach in confronting the French system, Bamba took a nonviolent philosophy to deal with the crisis. Bamba's nonviolent philosophy preceded and ranks equal with other proponents such as Mahatma Gandhi, Abdul Ghafar Khan, Martin Luther King, Jr., and many others.[7] The impact of Bamba's nonviolent philosophy is reflected in the stable and peaceful religious and political transformation of the country during and after colonialism. In 2005, the United States Institute of Peace upholds that "Senegal is a vivid illustration that political Islam can be a constructive and a regime stabilizing force . . . [and] has found balance between modernizing secular state and a religiously encouraged grassroots social conversation . . . Senegal's Sufi groups became pillars for the governing authorities."[8] Although the Qadiriyya and Tijaniyya Sufi orders had larger numbers, the Muridiyya Sufi group founded by Bamba has gradually become more visible in the West African region and exhibits greater influence over power relationships and wealth.[9] As a scholar, "Bamba developed his thoughts on education in the form of books and sermons that were presented as responses to questions asked by his adherents and colleagues."[10] Raised in the tradition and family of Islamic learning, Bamba had a passion for education which he sought diligently.

To Bamba, education is an essential part of the development process that helps to facilitate the development of "good Muslims who model their actions on the teachings of Islam and serve their community."[11] For him, knowledge encompasses both the esoteric or mystical sciences and the exoteric sciences (classical disciplines). In one of his major works, *Masalik alJinaan* (*Paths to Paradise*), completed around 1884/85, he wrote:

> According to the Masters, religious knowledge is divided into two sorts: Exoteric knowledge ('Ilm Zahir) Esoteric knowledge ('Ilm Batin). The exoteric one is in

charge of improving man's action while the esoteric one deals with his spiritual moods. The first one is known under the name of *Fiqh* [Islamic Law] while the second one is called Tasawwuf [Mysticism].[12]

Amadou Bamba founded and grounded the Muridiyya on educational, spiritual, and social pillars. The *Tarbiyya* (upbringing) was used by the Mourid leader as an educational and spiritual instrument to teach his followers.[13] He initiated a teaching method that completely departed from merely memorizing the Quran to a pedagogy that places emphasis on ethical and spiritual values. He contends that, knowledge should be for the purpose of combating ignorance, liberation of humanity, enriching the religious sciences, and to act and live in accordance with the teachings of the sciences. He cautioned, however, that people who pursue sciences only for the sake of participating in polemics or for the sake of status and glory would face God's wrath.[14]

Islam, Sufism, and the Education of Amadou Bamba

Islam as a monotheistic faith played a fundamental role in the education and development of the knowledge of God that is associated with Shaykh Amadou Bamba. His education was influenced first by the family he came from. His father, Maam Mor Anta Saly, was a great and respected Islamic scholar; likewise, Khaly Majakhate Kala, his father's colleague whom he also learned from. Thus, because he came from a background where scholarship and intellectualism was emphasized, Bamba had a solid foundation to begin his journey as an Islamic teacher. He stayed with his father and studied the Quran from a young age. He decided to study rhetoric and logic from Muhammad al-Karim Bani of Dayman, a Moorish scholar because he was passionate about Islamic education. During this time, Bamba started to write on a variety of topics, including Islamic law (*fiqh*), Sufism (*tassawuf*), God's oneness (*tawhid*), principles of moral behavior, language, and so on. The pursuit of knowledge in his immediate environment was highly valued. The culture of *wann* and *Lawaan* promoted debates and competition among peers who were inspired by theological debates among Islamic teachers in Senegal. In the past, the curriculum that dominated Islamic learning in the Western Sahara consists of "Qur'anic exegesis or *tafsir*, *hadith* or traditions of Prophet Muhammad, *fiq* or Islamic jurisprudence, *tasawwuf* or Islamic mysticism, and *siira* or biography and hagiography of Prophet Muhammad. In the Arabic sciences, *nahwu* or grammar, *luqa* or lexicography, *balaqa*, use of the language, and *uruudh* or poetry were taught. The ancient sciences were composed of *mantiq* or logic, *ilm al-nugum* or astrology and tibb *taqlidi* or traditional medicine" constitute the Arabic learning.[15] This shaped the education of many students in West Africa. Sufism was particularly essential in the spread of Islam in West Africa. According to Seesemann, Sufism is an individual devotion.[16] However, its mystical religiosity did not seem to have much influence on the people; rather, the combination of Sufism with the call for Islam along with social, economic, and political factors attracted Muslims and non-Muslims alike.[17] The Qadiriyya Sufi order, for example, teaches the practice of the ascetic life for the preservation of the spirit. To some Sufis, asceticism[18] is an essential path and process that allows one the ability to be able to commune directly with the supernatural (God).

The Sufis' capacity to comprehend the Prophet's teachings, which reflect Islam's inner knowledge and the achievement of inner calm, has historically been the most successful way of bringing the spiritual ideals of Islam to reality. Bamba's affiliation with the Sufi order of the Qadiriyya was influential in his path to Sufism. Most Sufis cultivate and teach peace, especially inner peace, as the yardstick for spirituality. Quietness and deep meditation brings peace. It is only when inner peace is attained that outward peace is achieved. Thus, Sufi adherents are integrated under the vision of peace that originates from God. Like any Sufi, Bamba was educated along the tenets of Islam, and particularly the basic provisions that define the attitudes and path of total submission to God. These are *Al-Iman* (the Muslim faith), *Al-Islam* (submission to God), and *Al-Ihsaan* (purification of the soul).[19]

The Muridiyya Sufi order was established on the basis of these principles. The pillars were religious and secular practical sciences, good actions, and Muslim etiquette. In his conception of Sufism, Bamba integrated the two legitimate dimensions of Sufism as conceived in Ibn Khaldun's commentary on Al-Ghazali: that Sufism as a "science of praxis rooted in sharia and Sufism as mysticism geared toward the education of the heart."[20] To Bamba, *tasawwuf* was a fundamental aspect of Islam, second only to *tawhid* (the knowledge of God's oneness) and Shari'a (Islamic law), which he believed to constitute the religion's spirit and body.[21]

Furthermore, *nafs* thought that man's heart is a mirror through which he may see God's visions, but that man's worldly desires and wants cause the mirror to become opaque. The worldly desires are identified with *nafs*.[22] *Nafs* must practice *Muhasaba* (self-examination), *Muraqaba* (meditation, that is, the love of God through meditation), and be detached from worldliness. Figuratively, the practice is known as *Safr* (journey) to God, and the phases of spiritual achievement are described as *Muqamat* (stations). At various stages and at the conclusion, the *Salik* (practitioner) experiences spiritual emotions known as *Hal* (states). As a result, the themes of Quranic spirituality such as attention, purpose, inner discipline, appreciation, charity, personal responsibility, and the fight for justice are only a few of the major topics raised by the Scripture.[23]

In terms of morality, piety, and religion, the Sufis emulate and draw inspiration from Prophet Muhammad. The attainment of God's wisdom is the goal of man's creation, and the Sufis believed that genuine knowledge from God can only be obtained via intuition. Perhaps, the Sufi philosophy guided Bamba such that at the time where he perceived the need to attain the state of quietness, meditation, and commitment to the supernatural, he retired from the public space in order to develop communities that he could fashion according to the teachings of Islam and practices of Sufism.[24]

With the demise of Amadou Bamba's father, Bamba developed a system of Quranic education that was different from the traditional teachings in the society. The new system laid the foundation for the emergence of the Muriddiyya Sufi order and the *Tarbiyya* educational system that is associated with it. The *Tarbiyya* system's differences from the standard teaching system was a result of its shift in focus. Rather than being centered around Quranic memorization, the *Tarbiyya* system was anchored on the Quranic principles of morality, the transformation of individual spiritual life, and the emphasis on works and religious practices rather than strict ideological persuasions advocated by the Qadiriyya. Bamba's deviation from the usual practice was informed by the exigencies of time and the need to reform the educational system that was fast declining in the face of religious knowledge practiced by the Sufi order.

Amadou Bamba and the Origin of the Muridiyya Movement in Senegal

When the word "Murid" is directly translated from Arabic, it means "one who desires." It is a term used by the Sufis to refer to someone seeking a spiritual guide to God. Murid beliefs and practices undergird the Muridiyya Sufi order, which is one of the largest Sufi orders in Senegal and Gambia today. Bamba's desire for Islamic knowledge, especially the purification of the soul and the attainment of the status that will enable it (the soul) to commune with the supernatural, prompted Bamba to establish the order. This effort was also inspired by the changing dynamics of the relations between the centers of Islamic teaching and their mandate for educating people which was fast dwindling.

French colonial activities were also changing the sociocultural and political space for ideal Islamic knowledge. Therefore, it became necessary to revive and protect the culture of the people in any way possible. To fulfil this responsibility, Bamba established an intellectual movement that instilled discipline, hard work, and the pursuit of religious education that earned him a special place—even today—in the history of Senegal, and indeed in the world. The effort to establish the Muridiyya brought him into direct confrontation with French colonialists as well as local rulers who were jittery because of his growing influence.

We mentioned that Bamba served as teaching assistant at his father's school. His quest for Islamic knowledge compelled him to move to Mauritania where he learned the practices of different Sufi orders, especially the Qadiriyya, Tijaniyya, and Shadilliyya. Mauritania was one of the centers of Islamic education with scholars from different aspects of Islamic knowledge. Upon his return from Mauritania, it was alleged that Bamba began to see the Prophet Muhammad in his dreams. Additionally, the prophets gave him directives. With the demise of his father in 1883, Bamba took over the school and continued his father's legacy.[25] Shaykh Amadou Bamba addressed the students and teachers in the school on Friday, Ramadan 27 1302 Hijri (1882-3)[26] to inform them that he had instructions from the Prophet to educate them who are attached to him in order to cleanse their souls and achieve spiritual fulfillment. As a result, Bamba taught his followers the art of purification (*tahliya*) as a means of attaining spiritual perfection (*takhlliya*). From then on, spiritual education became grounded in the actions and knowledge that Bamba propagated.

Although at the beginning of the establishment of the Muridiyya order, Bamba had the opportunity to assert himself as a force to reckon with in Senegal's politics, he never displayed any interest in politics and he never held any political appointments over the course of French colonialism or prior. Bamba was preoccupied with his religious endeavors. As mentioned in some of his poems, his ultimate aim was to revitalize the *Sunna* (traditions) of Prophet Muhammad which he believed were stained by the practices of the local aristocracy. He taught his disciples spiritually and according to Sufi concepts such as *tarbiyya* and *tarqiyya*, as well as the Sunna tradition. Creevey postulates that, "More potentially valuable as support for the argument that Murid founder was not concerned with politics are his poems and books, both published and hand-copied."[27] These documents show that he was far more interested in religious matters than in politics. However, this does not imply that Bamba considered politics to be irrelevant. His classification of knowledge into esoteric and exoteric indicates his interests in both worlds. However, he believed more in the spiritual development of humans as the basis for the development of other spheres of human progress, such as politics.

The establishment of the Muridiyya coincided with the period of French colonial activities in Senegal. Typical of colonial activities, French colonialists destroyed all forms of resistance by the indigenous population. The so-called "civilizing mission" was constantly in conflict with local values. Many resisted violently and were killed by the colonialists. Secondly, as mentioned elsewhere, the rise of Muridiyya also corresponded with the decline of the traditional system of Islamic education as well as societal values. It was a period when the *Mujaddid* was required to reform the system. While the colonialists branded Islam as an anti-colonial religion in Senegal, the aristocracy perceived the emergence of Bamba and his growing influence as threatening to destroy the loyalty and support they enjoyed from their followers.

In order to fully comprehend Bamba's viewpoint on politics, one must examine it from a secular standpoint, particularly if one wants to understand his view of state administration as it involves both politicians and political groups. A secular understanding of politics addresses ways, means, and strategies to agree to and wield political power as opposed to spiritual power. To retain Sufi principles, Muslim leaders, such as Bamba, desired to maintain considerable distance between themselves and non-spiritual matters. Clearly, Muslim leaders' view of the relationship between politics and religion can be interpreted in a variety of ways. However, during Prophet Muhammad's time, politics and religion were inseparable. Bamba, however, chose to seclude himself so that he could attain a more powerful spiritual height.

Worried by the need to establish himself as a Sufi Islamic scholar, Bamba founded *Daaru Salaam* around 1886; and years later, he founded *Touba* around 1889. The establishment of *Daaru Salaam* was essential for Bamba to assert his authority and to be able to separate himself from the traditional rulers as well as to seclude and secure himself from being deterred from achieving his dream of becoming a spiritual force. Babou states that, "the founding of Touba was important in the construction of Amadou Bamba's status as a saint and Sufi leader."[28] While Bamba was not the first to search for *Touba*, past religious individuals' attempts to search for and find Touba proved futile. There is a general belief among the Murids that Touba is one of the secrets of God that is only revealed to whosoever is close to Him. Bamba found favor from God and established the city which is today celebrated as a holy city by all Murids globally.

The city has since evolved into a cultural and intellectual capital for Muslims in Senegal and the diaspora. In *Matlab ul Fawzayni* (Quest for happiness in the two worlds [this world and the hereafter]), the poem he wrote just after founding the village, Amadou Bamba prayed for God to make Touba a place of knowledge, worship, and mercy.[29] Touba grew exponentially such that it became crowded with Bamba's disciples who got married and populated the city. Touba's growth would come at the detriment of Bamba especially, as the growing followership around him resulted in the intimidation of authorities who expressed concern over his growing influence and the possibility of Bamba waging jihad against the colonial government as well as the local chiefs. The French colonial government became worried over Bamba's influence and decided to arrest him in 1895.

Bamba's arrest and exile signaled the start of the Muridiyya's second phase in Senegal's history. He started to build his marabout pedagogy while in jail. He was committed to the pursuit of knowledge as a devout Muslim. He found the Hadith, Quran, Arabic, grammar, jurisprudence, poetry, and didactics all interesting. Based on his knowledge of the Quran and the jihad al-nafs (the jihad of the Soul) or Jihad al-Akbar (the Greater Jihad), as declared by the Prophet, and failed militant jihadist onslaughts—especially by the Tijaniyya—Bamba decided that the pursuit of righteousness and power were incompatible. Thus, it was incumbent on Muslims to live a nonviolent life in his view. This principle of human relations was propagated by Bamba alongside the doctrine of work which became the hallmark of the Murids society. Today, Murids in Senegal and the diaspora are among the most philanthropic Africans because of the Islamic virtues that were spread by Bamba.

All attempts by the French colonialists to silence him failed. Bamba became prominent in Senegal, the Gambia, Gabon, and Mauritania, deriving from his noble character and the followership he commanded, and he became a target of the colonialists who charged him with sedition and exiled him to Gabon. For seven years, Bamba lived in Gabon where his pursuit for knowledge was deepened along his calling as a Sufi. His philosophy of knowledge, worship, and work spread among the Murids who were already practicing these virtues and were successful. The colonialists were impressed by their hard work and decided, through a show of benevolence toward their leader, to allow him to return. His return was celebrated by Murids, and his influence and power over the people went against the wishes of the French and local chiefs.

The colonialists also thought the return of Bamba could allow them to maintain a grip on the economy of Senegal and particularly exert some degree of control over the Murids, who were mostly workers. Unfortunately for the French, it did not turn out this way. As a result, and upon request by the chiefs, Bamba was once more exiled—this time, to Mauritania. His deportation to Mauritania was to ensure that Bamba compromised his position on French colonialism. He refused to be an apologist, had already declared the Muridiyya as a separate Sufi order, and was ready to accommodate French colonialism, though according to his own terms.[30] Furthermore, it should be noted that twentieth-century Africa witnessed violent anti-colonial struggles; Bamba's Murid society focused on peaceful living while also promoting the need to live in accordance with the Islamic virtues of nonviolence and industriousness. The Murid revolutionaries undermined French aspirations for domination by redefining success, power, and autonomy, thus ending efforts to govern Senegal with intimidation.[31]

The Life and Works of Amadou Bamba

Bamba lived a life of spirituality, scholarship, and service to humanity. He dedicated a great part of his life to fighting against injustice and oppression by the local Wolof aristocracy and the French colonialists in Senegal. In order to promote scholarship among his disciples, Bamba encouraged them to reverently study Islamic sciences in order to know all the required elements of their religious practices. Through a pact of allegiance to learn theology and ethics, he encouraged the practice of purity, prayer, fasting, and everything a follower would know in his religious practice and communion with God. Bamba worked toward achieving his objectives by preaching, teaching, and writing books and poems. He promoted religious science among his followers.

Additionally, he promoted the order through his character, his actions, and his writings. Bamba emphasized sciences, which to him represents the foundation upon which worship and ethical conduct should be built. He also cherished the life of service. Service (*khidma*) is one of the most solid principles that Bamba incorporated into the Muridiyya. *Khidma* is a concept that encourages hard labor, independence from others, and self-reliance. The concept plays a key role in the propagation of the Muridiyya in Senegal and across the West African region where Murids play an important role. It encourages individuals to eschew harm to others while simultaneously leading them to righteousness and piety and participating in service to not only bring good to others but also to satisfy God. Bamba promoted good manners throughout his life which transferred over into his teachings to the Murids, where he encouraged them to live a life of good manners.

The Muridiyya is closely associated with pristine etiquette. After all, admirable conduct is the essence of Sufism. Each moment has its suitable behavior; each condition has its correct behavior; and each step has its proper method. Thus, the compliance with the established ethical conduct in any circumstance is essential. Good manners are believed by Murids to be a yardstick that enables one to assess the degrees of sainthood. However, if one ignores the established ethical conduct, one will undoubtedly be lost or even rejected. As a Sufi, Bamba emphasized upholding one's allegiances, which occupies a high position in the tenets and principles of the Muridiyya.

The concept implies the quest for one to find the guidance of a Sheikh who is connected to God and who is devoted to enhancing the wisdom of God among disciples and to teaching them the Quran and *hikmah* (divine wisdom). Bamba believed that the path to righteousness is difficult, thus, anyone who engages on the duty and commitment to walk on the path without a wise guide, is doomed to perdition. With this, Bamba encouraged his disciples to find a religious teacher that they could swear allegiance to just as the disciples of the Prophet Muhammad once did under a tree. This became the guiding principle of the relationship between teachers and students in Bamba's philosophy of education in the *Daara Tarbiyya* schools that he established in Senegal. These values were instilled in both the students and their instructors. The virtues promoted both love and a desire to learn among the students.

One of the distinguished contributions of Amadou Bamba is his conception of religion and education. Bamba established the *Daara Tarbiya School* so that he could impart knowledge to his people. The philosophy of Bamba's education is built on the pillars of Islam, the significance of work, and the proper upbringing of people for the betterment of their societies. He was strategic in thinking out the direction and the kind of change that was required to revive education and Islam in Senegal. In *Masalik al-Jinaan* (*Paths to Paradise*), which was completed in 1884/85, Bamba contributed to so many issues regarding religion, piety, *tassawuf* (mysticism/Sufism), devotion, righteousness, education, and many more. He divided religious knowledge into two components: the esoteric and exoteric.

While the esoteric is concerned with the spiritual mood of a person, the exoteric deals with improvement of a person's action. According to Bamba, those who are in the business of education are often required to have certain skills and competence that will guide them through. Thus, he identified three types of teachers that should be considered as essential to the profession. The first is the Shaykh of instruction, who is in charge of traditional Quran teaching as well as Islamic theory and practice (law, mysticism, Prophet Muhammad's tradition, Quran interpretation, and worship). The second is the Shaykh of education, whose goal is to educate the soul and lead the students to spiritual perfection. The third is the Shaykh of *tarqiyya* or ascension.[32] Shaykh Anta Babou explains this as follows:

> First, he must understand the nature of the soul in its different states and he should master the means of curing its defects. He also must be capable of identifying the sources of sicknesses that can affect the soul and the instruments that can assure its protection. In order to fulfil this task, the Shaikh needs to combine scholarly insights and practical knowledge derived from experience with his soul. Second, the Shaikh of education is required to understand the subtleties of the world and the practical and religious laws that govern the existence of matter and of the soul so that he can always apply the adequate remedy to the different problems submitted to him. Third, to act in this way, the Shaikh must analyze every problem without passion and prejudice. To do so, he needs to fear God and to show repentance by shunning all self-glorification and by ridding himself of anything that distances him from his Lord.[33]

These qualities are required and should be adhere to as guiding principles of the education for whoever may choose this path. He maintained that, "There is no doubt that a limited amount of time devoted to scientific work is better than a lifetime spent in ignorance."[34] He further stated that, "It is an obligation for one to accord the same attention to the Quran and the religious sciences as to mystical science." Bamba sees that "the acquisition of knowledge without practice was a waste of time."[35] However, in verse 86 of Masalik Al-jinaan, he stated that, "is it considered compulsory for any servant to combine respect for the established Rules of Worship [*fiqh*] with concern for mystical aspects [*Tasawwuf*] so as to obtain reward." As a teacher, Bamba was concerned with the development and protection of the individual's life as a key to the development of society and religion. He identified the *nafs* as one of the greatest enemies of mankind; thus, when one is able to overcome *nafs*, he could attain some level of discipline that could propel him/her into a super realm. Thus, he mentioned in *Tazawudu shubaan*, some of the organs that could be put into control so that the soul can be gratified to perform the greatest jihad. These are:

> The stomach, the tongue, the genitalia, the feet, the eyes, the hands and the ears. Referring to the stomach and the adverse effect it can have on the faith, Bamba warns against consuming illicitly acquired food and eating too much. He argues that behaving in such a way only leads to corruption of the spirit, the drought of the heart and to laziness. As for the tongue, it should be prevented from lying, slandering or engaging in [futile] controversies. Bamba advised disciples to refrain from seeking unlawful sexual pleasure and recommends chastity before marriage. The feet should be restrained from walking to do illegal acts or from visiting unjust rulers. Instead, they should be used to frequent the mosque and to build and strengthen ties between members of the Muslim community. The eyes should be taught not to look at forbidden things, to threaten, or to embarrass people. The hands must respect the body and property of Muslims, and must be banned from writing indecencies or anything one would be ashamed of saying in public. As for the ears, Bamba recommended keeping them from listening to futile conversation, such as slander and gossip, or violating people's privacy.[36]

These virtues drove Bamba's philosophy of education while simultaneously laying the foundation for the disciplines found in the *Daara Tarbiyya* and among the Murids. Bamba's philosophy of education does not only identify requirements for teachers, as the students are also expected to incorporate certain virtues that will help promote the culture of learning, assimilation, and discipline. According to Fallou Ngom, "Bamba's major educational goals were the dissemination of values such as solidarity, hard work, self-reliance, political stability, cultural autonomy, and Sufi spiritual elevation among disciples from many different walks of life."[37] For the students, Bamba posited that students must be ready to endure hunger; they must be humble enough to learn for the purpose of liberating the mind from ignorance rather than engaging in polemics. Students should be able to respect their teachers; he placed the teachers right higher and above that of the parents as he regarded the education of the spirit as essential. The teachers take care of the spiritual, and the parents can take care of the body.[38]

For Bamba, it is important that a child is educated at an early age rather than to having to catch up as an adult, when his mind may already be preoccupied with challenges associated with adulthood. In Touba, a settlement established by Bamba for learning around 1888/89, the disciples were enjoined to cultivate knowledge, courage, discipline, and physical labor. Studying the Quran was key, but learning craft and other rewarding activities was encouraged as well. In any case, idleness was not an option in Touba.

However, it is noteworthy that Bamba is not only renowned for his contributions to the development of the philosophy of education. The history of the development of Ajami writing in the process of education and the Wolof language is one of Bamba's most important contributions to knowledge. It is imperative to note that West Africa was one of the earliest regions that was exposed to Islam. In particular, Senegal is close to some of the centers of learning in the Maghreb as well as other centers of learning developed in Africa as a result of some of the continent's interactions with Islam.

Because of this, Senegal has played an important role for the growth and distribution of the Arabic language and scripts that promoted the production of literary works, such as poems, in the Arabic language. The emergence of Bamba and the Muridiyya Sufi order contributed to the production of Ajami writing in Wolof. Ngom maintains that the reason for the flourishing of the Wolofal (Wolof Ajami) among Murids is because of the desire for cultural autonomy and the pedagogy of Bamba, the founder of the Muridiyya Sufi order.[39]

While in exile, Bamba wrote about his experiences and how he overcame his tribulations in classical Arabic; the material became popular, widely read, and was translated into Wolof by his disciples as well as distributed in classical Arabic writings. Sacred words had emerged with tremendous power. The words spawned a hagiographic literature used by his followers as a source of inspiration and reverence for Bamba.[40] The use of Wolof Ajami to disseminate Bamba's teachings among the Murids helped in the preservation and sustenance of the intellectual and spiritual life of Murid schools and communities. The writing was also used as a medium of communication for the dissemination of Bamba's teaching and for writing of polemical poems, eulogies, and other literary genres that were used by students.

It should be noted, however, that the Ajami manuscripts produced in Africa were contributive to the spread of Islam in the continent. This is because it was the dominant means of teaching Islamic texts, including the Quran. Thus, Ajami, which resulted from classical Arabic scripts, emerged among the growing Muslim communities in Africa. What followed was the production of religious works and secular literary pieces that supported communication and learning on different issues that concerned the societies. In Senegal, the Muridiyya Sufi order is reputed to have produced a significant proportion of works in Ajami because of the influence of Shaykh Amadou Bamba.[41]

Furthermore, Bamba provided perspectives that contributed to a nonviolent form of proselytization other than jihad in his country. Bamba was distinguished in his commitment to conflict resolution and the promotion of peace in Senegal and the West African region in general. This is in contrast to other celebrated West African jihadists known for violent resistance against the colonialists and local aristocracies. This category included Usman Dan Fodio, El-Hadj Umar Futiyyu Tall, and Maba Diakhou, among others. Bamba projected, more than anyone else in the region, a nonviolent form of proselytization to deal with political and religious issues. In his *Mafatihu al-jinan wa Maghaliqu al-Jinna* (The keys to paradise and the bolt to the doors of hell), he discussed the ideals of Jihad al-Akbar (Greater Jihad/Jihad of the Soul) otherwise known as jihad al *nafs*. Learning from the tradition of the Prophet Muhammad who elevated the Jihad of the soul as the greatest of all, Bamba did not only write about jihad *al-akbar* but also practiced this form of jihad. His belief in Sufism provided the method for solemn practice of jihad *al-akbar*.

Like Prophet Muhammad, Bamba believed that evil can be destroyed by the good. Intimidated by his rising influence and the possibility of a violent jihad on the French colonialists, the French confronted Bamba, who declared that his jihad was that of knowledge and reverential awe.[42] In *Ya dha'l-Busharati* (O source of Happiness), he asserted that the presence of God is able and enough to protect him from all attacks. And for those who use arms and ammunitions against him, he wrote, "they do so to their dishonor."[43] He was certain that God would help him and "the creatures of the land and sea will follow me and I will be beneficial to them without harming them."[44]

Bamba is renowned for his focus on work ethic, an austere marabout concerned with producing works based on meditation, rituals, labor, and Quranic study; and his followers were known for their productivity. His teachings accentuated the benefits of a life filled with hard work and pacifism and influenced the contemporary life and culture of the people of Senegal. He neither set out to violently confront the French colonialists, nor did he plan to reform his society in a violent way. He is revered as one of the paramount spiritual leaders in Senegal's religious, economic, and political history. In modern day Senegal, and in other parts of the world, the Muridiyya Sufi order is one of four Sufi movements with a significant number of followers. Grounded in traditional Sufi philosophy, Murids yearn for a deeper connection with God and insist that their lives are modeled after the religious life of the Prophet.

Amadou Bamba and Nationalist Activities in Senegal

By the nineteenth century, European colonial activities had overtaken Africa with a colonial administration that was already established in other European-conquered territories. Political and economic activities were reoriented to serve European metropolitan companies to the detriment of Africans. New cultural identities were forged arising from the emergence of new civilizations. Although Islam was established in Senegal centuries earlier, the presence of French colonialists signaled a new era in the remaking, unmaking, and making of a new form of identity and cultural values determined by the foreign powers. The natives saw this as an interference in their norms and values; thus, many decided to resist the attempt to impose the alien French culture on themselves. Many decided to wage jihad on the French as a demonstration of opposition to the new arrangements, while others decided to bow to the superior military power of the French. Resistance struggle erupted and took on different dimensions in Senegal. The battle was set between political Islam and the French Western model of politics.

The relationship between French colonialism and Muridiyya, particularly the encompassing theme of a colonial mega power versus the dominance of Islam in West Africa, can be characterized as a dynamic and difficult relationship. The battle for dominance among the local aristocracy, who seemed to have a grudge toward the Murid leader for garnering so much authority, exacerbated the growing animosity between Shaykh Amadou Bamba and the French. This was because, despite his lack of interest in power and authority, an increasing majority of Senegalese people at the time regarded Bamba as the rightful ruler. Despite his aversion to politics, the French, as well as certain local authorities, labeled Bamba as a religious man with political aspirations and a danger to French interests. According to Diop, "the difference between [Shaikh Ahmadou Bamba] and those who seek this world is comparable to the distance between East and West."[45] His charisma, as well as the popularity of the Muridiyya Sufi order he had just established, were seen as roadblocks to French colonialism in Senegal. The situation became tense because of the continuing movement of local populations who flocked to revere the spiritual leader and to seek his blessings. As his following multiplied, French suspicion intensified, as they feared that the rise of a new spiritual movement could jeopardize their interests in Senegal. Subsequently, Bamba was accused of causing the *Jihād* (holy war), "a tradition which [he] never embraced."[46]

It was not only the French colonial authorities that nurtured feelings of insecurity and threat by the new religious group founded by Bamba but also the local chiefs and colonial agents, according to Glover, who planned and coordinated the libel—allegations of inciting jihad—because they saw the Murids and their leader as a danger to the efficient governance of their area.[47] Babou explains the situation thus:

> Chiefs also protested that their power was undermined by the prestige of Mourid sheikhs, who snubbed them and bragged that they recognized only the French commandants and residents as superior authorities. They asserted that the Murids were trying to create a state within the state, an idea that was later endorsed by the French administration. They also denounced the reluctance of Murids to pay taxes even as they lavishly donated to their sheikhs.[48]

Local chiefs became more fearful of Bamba's influence; the attention of the colonial authorities was drawn toward the Muridiyya and its leadership. Thus, the Murids' activities were placed under surveillance. The Senegalese economy suffered as a result of the Murids' reluctance to pay taxes, while many members of the royal courts that were conquered by French invaders joined Shaykh Amadou Bamba in Jolof and became his followers.[49]

The campaign against Bamba continued unflinchingly until the French arrested him in 1895. Bamba was taken to Saint-Louis where he was tried and exiled to Gabon. He lived in exile for seven years. While in exile, the members of his Sufi order frustrated the economic activities of the French colonialists in their territory especially with their continual refusal to pay taxes. Upon his return from Gabon in 1902, he was exiled again to Mauritania from 1902 to 1907, and subsequently kept under house arrest from 1907 to 1912 in Jolof and 1912 to 1927 in Diourbel. In 1912, the religious leader was released from exile. He was taken to Bawol—his ancestral land—to counteract his growing status as a martyr.

On the contrary, Murids viewed this as a positive development that would provide direction to their growing population. He was kept under strict surveillance in Diourbel, so that he would not move to Touba.[50] His stay in Diourbel was seen by the Murids as an attempt by the French to frustrate the group because Diourbel was a growing city with a great deal of Western culture and influence and undesirable for the Muslim *ummah*. In one of his works, *Matlab ul Fawzayni*, Bamba maintained that while the city may provide happiness, the culture of the city only attracts punishment in the life hereafter.[51] An Islamic city should be shaped by the ideals of Islam and through the piety of Muslims, so that their social and geographical space can promote spiritual and social functions of their faith and their survival as humans. The spiritual and social function of the Murids, according to Babou, are education, prayer, and farming. Bamba was not interested in politics, rather his focus was on the development of the people's mind while also teaching them the path to righteousness. Rather than participate in politics as insinuated by the authorities, Bamba made his intention clear when he wrote to the French Governor General that:

> I am writing to tell you what I have in my heart. I want you to know that I do not want anything from what you look for in this world and that you cannot help me with what I want in the hereafter. You all should know that I have left your world to you and my main objective is the face of the exalted and Great, Allah. Let your soul rest and your eyes gladden and delight to the fact that I am not quarreling with anybody on anything belonging to this world. Rest assured that, whoever comes to you with anything other than what I have just stated, is a liar and do not listen to him. Peace is upon those who follow the path of guidance.[52]

Bamba's persistence in demystifying the fact that he was not ready for any violent confrontation was further reassured as he concentrated on the activities of the divine world he so cherished. In agitation, Bamba was moved to make an appeal to the leader of the French for independence of geographical space that would guarantee his religious activities and shield his followers from the raging cultural hegemony of the French. Thus, Bamba's agitation came from both his opposition toward French colonial political systems as well as his defense of the cultural values of his society that were seriously endangered by French colonialism.

Due to French political and cultural imperialism, in order to promote the renaissance of his people, Bamba embarked on a journey to instill in his disciples, both spiritual and cultural values. His initiatives were to the detriment of the French, who went as far as to require the children of local leaders to go to French schools, which is precisely how the "*Ecole des fils de chefs*" (the school for the children of chiefs) came about. With regard to the Murid disciples, they abstained from the French educational systems by prohibiting their children from attending French schools out of fear of their children being "assimilés" (culturally assimilated by the French). Robinson observes that "Education is a revealing arena because of the emphasis that the French put on their language, culture, and school system, in its metropolitan and imperial dimensions, and the close relationship that they assumed between knowledge and power. The French often said that an 'educated native' could not be 'fanatic,' by which they meant a Muslim hostile to French imperialism."[53]

In the French perspective, colonization of West Africa was associated with a cultural agenda, which was a defining feature of French cultural imperialism. The primary ambition of the French was to culturally assimilate Senegal through the indoctrination of French culture and civilization to the people. Thus, the period in the history of the Muridiyya and colonialism during the house arrests of Bamba was characterized by a pacification process that reconciled a relationship that was once hostile especially between spiritualism (the Muridiyya) and colonialism. The French colonizers minimized their persecution agenda against Bamba and became concerned about the instantaneous development of the Murid order, which was a local socio-religious movement to address the French imperialist invasion of Senegal. Ed Van Hoven notes that French colonial activities transformed the Muridiyya Sufi order which was previously a "loosely organized order into more or less an institutionalized hierarchy of spiritual leaders and adherents."[54] By 1913, the relationship between the French and Murids changed for the better such that the French acknowledged that:

> Our relations with Amadu Bamba have entered a normal path, and the attitude of the Murids has in general been very proper. One can therefore hope that the chiefs of this powerful organization, who are already waiting for the division [of the estate] at the death of Bamba, will not attempt to stray from the economic path in which they certainly make their contribution to the development of the country.[55]

The declaration by the colonial government signaled cordiality, but the usual suspicion against Bamba continued. Bamba was being monitored in Diourbel with the French not fulfilling his request and desire to move to Touba. While this was ongoing, the First World War preparations were simultaneously taking place. The French needed support in terms of human and material resources. The right man for the job to secure the needed support was Bamba, in the eyes of the French administration. Because of his influence, the French government contacted Bamba to publicly declare his support of and loyalty to the French government; thus by 1913, the marabout declared that:

> One of the greatest benefits of the Most High is this magnificent order which presides over the affairs of the earth and which causes everything, hidden and evident, to be subordinated to the great men of the French Government, who have received their mission from God. They have established justice and equity towards the people.[56]

This statement confirms Bamba's commitment and willingness to cooperate with the French government. Additionally, the French realized that they needed soldiers more than they needed traditional chiefs. Bamba had also appeared to be more important with a huge following than the traditional rulers who were earlier opposed to his influence. When the French government made the appeal for soldiers, Bamba supplied 1,400 troops. In return for his service to the French, the colonial administration appointed Bamba to the Consultative Committee on Muslim Affairs in 1916 and offered him the award of the Cross of the Legion of Honor in 1918. The soldiers he supplied to the French on request was appreciated as well as the Murid industriousness in agricultural development, particularly in the production of peanuts.

Additionally, Harrison states that Bamba made a financial gift of 500,000 francs to the French to assist them in coping with currency depreciation; the sum constituted a fifth of the financial contribution made by the whole Senegalese colony.[57] Robinson claims that after he made this financial donation, the colonial authorities granted permission to the Murid leader to construct his mosque in Touba.[58] The distrust between Bamba and the French government had fizzled out—courtesy of Paul Marty's[59] demystification of all the alleged ties between Bamba and Pan-Islamic and Pan-Arabic groups—restoring the hope and confidence that was required to build a more trusting relationship.

Conclusion

Amadou Bamba remains one of the most revered individuals in the history of the state, religion, and the people in Senegal. He is celebrated as a reformer, a teacher, and an ambassador of peace by the Murids and among other Muslim groups in Senegal and Gambia. Bamba was one character who preserved and transmitted the inner traditions of Islam through his teachings on Sufism, "non-violent jihad," peaceful coexistence, knowledge, and work ethic. Bamba's influence on his people's cultural and spiritual renaissance shows the deep relevance of his ideas on long-term peace and concord, as well as the power of Islam's nonviolent traditions. Bamba gathered knowledge from people's previous experiences in order to safeguard his own future. The violent jihads by other Islamic scholars that came before him was a critical moral lesson to evoke a new perspective in the various existing forms of jihad.

Evidently, Bamba and Dan Fodio are practical leadership examples of how African religious/spiritual power translates into political influence and power in their regions. Perhaps, the only contrast between the two is in their interpretation of what method should be used to advance the course of Islam, and particularly what Sufism is about. While Dan Fodio declared war on infidels, Bamba preached peace to achieve what many now regard as the jihad of the mind and soul—inner revolution. Bamba's style and methods, especially in the face of Western/Christian expansionism into his region, nonetheless still got him followers—adherents who followed his teachings and the tenets he preached. Indeed, following his footsteps, they did not raise up arms nor embark on violent campaigns. Even the European colonizers recognized the leadership and political influence of Bamba on the people in the region, which explains and justifies their careful treatment of him. Like Dan Fodio, while he contributed to knowledge production on Islam, he wielded political power just as well and as much as religious power, although in contrasting utilization.

Indeed, Bamba's approach should not be misconceived given the fact that he could have carried out violent jihad against the French because he had the followership that is required; however, Bamba was a committed pacifist Sufi, whose heart was inclined toward seeking inner peace and the knowledge of God. Rather than resort to violence, Bamba took a different path that sought knowledge and wisdom as a necessary precondition for changing the tide. One of the ways this was achieved was through his contribution to the knowledge of jihad *al-nafs* and its elevation among the Muslim community through the production of texts in the form of poetry that defined his quest for knowledge. This would not have been achieved if he had not first accepted the responsibility of becoming a teaching assistant at his father's school which propelled his journey of becoming a teacher of faith.

His categorization of knowledge into two components did not only provide understanding of the existence of the human world but also of the forces that control mankind in the quest for service to the supernatural. He elevated the spiritual world higher and above the physical world. He contended that the *nafs* is one of the greatest enemies of mankind. Thus, it must be suppressed to ensure righteousness to God and to mankind. While the pursuit of spiritualism is essential in Bamba's teaching, he also contended that work is an essential part of human existence. His role in cultivating religious values is also worthwhile. Though the religious value of work does have importance in Islam, in general, Bamba's contribution to the dignity of labor propelled many into work as a religious ideology that must be committed to.

Part Three

Christianity

Missionaries and Knowledge Production about Africa

Introduction

The history of missions in Africa is a huge enterprise that has been a point of discourse and debate in and about the effects, contributions, and implications of its introduction to the African milieu. The impacts of Western missionaries in Africa are myriad in terms of the introduction of Western education, Western medicine, Christianization and expansion of the church, development of some African languages, establishment of the printing press, and a host of other engagements. The history of missionary engagement in Africa has tilted rather precariously toward the contributions of Western missionaries to Africa, while the impacts of Indigenous missionaries toward knowledge production about their continent have resulted in minimal discussion.

The history and success of Christian missions in Africa would be incomplete without the inclusion and discussion of the contributions of African missionaries to the expansion, dissemination, and publication of knowledge about Africa. This chapter will examine the contributions of African missionary writers to knowledge about Africa. In this chapter, missionary writers from Africa will be examined—their works, writings, and activities in areas such as expansion of anthropological, historical, linguistic, and literary knowledge about Africa. The contributions of these African missionaries to knowledge about Africa are extensive, more than a single chapter of a book can adequately discuss. However, the essence of this chapter is to encourage more debate and discussion about the occupations of these African missionaries in African science, religion, history, and other institutions of knowledge.

African missionary writers are clergymen of African descent who have been engaged with mission works in their countries and have been influential in producing works about Africa, thereby increasing scientific knowledge in and about the African continent. The contributions of these African missionary writers are significant in that through their knowledge of the African space, oral tradition, history, customs, traditions, geography, culture, and languages they are in the most favorable positions to expand and contribute to knowledge about Africa. These African missionary writers have enhanced transnational exchange of ideas about Africa and opened the channels of transmission of knowledge into and out of Africa.

African Missionary Writers

While discussing the impact or contributions of African missionary writers to knowledge about Africa, it is imperative to first explore the purview of the identities of these African missionaries. Missions and missionary ventures originate from the auspice of European intervention and engagement with Africa. The activities of European missionaries in Africa are enormous, and though not the focus of this chapter, it is important to discuss briefly the impact of the aforementioned to the works and development of African missionaries in Africa. The notion of mission encompasses the transmission of Christianity through some special people who are sent to other places for the implantation, propagation, and growth of the said faith.

The activities of many of the missions in Africa were not fully successful because of the peculiarities in the African milieu which informed the introduction of repatriated slaves who had been trained in missionary institutions to assist in the propagation of the Christian faith in Africa. For example, Sierra Leone has played a significant role in the education of slaves in mission works who have been saved from slave traders and ships. The significance of this African country to the whole continent in terms of raising and grooming African missionaries and their occupation with mission works in Africa is very crucial to the understanding of the indoctrination of the Indigenous missionaries and their intellectual engagements with their African heritage and interactions with their Western superiors and colleagues.

Because many of the missionary activities were conducted in the foreign languages brought over by colonizers which yielded little to no results, and coupled with several other significant circumstances that impeded their activities, European missionaries in Africa were somewhat unsuccessful at bringing natives to the knowledge of Christianity. The former slaves who had been educated in Sierra Leone in mostly missionary institutions realized the need to retrace their steps back to their places of origin to bring their people to the knowledge of Christianity. One of these slaves is the famous bishop Ajayi Crowther whose story of freedom from Fulani slave traders led to his legacy, as he was instrumental to the production of knowledge about Africa.

Carl Christian Reindorf, Samuel Johnson, James Johnson, Apolo Kivebulaya, A. B. C. Sibthorpe, E. M. Lijadu, Akrofi Clement Anderson, and many others like them have contributed to knowledge about Africa. Their contributions to knowledge about Africa spanned areas such as history, philosophy, anthropology, education, oral tradition, mythology, and theology of African societies. It is important to also note that their education and contact with European legacies, such as Western education, played a very crucial role in their preoccupation with African culture, traditions, philosophy, values, oral tradition, music, art, and crafts. It is also significant to add that the attitudes of the colonialist and European missionaries also informed these African missionaries' decision and preoccupation with Africa and African epistemology. According to Bascom:

> The conversion of Africans to Christianity was, of course, the primary objective of the early missionaries, and African religion was attacked directly and often vigorously as idolatry and superstition. There was often more success in gaining

worshippers than in getting them to abandon the old beliefs and rituals. Many Africans were willing to try the white man's religion who were not yet willing to cut themselves off from the religion of their forefathers, or who wanted to be safe and play it both ways.[1]

One of the African traditions that came under attack by the colonialists and missionaries was the African Traditional Religion. Bascom noted that through a variety of means, the missionaries tried to undermine African religion with varying success. The European missionaries adopted a negative approach where they condemned African religions as evil since the positive approach of showing the virtues Christianity did not prove adequate.[2] Many aspects of African tradition, such as polygamy, ritual, ancestor veneration, sacrifice, and belief systems were heavily criticized and undermined by European missionaries and colonialists in the bid to promote Christianity among African "pagans."

Missionary Activities in Africa and the Indoctrination of Indigenous Missionaries

Missionaries' activities in Africa have resulted in major debates due to their activities being riddled with paradoxes that have either affected the continent or have spurred the African people to rise up to the demands of the past and present, in reshaping their future through the employment of tools and opportunities the missions and colonialism have afforded them. Missionaries, through their activities in Africa, introduced Western education so that they could learn and understand the Christian message being delivered to them. The training of African people was the means used to achieve the goals of the missionaries in Africa.

Due to the paucity of knowledge about African culture, language, and traditions, missionary societies, such as the Church Mission Society (CMS), Basel Mission, London Missionary Society, Baptist Missionary Society, etc. had to devise means to bridge the gap and launch their missionary works upon the African people. These societies engaged the Indigenous people, ex-slaves, and clergies through their education in missionary schools, like the Fourah Bay College in Sierra Leone, to penetrate and make inroads into the African cultural and theological space. The introduction and indoctrination of these Africans made the activities of the Christian missions a huge success. The indoctrination of these Africans into mission works proved to be successful, as it marked the optimum advancement and engagement of Christian missions and occupation of Africa.

African Missionary Writings

Missionary writings by African scholars have received little attention in terms of their contributions to knowledge about Africa. Much of what is known about African missionary writers revolve around Carl Christian Reindorf and Samuel Johnson, and, even so, their contributions to knowledge about Africa are yet to be fully investigated. Theological writings and rhetoric about African knowledge were handled by Europeans who had little knowledge of the subject of their writings, and European theological writings pertaining to Africa revolved around the denial of the diverse aspects of African culture. African missionaries discovered that the way to truly emancipate themselves from the cloak of ignorance and subversion was to genuinely engage with the systems of knowledge in their culture, oral traditions, history, religions, language, and beliefs.

Some of these African missionaries began by translating the Bible and other literary works into their own languages as a way of expounding knowledge into the African knowledge base. Their translation of works soon developed into a medium where African language was utilized in written form to expand and preserve African ideas of knowledge, values, literary, and linguistic creativity. The standardization of these African languages through the publications of grammars, dictionaries, spelling books, etc. enhanced the production of African literatures of different subjects, such as poetry, history, mythology, anthropology, and music.

African missionary writings for the purpose of this chapter will include works by Indigenous clergies on African history, oral literature, African Traditional Religion, mythology, belief systems, language, etc. Works by Indigenous missionaries on/about Africa expounding on African life, theology, cosmology, belief systems, music, arts and crafts etc, are considered African missionary writings. On this premise, this chapter will engage discourses of knowledge production and contribution about Africa by African missionary writers.

The Development of African Historiography

African missionary writers' reconstruction and development of African history through the documentation of oral historical narratives has contributed immensely to knowledge about the continent. Many written accounts of the African continent are systematically riddled with assumptions from Eurocentric writers, who do not possess knowledge or a basic cultural understanding of Africa. These misconceptions have stimulated African missionary writers, like the Ghanaian Carl Christian Reindorf, to document the existence of the huge cultural and historical knowledge inherent in the continent. The production and contribution of knowledge on African historiography started with these early African missionary writers who have used their knowledge of the colonial language and education to record the history of their people.

Historiography is often used to refer to all human efforts to convey and preserve knowledge or recollections of previous experiences, events, circumstances, processes, and expectations in permanent and frequently aesthetic forms.[3] Reindorf's writing engaged the history of the Gold Coast (Ghana) people through the collection of oral data from the older generation who had knowledge of their heritage. According to Hauser-Renner, Reindorf's *History of the Gold Coast and Asante* is representative of a corpus of historical works produced by Western-educated Africans between the 1850s and the 1940s.[4]

Activities of missionaries in Africa are vaster than the scope of this chapter; however, activities of African missionaries can be traced to the freedom and return of ex-slaves from the West. Carl Christian Reindorf, a missionary writer, documented and contributed to knowledge about Africa, specifically Ghana. The contribution was a carefully researched and written history of the Gold Coast and Asante. Reindorf undertook the responsibility of documenting the Ghanaian people's history and their state of politics, which vastly contributed to current knowledge. One of the problems facing the growth of the African continent is the lack of sufficient knowledge of the African past and history which the new generations of African people do not possess but which is crucial in order to reconstruct their future from the past.

Adequate knowledge of their history is pertinent to the restructuring and development of Africa by its people. Reindorf's utilization of oral traditional sources in writing the history of the Ghanaian people is not only commendable but also futuristic, as it keeps the posterity aware of their history and heritage which informs them of where they have been, who their ancestors were, and how events that are replicated from the past will alter the route pursued by later generations. When the history of a people is not documented and passed on to its younger generations, authentic historical knowledge about their predecessors, as well as a national identity that is necessary for nation-building, are at risk of extinction. Hauser-Renner noted that some of these African authors of early written historical works have been "analyzed" and termed amateur historians, of missionary/Christian background, cultural nationalists, and that they wrote history to preserve oral traditions and in view of presenting the African perspective of history vis-a-vis contemporary African historiography written by Europeans.[5]

Safeguarding and protecting the history of the people includes protecting their culture, traditions, customs, values, literature, arts and crafts, etc. This foregrounds that African missionary writers have promoted and contributed to knowledge about Africa especially in the documentation of the people's culture, traditions, and folklore as seen in the writings of Reindorf. Cultural materials such as dances, music, folktales, and oral literary forms are essential parts of the history and heritage of the African people. Embracing the history of the African people will enhance the growth of some of these cultural institutions. However, the arrival of colonialists and missionaries in Africa did not bode well for the future of some of these traditional institutions. Colonists and missionaries began with crusades that dismantled these cultural heritages and institutions, dismissing them as barbaric and evil while simultaneously colonizing the minds of the African people. Hauser adds:

> Reindorf was well aware of the importance of history and cultural expressions, and with his History he made a very early and therefore pioneering contribution to the conservation, preservation and dissemination of the Gold Coast heritage knowing that it is/was part of the people's cultural identity.[6]

Hauser recognizes the contribution of Reindorf's work to knowledge about the history of his people and the preservation of the same. His contributions extend beyond preservation, bringing awareness and spread of African cultural and historical knowledge to the rest of the world. Therefore, his works are still etched on the world's memory because of his production and dissemination of historical knowledge about the Gold Coast. Hauser noted that the contribution of Carl Reindorf is quite a unique project in African historiography, aimed at sensitizing the elite community of the Gold Coast to rise to the task of an authentic national history.[7]

The need for an original national history is very important, as it is the history of all the Indigenous people, and the revival of an original national history will give modern Africans the opportunity to resonate with their ancestors' struggles and achievements. Hauser also opined that according to Reindorf, a national history should embrace the 'histories' of all the peoples of the Gold Coast including the renown and powerful Asante, 'as the histories of both countries [i.e. Asante and the Gold Coast] are so interwoven' and, of course, it included the *Fante* in the western part of the Gold Coast, 'principal and important portion of the Gold Coast.[8]

Reindorf translated oral traditions into writing which, as acknowledged by Hauser, contributed to the knowledge and insights into African culture and history. The significance of this missionary writer in documenting the history of his people as well as their traditions was motivated by his early introduction to history and folktale narrated to him by his grandmother.

> I have had the privilege of being initiated into, and also of possessing a love for, the history of my country. (. . .) My worthy grandmother Okako Asase, as in duty bound to her children and grandchildren, used to relate the traditions of the country to her people when they sat around her in the evenings.[9]

This is one of the methods of education in the preliterate African society, where the elderly serve as the instructors, imparting cultural wisdoms and values through folktales, legends, myths, and proverbs. This process of African education is part of the African historiography that Reindorf has explored, in order to contribute to the knowledge about Africa as a continent with its own system of education, values, culture, and tradition prior to the advent of Western education and values. Heinz writes:

> In 1889 Reindorf perceived the advance of European formal education and Chris-tianity as a very real threat to the traditional transmission of history. Children and teenagers who attended schools missed traditional African education, including historical oral narrations as guidelines for and/or explanation of the present pre-serving the achievements of the ancestors in the memory of the living. Reindorf was well aware that Western education also created a widening gap between the literate Christian and the non-literate and/or non-Christian members of the community.[10]

The documentation of African history from oral narratives and traditions demonstrates the contribution of Reindorf which espouses the rich resources of knowledge in the African milieu and its various cultural institutions. Hauser noted that Reindorf envisaged the devastation of the African heritage, education, and history through the installation of Christianity and Western education. Heinz, in the previously quoted passage, alludes to the African system of education as being replete with historical materials, but because these African children have been removed from this system, the acquisition of knowledge that should have been imparted to them is lost; therefore, their history is fading away in the cacophonies of Western education, colonialism, migration, and the economic scramble. The documentation of the history of the Gold Coast and Asante in Reindorf's *History* was a concerted effort to disseminate informed knowledge about Africa, which has been variously regarded as the "dark continent" and with barbarians who needed to be saved by the colonialists. His book was a means of reeducating both Africans and Europeans about Africa and the multiple bands of knowledge that had been deliberately silenced and ignored.

Culture and traditions of the African people are natural materials of history, and in them history is preserved and disseminated from one generation to another in its most natural state. The minds and brains of the older generation serves as the storehouse for the history of the people which attested to the mental powers and capacities of the African people before the introduction of writing and the printing press. These generations of older Africans committed these oral histories and narratives to memory and, through the many mnemonic devices and retentive memory, were able to recount, chant, and narrate them to the younger generations. The implication of this system of oral transmission of historical facts at that period in African history was already fading and dying with the older generation who do not have knowledge of documentation neither of publishing their history.

Reindorf's contributions counteracted the narrative being circulated by Europeans telling the history of the African people, the latter being a fictitious historiography that molded to the Europeans' perceptions of the African people. Reindorf's publication of the *History of the Gold Coast and Asante* stimulated other Africans to seize the opportunity to tell their story and history, producing knowledge and accurate accounts of their own histories and narratives to the world, thereby highlighting and buttressing the untapped resources of the land. Furthermore, Hauser emphasized that Reindorf's writing was rooted in the notion that national development was hinged on the "nation's history and that historical knowledge facilitated the process of identifying ideas and strategies appropriate for this development."[11] The significance of this history lies in the guidance it provides Africans and the assistance given that causes them to reflect on the nation's progress and to ruminate on past experiences in order to devise ways to improve the nation's output.

Most ethnographic writings about Africa and its people by European missionaries and other colonialists, in the form of migrant stories and travel accounts, neglected the African traditions, history, values, religion, and their importance. Hauser noted the contribution of Reindorf's works to Africa's intellectual vastness in many aspects such as oral literary narratives, customs, and values. Reindorf's work positions African knowledge on display where the rest of the world can perceive the cultural diversity, traditions, and linguistic variations that have earned the continent a major place in the world. Reindorf has combined his training in Western education with Christian values to document the African way of life.

Reindorf was well aware of the differences between oral traditions and written European travel descriptions as expressed in the sub-title of the History "based on traditions and historical facts," and he was one of the first—if not the first—to attempt to reconstruct history by critically using both kinds of sources. Due to the differences between the two sets of sources, Reindorf saw himself confronted by a problem that had no ready-made solution: how to transform and translate oral traditions received by his informants into a form of history that befitted modern times.[12]

As part of his project in writing and publishing the history of the Gold Coast, Reindorf had to contend with the problems of translation and differentiation between oral traditions and the Eurocentric history of Africa. The transposition of the oral tradition into a written account of the history of people's groupings placed his work as a revolutionary effort in reconstructing the image of the African continent. Hauser noted that Reindorf's work as a source of knowledge of Ghana's past and history is still unsurpassed.[13]

Hauser argued that "Reindorf was the first author to present a comprehensive history of the Gã people who had created the powerful state of Great Accra in the precolonial era before the emergence of the major known Akan-speaking states of Akwamu, Denkyera, Akyem, and Asante."[14] Reindorf's significant and commendable contribution to knowledge about the Ghanaian people serves as a testament to the knowledge resident in the continent which its people had to document and disseminate to the world. Such an enterprise marks the beginning of other projects: Of particular interest are initiatives where African missionary writers and scholars undertook reconstructing the prevalent Eurocentric narrative of the African people and ensuring the release of the true version of African history. Jenkins affirmed that in the context of the development of the Gold Coast Euro-African historical studies, Reindorf's *History* of 1895 was a revolutionary departure, in several senses. In spatial terms it was the most comprehensive history of the area which Reindorf had defined and described as the Gold Coast.[15]

The Origin and History of the Yoruba People

One of the notable contributions of African missionary writers to knowledge about Africa is the work of Samuel Johnson on the origin, history, culture, political, and socio-religious aspects of the Yoruba people. The invasion and scramble for Africa among the Europeans was done without much knowledge of the cultural and sociopolitical history of the people. The work of Johnson covers more than a historical account of the Yoruba as enunciated by scholars of anthropology, sociology, linguistics, and history because of the scope and varied branches of knowledge in the book, *History of the Yorubas*. African oral narratives and traditions have been noted as the sources of Johnson's work. The oral traditions are the most common sources of these Indigenous missionaries' writings of their culture, history, literary narratives, socio-religious, and political realities. In Johnson's book, several aspects of knowledge about the African people, especially the Yoruba people, are documented, discussed, and disseminated:

The *History of the Yorubas* consists of a chronologically arranged historical narrative concerning the dynastic history of Oyo from mythological to modern times, and the political and military history of the early nineteenth century. In it, Johnson offers his readers his interpretation of the traditional version (or versions) of Oyo history.[16]

The work of Johnson has undoubtedly been a monumental contribution to knowledge about African history, especially in the case of the Oyo dynasty of the Yoruba in what is the present-day southwestern part of Nigeria. The Oyo history, like many others of the African continent, illuminated the histories of the different kingdoms, empires, dynasties, cities, and how their traditional kings, rulers, and chiefs have been able to rule and govern their people in a unique system of governance prior and during the colonial invasion of Africa. In the case of the history of Oyo, Johnson has rendered the account of the Yoruba people a Western scholarship which remains an epic to date. His work shows that oral traditions can be an important source of African history and their survival the bedrock of modern Yoruba historiography.[17]

Translation as a Tool for Knowledge Expansion of the African Languages

Translating the Yoruba language to the written word was the first contribution of the missionaries to the development of Western education in Western Nigeria. Subsequently, they translated several books of the Bible into Yoruba. A Southern Baptist missionary, Reverend Thomas Jefferson Bowen, produced *Grammar and Dictionary of the Yoruba Language* in 1858. Other missionary groups, such as the Church Missionary Society (CMS) and the Methodists, also produced textbooks, primers, and dictionaries that enabled the missionaries to teach their converts to read the bible in Yoruba.[18]

The missionaries represent the foremost people who used translation as a tool for knowledge production about Africa and its languages. Translation becomes knowledge through the dual transmission of linguistic codes and meanings. Moreover, translation entails the employment of linguistic and semantic skills to reproduce new ideas, concepts, and epistemic writings. African missionaries have contributed an amplitude of knowledge about African languages through the process of translation and transliteration of works into European languages. Although the process of translation began as an alternative way of bringing the Indigenous people closer to Christianity and aiding their comprehension of the Christian values, it soon became a larger preoccupation of penetrating the knowledge in many African languages.

The works of Apolo Kivebulaya and many other African missionaries began as translation of Christian pamphlets, books, hymns, and even the Bible into their respective African languages. Apolo Kivebulaya's translation of prayer books, parts of the Bible, and religious pamphlets to Nyoro reveals that this and many

African languages possess and hold knowledge useful in the communication of ideas whether secular or religious. The translation of biblical writings to African languages by many African missionaries had a dual significance of indigenizing Christianity and production of works in African languages. Their activities proved that Africans are capable of knowledge production and linguistic and literary engagement with European languages. The translation writings and activities of these Indigenous clergies have placed these African languages on the same pedestal as their European counterparts, demonstrating that African languages are also capable of holding and disseminating knowledge.

Bishop Ajayi Crowther is the name of an African missionary; whose name resounds in and outside the African continent for his commendable and revolutionary works and ventures in translating the Bible into African languages. His translation works unlocked the minefield for knowledge about African languages and the dynamic use of these languages to situate knowledge about the cultural dimension of the continent. The use of English and other European languages introduced into Africa by the Europeans have made the African languages ineffective and of inferior relevance in the African milieu. This ineffectiveness and irrelevance were a direct result of the dispositions of European colonialists and missionaries to these Indigenous languages, which was condescending as with other aspects of the continent.

The European languages were given positions of eminence and precedence and, most importantly, were used as a medium of instruction and governance of the activities in the colonies. Walls highlighted Ajayi Crowther's literary journey and career with the publication of *Yoruba Vocabulary*, which included an explanation of grammatical structure, perhaps the first book of its kind by a natural speaker of an African language.[19] The knowledge of the Yoruba language and its grammar was significant in contributing to knowledge about the Yoruba people and their language. This translation work did not only contribute to knowledge about this African language, but it also proves that Africans possessed the mental capacities to learn, read, write, and understand their languages and European ones together. The translation of works from their original African foundations to European languages enabled the current free flow of knowledge from African oral sources to European languages.

As Walls noted, the translation of the Bible into Yoruba was not the first into an African language; nevertheless, since Crowther was the primary influence on its creation, it was the first by a native speaker.[20] Indeed, according to Walls:

> Crowther insisted that the translation should indicate tone—a new departure. In vocabulary and style, he sought to get behind colloquial speech by listening to the elders, by noting significant words that emerged in his discussions with Muslims or specialists in the old religion. Over the years, wherever he was, he noted words, proverbs, forms of speech.[21]

Rather than being simply a literal translation of English into the Yoruba language, the work was a systematic translation that reveals the tonal difference, semantic, structural, and grammatical arrangement in the Yoruba language. This translation involved the phonological, lexical, morphological, and semantic complexities in the Yoruba language. The translation's orthographical connotation and the eventual development of the Yoruba vocabulary through the translation of the Bible into Yoruba added a new depth to the information inherent in this language as well as other African languages. These writings and activities of African missionary writers inspired other writers to write in the Yoruba language which resulted in pieces of literature that expound, promote, and disseminate knowledge about the Yoruba people and their distinct culture. As noted by Akangbe, Crowther had a special interest in languages, as well as a tenacity in developing languages for expansive study by his people and others who may be interested in gaining a deeper understanding of Yoruba culture. Akangbe wrote:

> A prolific writer, translator, and enviable linguist, Crowther published his *Yoruba Vocabulary* and *Journal of an Expedition up the Niger in* 1841 (with J. F. Schon) in 1843, *Journal of an Expedition up the Niger and Tshadda Rivers* in 1855, and *The Gospel on the Banks of the Niger* (with J. C. Taylor) in 1859. Following the British Niger Expeditions of 1854 and 1857, Crowther produced a primer for the Igbo language in 1857, another for the Nupe in 1860, a full grammar and vocabulary of Nupe in 1864. He also published the Yoruba version of the *Anglican Book of Common Prayers*.[22]

Crowther's interest and writings on many African languages comprise a large proportion of the contributions of African missionary writers to knowledge about African languages. With his works on translation, orthography, and grammar, many European writers can access works on African languages and conduct research on the dynamic properties of the African languages. Crowther's works of translation paved the way for dual enterprise and research as Adesola noted that Bishop Ajayi Crowther was the leader in using the Latin alphabet to write Yoruba. Crowther's work in the 1840s, when he labored on the Yoruba Bible and Yoruba grammar, exemplifies his position as a leader in dual enterprise.[23]

Moreover, his dual enterprise and research efforts are reflected in his efforts to codify Yoruba after the Latin alphabet. Additionally, Adesola observed that some of the unique features of the Yoruba language in the Latin alphabet include the use of diacritic marks on vowels and under certain letters.[24] This unique comparison between Latin alphabet and Yoruba shows that similarities and differences can be worked with and researched on simultaneously, thereby producing dual knowledge about the Yoruba language and the Latin alphabet.

The pioneering works of Ajayi Crowther has created works of different dimensions such as the ones noted by Adesola:

> Several foundational Yoruba grammar and history were produced by Ajayi Crowther, J. T. Bowen, Samuel Johnson, Ida Ward, and others. Many literary books were also produced in the language based on the evolving Yoruba orthography. Some of the foremost authors of Yoruba literature include I. B. Thomas who was credited with the first Yoruba novel, *Itan Emi Segilola Eleyinju Ege*, (. . .) Hundreds of Yoruba literature and grammar books have been produced with the Latin alphabet.[25]

The works of these African and European missionary writers have enhanced knowledge about African literary traditions, as well as the facts and ideas that stimulated a diverse range of literary genres. Initially, these literary traditions started with translations of the oral narratives such as folktales, myths, legends, etc. as displayed by the works of early literary writers. At first, literary writings were mostly a product of translation of the oral literature of the African languages into English and documentation of the oral traditions in African languages. However, with the establishment of a Yoruba newspaper, *Iwe Irohin,* which aided the translation of English poems to Yoruba, African leaders and missionaries were encouraged to establish a number of sociocultural organizations charged with the collection, translation, and publication of folkloric materials.[26] For instance

> The Egbe Onife Ile Yoruba, organized periodic lectures on issues relating to history culture. The Egbe Agba-O-Tan actually had a publications committee (with I. B. Akinyele as its general editor) and published works of history and philosophy.[27]

Some of the committee's prominent titles with extensive oral data translated to English are Ajisafe's *History of Abeokuta* (1921) and *The Laws of the Yoruba People* (1924), D. O. Epega's *Ifa* (1908) and *The Mystery of the Yoruba Gods* (1932); E. M. Lijadu's *Ifa* (1897) and *Orunmila* (1907), J. B. O. Losi's *The History of Abeokuta* (1924), and J. Ojo-Cole's *A Collection of Yoruba Thoughts* (1931). The publication of books on African history, culture, customs, and taboos resulted from the direct influence of African missionary writers who have stimulated and encouraged both foreign and Indigenous scholars and researchers to pursue those literary undertakings. African missionary writers influenced the epistemologies of the African milieu through urging and motivating others to write about the African oral traditions and even translate them to other European languages for further engagement with the diverse range of global literature.

African Missionary Writers and West African Cultural Nationalism

African missionary writers have contributed to knowledge about Africa especially around cultural nationalism and national heritage. African nationalism is concerned with the celebration, propagation, and promotion of African values and heritage as a countermeasure to the effects of colonialism that accompanied the arrival of the colonialists. From the perspective of the colonialists, reeducation of the African people was necessary to purge them of their traditional African ways and values. The condemnation of African customs and cultural practices by European colonialists and the enforcement of their cultures and values through education and Christian mission activities impacted the development of African culture negatively. To counteract these negative effects, African missionary writers had to change the African people and Europeans' perception of the African culture.

These African missionary writers, through their writings and actions, embraced African culture and its recognition as one of the means for cultural emancipation from European cultural domination. The teachings, writings, and publication of works in African languages were some of their contributions to knowledge about cultural ideologies carved from their literary activism. The likes of E. K. James Aggrey Mojola Agbebi, E. M. Lijadu, Rev. Moses Ladejo Stone, etc. were the people who defied cultural imperialism through their dogged determination to retain African cultural, linguistic, and ministerial autonomy. Their efforts on nationalism were a pre-figuration of pan-African ideologies, a movement that emanated from European subversion of African culture. Moreover, their writings and efforts were instrumental to the independence and creation of the African churches and missions. Their writings were espousing proto-nationalist ideologies and stimulated liberation from colonial hegemony.

The Contribution to African Languages by Missionary Writers and Linguists

Many African languages that have been reduced to writing were first undertaken by European missionaries who discovered that the transmission of Christianity and its teachings were limited in terms of the reach and accessibility to Africans because of the paucity of materials, especially of the Christian nature in African languages. There they were, the first set of missionaries to pioneer works on African languages; however, their works were concerned with primarily advancing their cause and Christianity, rather than appreciating African languages. The activities of the European colonialists and missionaries indirectly resulted in the stimulation of African missionary writers to embark on the writing, publication, and dissemination of works on African languages.

> As more and more indigenous missionaries were trained to evangelize their own people, emphasis was laid on the literary and linguistic study of African culture. Yoruba language had a significant place in the scale of things around this period. Through the efforts of Samuel Ajayi Crowther, a Yoruba freed slave who was trained at Fourah Bay College, Sierra Leone, and who later became the first African bishop from West Africa, Yoruba was reduced to writing and the Bible was also translated into Yoruba language.[28]

African missionary writers produced works on African languages thereby promoting knowledge about Africa and their linguistic repertoire. Notable among these African missionary writers is Akrofi Clement Anderson, a Ghanaian linguist and translator of the Bible. Anderson created works in the Twi language, which was nurtured from his conviction that effective teaching of the Christian values to the Indigenous people had to be indigenized and situated in the language of the people. This Ghanaian missionary writer is the author of many publications, including Twi Grammar, A Twi Spelling Book, Twi Mmebusem, an annotated collection of 1018 Twi proverbs, and an English-Twi-Ga Dictionary.

The investigation and development of the African linguistic repertoire and proverbs by Anderson stimulated a lot of research to produce works on African proverbs and linguistic tools. These literary, linguistic, and theological works are phenomenal works about the collection of knowledge on African literary traditions and knowledge in the African proverbs. His work opened doors and interests in the development and standardization of the Twi language. According to Ansah, Anderson did study both spoken and written Twi as a researcher. He based his study and final publication on Twi orthography on the works of J. G. Christaller and A. N. Rii.[29] The works of these African missionary writers and linguists were essential for the production of knowledge about African languages and literary outputs. Ansah documents thus:

> He was commissioned by the Christian Council of Ghana to revise the Twi Bible, a job which was jointly undertaken with Rapp. Some major decisions taken by Akrofi and Rapp included the removal of diacritical marks from some letters in the Twi Bible. The revision was guided by the principles documented in the "Twi Spelling Book" yielding a new version of the Twi Bible, devoid of diacritical marks, which was initially opposed by a section of the Christian community. The rules and principles, guiding the writing of Twi (Twi Spelling Book) were however approved by the Education Department of the Gold Coast, now Ministry of Education, Ghana (Asare Opoku 1967; Souvenir Brochure 1974). His research into Twi was recognized at both national and international levels. Subsequently, he was appointed the External Examiner in Twi by the Universities of London and Cambridge for their overseas examinations.[30]

Anderson's work on the orthography of Twi was a progressive attempt at producing works on African languages and standardization of the same. According to Ansah, Anderson's work, particularly the book *Twi Kasa Mmara*, defines Twi's grammatical and stylistic rules, describing how Twi should be spoken and written.[31]

> Yet another feat of C. A. Akrofi is the Twi Spelling Book (Twi Nsem Nkorenkore Kyerewbea) which was authored with E. L. Rapp and published in 1938. This book is principally on orthography, rules governing the writing and spelling of Twi. In this book, words are arranged in alphabetical order where the first letter of the root is used. This work replaced the script adopted for Twi language in 1927, and also that which was revised by Christaller and published in 1933. It is important to note that the authors followed the 1933 edition as far as possible. However, it became necessary for Akrofi and Rapp to revise the two earlier versions: 1927, 1933 to resolve a number of inconsistencies in spelling. Some of the topics the Twi Spelling Book (Twi Nsɛm Nkorɛnkorɛ Kyerɛwbea) treats are rules concerning the division of syllables and writing reduplications and repetitions. In addition, the book presents twenty specimen paradigms of verbs, conjugated in the various tense/aspectual forms, operational in Twi. Upon outlining the rules of spelling, a new edition of the Holy Bible in Twi was done by C.A. Akrofi and Rapp.[32]

While Anderson is distinguished for his contribution in standardizing Twi, his work was motivated by the pioneering contributions of the European missionary writers before him. He revised their works and made them truly African works from his sufficient knowledge of the African language. His and other African missionary writers' contributions to linguistic epistemologies about Africa laid the foundation for other researchers to produce books on the scientific study of African languages. Anderson's writings included the publication of books for teaching in Twi and the translation of the Bible into Twi.

His writings and production of knowledge also explored literary and religious works written in English and literary works in Twi, such as the *Wiase Abasem*. The contributions of Anderson and other African missionaries, such as David Asante, to knowledge about African languages are so numerous in terms of their scope that this chapter will not be able to sufficiently discuss all of them; however, it should still be apparent that their works are engaging and producing knowledge about Africa to date.

African Missionary Writers and Their Works on African Oral Literature

Akrofi's collection of 1,000 proverbs, Twi Mmebusem (Twi Proverbs), was from discussions with elderly men, chiefs, akyeame (the chief's spokespersons) and Twi speakers over a period of years. Twi Mmebusem (Twi Proverbs) is structured as follows: the text of each proverb is given, accompanied by a literal English translation. An explanation of the proverb is given in Twi, and for some, the use or the context in which the proverb may be used is given.[33]

African proverbs, idioms, metaphors, aphorisms, etc. are part of the linguistic and literary sociocultural aspects of the African people that permeates every aspect of their lives. Proverbs are known to be extracts of truth, belief systems, culture, and customs of people, especially in African societies, that are used for various reasons because of their invaluable functions in sociocultural, political, and religious activities of the people. African proverbs result from oral traditions, but they are also sources of African knowledge that are embedded in the African oral literature.

The significance of the collection, writing, and publication of these African proverbs, folklore, legends, myths, and stories is the reproduction of knowledge of the African system of education and literary traditions. Research regarding African proverbs and idiomatic expressions contributes a counternarrative to the Eurocentric notion that Africa does not possess a body of literature whether written or oral. The collection of these Twi proverbs by Akrofi Clement Anderson attests to the literary wealth and treasures of the African continent.

Other notable contributions of African missionary writers to knowledge about Africa are the works of E. M. Lijadu and Mojola Agbebi. A collection of Yoruba riddles and stories on Yoruba wars was published in 1887, and Lijadu put together the works of a nineteenth-century Egba poet, Aribiloso.[34] The collection of these stories was not only a phenomenal enterprise, it was also an attempt at producing African stories; the start of a literary tradition that will enhance research into and about African oral literature. In many African societies, stories, poems, parables, and folklore are a huge part of the children's education regarding their culture, customs, and traditions. The pioneering works of these African missionaries have enabled scholarship into the literary tradition of the African people.

The riddles, folktales, and stories are extracts of African oral literature where African wisdom, culture, and knowledge are dispensed through an educative and entertaining medium. Lijadu's writings and works reflected African consciousness, values, identity, pride, and literature. Okonkwo observed that in addition to racial patriotism, there was a striving—in what used to be considered Lagos—for an African cultural identity. Agbebi established himself as the leader of the Yoruba party which advocated the sponsorship of competitions and scholarships to promote literature in Yoruba.[35] African missionary writers fostered the development of literature in African languages. The productions of literary works on African folklore, proverbs, riddles, poetry, myths, legends etc. are some of the contributions of these African missionaries to knowledge about the African continent.

Furthermore, Lijadu's works on Ifa and Orunmila contributed to knowledge about the Ifa literary corpus. The *ese Ifa* (divination poetry) are instances of the production of epistemological works into the hidden codes in the Ifa divination poetry. The writings of these missionaries have enhanced knowledge acquisition of the different poetry associated with the Yoruba pantheon. The publications of these oral texts have stimulated research and discussions on/about panegyric poetry and its different forms in the ritualistic veneration of the Yoruba Orisa.

Knowledge About African Politics and Leadership

The works of African missionary writers captured the political and military sagas of the African continent, displaying knowledge about African system of governance and military strength.

> To understand nineteenth-century Yoruba historiography, and, by extension also to understand twentieth-century Yoruba historiography, we have to look at the political climate in the region at the time. In the rather confused political and socio-economic circumstances of nineteenth-century Yorubaland two new elites emerged that were to set the scene of colonial Western Nigeria for the remainder of the nineteenth and the beginning of the twentieth century. The old order of Oyo Empire in the north of the country was destroyed and replaced by a number of smaller, rather bellicose states, headed by men who, in general, had no loyalties toward older power structures.[36]

The political and military intrigues of the Yoruba were captured in the historical writings by Indigenous missionary writers. The documentation of the political and military activities of the Yoruba people demonstrated that this set of Africans possessed sufficient knowledge of politics and political systems of governance that was appropriate for them. Doortmont opined that in Yorubaland, as with many other parts of Africa, the past was and is an important legitimizing source for the currently existing political and social order, and such changes in the conception of history gives us an insight into the way in which the Yoruba collectively perceived the social order in which they resided.[37] The political state of affairs and social order of the Yoruba people were documented in Johnson's *History*, giving them a distinct image of how they could govern and be governed by their Indigenous rulers.

> In the period of the Yoruba civil wars, a number of strong military states emerged, led by soldiers without obvious connections with, or loyalties towards the old power structures. New towns like Ibadan under Oluyole, Ijaye under Kurunmi, New Oyo under Atiba, and Abeokuta under Sodeke all started their existence as war camps or refuges in the civil war period.[38]

The historiography of the Yoruba included the civil wars and military camps that seceded from the older power structures. The emergence of these states led by military men and other older states were captured as part of the political and military structures of the Yoruba in the writings of African missionaries, especially those of Johnson. These works contributed to knowledge about the Yoruba military structures and states that were established as military camps by the warlords and soldiers of that time. Additionally, Doortmont opined that due to the needs of the time, older, long-established states militarized.

This is true for the Ijesha in the 1870s, when they were de facto ruled by the *Balogun* (war chief) Ogedemgbe, rather than by the *Oba* (king). The militarization of states was also valid for the ancient and sacred city of Ile-Ife under the Ooni-elect Derin, after its destruction by Modakeke.[39] The record and documentation of these political and military intrigues by these missionary writers of African descent demonstrated the consolidation of political and military powers in the preliterate African society and the development of an African system of government.

The implication of the change in the system of governance from the old power structures to the establishment of new military states in history, captured by these missionary historians, establishes that the Yoruba people possess adequate knowledge of power and political schemes. These African missionary writers explored, wrote about, and published these military power plays and political turns in the Yoruba states through the gathering and collection of oral data and personal experiences. Moreover, Doortmont observed that in the new systems of government, the warlords of Ijaye and Ibadan took up the Old Oyo titles of *Basorun* (prime minister) and *Are-Ona-Kakanfo* (commander-in-chief) respectively, thereby conveniently fitting themselves into and recreating the administrative order of Old Oyo.[40]

The works of African missionary writers illustrated the recreation of a new government from the old order of power structures, thereby establishing that Africans, specifically the Yoruba, possessed military and political knowledge as demonstrated by the ingenious creation of a new system from the old administrative and political power. The development of historical writings from oral traditions, eyewitness accounts, and personal experiences by African missionary writers, such as Samuel Johnson's *History*, contributed to the knowledge and study of civil wars, military strengths, and political machinations and structures of the African people in the preliterate Yoruba societies. Oral traditions about the Yoruba political and military sagas, especially concerning the Oyo Empire, bring to the fore, knowledge buried in African history. These African missionaries have disseminated the knowledge of African politics, systems of government, and military escapades before and during the colonial invasion of the continent.

From the 1840s and 1850s onwards these people developed an interest in their cultural and historical background, especially after 1880, when they were increasingly barred from higher functions in the mission and the colonial government, due to the development of racialist attitudes and the formation of a more colonial system. This put the Western-educated Yoruba in a position of relative deprivation, and to better their position independently of the colonial structures, they were forced to search for alternative modes of development.[41]

Furthermore, Doortmont argues that the output of the Yoruba historiography includes the sociopolitical, religious, and cultural aspects of the Yoruba. He also noted that with these historiographies, Yoruba historians founded a school of Yoruba history that was to influence not only the attitudes of the British government toward the Yoruba hinterland, but also many of the actions of Indigenous Yoruba in their dealings with the British that extended far into the twentieth century.[42] One of the influences of the African missionary writers is the contribution of historical, political, and military history of the Yoruba. These African missionary writers provided exceptional knowledge about their sociopolitical and cultural milieu. Doortmont writes thus:

> Samuel Johnson, CMS missionary, raised in Ibadan in a period of continuous civil war, sent his *History of the Yorubas* into the world with the message that the only way to civilization was through Christianity and British colonial protection. Emmanuel Lijadu, also a CMS missionary, saw more in an independent Yoruba development through Christianity.[43]

These missionaries may have conflicting reasons for undertaking such works, but the underlying significance of their works on the African continent and abroad remains evergreen due to their contribution to epistemologies about Africa. Their works have instigated research into many areas such as Yoruba religions, knowledge of healing properties in herbs and plants, arts and crafts, oral literature, customs, and traditions.

African Mythology and the Contribution of African Missionary Writers

Lijadu, an African missionary, engaged aspects of African mythology in his writings, establishing that African religions have mythological similarities to their Greek counterparts. African missionary writers, such as Euler Ajayi and Emmanuel Moses Lijadu, produced first of their kind works about African mythology, specifically on

African traditional deities such as Ifa, Orunmila, Shango, etc., making comparative discourses about their origin with the Grecian gods. These missionary writers were intentional about the promotion of African mythological knowledge through the exploration of the Yoruba deities.

Doortmont noted that the gods of the Yoruba have an identical counterpart with those of Greek and Roman mythology: "Oya becomes Neptune, Shango is Jupiter, the god of thunder, Ifa is equated with Minerva as the god of intelligence and wisdom, and Ogun becomes Mars, the god of war."[44] The comparison of these African deities with their Greek equivalents is one of the areas of knowledge that has emanated from the writing and dissemination of knowledge about African mythology that these African missionaries have pioneered.

The production of knowledge of the Yoruba pantheon substantiated that Africans and Africa possess their own deities and spirituality, and there are mythological accounts to back them up. The Indigenous missionaries' writings on Ifa as a deity of wisdom contribute to the expansion of knowledge about African culture and theology, which is evident in the increase of vigorous efforts of Indigenous and foreign researchers to study Ifa. African missionary writers' decisions to document the Yoruba pantheon on the same level or space as the highly revered classical mythology of Greece and Rome reveals a degree of boldness and tenacity that is to be admired. These writings and contributions placed Africa on the same epistemological level with the same European countries that have historically reduced the African continent to a land of barbarians who needed the intervention of colonialists.

Furthering his point, Doortmont opined that the work of Euler Ajayi on Yoruba mythology was an instrument of reeducation, where one explains to the "civilized" Yoruba readers in Lagos, the Yoruba pantheon. He equated the important Yoruba gods with equivalents from classical mythology, implying that these appealed more to the imagination of the average Lagosian than the Indigenous deities.[45] Ajayi's work on Yoruba mythology was more on reeducation as well as celebration and promotion of the African mythology than it was to appeal to the imagination of the elite Indigenous people.

The comparison of African deities with Greek deities was, to an exceptionally large and reasonable extent, the promotion of the African mythology, especially the Yoruba version and finding similarities in knowledge about their equivalents in the Greek mythology. The writing and publication of the Yoruba mythology was phenomenal in that it was collected from bards, eyewitnesses, and/or participants in the African Traditional Religion. The works of these African missionaries have contributed immensely to anthropological, literary, archeological, and scientific investigation about the African landscape, mythology, and oral literature.

The comparison of Christ to Yoruba deities and Ifa is a production of knowledge about the African deities. Lijadu's works stimulated epistemological research into the particularities of the Yoruba deity of wisdom. The work of E. M. Lijadu conveys the knowledge in Indigenous traditions and religion that Western education, European missionaries, and colonialists have no interest in. Lijadu is known for the incorporation of African traditional practices in his mission works. Peel noted that the literature and knowledge of Ifa started with works by Yoruba priests such as Revd. James Johnson and Revd. E. M. Lijadu, who were primarily concerned with the theological content of Ifa divination poetry (ese Ifa).[46]

The production of literature on Ifa enunciated the production of knowledge inherent in the African mythologies which have been largely ignored and distorted with the introduction of Western education. The works of these African missionary writers have encouraged African and European researchers to undertake meticulous research into the neglected African mythology. The infinite corpus of Ifa is a testament to the dissemination of African wisdom and philosophy which these African missionaries recognized and painstakingly documented to enhance the study of African theology by Africans. Bishop Johnson pushed for the church to acknowledge and integrate a broader range of African traditions in his 1899 book, *Yoruba Heathendom*. He would, for instance, baptize children with Yoruba names.

> A number of younger pastors and laymen pursued with more deliberation the path which Johnson had opened up. Most notable was Revd. E. M. Lijadu, who came from an early convert family at Abeokuta but made his career in the eastern Lagoon country. Lijadu went to the length of taking formal instruction from a babalawo, "pursuing my investigations in Yoruba theology," as he put it, as well as in native medicine, at considerable personal expense. In his pamphlet Orunmila (1908), Lijadu drew especially on Orunmila's oriki, seeking to show that there was in Yoruba culture—i.e. as expressed in the oral literature of the Ifa cult—a large degree of anticipation of Christian themes. For example, he argues that the true etymology of Orunmila is "Orun li o mo ilaja" or "it is Heaven which knows reconciliation," and relates this to its conceptual background, in terms of the antagonism (ija) between heaven (orun) and earth (aiye).[47]

Peel noted that some African missionaries followed the path of Rev. James Johnson in seeking knowledge into the Yoruba mythology to the extent of receiving education from an Ifa priest; the theological knowledge in Yoruba mythology. This occupation of the African missionary writers with their Indigenous knowledge of the Yoruba deities and pantheon exposes the similarities in the veneration of the Yoruba pantheon and Christianity. Lijadu's investigation into Orunmila's praise poetry and the Ifa Corpus uncovered underlying Christian themes and values. This is enunciated by Peel when he avers that Lijadu's works laid a conceptual framework of the origin of Orunmila in the work of Jesus Christ as the intermediary between heaven and earth.

It is true that a great deal of Yoruba religious action, such as divination, sacrifice, spirit-possession and masquerades, can usefully be seen as attempts to establish life-giving and confirmatory links between orun and aiye. Lijadu's conclusion is that Christ, by his self-sacrifice, is the ultimate means of reconciling heaven and earth. Throughout the pamphlet parallels are noted between Bible texts and quotations from *ese Ifa*. One strand in the modern tradition of Ifa scholarship was in the making.[48]

The works of these African missionary authors have instituted productions of knowledge about the Ifa poetry, ese Ifa, which African and European researchers have worked on to produce an extensive body of works on the Ifa literary corpus. Lijadu's work on Ifa and Orunmila became a pre-figuration and foreshadowing of the development and production of epistemological works and research into Ifa and several other African deities. The exploration of African myths and mythology by African missionary writers is a reflection of the extant knowledge in African Traditional Religion. Further evidence of the surviving African Traditional Religion is provided by Falola who opined that a formidable work comes from David Onadele Epega on Ifa among the Ijebu. Like Lijadu, Epega apprenticed with a Babalawo (diviner) from 1900 to 1904, where he learned about the religion, divination, and charms.[49] Falola believed that D. O. Epega's Ifa was an accepted religion, proof of God's real divine revelation to the Yoruba.[50]

Knowledge Production on African Religion and Philosophy by African Missionary Writers

One of the outstanding contributions of African missionary writers to knowledge about the African continent is the promotion and publication of works about African Traditional Religions. African missionary writers like John S. Mbiti have contributed to knowledge about African Traditional Religion through the publication of the book *African Religions and Philosophy*. Mbiti took the subject of the African religion to an overly broad perspective and length, like his colleagues from other African regions. Mbiti's phenomenal work was a counternarrative to the Eurocentric assumptions of African Traditional Religion where traditional religion was framed as animism, idolatry, and fetishism; however, Eurocentric assumptions resulted from their ignorance and dismissal of the spiritual and ritualistic elements of African religion.

Mbiti's work engaged the existence of the Supreme God in the African Traditional Religion which also established the belief in a personal god by the African people. The veneration of the Supreme God in the ATR hinges on the presence and intermediating energies of the divinities that are called by different names in different African societies. Mbiti's work situates the universality of the Supreme God in African belief systems, cosmology, and philosophy emphasizing that African Traditional Religion to the Indigenous people is foregrounded on the ontological phenomenon of existing within and for religious reasons. The African people are a religious group of individuals whose worldview revolves around religious/ritualistic activities.

The African cosmology, thought systems, and cultures existed on the harmony of all the systems. African religion integrated with other aspects of African society. The theological enterprise of Mbiti and other African missionaries has contributed immensely to the theological knowledge and discoveries about African Traditional Religion and its relationship with Christianity. Mbaya and Cezula opined that it is apparent that Mbiti's work has made considerable impact. His work made had made considerable impact. It made some people raise issues or questions regarding the relationship between Christianity and African culture and religions, which hitherto had either been taken for granted, or had never seriously been thought through.[51] Through Mbiti's intensive academic study, ATR became an area where people sought to enquire more, to engage more seriously and authentically with the issues ATR raised.

Mbaya and Cezula opined that Mbiti's methodological approach was one of the phenomenal contributions of his work to knowledge about ATR and Africa as a whole. Mbiti's methodology drawn from his work, *African Religions and Philosophy*, is the result of the integration of African philosophy and religions; the appraisal and exploration of African religion is the acquisition of knowledge about the African people. To acquire knowledge about the African people, Mbiti considered it imperative to examine their religions and philosophies.

African Missionary Writers and African Music, Songs, and Rhythm

One of the entertaining aspects of African culture is the creation of songs, dance, and rhythm which are incorporated into different segments of African society. Songs, dances, rhymes, and rhythm are native to the African people and highly desirable. Music and song comprise a major role in the sociocultural, religious, and political features of many African societies. There are songs for many occasions, festivals, and events with their attendant secular, religious, political, and social functions. There are songs that are related to trades which may be spontaneous creations stimulated by sounds emanating from the beating of their work tools or songs composed to mitigate work stress.

The introduction of hymns which followed the European musical rhythm and style by missionaries undermined the appreciation of African musical style and even curtailed the promotion and usage of African music until the pioneering efforts of Amu Ephraim Kwaku, a Ghanaian preacher, teacher, and ethnomusicologist who sought to promote the African, specifically Ghanaian, culture, songs, rhythm, and musical instruments among his students. Ebeli espoused Kwaku's contributions to knowledge about African music, composition, and musical instruments.

> One of the reasons Amu is regarded as the father of Ghanaian Art music is that he was the first Ghanaian to build African music by writing the Western type of harmony with African rhythm, a technique completely unknown before his time. This transcended choral music compositions to atenteben music as demonstrated in his piece titled Pipes and drums for atenteben I and II with percussion accompaniment, Miato agblema in C for odurogya and atenteben I and II and many others. Amu's pioneering efforts in laying a foundation of how African rhythmic motifs should be organized was demonstrated in his works.[52]

Through Amu's pioneering work as a missionary in Ghana, he raised awareness on the excellence of African musical instruments such as the traditional drums. Kwaku's work spanned across research areas in African music from stressing the importance of the drums to the bold assertion that African musical forms should be integrated into the church. Even though his work was confronted with so much antagonism from his European missionary superiors, he was not dissuaded from his work and continued to espouse the significance of African music and musical instruments. Apart from

Amu's monumental achievements as a composer of choral works, Ebeli asserted that he delved into new areas and spent over thirty years researching Ghanaian musical instruments and all musical genres, constantly seeking to improve them in light of the musical knowledge he obtained both home and abroad.[53]

The legacy and contribution of Amu is celebrated in Ghana as a testament to the knowledge of African music, rhythm, and musical instruments, such as the incorporation and promotion of African drums and songs into the church. His work enhanced Africans' awareness of African types of musical instruments, rhythm, and music. The determination to break away from the hold of Western music to concentrating on African styles of music had enabled many researchers to produce works on the different musical instruments in Africa and to further encourage the development of these aspects of African culture.

Moreover, Koschorke observed that Mojola Agbebi asserted that the use of Anglican hymn books was not essential for the proclamation of the gospel.

It was recorded of the early disciples that after the celebration of the Last Supper "they sang a hymn," yet it should be remembered that neither the harmonium, nor the organ, nor the piano was known to them. Our dundun and Batakoto, our Gese and Kerikiri, our Fajakis, and Sambas would serve admirable purposes of joy and praise if properly directed and wisely brought into play.[54]

The engagement of these African missionaries with African music, rhythm, and musical instruments were attempts at producing intellectual occupation and development of African music.

Additionally, Ludwig asserts that Mojola Agbebi concluded his sermon with the following words: "in the carrying out of the function of singing, therefore, let us always remember that we are Africans, and that we ought to sing African songs, and that in African style and fashion."[55] The composition and writing of African hymns and songs by these missionaries with African rhythm and instruments are an example of their contributions to knowledge about African music and composition.

African Missionary Writers and the Preoccupation with African Culture and Civilization

Many of the African missionaries had been educated both in European languages and culture thereby promoting European sensibilities and culture to the detriment of the African civilization and identity. Western attire, food, names, culture, etc., through colonialism and Christianity, have negatively impacted African people's perception of their culture such as dismissive attitudes toward Indigenous missionaries and people appropriating African attire and clothes. This negative consequence was not counteracted until African missionaries engaged with the African culture and its sensibilities to reroute the narrative to the promotion of African culture. Many African missionaries encountered antagonism because of their choice to appear in African attire.

However, the attitude of the European missionaries toward African identity and culture showed the paucity and deficit on knowledge about African identity which are expressed through African names, clothing, food, etc. Many African missionaries are baptized and given European names which showed cultural disconnection, alienation, and in this case, psychological detachment from their identity as Africans. Europeanization acts as a psychological attack and colonization of the African mind and heritage. However, many African missionary writers like Mojola Agbebi, formerly known as David Brown Vincent, changed their names to decolonize their minds and reclaim their identity as Africans:

> In Nigeria, a leader in the Southern Baptist mission, David Brown Vincent (1860–1917), took to wearing only Yoruba clothes, founded a school with no foreign support, and in 1888 seceded from the Southern Baptists to form the Native Baptist Church in Lagos, the first indigenous church in West Africa. In 1894 he reverted to his original name, Mojola Agbebi. Similarly, another Yoruba, E. M. Lijadu (1862–1926), refused to be insulted by an Anglican agent, funded his "Self-Supporting Evangelist Band" (1900) through trade, and wrote two books in which he tried to articulate Christian theology with indigenous knowledge, arguing that the Yoruba deity, Orunmila, was a pre-figuration of Jesus.[56]

The writings of Agbebi, Akrofi, and many others were targeted at reclaiming their identity as Africans, exhibited through the changing of their European names to African ones, wearing African attire like the kente, eating African foods, using African methods of farming, etc. African missionaries decided to act in a way that upheld and promoted African culture and civilization, which ultimately resulted in the accumulation of more knowledge about African arts, craft, attires, names, beauty, and sensibilities.

Their actions encouraged African independence, dignity, and identity which would later metamorphose into works on cultural nationalism by the African people. African missionaries' efforts and works began to exude cultural ideologies about the necessity to embrace the totality of the African identity which are expressed through their names, traditional attires, music, dance, art, crafts, etc. The writings and activities of these African missionaries may not have been fully developed into modern ideologies but have shown signs of intellectual engagement with cultural ideologies about Africa. These missionary writers produced knowledge about national consciousness and emancipation through cultural engagement.

Production of Knowledge on African Cosmology

Throughout the continent, African missionaries have produced works on African cosmology. According to Olupona, Indigenous authors, particularly the Reverend Gentlemen of the Church Missionary Society, replied to these early writings by claiming the Egyptian origins of Yoruba religion and pursuing study into the Ifa divination system as a *preparatio evangelica*.[57] African cosmology encompasses

African knowledge systems, belief systems, the structure of the society, and the metaphysical interactions of humans and their environment. The production of knowledge about African practices, worldviews, origins, and structure of the African societies were observed, researched, and recorded by these African missionaries as a way of expanding knowledge about them and correcting misconceptions about these practices that have been propagated and upheld by European missionaries' negative attitudes and assumptions about African practices.

The structure of African belief systems, organization of society by traditional rulers and kings, administration of justice, education and the different social institutions, cults, and groups that act as stabilizers of these societies are observed and recorded by African missionaries. Some of the belief systems about reincarnation, spirit possession, and life after death are recorded by African missionaries. Venerable J. Olumide Lucas, a renowned Egyptologist and an intellectual among the Anglican clergy in his day, was the first Yoruba native to write about religion among the Yoruba people. His work, *Religion of the Yorubas* is a significant contribution to Yoruba religious studies. He stated that the Yoruba religion originated in ancient Egypt, which he considered as the hub of World Civilization after rigorous investigation and exploration. The cosmological connection of the Yoruba religion with ancient Egyptian civilization attested to the production of knowledge into the African cosmology and belief systems. Olupona believes that the value of Lucas' work lies less in the language affinity he established between the ancient Egyptian religion and Yoruba society and more in the subsequent use of his work.[58] Lucas' work may not have contributed much to knowledge at the time of its publication; however, it has aroused research and works on the establishment of Egyptian civilization with African connection.

The encounter with some African beliefs such as the belief in reincarnation, death, and sacrifices were handled by these African missionaries who discovered that some African beliefs had connection in many ways with the Christian themes of resurrection, death, and the sacrifice of Christ. The Ifa divination system is a product of the African knowledge systems that the Indigenous people believe in which guide many of their cultural and ritualistic activities. Ifa divination and poetry (ese Ifa) are employed by diviners to provide solutions to different problems in society because Ifa is the deity of wisdom, who according to Yoruba cosmology was present at the time of creation.

These African missionaries were the first set of Africans to engage polemically with diviners' knowledge about these belief systems. Olupona noted that following Lijadu's lead, "Rev. David Epega published his own book *Ifa Amona Awon Baba Wa, Jesu Kristi Amona Wa* (literally, Ifa our forefathers' Savior God and Jesus Christ our Savior)."[59] This work showed how the Indigenous people relied on Ifa as their guide like the Christians look up to Christ as their spiritual leader. Ifa becomes a spiritual and literary text for the Indigenous people through the efforts of these African missionary writers' quest for knowledge about the African cosmology.

The work of E. B. Idowu, *Olodumare: God in Yoruba Belief*, is proof of the impact of African missionary writers and production of knowledge about African cosmology gathered from oral poetry, myths, proverbs, and folklore. The work dwells on the essentiality of the metaphysical presence of Olodumare, the Yoruba High God, and is encapsulated in the veneration of the Yoruba Orisha. The Yoruba worldview perceives that Olodumare is spread across the different Yoruba beliefs and practices, such as the veneration of the Yoruba pantheon. *Olodumare: God in Yoruba Belief* engaged the Yoruba belief of reincarnation and life after death. The Yoruba worldview did not only acknowledge the presence of the Supreme Being in the Yoruba belief system but also the transience of human life on earth and the existence of an after-life, where all souls must come to rest.

The cosmological structure of the Yoruba substantiates the sovereignty of Olodumare as the Supreme Being who serves as the creator and maker of heaven and earth, with the assistance of the divinities, the Orisas, who act as intermediaries between Olodumare and humans. The work of Idowu engaged the cosmological structure of the Yoruba divinities and has argued the Yoruba pantheon are intermediaries just like saints in the Christian theological teachings. The engagement of African missionary writers with production and contribution of knowledge about African cosmology is enormous and may be too vast for the scope of this work to adequately explore; however, from the discussions above, it is evident that Indigenous missionaries have contributed a great deal to knowledge about African cosmology.

Additionally, Idowu emphasizes the notion of Orisa (divinities) who inhabit the living world and to whom daily sacrifices are made. They are, in his perspective, manifestations of the Supreme Being, God.[60] Idowu concludes that the Yoruba traditional religion is best captured as diffused monotheism instead of the many popular notions of polytheism. Diffused monotheism suggests that there is a uniform belief in a single creator, the Yoruba High God, but varied means of veneration through the Orisa ministers. According to Olupona:

> *Ese Ifa* is the most detailed form of Yoruba religious texts. It has been described as the storehouse of information about Yoruba mythology and cosmology. For one thing, research into *Ifa* texts has provided a possible alternative view to the theological works produced by the Ibadan School.[61]

The Ifa Corpus engages the Yoruba myths of creation and the organization of the Yoruba divinities.

Conclusion

This chapter is about the contributions of African missionary writers to knowledge about Africa. The contributions of these Indigenous clergies span the fields of history, archeology, anthropology, mythology, etc. These missionaries engaged both European and African discourses to produce books on African Traditional Religion and its interaction with other religions, especially Islam and Christianity. Their contributions to epistemological research about Africa were stimulated by the desire to engage their continent and explore its hidden epistemological treasures. This chapter has discussed African missionaries' activities where they engaged with knowledge of African belief systems and practices which have been attacked by the European colonialists and missionaries as barbaric and evil. Their writings have shown modern and intellectual methodologies espousing scientific ideologies about their language, mythology, culture, and tradition. African missionaries, such as Reindorf, Samuel Johnson, Mojola Agbebi, A. B. C. Sibthorpe, Bishop Samuel Ajayi Crowther, James Johnson, etc. have contributed immensely to knowledge about Africa and its people.

It is important to note, however, that the study of African Indigenous missionaries is not limited or confined to their contribution to knowledge production and exportation, but also in how their knowledge at that time translated into power and influence over people, especially adherents of the then newly introduced Christianity, which was just penetrating Africa. The influence of these missionaries manifested in several ways especially as they served in considerably religious and administrative positions owing to their relative high level of literacy. Beyond serving in administrative roles, they were the first/immediate link between the Europeans and Africans, especially serving as interpreters. With their capabilities, chiefly from the learnings derived from the Christian religion and interactions with Western practitioners, they were able to influence the early politics in the era of colonialism.

The works of these African missionary writers have and are still producing scientific research and knowledge even after their deaths. Their writings have constructed a solid foundation for many current researchers to critically engage and explore modern ideologies and concepts, such as cultural nationalism, cultural and literary theories, ideas, and concepts which have emanated from engagement with traditional knowledge. The activities and writings of these African missionaries have established interdisciplinary scholarship through their preoccupations with various fields of knowledge including Greco-Roman mythology, Egyptian cosmology and civilization, Western literary traditions, etc. They have combined intertextual knowledge of African theology, oral tradition, mythology, philosophical, art and craft, music, etc. with Western language, education, theology, musical, literary, and scientific knowledge to contribute to interdisciplinary research and publications into many aspects of world knowledge. This chapter has investigated some aspects of knowledge that have been produced by African missionary writers but is nowhere near an exhaustive documentation of the contributions of these Indigenous clergies. This chapter seeks to encourage exploration and investigation of the contributions of African missionary writers to other fields of African knowledge such as psychology, medicine, agriculture, economy, trade, and commerce.

Pentecostalism

Philosophies and Practices

Introduction

The word "Pentecostal" is primarily used to discuss a pneumatic Christian faith, doctrine, and church. As a movement, Pentecostalism differs from other Christian movements for its emphasis on spirit baptism and cultivating a direct relationship with the Holy Spirit that is usually expressed through "glossolalia" or speaking in tongues.[1] It exists in Africa as continuities and discontinuities from Roman Catholic and Protestant mission churches that brought orthodox Western traditions, also shaped by African independent churches that have spread various denominations across the globe. Politics, culture, race, and other factors have contributed to the global development of these denominations.[2]

As a word and as a movement, Pentecostal is derived from the biblical narration of the experience of Pentecost.[3] Kgatle describes it with the following excerpt:

> Pentecostalism has other characteristics such as faith healing, spirited music, certain theologies, and a particular kind of piety, but in tongues is the movement's most distinctive feature . . . The essence of Pentecostalism is the baptism of the Holy Spirit and the gifts of the spirit, especially the gift of speaking in tongues as the initial evidence of baptism in the Holy Spirit . . . In addition the Pentecostal movement refers to that radical expression of Christianity which emphasizes ecstatic speech in an unknown tongue as proof of the presence of the Holy Spirit.[4]

Scholars, theologians, historians, and others attribute the Pentecostalism movement to the Azusa revival in Los Angeles, led by Charles F. Parham and Joseph Seymour.[5] Others have disagreed. Scholars such as Olufunke Adeboye challenge the assumption that Pentecostalism originated in the United States, questioning whether a single catalyst is responsible for a global trend in Christian religiosity. Adeboye notes that Pentecostalism in Africa was encouraged by several indigenous factors, including "indigenous prophet figures" whose uncommon spirituality led to their immediate expulsion from their respective mission churches.[6]

Allan Heaton Anderson describes different religious revivals occurring in various regions around the world, at different periods during the late nineteenth and early twentieth centuries. These revivals include experiential confirmations of the gifts of the spirits, including healing, prophecy, tongues, and other miraculous signs that are globally ascribed to Pentecostalism today. It implies that there were conscious efforts from Christians in different regions, in various local contexts apart from the Azusa revival, to experience a more spiritually inclined religiosity and the power of the Holy Spirit. Although Adeboye finds obvious Western influences in what is considered African Pentecostalism today, scholars should engage in more regional historical exploration to explain the rise of Pentecostalism in ways that do not rely solely on the broad generalization of Pentecostalism's inception at the Azusa revival.

African independent churches emerged prior to the advent of Pentecostalism, developed as a nationalist reaction to the doctrines of missionary Christianity. These churches were on a mission to Africanize Christian faith for the continent by breaking the Western monopoly on worship patterns and symbols.[7] This Africanization was part of the changes experienced by Christianity in Africa at the end of the missionary era, in the mid-1950s, when the leadership and policies of African churches were left in the hands of Africans.[8] The African independent churches derived from traditional Christian practices while remaining conscious of the worldview held by African Traditional Religions. Pentecostal churches are quite similar to African independent churches, but they tend to focus on personal salvation and place a different emphasis on the Holy Spirit.[9]

The African continent's extreme religiosity cannot be overemphasized. Ogbu states that "Africa is currently boiling with much religious ferment and has, indeed, become a 'great theological laboratory,' dealing with issues literally of life and death, of deformation and reformation, of fossilization and revival."[10] Prior to the incursion of Islam and Christian missionaries, Africa had been firmly rooted in celestial and mystical explorations. The current religious interactions and expressions within the continent are not far removed. They are a representation of belief in the existence of supernatural and extraterrestrial forces controlling humanity's fate; the people link their constant search for identity and power with appeals to the powers that are believed to be. This belief is at the heart of African cultural and religious beliefs, accounting for the endless worship, appeasements, and sacrifices.

According to Johnson et al., Africa had the world's biggest Christian population in 2018, with an estimated 600 million Christians, compared to about 597 million in Latin America and 550 million in Europe.[11] Within these Christian groups, Pentecostal churches are the fastest-growing churches currently on the continent.[12] How has the Pentecostal doctrine woven itself into the fabric of Africa's religious landscape and its sociopolitical affairs? To address this question and its implications, as well as Pentecostalism's role in shaping postcolonial Africa, this study will examine the relationship between Pentecostal philosophies and the African worldview. It will explore the convergent and divergent aspects of this religious phenomenon and African cultures and belief systems, identifying the relevance of Pentecostalism's philosophies for contemporary Africa. It will also contemplate whether the knowledge and the thought system derived from these philosophies should be incorporated into the African educational system.

History, Texture, and Growth of African Pentecostalism

Western historiography of the global Pentecostal phenomenon traces it to the 1906 Azusa revival in Los Angeles that was championed by William J. Seymour, suggesting that African Pentecostalism is a Western import. But many African theologians and scholars have debunked this notion, establishing that Pentecostalism in Africa developed from the continent's cultural, linguistic, and ethnic ecology. The phenomenon was subject to Western influence—Christianity itself is a Western import.

The advancement of Pentecostalism in several regions of the world was enabled by indigenous influences that had no affiliation with the Azusa revival. Asamoah-Gyadu summarizes the situation by stating: "The intercultural view of Pentecostal history rejects conventional interpretations that consider what happened in the course of western Christendom as universally normative for Christian history."[13] Scholars emphasize the ambivalent, pluralistic nature of the Pentecostal movement that manifested into diverse Pentecostal doctrines and churches around the world.

Mayrargue has noted that Christian missionaries began evangelical movements in Africa dating back to the 1910s, but the Pentecostal renewal in Africa was evident in the 1970s and 1980s in countries that already had functional, dominant Christian movements.[14] This was an obvious reinvention of Pentecostalism in Africa, separate from the Azusa revival, which began in English-speaking countries such as Kenya in East Africa, Nigeria in the West, and South Africa. The movement progressed more slowly into parts of French-speaking West Africa and Central Africa in the 1990s.[15] The Islamic predominance in some parts of Africa meant that the movement did not have free rein in countries like Senegal; anchors for Pentecostal development were established in other parts of the continent. Even its development within countries was often disproportionate—the dissemination of Pentecostal movements has been uneven, with churches flourishing in urban regions that have a predominance of rich and youthful citizens.

Pentecostal churches with messages of prosperity became the heart of missions in various African countries. Youths and rich individuals had advantages that allowed them to afford a more open-minded approach to religion, comprising the majority of members in these Pentecostal churches. However, Pentecostalism has gradually spread to rural areas and more interior parts of various countries. Mayrargue notes that cities serving as anchors for the continent's Pentecostalism movement are often overcome by its aggressive religiosity. Nearly all city structures have been transformed into churches and other houses of worship, including "old hangars, abandoned cinemas, and so on . . . [while] stadiums, conference halls, crossroads and squares, wasteland— are periodically taken over for evangelical crusades, deliverance sessions, special programs, and so on."[16]

Despite the aggressive proliferation of Christianity in some parts of Africa, many parts of Europe and the global North are experiencing the opposite. Asamoah-Gyadu has noted that while Africa is progressively becoming more Christianized, the Western countries that originally spread Christianity's message are gradually losing interest. He posits:

The current renewal of African Christianity stands in sharp contrast to the state of European Christendom where, as Forrester writes, Christianity has been marginalized through the forces of "secularism, atheism, and materialism." At a time when chapel buildings in many parts of Western Europe are being painlessly converted into pubs, club houses, restaurants, warehouses, cinema halls, museum monuments, residential facilities, and in other instances Buddhist and Hindu temples, these same secular facilities are being refurbished and transformed for the use of churches in sub-Saharan Africa.[17]

African Pentecostalism and its expressions are no longer confined to the continent; their evangelical mission has led back into parts of Europe and the global North. Most of the fastest-growing churches in these parts of the world were established by immigrants and settlers from Sub-Saharan Africa, which reinforces the idea that Pentecostalism in Africa could be the global future of Christianity.

Kalu considers Pentecostalism in Africa to be a "unique character" acquired by Christian religion through its contact with Africa[18] and a product of the "seismic transformations" experienced by Christianity in the hands of Africans. Asamoah-Gyadu describes it as "represent[ing] the changing face of African Christianity and therefore of Christian mission on the continent."[19] Pentecostalism's growth and development on the continent has occurred in three different stages: the classical Pentecostalism that was the first wave of Pentecostalism to hit Africa, the charismatic movement that was the second wave, and finally the charismatic renewal movements.[20]

The concept of Pentecostalism is expressed through churches and Christian groups emphasizing the Holy Spirit's embrace, proven through speaking in tongues. The practice of tongues is considered to be a physical manifestation of the transformative experience that is salvation in Christ. Pentecostalism promotes beliefs in the spirit, prophecy and healing. Pentecostalism's vibrant form of spirituality engenders creative rituals and ethics based on the proselytization of the gospel and a desire for the growth and continued welfare of its adherents.

Pentecostal ministries and African independent churches remain aware of the spiritual ecology in African communities. This perception of spirituality may have eluded mission churches, which explains their less aggressive approach toward spiritual warfare.[21] Modern day Pentecostals in Africa not only recognize the spiritual temper of the continent, but they also embrace its aura; their notion of and belief in spiritual warfare is connected to their perception of the African view of the world. Anderson argues that the growth of Pentecostalism on the continent is justified: "Pentecostalism's emphasis on 'freedom in the Spirit' renders it inherently flexible in different religious, cultural, and social contexts and makes the adaptation of its central ideas easier in Africa."[22]

Africa's specific expressions of Pentecostal spirituality involve energetic and emotional worship sessions that entertain the audience, especially in comparison to the dogmatic religious traditions of Catholic and orthodox Christianity.[23] The effusive quality of Pentecostal worship complements the expressive African culture, accounting for its public appeal. Electronic instruments, combined with African free modes of worship, such as dancing and clapping, have also improved the experience of worship. The flexibility of Pentecostalism allows many Pentecostal preachers to play multiple roles. MacArthur explains that their work as "comedians, storytellers, therapists, showmen" sustains and increases the size of their audience.[24] This can also explain the number of Pentecostal churches on the continent, which has grown in comparison to orthodox mission churches.

Specialized worship and music practices are an integral part of Pentecostal expression; they have become crucial tools and strategies for the growth and sustenance of Pentecostalism around the world. Worship sessions—particularly in Pentecostal mega churches in Africa—effusively mix personal performativity with learned and embodied practices that inform the singer's expression of self and the Pentecostal experience. Nel states that "It is not unusual to find emotional reactions as a part of Pentecostal worship experiences, whether in the communion or privately, where believers laugh and cry, dance and wait in stillness, weep in remorse or joy."[25]

Contemporary Pentecostal musical experiences are enriched by technological advancements, facilitating individual experiences with the presence of God. These specialized musical experiences often mirror similar Pentecostal experiences from the global North; African Pentecostal promises to link their born-again members with global circuits[26] setting them apart from orthodox Christian groups. The worship practices and Euro/American/African mix of musical culture offer an attractive novelty for their predominantly youthful, elitist members.

Mashau opines that the adoption of "spontaneity and dynamism" by continental Pentecostal churches is one of the leading tools for the movement's expansion and growth in Africa.[27] These factors appeal to the predominantly youthful African population, and the incorporation of "contemporary music and dance" has further energized younger members.[28] Abraham emphasizes music's integrality to Pentecostalism, writing:

> Music is a key medium through which Pentecostalism has grown; Pentecostal worship music circulates in physical and digital formats through formal and informal networks, laying down the cultural and theological infrastructure for new churches and new individual experiences.[29]

It can be argued that Pentecostalism has gained doctrinal prominence in Christendom, and Abraham explains that the movement seems to be "laying down cultural and theological infrastructure for new churches"[30] in sites that include former mission churches. In other words, there is an ongoing Pentecostalization of African Christianity. Anderson writes:

> Christianity is fully an African religion today, the largest religion on the continent. But what is often not appreciated in the bare statistics is that there is not only a remarkable demographic growth in Christian Africa, but also a change in the character and orientation of these Christians. African Christianity as a whole— Roman Catholic, Anglican, Protestant, and independent—has moved considerably in a Pentecostal/charismatic direction.

Anderson explains that the departure of worshipers from the Christian sects listed above has led to a Pentecostalization of their doctrines. Asamoah-Gyadu states that the expansion and growth of Pentecostal churches on the continent, and the constant defection of members from other Christian churches to Pentecostal congregations, has driven other religious services to follow the Pentecostal example. Some members of mission churches created cell and unit renewal groups, hoping to offer the spiritual attractions of Pentecostalism within their own houses of worship. These efforts were attempts to stop the gradual departure of worshipers from mission churches who left for Pentecostal churches.[31]

The departure of church members can occur in two ways: one is a complete, unrepentant move away from mission churches to Pentecostal churches. The second method begins with what Asamoah-Gyadu refers to as "plural belonging," or the process of maintaining ties with mission churches while attending Pentecostal churches for the fulfillment of spiritual needs. Ryan discusses how Catholic churches in regions of West Africa devised a partial answer to the problem of migration from mission theology to Pentecostalism:

> . . . Ghanaian Catholicism with a partial answer to the problems posed by neo-Protestant Pentecostalism. Too few priests have recognised the importance of that answer and have tried to ignore or even relegate that answer to an insignificant corner. Catholic Charismatic renewal-fully Catholic and fully Charismatic-can and does offer Catholics all that might otherwise attract them away from the humdrum Masses and devotional exercises to the religiously attractive realm of neo-Protestant Pentecostalism.[32]

Through the integration of Pentecostal practices and the shift in theological emphasis for mission/orthodox churches, Pentecostal churches have indirectly informed the theological and cultural infrastructure of African Christianity.

Philosophies and Features of African Pentecostalism

Pentecostalism as a concept and movement is a global phenomenon, regardless of its plural and localized expressions; it is not restricted to the continent. These pluralistic expressions share a number of related philosophies and ideologies—in this context, the phrase "Pentecostal philosophies" is used to describe philosophical thought emanating from Christian engagements or commitments, influenced by a Pentecostal worldview.[33]

As a field of study, philosophy is tied to critical inquiry and rationality. It involves a systematic cross-examination of worldviews and belief systems.[34] Pentecostal philosophies are the products of critically cross-examining various Christian belief systems, and this critical inquiry proffers guiding principles and epistemologies that inform the practice of Pentecostalism on the continent and around the world. Pentecostalism, as an ideology and a movement does not encourage an "arid, rationalistic, formalistic, unemotional, non-experiential and non-charismatic approach to religious life."[35] It does not necessarily separate experience from reasoning, which sets the tone for an exploration of Pentecostalism and the identification of its philosophies. These guiding principles are implicit belief systems that instruct Pentecostal behavior and practices.

Pentecostals, irrespective of geography, believe in a radical openness and closeness to God. This form of Pentecostal spirituality informs several religious practices, showing their readiness for the diverse new approaches of God that comprise the lived religious experiences of Pentecostals.[36]

The foundation of Pentecostal spirituality, locally and globally, is often considered to be the emphasis on the baptism of the Holy Spirit and the direct personal relationship with God. Scholars like Nel have examined this notion of a direct personal relationship and found it to have made room for subjective interpretations of the gospel based on the revelatory abilities of the Holy Spirit. Nel also claims that these revelatory capacities have been superimposed on biblical injunctions, and eventually, practices that are not measured against the Bible.[37] In more explicit terms, MacArthur writes:

> The charismatic movement has supplanted doctrine with experience. Psychology has elevated "felt" needs over *real* needs and behavioral theory over revealed truth. All this has accelerated the move away from doctrine and focused the pulpit message on everything *but* the objective truth of Scripture. Preachers have become comedians, storytellers, therapists, showmen, and entertainers rather than powerful envoys of divine truth.[38]

Diara and Onah corroborate MacArthur's observation, examining the entertainment value of worship sessions and measuring the extensive performance of the self that is found among Pentecostal choristers. The outpouring of self is in line with the "feeling" and closeness to the Holy Spirit described in Pentecostal messages—it is an expression of their radical openness to the will of God. This extensive expression of emotional worship embodies the meaning and concept of spirituality, which is the act, manner, and attitude of a religious community.[39] These attitudes and acts emanate from the internalization of practices, principles, and beliefs specific to a particular religious community.

The prominent concept of "as the spirit leads" in African Pentecostalism is a perception of the Holy Spirit's free rein manifested through glossolalia, emotionalism, and spontaneity.[40] According to Nel, within the Pentecostals, "the Spirit endows and guides the believer and the community as a whole."[41] It guides the interpretation of the scriptures, which is often attributed to insight derived from the nearness of God. MacArthur speculates that among Pentecostals, the Holy Spirit is elevated above the Bible, which means that Pentecostals believe in the revelatory capacities of the spirit outside the provisions of the Bible.[42] Although MacArthur's opinions have been described as generalizations, Nel recognizes that they contain some fragments of truth.

The gospel of prosperity is a characteristic message of Pentecostalism in Africa and the world. This is accompanied by a preference for global networks, which can be inferred from various names associated with Pentecostal missions in the country—words like "global" or "international" in organizations such as "Streams of Joy International" and "Living Word Global Ministries." Mayrargue notes that the theology of prosperity in Africa can be traced to ideologies developed by American variants of Pentecostalism.[43]

The gospel of prosperity in African Pentecostalism clearly appeals to the economically challenged and the wealthy in Africa, encouraging a thirst for wealth that is interpreted as a sign of God's blessings and presence in a person's life. For Pentecostalism's adherents, prosperity and wealth are an indication of God's love for humanity. This is the reason for the doctrinal emphasis on tithing, where a person ceremonially surrenders ten percent of their income to the church, which is believed to be followed by messages of abundance that emanate from their act. This "givers never lack" ideology is derived from Christ's injunction to "give and it shall be given unto you."[44] The ostentatious lifestyle of African preachers is seen as a display of this ideology that validates their wealth and prosperity. Mayrargue engages this phenomenon in Africa extensively, analyzing the origin and infiltration of the prosperity gospel in Africa:

> Prosperity theology was formed in the United States in the 70s. According to this ideology, personal success, especially financial and material success, is valued. Individual success is encouraged and legitimised because it is seen as the result of divine blessings. Richness is a sign that one has been chosen by God. Such a discourse works both for impoverished populations and for social elites, who find justification for their behaviour. The ideology also legitimises the ostentatious comportment of pastors and external signs of wealth. The dictum that the more one gives (money to one's Church) the more one gets (from God) acts as an important levy on worshippers. Tithes (followers are supposed to give 10% of their income to the church), collections after services and offerings given in thanks for help are all sources of church income. Even if more precise observation tempers the relative success of these payments, a few religious entrepreneurs manage to accumulate vast amounts.[45]

The belief and practice of miracles and healing is another core characteristic of African Pentecostalism; these acts are considered to be a manifestation of God's love. According to Diara and Onah, the practice of miracle-working and healing is one of the strongest components of Pentecostal spirituality in Africa.[46] These acts may be the biggest attraction for Pentecostalism's African audience, accounting for the growing membership of Pentecostal churches in Africa. The preaching of miracles and healing has been and remains attractive to the average African because it addresses common fears that include poverty, unemployment, and poor medical service or restricted access to existing care. Anderson examines how these continental struggles have indirectly heightened the clamor for miracles in the Pentecostal Christian faith:

> Poverty is probably the single greatest challenge facing Africa today. Unemployment is growing as the continent's economy is unable to keep up with population growth, and access to essential services is unequally distributed . . . higher education is still out of the reach of most Africans, especially for women. The percentage of primary school age children in education has declined since

the 1980s, because Africa, with the highest proportion in the world of children in large, impoverished families, struggles to keep pace with creating adequate educational provisions for these children . . . Disease is a major problem for the poor, as infectious diseases and poor nutrition affect children in particular, and safe water and health services are inaccessible to a large proportion of Africa's people.[47]

The current economic temper of Africa, its history of colonialism, and the continent's resulting debt and dependence on other nations of the world brings some perspective to the Pentecostal ferment on the continent. The overwhelming, disillusioning reality of life in postcolonial Africa can drive people to seek refuge in the arms of supernatural authorities—when physical authorities have failed in their responsibilities to care for their citizens. A religion appearing to offer health in the absence of good medical care, happiness in the presence of palpable poverty, and security in the face of rampant insecurity will doubtlessly sound like good news for the continent. Most of the continent's challenges are attributed to spiritual causes, which means that Pentecostalism complements the region's supernatural and fantastic worldview, which makes little distinction between the physical and the supernatural. The movement has flourished on the continent for many reasons, not just because of depressed socioeconomic and political environments.

The Pentecostalism movement has offered a religious promise of respite from overwhelming socioeconomic hardship, which has expanded its membership. Aggressive advertisements publicize miracle sessions and testimonies through various media used creatively and extensively. Various cultural backgrounds have been innovatively combined to form a hub of traditionalism, modernity, and globalism. They have adopted new strategies that afford inclusive services, such as Bible study; cell group meetings, fasting, and prayer; organized retreats; magazines and newsletters; door-to-door evangelism; stickers displayed on cars; and billboards.[48] These efforts have led to the tremendous growth and expansion of Pentecostalism on the continent, which is seen in the large-scale conversion of warehouse spaces and schools into churches.

The concept of miracles and healing is common in Pentecostal theology, implying a flexibility of epistemology where God freely intervenes in human affairs—God can suspend the natural order of the universe for the sake of humanity, and the knowledge of God is free to all who seek it. This flexibility allows God's intervention to heal all illnesses. This belief might not be derived from previous experience or evidence, but is instead supported by an understanding of God's capacity to heal.[49]

This view encourages a philosophy of vibrant expectation for divine intervention, especially in very difficult or seemingly impossible situations. The worldview is derived from the gospel of salvation and liberation in Christ Jesus; the liberation from sin and its repercussions usually includes remedies for sickness, disease, and even poverty. The practice of miracle working is informed by the life and ministry of Jesus, who performed good deeds, healed the sick, and raised the dead. The gift of healing is also included in the ministry of the spirit, perceived to be part of the packages and endowments of the Holy Spirit.

The coming of the Kingdom of God and the end of times, which is commonly referred to as eschatology, is a core tenet of Pentecostalism. The apocalyptic worldview of the Pentecostal mission explains its notions and attitudes toward the expected end of time for humanity. Nel writes that "the faith, worldview, experience and practice of Pentecostals are thoroughly eschatological."[50] The entire Pentecostal theology and system of doctrines is woven around a consciousness of death, the apocalypse, the second coming of Christ, and final judgment.

Although the outpouring of the Holy Spirit is often considered the foundation of Pentecostal spirituality, Smith finds the eschatology signaling the end of time to be equally important—primarily because the outpouring of the spirit is believed to be proof of the last days approaching.[51] The significance of the outpouring of the spirit is tied to the advancement of the last days, and without the last days there would be no outpouring of the spirit. Althouse explains this ideology by stating that "The ability to speak in tongues was thought to empower the recipient to proclaim the 'glorious fulfillment' of Jesus' imminent coming to establish his kingdom."[52]

There is an inherent transformative epistemology in this eschatological view; the coming of Christ will bring transformative change on earth. There is also the expectation of Jesus' one-thousand-year reign on earth, where justice and fairness will prevail, which supports Pentecostal claims that the church and Christians in general will reawaken to the consciousness of an imminent apocalypse and coming of Christ. These beliefs are implied in the various cognomens adopted by African Pentecostal missions. Lands opines that the spirituality of Pentecostalism is a founded in an "apocalyptic vision,"[53] and Khathide identifies the rapture of the saints at the time of the second coming of Christ as a core ideology and teaching of the Pentecostal movement.[54] Through their messages and doctrines, Pentecostal organizations have positioned themselves as revivalist churches that hold the task of reawakening society to the reality of the biblically promised end of times while also equipping humanity for its inevitability.

Althouse corroborates the transformative epistemology derived from the Pentecostal idea of the end times, stating that contemporary Pentecostalism legitimizes discourse on society and societal justice.[55] Given the general reputation of spirituality and "otherworldliness" associated with Pentecostals, it is surprising that the Pentecostal philosophy is invested in improving the welfare of the marginalized and advancing social and political justice during their time on earth. However, it is inferred from their vision of the present world's replacement—instability and financial disequilibrium will give way to an equitable and just society during the millennial reign of Jesus Christ on earth.

The millennial refers to the period when Christ shall personally reign over the earth. This reign is described in Rev. 20:4, "As they lived and reigned with Christ a thousand years" and it can only materialize once the church has ended—this is the rapture, given that the church began with the Pentecost. This further emphasizes the relationship between the message of Pentecost and eschatology in the Pentecostal mission.[56] The millennial reign of Christ will maintain a society of justice and peace, with an equitable distribution of wealth:

There will be no piling up of wealth. The Son of God shall mete out to every man his portion. Conditions today are tragic. Men are starving to death for lack of food, while others are accumulating masses of wealth which they cannot possibly use. Some today are worth billions of dollars, while countless others cannot find employment. Jesus is going to solve that problem! It is not going to be solved by Socialism or Communism, but by the Son of God Himself! Someone once asked, "What is the difference between Communism and Christianity?" And the answer was this: "Communism says, 'All you have is mine'; while Christianity says, 'All I have is yours.'" And that is true, too; and when Christ rules, there will be justice for all.[57]

Visions of social justice and empowerment for the marginalized are endemic to the Pentecostal mission, which Smith traces not just to the notion of the millennial reign of Christ but also to the concept of the fishermen on the day of Pentecost.[58] The idea of Peter and other disciples, who were mere fishermen, receiving the gift of the Holy Spirit and speaking in different languages is similar to the circumstances of the Azusa revival, where a marginalized African American man led the groundbreaking Pentecostalism movement. They display the revolutionary capacity of the spirit and its ability to subvert normalcy, which can enable the subversion of the powerful by the weak.[59] That is why the subject of social justice is ingrained in the Pentecostal mission.

Indigenous African Religious Views and Pentecostalism

Africa's cultural and religious (dis)continuities must be unraveled to understand Pentecostalism's relationship to African belief systems. Anderson states that "Pentecostalism draws from . . . ancient sources in continuity with them, while also simultaneously confronting them in discontinuity."[60] Paradoxes in African Pentecostalism validate and reinforce claims of continuities and discontinuities with Indigenous cultural and religious praxes and belief systems in the movement. Pentecostalism in Africa makes a show of rejecting the religious practices of its African host communities—it thrives on its war against spiritual forces that are believed to interfere in the affairs of the people. This confrontational attitude toward existing religious rituals and practices shows that the movement accepts and believes in the existence of spiritual forces. It has accepted local ontologies and indirectly aids the furtherance of such worldviews and cultures.[61] Smith asserts that Pentecostalists possess an enchanted worldview, seeing spirits of good and evil constantly interact with humanity.[62]

Anderson has identified distinctive characteristics of Pentecostalism that set the movement apart from other Christian movements, which include "the practices of spiritual gifts like healing, exorcism, prophecy, and speaking in tongues or glossolalia—practices found in Pentecostalism throughout the world."[63] These practices share similarities with some pre-Christian religions in Africa. Prophecy, exorcism, healing, and even speaking in tongues are not novel to African societies, and most of the core features of pre-Christian religious practices have continued in contemporary Pentecostalism.

Africa had been pulsating with a religious and spiritual consciousness since before the incursion of Christianity. There was a clear belief in strong connections between the world of the physical and the spiritual within the African cultural space. Many cultures of Sub-Saharan Africa recognized the existence of spiritual powers and their capacity to influence human affairs; there was almost no distinction between natural and spiritual causes of various disasters that befell humanity. Most disasters and misfortunes were attributed to spiritual causes, as reactions to the universe's misalignment and man's inability to appease spiritual forces.

Ashforth has noted that the endemic reasons behind the absence of a healthy dichotomy between natural and spiritual can be found in the obvious sense of safety that is found in interactions between human and spiritual forces. It champions the idea that a person's situation can be influenced and guided by spiritual forces.[64] The predominant belief is that a supreme God's relationship with humanity is facilitated by smaller gods, spirits, and other divinities in a hierarchy. It also recognizes antagonism from evil forces, which can be mitigated by a superior power's intervention. Belief in these metaphysical entities and supernatural forces influence the people's existential decisions and outlook toward life. Mbiti describes the African worldview in relation to the spiritual world:

> The spiritual universe is united with the physical, and that these two intermingle and dovetail into each other so much that it is not easy, or even necessary, at times to draw the distinction or separate them.[65]

The intricate interaction between physical and spiritual in the African worldview is no surprise for scholars like Anderson, Ogbu Kalu, and Olufunke Adeboye, who draw a connection between traditional religious praxes and the current Pentecostal frenzy.[66]

Although Pentecostalism trumpets its mission to abolish the spiritual practices that characterized pre-Christian religions in Africa—they consider such practices to be incompatible with their faith—they are ironically preserving them. Anderson considers the two religious forms to be in dialogue with one another,[67] while Kalu describes their entanglement as "a correlation of two entities thought to be independent."[68] These interactions are illustrated by reports of African Pentecostalism seen in ethnographic research on Pentecostal and African cultural religions in South Africa. Although Anderson's findings were collected from Pentecostal and cultural religious practices in South Africa, secondary research that relies on publications from various scholars in different parts of the continent corroborate these findings, making the observations admissible for almost all of Sub-Saharan Africa.

The idea of angry, hateful spirits intervening in earthly affairs to torment humans is a dominant belief in African religions across the continent. There is an idea that unseen spiritual forces can affect the physical world, and this spiritual impact usually manifests through hexes, curses, witchcraft, and other spirits that people must protect against. Although Pentecostalism shares a similar worldview, it offers protection through its emphasis on the potency and effectiveness of the Holy Spirit.

Pentecostalism believes that the Holy Spirit's power can provide the luxury of deliverance, not only from the wasteful life of sin, but also from the attacks of evil spirits, demons, spiritual possession, poverty, and diseases. Through the Holy Spirit, Christians are believed to have been given power and dominion over these spirits. This ideology of spiritual warfare and the concept of supernatural forces influencing life on earth are predominant Pentecostal beliefs. Their weapons are verses of Scripture that offer protection from enemies and healing from diseases by proclaiming the name of Jesus—the belief is that the name of Jesus is more powerful than any other force. Pentecostalism and African Traditional Religions alike acknowledge the presence of witchcraft, demons, and other spiritual forces.[69] Where traditional practices would require ritual cleansing or animal sacrifice, Pentecostals believe in the power of prayer and God's superiority over all other forces. This is expressed through the fervency of prayers supported by glossolalia.

Existing aspects of African traditional belief systems were emphasized by Christian religious practices, which continue to address the realities of African religious beliefs. The language of power and evil is common to both religious forms. Kalu explores the similitude of these evil powers in the Jewish literature that undoubtedly informed Christianity. In his opinion, African Christians did not manufacture the idea of spirits and demons, but neither are they completely derived from the African worldview. "These demons abound in Jewish literature as defecting angels; they sired giants who were drowned in the flood, their spirits live on as demons, evil spirits or 'powers of Mastema.'"[70]

Covenants are also understood and acknowledged in Pentecostalism and African Traditional Religions. However, Pentecostal belief systems hold that there is a place for godly Christian covenants, while indigenous covenants are considered ungodly. Visions and dreams are as much a part of African religious practices as they are part of Pentecostalism. Others abound in moral values and lifestyles. The purist commandments and behavioral injunctions espoused in the book of Leviticus make the Old Testament a relatable book for African Christians.

One might expect that ancestor worship, which is a strong aspect of traditional African religious practices, would be omitted from African Pentecostalism. Traditionally, ancestors are thought to protect and guard various African communities. They led moral, dignified lives that did not provoke physical manifestations of divine displeasure, meaning that they did not die under suspicious circumstances. They have earned the privilege of being venerated as ancestors, granting them the power to guide and protect their families on earth.[71] Africans aspire to attain the status of ancestors, which indicates that their lives have been well spent. Living descendants are obligated to remember and revere their dead, which can be expressed in the performance of ritual activities, burial ceremonies, and even "covenanted obligations with the spirits woven by the dead person."[72] These ongoing relationships could be a deciding factor in the ancestors' decisions to intervene on behalf of their families on earth.

The existence of such ancestors is acknowledged in the beliefs and practices of African Pentecostals, and the ancestors' role as an active influence on humanity's fate is not denied. However, Pentecostalism rejects the idea that ancestors are neutral entities capable of either empathy or wrath. Some Pentecostals have demonized the concept of ancestorhood in Africa, and Anderson's research has found that most Pentecostals believe that ancestors are demons who should have no interaction with Christians:

Ancestors do appear to Christians, but their response as believers is usually to reject any visitation. The ancestors, they believe, are not really ancestors, but demon spirits impersonating them that need to be confronted and exorcised—for they only lead to further misery and bondage. They have no power over Christians, because Christians have the greater power of the Holy Spirit within them to overcome all Satan's power . . . Both Pentecostals and Zionists said that ancestors were really demons and that they did not believe in their power at all.[73]

Some participants in Anderson's research were clearly indifferent to the role of ancestors in their lives, which has a lot to do with the replacements that Pentecostalism seems to offer for the roles played by ancestors in the lives of pre-Christian Africans. Programs such as "prophetic therapy" seem to be providing the guidance and protection that was formerly sought from ancestors.[74] The supremacy of Jesus Christ is emphasized by Pentecostal missions, which justifies their role in providing protection and guidance.

Anderson's Pentecostal respondents revealed differing ideologies regarding the belief in African ancestors. Their beliefs are often supported by the Bible and elements of Pentecostalism, including the visionary capacity of dreams where God might use a deceased family member to reveal hidden truths. These kinds of beliefs are often demonized in Christian settings; various expressions of pre-Christian religions in Africa, which include ancestor worship, have been translated into symbols of evil that demonstrate the types of dark powers that should be shunned and rebuked. However, these beliefs have persisted even through the brutal battle of Christianity, and Pentecostalism continues to foster them unintentionally.

Among Pentecostalism and African religions, time is conceived in two contrasting patterns. In the old African religious context, the cyclical pattern of time moves life from birth through death, returning through birth in a process of reincarnation. It is commonly believed that the living, by fulfilling all their burial obligations, can assist the dead in travelling through the world of the spirit to return through reincarnation.[75] In contrast, Christian religions conceive of linear time as a continuum. In Kalu's opinion, the African worldview is informed by their concept of cyclical time, and the Christian conception of linear time has affected the African imagination.[76] Religion plays a huge role in shaping a people's view of the world.

Regardless of the varying conceptions of time, Christianity and traditional African religions are consistent in their conceptualization of space, which Kalu refers to as the "three-dimensional space structure" ideology.[77] The Bible describes the existence of a heaven, which is believed to be the abode of the supreme God even within African religions, and an earth consisting of land and water that is home to spiritual forces seen and unseen. The earth below is frequently considered as the ancestral world and the devil's dwelling. This shared perspective informs the belief that spiritual actions often determine physical outcomes, or as in Hebrews 11:3b, "things which are seen are made of things which are not seen."[78]

Christianity spiritualizes human existence and the world just as much as traditional African religions, viewing it as spiritually dangerous and insecure. Both groups are keenly aware of the existence of evil forces—to Christians, they are the principalities and powers that cause spiritual harm. The conception of witchcraft is almost equally established for both groups. Ashforth defines witchcraft as "the capacity to cause harm or accumulate wealth by illegitimate occult means."[79] Both religions accept the idea that evil persons can possess spiritual powers, derived from occult methods, which are capable of harming family members, friends, and others.

In contemporary Africa, Pentecostal groups and traditional African religions have spiritualized the struggle of modernity by sustaining a fervent spiritual temper. Biological ailments that can be explained through science are instead attributed to witchcraft and bad luck. Incompetent or corrupt government officials are assumed to be possessed, and economic setbacks or political upheaval are attributed to spiritual causes. Witchcraft is suspected to cause diseases that range from superficial sickness to debilitating medical conditions. These views dispel the expectation that modernity's expansion would banish most forms of religiosity. Ashforth expounds on this idea:

> Illness and health were not interpreted simply as products of biological processes, but rather as outcomes of decisions by, or struggles among, spiritual entities responsible for preserving the good in human life and those agencies—human and spiritual—seeking the destruction of the individual his family, and community.[80]

Pentecostalism and the African School System

Expressions of Pentecostal epistemologies and thought systems can be identified in various aspects of society, such as schools and workplaces, including Pentecostalist secondary and tertiary schools. Pentecostal knowledge systems can positively affect and influence African school systems. How can the knowledge and thought systems derived from Pentecostalism be introduced into the African school system?

The practice and ideology of personal testimony, considered to be at the heart of Pentecostalism, could be useful for the African education system. Demonstrative, passionate expressions are often externalized through worship and personal testimony. The predisposition to narrative that is found in the Pentecostal practice of testimony can be applied to non-religious learning. The benefits of narrative can be maximized by teachers and students to ameliorate the drudgery of complex subjects.

Pentecostalism also emphasizes the personal nature of God's relationship with people and the personal nature of spiritual growth. This principle can be applied to the teacher-student relationship. With this perspective, teachers can recognize the individual nature of human education, exercising patience to suit the pace of learning for each student while also adapting their teaching methods to suit individual needs.

Hittenberger has identified the Pentecostal philosophy of expectation from God as a driving force for youth educators.[81] This philosophy is derived from optimism and belief in God's constant intervention to resolve seemingly difficult and impossible challenges for humans. It is contextualized for the challenge of dealing with difficult, unyielding students that are often considered lost to the rest of the world. Educators and school systems that remain true to this philosophy are expected to deal with students patiently, refusing to abandon them just as God will not abandon them, believing that divine intervention will address any serious concerns. There is also a conception of the ethical relationship between teacher and learner—the relationship is meant to be derived from consciousness of a shared love of God and based on mutual respect.

The thoughts and principles of social justice found in Pentecostalism can be applied to education in Africa. The search for justice and equity, as professed in the Pentecostal mission, can be introduced to the educational system and the curricula, incorporating subjects that expose the evils of injustice, discrimination, and oppression. Educators can strive to eliminate all forms of discrimination and partiality among the students and in their administrative duties. The inculcation of such principles and knowledge systems will ensure that students will not be treated unfairly based on economic, religious, ethnic, or racial backgrounds, and they will not receive special treatment due to family connections. In applying these principles, educational systems will curtail or eradicate the prevalence of bribery and corruption that is common in educational institutions across Africa. It would also address the issues of sexual harassment in tertiary institutions across the continent and prevent the misappropriation of funds intended for educational institutions.

An understanding of God's love for humanity, which manifests in the various miracles and healing that is foundational to the Pentecostal movement, can positively influence educational systems across the continent. Pentecostals try to model their lives after the will of God, which means that they are also expected to value human life. In the context of educational systems, they are supposed to be actively involved in the educational process, taking their teaching responsibilities as seriously as God takes the affairs of humanity, which also applies to the administration and governing boards of these institutions: the educational interests of the students should come first. As Christians, their responsibilities go beyond teaching a secular curriculum. They are expected to model the Christian lifestyle for children while inculcating moral values and proper behavior through their interactions.

To conclude, it is important to assert that the religious practices of Pentecostalism not only generate huge followership or engender adherents and a belief system. Indeed, Pentecostalism also influences a new way of life for Africans who believe the religion is the true way to God. This chapter examines Pentecostalism, similar to the way it elucidated Divination, Shamanism, and Sufism in other chapters. The belief in them means the spiritual leaders interpret and preach these practices, the doctrine of Pentecostalism, which was not a predominant practice until recent years and influences the belief, practices, and actions of African Christians who embrace the doctrine.

Further, Pentecostalism enabled the wielding of considerable influence on not just converts, but also on African Traditional Religion (ATR). Indeed, Pentecostalism is one of the major catalysts for ATR's decline and dwindling patronage as it disagrees with many of ATR's practices and activities, which are considered ungodly. Particularly, Pentecostal active proselytism ensures a considerable power shift, which continues till today, from the traditional African religious setting to African modeling of Western-introduced modern religious practices and settings.

African Spiritual Churches

Introduction

The expansion of European domination beyond the shores of their geographical reach involved a very comprehensive plan for which the spread of Christianity is a strategic mechanism.[1] Valid questions are raised concerning the necessity of introducing religion as the instrument of penetration into the cultural traditions and fabrics of their potential subjects, chief of whom are Africans. Their overtaking of the continent is absolute, leaving the ground for the interrogation of their employed strategy. This is because without the introduction of a religious tool, having such a level of penetration into their worldview could probably have achieved no success. Europeans are left to consider this possibility carefully, for the potential rejection of their spirituality would possibly be a direct assault on their imagined intelligence and a great impediment to their imperialist expansionist goals and agenda. This, therefore, explains the reason for the employment of the religious approach and the irrevocable commitment to making it effective. In essence, the effectiveness of this method is largely determined by the extent of ruthless campaigns against existing spiritual structures so that the nascent religious identity would have a soft landing and a solid foundation from which to elucidate the African epistemological perception. It is important to note that African spirituality, knowledge systems, and ontological reality are intricately linked.[2]

The mission to educate Africans begins with the denaturalization and disarticulation of their indigenous educational and spiritual structures. Their embrace of a different structure would depend on their conviction that their indigenous cultures, handed down from one generation to another, are incapable of supporting their mission for modernization and civilization and unsuitable for guaranteeing quality intellection. The same thing happens to their spirituality. For Africans to accept a foreign religion, seeing their indigenous spirituality as evil became necessary and important to the actualization of the European expansionist agenda. In essence, the native religious systems were dressed down, ridiculed, blackmailed, and badmouthed so that Christianity, the European religion, would infiltrate the people and begin the exploitations in the different manifestations in which it would eventually occur. As such, for the first generation of Africans who were baptized into Christianity during slavery, there was a process of spiritual detachment from their indigenous backgrounds, but this would not last long.

Immediately after realizing that the new faith, even when it had successfully displaced indigenous spiritual mechanisms, was inherently incapable of, or maybe inadequate to, replace the seriously tainted African spirituality—perhaps because the ties between the people and the spirituality was not something that could be severed physically—some Africans began to nurse the ambition to Africanize the religion. The sudden feeling of hollowness, disconcertion, and want and the desire for reconciliation with their old self compelled them to begin searching for spiritual rediscovery so that they would not be completely dispossessed of their cultural and religious inheritance as that might erode all their existential essence. Apparently, the reunification that the people were seeking could no more manifest in the usual uncontaminated religious forms, for they have not only been detached from the systems through long-term abandonment, but they have also lost their sense of originality. In other words, what was left for them to cling on to was the debris of the ancient indigenous structures, mostly made available by individuals who were inseparably protective of their ancient religion and its values. However, it appears that these Africans were determined, and to show that they were on their search for their displaced spiritual treasures, they recreated them in the churches, hence the African Indigenous Churches (AIC).

African Spiritual Churches in Context: Motivations and Aspirations

Central to the objectives of African Indigenous Churches is the emancipation of Africans from the shackles of colonialism to which the missionaries had ineluctably turned. Contrary to the teachings of solidarity and tolerance that were domiciled in the Bible, the missionaries demonstrated very extreme attitudes of rejection that complicated the possibility of integrating them as members of the same spiritual identity. More insidiously, the evangelization of the missionaries, preaching oneness in Christ and therefore compelling potential Africans to convert or identify with the religion, did not extend to racial tolerance, sending a very strong signal to the African Christians.[3] While white missionaries provided academic opportunities for the Black missionaries, it was revealed that the education of these Blacks was not designed specifically for their all-round transformation so that they could be at the same level as the European missionaries. Instead, their education was restricted to serving an adjunct position to the white crusaders. It stands to reason that the acquisition of colonial education was aimed at using the converts as agents of Christianization or evangelization. Even when they were willing to offer the latter services gleefully, the realization that their usefulness ended with converting their people reignited their determination to create a Christianity that would represent their African interests.

In essence, these Africans believed that if colonizers were loathed for their perceived injustices and pervasive intolerance, there was no solid justification for the missionaries who were putting up similar behavior against them. Discrimination against Africans in the church did not necessarily have to do with racially profiling them or keeping distance from them. The understanding that African spirituality and epistemology were discouraged enraged certain activist Christians who believe that the success of a nascent religious identity in the continent is reasonably dependent on their ability to integrate the indigenous systems. One would possibly question the fact that those Africans who have been transferred to the trans-Atlantic environment due to slavery, which once swept the continent by storm, and the ones in their homeland, have an almost identical dream under different treatments. This is necessary because, while those in the trans-Atlantic areas made concerted efforts to integrate their indigenous African spirituality into the church in diaspora, those at home pursued a similar agenda. The goals appeared identical, perhaps because they felt the same way about their ancestral spiritual sources. It was a connection that was continuously difficult to sever ties with.

African Spiritual Churches developed essentially to accommodate the various cultural traditions and epistemological perceptions that reflect their true nature or identity.[4] By doing this, it was estimated that the reduction of Western representation and influence in the church was very imminent, and as a substitute for this, it would immediately motivate the people to accept some of their past histories from which they had been distanced for a long time. There was a consensus that African spirituality would ultimately cater to the indigenous system to the extent that it would redeem the image that had been ridiculed, molested, and shattered. Domesticating the Christian religion was very important for a variety of reasons. Modern Christians have a hazy recollection of their religious history, which naturally rendered them incapable of creating an environment for the practice of their indigenous systems. Even if they did, the question of power that Christianity represented would be a challenging issue to address. As a result, it was technically sensible that they recreated themselves in the new religion and demonstrated their creativity in domesticating it. It is important to reiterate that the antagonistic reactions to the European version of Christianity started for a very long time in Africa, and this is because of the early realization that Africanizing such religious identity is a progressively important step toward their identity rediscovery.

A very strong motivating reason for the integration of African spirituality into the Christianity introduced to them was the widespread spiritual consciousness of the people all over the continent. There was not a single African social group of people that did not have indigenous systems of spiritual connections. Although they might not have had the Christian version of the trinity to spirituality, they had a well-designed spiritual system that emphasized personal connections with the Supreme Being, making the duty of worship significant. Ghanaians of the Asante ethnic identity identify God as "Onyame," and they could not be alleged to have been ignorant about the existence of a Supreme Being.[5] It betrays every aspect of logic to suddenly describe the Yoruba people of Nigeria, who are steadfast in their relationship with supernatural figures, the head of which they call Olodumare, as irreligious, perhaps because one has a low understanding of their spirituality. We should also mention that the formulation of a religious tenet as found in Christianity could not have been in practice among the Ethiopians of East African before the coming of the Europeans, but this does not invalidate their relationship with God for whatever reason. As such, African spirituality was ubiquitous as long as it was in an African environment, and motivations for assimilation would be ascertained because of this socio-religious consciousness.

To corroborate the arguments of many of these Africans, the extreme castigation by Europeans of African cultural practice became a strong motivation for the pursuit of Africanization of the Christian religion. Western missionaries could not separate their religious inclinations from the trappings of sentiments that beclouded their judgment of Africans, which ineluctably led to their indicting evaluation of Africans' indigenous structures. Everywhere across the world, religions are meant to guide individuals toward the unification of the people with the Cosmic Intelligence and not, in most cases, challenge their cultural traditions.[6] This is usually because an indictment of a people's cultural identity serves as an assault on their intellectual capacity and ancestral thoughts. Such epistemicide would usually have greater consequences for the people, which explains why they always challenge such developments. It was evident that the Western missionaries were uncomfortable with the practice of polygamy in many African countries, even against the fact that certain Biblical characters consciously chose the polygamous system in their time. Perhaps, the agitating Africans would have found no reason to challenge this inconsistency if they did not have the intellectual capacity to interpret the Bible. However, the fact that Biblical characters practiced it while the crusaders of the religion frowned at it suggested a different thing to them. They believed that the Christianity brought by these people was on the road to cultural genocide. They obviously would not accept such.[7]

Thinking that African cultural practice of polygamy is just an insignificant part of the Eurocentric discrimination underpins the increased rigor diverted into Africanizing Christianity. Segregations along the color line constituted an insurmountable challenge that the Africans faced at the hands of Europeans because of their awareness of its underlying consequences. For one, having the opportunity to attain a leadership height would be potentially jeopardized because of the existing bias that Western missionaries had erected. We should remember that already concluded remarks about Africans, even by missionaries, were that they were barbaric and outrageously backward[8] and that a people with such receding intellectual capacity cannot be entrusted with any leadership position in the church—although they would be allocated marginal positions. Underneath this idea was a practical depiction of Africans as subhuman, against whom the colonization of their minds must be ruthless. Getting this impression created the necessary motivations in the hearts of the African converts, and therefore, a necessary countermeasure was to indigenize the religion.

Meanwhile, the contributions of natural events cannot be underestimated. Perhaps because nature was also complicit here, the motivation to Africanize the religion was further strengthened because there are certain impenetrable regions in the continent. The missionaries were reluctant to pierce the geographical environments that were reasonably harsh on their color and identity. This means that the expansion of Christianity into the interior environment would largely be dependent on insiders' efforts to carry on the evangelical assignment. It gives sufficient justification for the ordination of people like Samuel Ajayi Crowther to enhance the Christianizing agenda. Ajayi Crowther was an erstwhile enslaved African who got his freedom in Freetown, Sierra Leone, en route to the trans-Atlantic environment. Being a Yoruba man, he was well-suited for the spread of the religion because of his knowledge of the environment. More importantly, his involvement in the evangelization of the people attracted more participation from indigenous people who would naturally fraternize with the idea that their own is among the movement. We would understand the significance of this reason when we realize that Bishop Samuel Ajayi Crowther translated the Yoruba and Igbo languages to English.

It became extremely important for Africans to develop their identity in Christianity, even if it meant they would not secure the necessary European backing. Of course, the Europeans were not going to accept the redefinition of Christianity that the Africans were making substantial efforts to achieve. However, because of the understanding that their identity was under a serious attack and their survival was subjected to threats of unimaginable magnitude as a result, the early African Christian converts began to promote a version of Christianity that would not only validate their epistemic perception but would also essentialize their indigenous understanding of life. Therefore, polygamy was seen as an expression of cultural thought that would not be subjected to the external molestations that the Europeans brought. In the same way that the Africans identified and appreciated these things, they provided means of cultural reconstruction into religious belief. Cultural practices, such as songs and dances, which were an integral part of the African heritage, were incorporated because all attempts to separate them from the activities were unsuccessful.[9] It thus appeared like Africans were intricately connected to their cultural traditions and would rather reinforce this than deny them.

African Spiritual Churches and African Spirituality

The African people, as already indicated, are extremely religious people because a form of spirituality resides historically with them. This form of spirituality exists in various dimensions in different African civilizations, but what remains constant is that they are usually socially constitutive, precisely because individuals are sometimes exposed to them unconsciously so that they begin to inculcate spiritual thoughts that are appropriated culturally. Africans accept the limitations of human knowledge because they consider the cosmological existence a gap that cannot be accounted for by using human logic.[10] Although they consider humans the center of the universal organization, many of these African social groups accept that unseen forces exist and influence their physical events. African spirituality is developed not from the hallucinating disposition of an average individual about unknown events; rather, it comes from acknowledging their intellectual limitations about life. No system of thought can explain certain phenomena, much less the underlying reason behind their existence. In other words, certain events defy logical explanations, and no matter the level of systematic evaluation or rationalization of the occasion, the knowledge gap is always there. Why is the world existing? What are the specific reasons for human evolution to a level above other animals? These, among other questions, usually crop up but are mostly unsatisfactorily answered.

Whereas the understanding of the cosmological body differs considerably from culture to culture in Africa, it remains prevalent among them that the triad of the unborn, the living, and the dead constitute the circle of existence. This circle is connected by an umbilical cord, and the actions of the dead are understandably affective of the other two. Based on his understanding, John Mbiti observed that Africans are intricately religious, as they connect their life experiences with unseen forces, believing that their day-to-day experiences are subject to manipulations by these powers from whom a number of them receive communication in very different realizations.[11] Africans are extremely conscious of the unseen presence, so much that they usually evoke their spirit for intervention and support in different human circumstances. Unlike many other civilizations, Africans consider death, for example, not as the finitude of human existence but as a transition from one phase of living to another. Given that these humans have acquired a reasonable level of social and spiritual knowledge and awareness, their death does not render them inactive in the matters of the living; they, however, can play their roles using different means. The fact that the dead appear to people in their dreams underscores the conclusion that they intervene in human affairs.

There are some cultural identities in Africa where the departed members of the society are given symbolic treatment at their departure to the great beyond. In fact, the Yoruba people of Nigeria have political offices for spiritual emissaries for some kings, under the assumption that they would guide the passage of these kings to the great beyond. This is apart from the fact that an elaborate ceremony is organized for deceased people. It is a cultural and spiritual behavior that developed from the thinking that transition from one phase to another requires the level of respect accorded to the dead so that they would intervene on their behalf on matters of significant import. The presence of deep spirituality in Africa is corroborated by the celebration of Egungun in many of their settlements or societies. The Egungun cult exists almost in every country on the continent, and their underlying spiritual essence is that they serve as the physical manifestations of their ancestors whose spirits are evoked occasionally for the enhancement of their intervention into human affairs. Even when specific lineages are usually associated with a particular Egungun, their ancestral spirits are believed to have transformed to occupy a human body through whom they communicate with the living. In essence, the communication with the unseen manifests in dreams and through the ceremonial arrangement of the Egungun festivals.[12]

Sibusiso Masondo observed that in South Africa house dedication ceremonies represent a ritual organization that answers specific spiritual questions about their existence.[13] This validates the thinking that completing such projects depends on the relationship between humans and their ancestral sources. We should carefully emphasize here that the notoriously spiritual African is aware that their activities, even when logically explained, are not something whose planning can be attributed to them, as they are conceived only as the physical body to execute them. So the fulfillment these South Africans attain by successfully completing a physical structure, and their dedication to the ancestral sources underscores their awareness about the presence and influence of the unseen forces. Logically, and maybe psychologically, the accuracy of this thinking would be brought to bear by the time we understand that individuals of the time past have a substantial influence cn us, apart from their genetic history transferred into the living. Their achievements, activities, social contributions, and personal record are what the society keeps in their public memory and what reminds generations to come about the past activities of these individuals. For example, the Yoruba people have a group of griots who keep the social history of virtually all the people of the community intact in their memory. Turning this to artistic production, they remind the living of the activities of their ancestors from which they can never be dissociated.

These are the various manifestations of African spirituality that cannot be disconnected from the people regardless of the religion they embrace or profess. For instance, the concept of a generational curse, popular among the African Indigenous Churches, finds similar sociocultural import in the Bible, and it is an integral part of the African spirituality.[14] Generational curses remain valid as long as the individual believes that humans are the product of their ancestors, and records associated with these departed souls continue to influence the activities of the present ones in various ways, to the extent that this spiritual construction extends to their traditional social involvements and the career choices of the people. A lineage known as hunters keeps the hunting tradition because they understand that the transference of knowledge through their ancestors cannot be denied. The same thing happens to lineages socially known for other professions. This comes from the thinking that members of the same family group would more easily coordinate the consultation of these ancestral beings. In essence, when one comes across Christians in the Indigenous churches, one would immediately link their conferment of titles to the cosmic forces because it is a tradition that developed from their indigenous systems. Passive references are made to ancestral accomplishments, which is a special way the living expects the activities of the departed to determine what happens in their current existence.

One need not look far into the African Indigenous Churches to understand the deep-seated connections between them and their indigenous spirituality. For example, the Aladura Church usually demands personal communication between themselves and supernatural forces that would, in most cases, have immediate manifestations in their physical existence. This is usually the case because there is an inherent belief that spiritual forces, while they remain the powerhouses that determine physical events, are susceptible to manipulations, hence the persistent engagement of these forces by the AICs, including some Pentecostals. The thought originated from the spiritual conceptualization of Africans, different in practice and from the ones identified by the Western missionaries. It could readily be linked with the consultation of the diviners among the custodians of traditional worship in Africa. In fact, it is a general spiritual practice that people consult diviners in their day-to-day engagement so that their physical activities would not be overcome by violence or unimaginable melancholy. The thinking is thereby transferred into Africanized Christianity because the people find it difficult to dissociate themselves from their indigenous backgrounds.

The culture of dancing introduced to African Christianity comes from the indigenous system of religious practices. As already indicated, indigenous spirituality is a cornucopia of systems where social functions are combined with political issues, the same way that economic issues are interwoven with institutional activities. For example, in an Egungun festival, there appear to be many social events that are brought together, the most popular of which is the invocation of the ancestral spirits (which gives spiritual import), the intervention of these spirits in controversies between or among different family members (which qualifies them as the social justice system), and the distribution of one's products to the attendees of the program, in which case, economic issues would be solved. All through these processes, dances, jubilation, and merrymaking would be circulated. Therefore, such practice is imported into African Christianity in the Aladura Churches, the Church Missionary Society, Cherubim and Seraphim, among other denominations. These churches incorporate dances into their program with the belief that it places the people within the appropriate frame of mind to enhance spiritual conversation between them and the unseen.

Spirit in the African Indigenous Churches constitutes the foundation of their spiritual principles to the extent that it is the basis of their prophecy, revelation, flushing out evil, securing economic opportunities, getting dream appointments, among other things. Africanized Christianity believes that when confronted with overwhelming challenges, humans need immediate spiritual delivery from unseen forces that have been placed against them. In essence, they become the sources of restoration of lost glories and the advocates for their rights at the spiritual realm, the crucible where people's destinies and fortunes are determined. These churches place emphasis on divine healing, supernatural delivery, glossolalia (speaking in tongues), Holy Spirit, revelation, prophecy, among other things. Because of the socio-religious disposition of the African Indigenous Churches, Africans found their identity in their practice and, therefore, preferred these churches to orthodox types and the Western missionaries' ones. The Zimbabwean African churches, their Ghanaian colleagues, and their Nigerian neighbors all follow the system of their ancestral worship, where the place of spirituality remains central to all their engagements.

African Spiritual Churches and Knowledge Production

Africa's epistemological structure forms the basis of knowledge production for religious principles, social behavior, and even political systems. The inseparableness of these products of their epistemological design underscores the reason for the promotion of their indigenous systems in an available means in the society. Thus, while it would reinforce their spiritual principles and significance to society, religious platforms would not refuse to interject moral principles into the people or build their political systems with ideas associated with these structures. In other words, African spirituality cannot be divorced from their epistemic intimations because that was the source from which it is drawn. Consequently, the African Spiritual Churches (ASC) follow a foundational pattern that stresses the importance of education to members of the religion so that while they are serving as the spiritual guide for the people, they would simultaneously construct good moral philosophy in them.

The contributions of ASC to knowledge generation and circulation can be discussed at two different levels. Firstly, they have made a substantial effort to reclaim African identity by restoring their education models in the Western ones. Secondly, they operate at the level of religious society to inculcate values into their members. On the first note, the development of schools in different realizations by these churches seeks to achieve an important role in the advancement of their cultural agenda.[15] One of the shortcomings of the Europeans is their silence in the investment in African education, presumably because their ambition toward Africans is to evangelize them, not develop them intellectually. Apparently, such determination sought to promote Western civilization and agendas while their subjects, the Christianized Africans, are not afforded quality human development opportunities. Training given to them is usually meant to develop their speaking skills to facilitate communication between the Western missionaries and their potential African converts. Although it assisted in the flourish of Christianity, the Africans' human development index would enjoy only minimal social and economic benefits. Despite this, the development of African churches brought about their emancipation in academic areas so that while they achieved a redoubtable spiritual growth, they would equally have been increased in knowledge to develop themselves and their immediate society. In essence, the South African indigenous churches, the Ethiopian churches, the Ghanaian churches, and their counterparts in Nigeria have directly undertaken the responsibility of creating schools so that they would become centers of knowledge production and information circulation.

Quite a large number of African Indigenous Churches have concentrated on the establishment of schools so that people would have access to quality education with which they can develop the larger society to meet up with the global academic system. In Nigeria, for example, there has been a radical development of schools by the indigenous churches so much that they constitute a formidable structure in the academic development of the people. For example, in Bayelsa State, the impact of the Zion brand of Christianity and the Cherubim and Seraphim Church cannot be underestimated. They have continued to create educational centers where knowledge distribution has been serious and efficiently delivered.[16] This is consolidated by their constant improvement on the standards of delivery so that these students can compete with their global and transnational colleagues. Not less than twenty-one primary schools were established by the combination of the churches in these communities, which statistically represents approximately twenty-nine percent of the schools in that environment.[17] The successful establishment of these schools and their maintenance has substantially improved the academic enrollment there, making it easier for the intellectual development of the people, in general, to become socially relevant. The commitment is erected from the philosophy entrenched in the indigenous religious systems where the primacy of educational engagement is uncompromisingly emphasized.

These churches are confronted with death-defying challenges for reasons that are not unconnected to their financial incapacity to operate with such academic centers. However, knowledge distribution is a fundamental part of their spiritual awareness and should be embraced by members who have the financial oxygen to finance the project. For the highlighted schools above, churches spread the responsibility on members, and, through their contributions, they have been able to create a number of schools for the enhancement of their objectives. Levies on members, donations from different interest groups, and contributions from individuals who have experienced the spiritual prospects of the churches are used for the running of the school project because they believe that such would increase their social development and would inadvertently convince converts to embrace the religion. Essentially, they are considered progressives because all their academic projects are geared toward improving their intellectual conditions. When knowledge is acquired, the individuals would, in turn, employ their intellectual property to bring about ultimate development for the people. This means that the traditional roles played by the African spiritual institutions are still reinforced in contemporary times. This is consolidated by the understanding that people would rapidly develop if they have access to wide-ranging knowledge systems.

It becomes clear that the production of knowledge would have a substantial impact on the political participation of the people. For example, going to school helps to mold an individual to develop critical thinking and engagement of their political circumstances. It is not grandstanding to say that the eventual embers of independence that became widespread in Africa before the expiration of colonialism were consolidated by the educational foundation of these nationalists who have been deeply immersed in the teachings of their churches. Ayegboyi and Ishola reiterate the significance of these AICs with their assertion that they exposed Africans to the true spirit of nationalism as a strategy for the displacement of colonialism—which not only submerged their economic and political systems but also inadvertently proscribed their indigenous value system.[18] The Aladura Churches were excellently involved in these mobilizations as they emphasized the importance of integrating their congregation into African struggles so that they would identify with them in their endeavors and, more importantly, accept them as their own struggles. It thus confirms the speculation that the introduction of education to these people served as the launchpad for their emancipation in all respects. Western missionaries did not understand the struggles of these Africans, or perhaps they pretended not to, but the pure practice of their religion without the infusion of indigenous materials would neutralize the potential of these informed people in the aspirations of their general identity.

It is irrefutable that efforts given in the above respect have yielded positive responses because recorded enrollment of African children at the school has increased, thereby facilitating their nationalist commitments.[19] Beyond the provision of educational centers or the enhancement of a nationalist political culture is the repudiation of immoral behavior through the biblically mixed Yoruba morals. Knowledge productions, it should be emphasized, necessarily have more to do with the generation of ideas that would impact the lives of the individual than it has to do with the provision of centers where their learning would be enhanced. This is because the content of learning in most cases determines the intellectual development of a people as they would be persuaded to follow a predetermined trajectory through what they have internalized than what would make relevant the agencies of these processes. It means that if a school is erected where the content of another people is offered, the claim that the knowledge produced is attributable to the groups that erected the infrastructure is invalid. On this basis, a careful examination of the impact of African churches with relations to knowledge manufacturing was done.

The crucible of intellectual development lies in integrating the young individuals with the epistemic perception of their cultural traditions, and it appears that Christianity naturally brings up such potentiality in the church. For example, the creation of the Sunday school department in the church helps in the impartation of knowledge into the members of the same religion. Consider, for example, that the Sunday school avenue has seized several African churches, Aladura churches, Cherubim and Seraphim, Church Mission Society, The Apostolic Faith, and an assortment of others, to pass knowledge through into the members; it would be realized that the content of their education there is mostly the one that is drawn from their indigenous epistemology so that the people would find an adequate representation of themselves in the system. We continue to see a substantial relay of their message, such as the essentialization of human relationships, the creation of a social system where respect to constituted authorities was emphasized, and the purification of their spiritual existence was as equally necessary.

Individuals in the churches are usually taught about these values that are associated with their societal ideas. The fact that they are exposed to what constitutes morality as a way to encourage the development of strong moral principles reflects their determination to enhance good education through their churches. While they may share similarities with other people's ideas, moral perception and ideas are mostly culture-dependent. For this reason, the inculcation of morals that are African-specific became one of the ultimate concerns of the indigenous churches, which they promoted at every given opportunity. Individuals are introduced to strong philosophical constructs believed to assist them in navigating their ways through life. In essence, social behaviors, condemned by Western missionaries, were encouraged so long as they helped build a morally responsible set of people who reflect African ideas. This happened because they understood that the reliance on Western knowledge systems would potentially drift the people away from their cultural and religious focus. For example, the proliferation of same-sex marriage in contemporary times is what some AIC were against because of the superstition and myths built around the practice. Therefore, such engagements would be challenged through a knowledge position that corroborates their indigenous sentiment and invalidates the Western side.

Beliefs and the Power of Biblical Words

From the beginning, the foundation of AIC was built on the belief in the potency of words to propel their sayings into visible actions. Meanwhile, the Bible itself substantially validates the employment of words and their spiritual manipulations so that the results would have a physical effect. Geoffrey Nelson (1969) claims that the association of greatness to the people called men or women of God is directly based on their validated authority that has been divinely sanctioned.[20] Whereas anyone can usually lay claim to being exceptionally endowed by the Cosmic Intelligence, the production of physical results usually serves as a reinforcement of the people's position in the spiritual world. This means that the essentialization of the people called men and women of God depends substantially on their capacity to use Biblical words effectively and productively. Numerous indigenous churches have spiritual leaders who are legitimized through their extraordinary display of an uncommon gift. They are canonized by their manipulations of supernatural existence to the extent that the wishes of their members are usually propelled into existence. And because they usually give these results, it is believed that they are themselves superhuman and exceptional.

The sustenance of their religious significance depends largely on their ability to continue to display these extraordinary powers so that their manipulations of supernatural affairs come not only as permanent conditions but also that the possibility of changing even the otherwise unfortunate events remains constant. Pastors are seen as spiritually inclined and divinely ordained as long as measurable results and actions follow. They are understood as characters whose actions cannot be subjected to logical explanations or rational evaluations because they present results that defy human understanding. They become the preferred choices of the people in a way that makes them relevant to their social and even economic affairs. Words can be transformed into concrete results and have the potential to change people's conditions, and their exceptionality is confirmed by those who are ordained. Getting results from the use of words spiritually is not conferred on people who do not understand their usage but on people with the divine license to do so. The image of the pastors is not different from the ones of their departed ancestors, for they perform spiritually similar things.

Africans naturally believe that their ancestors are mediators between them and the supernatural world,[21] and because of the spiritual significance accorded to them, a number of these African indigenous pastors are automatically given the social roles of ancestors who are believed to serve as mediators between them and the Cosmic Intelligence. The process of Africanizing the Christian religion has converted the positions of pastors or other individuals who are believed to have superhuman qualities to that of their ancestors. In many African societies, divination is conducted to understand the positions of their ancestors so that they would come to the knowledge of what they should do or not do in order to continue on a prosperous path. In modern times, the roles of these ancestors are automatically transferred to their pastors so that they would use their powers to manipulate words to transform their lives positively. When understood very clearly, the African traditional religious institutions are erected to conscript certain extraordinary and superhuman individuals as voices who would appeal to the cosmic forces on their behalf. The Orisha worship, for example, is created with the impression that these deities would negotiate on behalf of the people with the Supreme Being so that they would have physical evidence of their lives' transformations. God is not usually approached directly, except through these agencies.

Mainstream Christianity depends largely on the potency of words, consolidating the fundamental principles of the religion itself. Western Christians understand that the biblical miracles recorded have a substantial relationship with manipulating words with a physical manifestation. African spirituality relies heavily on similar experiences, as the performative force accompanying their verbal declarations is domiciled and dominant in their traditional spiritual engagement. The Biblical miracles involve the use of the words, and, in the course of worship, the movement into glossolalia helps to make important their desire for it to be granted the effectiveness that the people desired. People speak in tongues, and the results manifest in what can be physically quantified. Western missionaries educate the early converts about these things to advance their desire for evangelization in its totality. Instances of powerful prayers that changed courses of action are evident in the Bible, but the lack of practical demonstrations from the missionaries resulted in the creation of several native churches.

Meanwhile, there is a culture of incantations among many Africans that have been historically preserved for centuries and ages. The Biblical reiteration of the power of words was a silent motivation for the people. If words are believed to be effective and powerful, as showcased in the Bible, the fact that such experiments have been successfully undertaken by their ancestors became a motivating factor for the incorporation of incantations into the new system. Even though they were aware that the excavation of such a practice would be taken through serious transformative processes, they still believed that it could be integrated into their new religion. As such, you would not have incantations in the manner of the indigenous practices. While it would have been given a Christian identity, it would also make a good heritage that can be depended on in the new religious system. To the extent that many African indigenous systems rely on the potency of their words, the reincarnation of that practice is justified by its duplication in the Bible. Therefore, the Christological potency of words cannot be differentiated from its African counterparts, and the fact that it is more accessible to African Christians makes it necessary to incorporate it. Western missionaries relayed principles of spirituality that highlight the place of words in the transformation of human life to their early African converts, but they did not showcase maximum practical demonstrations as the indigenous spiritual systems did.

An African Christian who comes from a family that uses words every day in their engagement, with physical results, tends to challenge what they are taught in Western churches by switching to their ancestral systems. The reason for this is very obvious. In the quest for the evangelization of the people, whose job would be substantially handled by the indigenous converts, they ended with something concrete that would attract their potential converts into what they are doing so that they would understand the significance of the new religious system. Explaining such developments to the Western missionaries would achieve no desirable results because they are not groomed in the cultural tradition of these people and are not in proper socio-religious positions to make objective evaluations. Therefore, these Africans were determined to employ the indigenous potency of words through the agency of the Biblical activities and events which could be used to justify their actions. Several places in the Bible depict when the words were relied on by the users until they became sanctioned divinely, so much that the physical manifestation of their request was realized. Meanwhile, similar events occurred among native people of the continent, and such experiences inspired them to export the idea into their newly found religion, Christianity. For example, I consider glossolalia, speaking in tongues, as an identical spiritual behavior to the incantations used by the Yoruba people of Nigeria.

We now divert our attention to what Pierre Verger calls the "vital power."[22] According to him, there is a spiritual equivalence between the orthodox Christianity's idea of *manna* and the concept of Àṣẹ among the Yoruba people. For this social group, there is the physical manifestation of the results of prayers or incantations among the people. The Biblical association of divine intervention on human requests to the word finds similarity among them as they also concede the responsibility of transformations of their requests to Olodumare, their own Supreme Being. The Bible's position that the creation of the world and the creativity displayed in doing it reflects a supernatural ability to command things to take a particular form. The universe was designed through the potency of God's words, and the place of words in shaping human affairs and the world cannot be overemphasized. In essence, the trees in the forest bow to the manifestation of the potency of words, the same way that the creatures in the ocean follow similar divine directives. The declaration by God in the book of Genesis "Let there be light" consolidates the assumption that the things of the world are the product of words that are divinely sanctioned. Therefore, it would be difficult to continue dominance or have maximum spiritual control of things without being grounded in indigenous spirituality. Àṣẹ is transported to the AIC in different dimensions.

Moreover, the association of power to the potency of words is underscored by the understanding that power is generally central to the organization of ideas and philosophies that would assist in guiding human conduct. This association would equally help in the conferment of authority to the individual, usually above all other things. It is important because, through it, humans can influence activities around them that take flight without their knowledge. Through the manifestation of the power of words, an individual's life would take a different yet encouraging trajectory. The residual power of words as it is domiciled in the Bible finds its way into Africanized Christianity in the indigenous forms. Because of the failure to show concrete evidence to the experience documented in the Bible, the Aladura, the C&S, and other variants of the AIC incorporated their native ideas of words, adding them to the regular Christian engagement. Nearly all the Africanized Christianity denominations in the continent and transnational communities have incorporated words into their spiritual systems and principles. The Aladura churches, most especially, proclaim words as something integral to their spiritual trajectory. It is reinforced by the commendable results that the congregants find in the course of their religious engagement, thus validating the reason for the initiation of an African-centered church identity.

African Spiritual Churches and Their Sociocultural Import

From inception, the primary aim of Africanizing the Christian religion was to establish a connection among Africans that will be nurtured by their cultural and social history. Against the understanding that Western missionaries would not enable the sociocultural effervescence of Africans needed to crystallize their cultural traditions and identity import, the early African Christians decided to use the church as a medium for reunification. We should consider the Sierra Leone experience of the freed enslaved Africans as an important example here. In connection with other Africans, Samuel Ajayi Crowther naturally wanted a platform that would unite them and serve as the basis for planning their approach to independence and freedom.[23] Including those in the trans-Atlantic environment, where they were subjected to unending repression, the organization of themselves using the platform provided by the religious institutions became inescapable. Apart from serving as a ground for exchanging numerous indigenous principles, it was meant to dowse the tension they were confronted with under the leadership of the Western Christians. Indeed, the promulgation of the

African church became a countermeasure for different issues of grandstanding and marginalization that had become synonymous with Christianity.

As there are social interactions that usually helped in the fraternization of the people, the need for simulating similar experiences in the African churches became unavoidably important. When there are forums for raising some issues, individuals will find solutions to challenges that are not even spiritually related. For example, placing their members into good positions in society was necessary because spiritual powers are usually consolidated by political power. When there is one, and the other is absent, the potential for expansion becomes dim and uncertain. As such, one of the important things considered in the social organization of church activities is that members bring forth their personal concerns so that other members in the capacity to proffer solutions to them would do so accordingly. During the period of migration to the Americas and other places around the world, many indigenous churches became the rallying ground for migrants to seek jobs and other important economic connections so that members would not only be transformed spiritually but would also be exceptionally developed financially.

Beyond the possibility of exchanging economic opportunities is the potentiality to seek partners in these churches. Usually, the indigenous social organizational structures where younger ones confide in their elders on issues that border on their personal challenges and experiences remain sacrosanct even in the new church structure. While the pastor is the head to whom the activities of the church and issues of its members are taken, there are elders also who are responsible for overseeing that the yearnings of the people are catered to. Some members are confronted with marital issues or are constrained by the morals of the Bible that emphasize the primacy of rights of one's emotional partners. For this reason, they come to these churches to consider the possibility of getting life partners. The elders there are keepers of people's records, and because they understand the peculiarities of each of their members, joining members together based on their compatibility becomes one of their primary assignments. Some marriages have been facilitated through the African churches. This means that religion is used to reinforce the indigenous practice of social integration. Basically, the duty of joining people together for marriage has become one of their functions in the current time. In contemporary times, more churches are emboldened to do this publicly as they dedicate a session for this.

The fact that these African churches understand the place of matchmaking is not only rooted in their indigenous social order; it is also considered as a beautiful method of social integration and regeneration. Beyond this, however, conflict resolution and management becomes inevitable because they know that homes, as social institutions, could falter in their social responsibilities when confronted with overwhelming challenges. This awareness has mandated them to create an appropriate platform for managing emerging conflicts among the people. From close observation of the activities of these churches, it cannot be contested that the ASC has become a perfect simulation of the African society themselves. In a typical African environment, conflicts are managed by the elders, in most cases by the ancestral spirits of Egungun, as in the Yoruba culture. This is underscored by the realization that humans are naturally more persuaded by unseen intervention into their affairs than by the prescriptions of some individuals, especially when the conflict is corrosive. However, when the issues of controversy are within the capacity of the elders to settle, they undertake the responsibility. The ASC has come to function in this respect as they mediate between couples in some cases and between warring factions in others.

It is important to know that while the African churches provide motivations for their members in terms of spiritual and metaphysical concerns, they also complement this by providing financial assistance to members who are confronted with economic challenges. Empowerment is essentially necessary for people who wanted emancipation in all respects. When financial rescue is not forthcoming, the human spirit would be especially low, which could frustrate them to seek alternative solutions elsewhere. As Africans, the awareness of this is strong and unshaken. To prevent their congregation from being attracted to some morally delinquent and ideologically condemnable activities, these churches provide financial support for members on many occasions. This is, however, achieved through different means. Some churches offer scholarship opportunities to members to pursue higher academic interests and subsequently add to society what they have added to their intellectual property. Others provide monies for medical assistance or even build hospitals where members would be given an utmost priority. All these engagements help to build a socialist system where members directly enjoy some benefits and, as a result, increase their sense of responsibility to the society itself. Thus, it is toward the actualization of an African agenda that the people are integrated into the system.

Included in the social responsibility of these churches is the organization of programs where the members are given spiritual support. In the traditional African society, indigenous systems recognized the sanctity of sanitizing the psychology of members who sometimes face one challenge or the other. Spiritual attacks are well-defined. Individuals who are perturbed by the constant confrontation from unseen forces are sometimes brought to diviners for personal healing. However, with the emergence of churches in Africa, the African churches have capitalized on this activity and expanded it. In Kenya, for example, and Nigeria, too, there are series of public organizations of programs that feature the onslaught of spiritual enemies who are believed to have impeded the development of the people in one way or the other. Hosting public programs where problems confronting members are solved is aimed at different objectives. Through their spiritual efficiency, pastors intend to use the opportunity to advertise their churches to members who have not accepted the religion or those who belong to other denominations. Africans generally accept that all persons have one or two spiritual challenges that face them, and through the engagement of spiritual people, they would get deliverance. This mindset prepares them to open their hearts to evangelists who have come on the mission to "set them free."

Additionally, a very strong component of African socio-religious belief is dance. With dance, however, comes musical performances that are capable of triggering people's emotions for participation. Dance was used for various purposes in African society because it was one of the most effective ways to draw people together on different occasions. To these people, dance fulfilled more than entertainment purposes, for it is sometimes performed during rites and procession of the diviners. And because this has become an important part of their cultural history, every member of various African societies is always inclined to participate whenever occasions call for it. The founders of these African churches are not isolated from the cultural activities that usually lead to dance, and neither did they understand the socio-religious import of that component of their culture. Western Christianity is averse to the culture of dance in the process of worship, especially during the period when Christianity was brought to the continent. It is not that the Bible itself is opposed to dancing but because there was something cultural and political that prevented the people from dancing. They saw Africans as their subordinates in whose presence dance would appear demeaning. But the Africans who intended to Africanize the Christian religion were not going to follow such sentiment because dance expressed their culture.

African indigenous spirituality places much emphasis on family and ancestors. Within the same social group, members are seen as one because they are usually joined by some paternalistic bond. Everyone is somewhat related to one another, which foregrounds the reason for organizing their activities in ways that would respect this arrangement. One of the beautiful ways to explain this is the peaceful disposition of Africans to their clan and social groups who may have different religious orientations. Africans are peaceful with their neighbors because they believe that antagonism should not be attracted based on their differences in religious orientation. This provides an easy way to continue with their social cohesion and bonding, and it became a vital part of their cultural movement during the period of creating African churches through the indigenization of European Christianity. The system continues because, in church, Africans have found the duplication of their social structure and organization, and the church itself serves this cardinal purpose to the people. In addition, some churches address their pastors as "daddy," expressing their emotional connection with the people around them because they understand that they are from one beginning. For this reason, it is difficult to come across AIC that are not immersed in the culture of emotional bonding with their members.

Conclusion

We have explicitly explained that the motivation behind the AIC is to create a religious identity and movements that would specifically incorporate their traditional ideologies around their spirituality. We explain too that African spirituality and epistemology remain intricately interwoven, which forestalls the possibility of separating one from the other. Without mincing words, African spirituality has been the foundational structure upon which African morality, political system, and knowledge systems are erected. The connection between them is so strong that they cannot be taken away from one another. This underscores the reason for the apparent impossibility of dissociating the African people from the indigenous system they inherited. On this basis, one would understand the simultaneous domestication of the Christian religion introduced to them in their different African countries and the Americas. Africans, without having a reliable communication system, created a Christian religion that makes way for the appropriation of their indigenous systems and practices without necessarily forsaking the new one given to them.

The domestication of the religion was thus necessary because it stood the potential to trigger a radical development that would push their emancipation dream. Africans needed political freedom, which might not come without having a reliable structure to galvanize ideas and philosophies in their bid for self-determination. It became more apparent that the need to use the church was important when it was discovered that the new elite growing from the continent had acquired Western education through different means. However, because they needed to guarantee a better academic experience for these people, the church would become a stakeholder responsible for producing knowledge systems for Africans. The combination of these ideas became so electric that even for the church (sometimes), the dream to restore African identity and respect was incubated. Basically, there was the need for the combination of spiritual power and intellectual might so that they would become a formidable structure fighting for the same course of action. As a result, the churches incorporated some African systems, including but not limited to their divination system, which was transformed to the idea of consulting the pastors, spiritual healing, which ultimately became a thing in the church, and a few others that have been addressed accordingly.

Therefore, the AIC had a comprehensive plan to become a formidable structure that would empower African people in all directions. They are believed to be united by the creed of Christianity and would not stop their agitation for the rejuvenation of their indigenous practices. From the well of their traditional spirituality, these churches have tapped the current of *Àṣẹ* and performative force for their spoken words so that their physical life would be transformed as desired. Contrary to what Western Christianity is doing, the indigenous African churches create unending opportunities for members so that the philosophy of socialism practiced in the continent before the ascension of the religion is sustained. It appears that the current religion of Christianity has therefore served as the rallying ground for the fortification of Africans wherever they appear. Scholars have emphasized how international communities are used for the enhancement of unity through the churches. These places help to seek economic opportunities for members and, in some cases, share their burdens so that they would have a sense of belonging and home. These churches continue to the present time, unrelenting in their integration of indigenous systems onto the platform that Christianity has provided.

Conclusion

This body of work has established the importance, position, and influence of sacred words in the African context. Sacred words inform and empower spiritual knowledge and engender leadership while having an enormous influence on the actions, practices, and beliefs of Africans across the continent. Afolabi agrees in his study on Nigeria's relationship with religion when he submits that "all over the country, religion plays an important role in the daily lives of her citizens; the way we interact with one other, our choice of dressing, food, and politics are mostly affected by religion."[1] Afolabi's cross-examination demonstrates religion as having massive cultural influence. However, this book went beyond the cultural effects of these religions on Africa to examine their origin—the foundation of the beliefs that inform them and the knowledge generated and produced through them. As promised, this book focuses on how guiding belief systems influence adherents and engineer practices.[2]

However, this book is not complete without harmonizing the ideas espoused with its contribution and future possibilities of knowledge production on African scholarship. African religious practices proliferate as African culture. Thus, a near-holistic examination of how sacred words inform belief and manifest in actions is impossible from a monopolized viewpoint. Put differently, there are multiple variations of Africa's three major religions, hence the need to examine the top picks (as divided into chapters) in each of the three religions with relevance to Africanism. In similar fashion, the approach to each of the chapters correspond to that chapter's context, instead of enforcing uniformity. This is deliberate in order to compartmentalize as many perspectives and variant contributions as possible while embracing the diversity and distinction in their knowledge production.

The opening chapter, "Diviners and Indigenous Knowledge," centers the discussion of knowledge production on the diviner, the "artisan" with divining skills. Through their works, relationships with the gods and humans, their tools, and society, one is able to learn the philosophy and principles that guide this practice. This is an example of perspective through leadership, although it was not specific, unlike the discussion on Amadou Bamba and Usman Dan Fodio. Conversely, shamanism shows from its volume the enormous significance of the subject matter, especially to Yoruba cosmology.

The approach in the second chapter focuses more on the knowledge of shamanism than the shaman (which is, of course, inclusive). The knowledge of shamanism in Africa as detailed here manifests in today's modern formal education as astronomy. Knowledge produced from shamanism is relevant for science and technology if properly developed and invested in. African shamanic practices can be developed through further academic research, taught in the academy as African astrology, using

African methods, not Western-imposed models. Even more interesting is the fact that, like other African Traditional Religions, continual academic knowledge production on shamanism will contribute to knowledge exported from Africa.

Magic and witchcraft followed a totally different path from the former topics. Knowledge production from the belief and practice of magic and witchcraft was illustrated via a comparison with Western science. Indeed, Western denigration of magic and witchcraft practices by demeaning colonialist ideology dealt irreparable damage. The break in its development meant that these knowledges could not effectively transmit to serve Africa in the present day. The positive values inherent in these practices were forfeited, along the negative. This is hypocritical especially when you consider the many evils of Western science, for which evolving African science was sacrificed. While there remain many debates about the authenticity or realness of the practice, whatever the outcome nonetheless bodes well for African and indeed global scholarship.

On the one hand, if the belief and practice of magic and witchcraft is/was all a trick or unreal, then the creativity of traditional African society should be lauded, documented historically in literature, and seen as a set of practices in times past that contributed to African progress and entertainment. Even more, it can be systemized as a practice in contemporary times in the entertainment industry if the spirituality is not taken as real. After all, there are Western tricksters in the entertainment industry who make money by "fooling" their audiences. On the other hand, if magic and witchcraft were real and effective in traditional African settings as often depicted—especially with ontological performances in Nollywood—then it means the knowledge system and its production should be incorporated into scholarship to preserve, teach, and advance for contemporary use. No matter what might be thought of the practices of magic and witchcraft, the knowledge derived from them is worthy of African scholarship, development, and even more importantly, practice in their varying forms and possibilities, contributing to the entertainment, health, or economics of the continent.

Altogether, it is apt to surmise that the study of African Traditional Religions should not be limited to the confines of religion or institutes of African studies, but also taught in several other disciplines in the humanities and sciences. In the humanities, it is essential for the preservation of the practices of African Traditional Religions, which wanes along with indigenous culture, owing to Western imperial influence and untiring Christian and Muslim proselytization. The production of volumes of literature on the knowledge generated from these practices not only preserve them as well as larger African cultural beliefs and practices, but encourages their teaching and export of African indigenous knowledge. This is especially important given the misrepresentations of African cultural ethos by Eurocentric thought.

On the other hand, in the sciences, if these knowledges are properly utilized, channeled, and developed, they could be useful in the evolution of African sciences and medicine. Though Western sciences and medicine have become predominant in Africa, there is no gainsaying the fact that Africans had indigenous systems of medicine that continued to evolve centuries before the first contact with Europeans. This is known as "traditional medicine" and usually sourced through herbs (*ewe ati egbo*— plants and roots), used for healing after diagnosis. African practitioners engage in both physical and mental healing, appropriating these plants using the right combination and the right measurement, without Western or any other form of foreign knowledge or guidance. Sobiecki expounds this better with his review of plant usage in Southern Africa for divination.

In his report, he covers eighty-five plant species being used for acts of divination in Southern Africa, specifically by Bantu-speaking peoples, thirty-nine of which have "psychoactive uses, and a number have established hallucinogenic activity."[3] The derivative conclusion is that these psychoactive plants have significant effects in traditional healing processes in the quoted region. More importantly and also corroboratively, Schultes and Hofmann traced the use of *cactus Echinopsis pachanoi* for healing through divination and sorcery to around 3,000 years.[4] Indeed, the continual existence of these plants and practitioners who are living repositories of this knowledge of traditional medicine means this knowledge is still being produced, and should be promoted as African medicine and as a uniquely African contribution to global medical research and practices.

For instance, *sangomas*, traditional healers in the Mpumalanga Province of South Africa, now exist as an institution with the head—a *gobela*—known as the senior teacher.[5] Here, the knowledge of these traditional practices no longer manifests within the scope of religion or confines of spiritual exercise but as an institution of learning where members of the *sangomas* community share knowledge and ideas and learn from each other. Robert Thornton divides their practices broadly into six disciplines, "divination, herbs, control of ancestral spirits, the cult of foreign *ndawe* spirits, drumming and dancing, and training of new *sangomas*."[6]

Also, a collaborative study by Zuma, Wight, Rochat, and Moshabela establishes how Traditional Health Practitioners (THPs) "play a vital role in the health care of the majority of the South African population and elsewhere on the African continent"[7] while also rebutting concerns raised over the safety of these traditional practices. In their findings in the rural area of Northern KwaZulu-Natal, they identified three different types of THPs; these include the *Isangoma* (diviner); the *Inyanga* (traditional medicine specialist); and the *Umthandazi* (faith healer).[8] This is another example of the uses of knowledge production in divination and African Traditional Religions beyond the religious fundamentals. If incorporated into learning in the humanities, they would serve as custodians, preservers, and teachers of the African Traditional Religions and associated customs to ensure the continual existence and development of its knowledge, mediators, and also counsellors; in the medical field, THPs could use "generic methods and practices to focus on the physical, spiritual, cultural, psychological, emotional, and social elements of illness."[9]

Beyond incorporations into academia for further study and theoretical development, "African medicine" should be further advanced into modern practice. African governments need to properly invest in traditional medicinal knowledge and practices as well as incorporating them into their respective ministries of health. A proper investment and development of traditional medicine could not only ensure the development and advancement of African medicine but also potentially solve some globally unresolved problems in medicine.

Sufism as a knowledge system was also examined generally through the study of Amadou Bamba. The significance of knowledge production under Islam helps readers to understand the cultural relativity of Islamic practices in Africa, as chiefly founded in and influenced by the socioeconomic conditions of their African environment. The fourth chapter of the book—"Sufism as a Knowledge System"—focuses on the theoretical knowledge derived from this syncretic belief system. The chapter itself concludes on the significance of Sufism to Africa and especially how the knowledge gained from it can develop education, science, politics, economics, and the "entertainment industry," while also relevant in African languages and linguistics.

The study of Usman Dan Fodio and Amadou Bamba is particularly significant to understanding the socioeconomic impact of two great Islamic scholars and how knowledge systems are manufactured in contrast to one another, although from nearly the same sources. Put differently, their narratives define and explain the existence of African Islam and the conditions that created it. Their study alongside Sufism helps to establish a fundamental understanding of African Muslim communities, their practices, beliefs, and cultural ethos. It also helps clarify the development of African Muslim communities not as a result of division but instead owing to prevailing circumstances. This was then coupled with what both leaders deemed the best approach to counter the menace they each faced vis-a-vis their interpretations of their guiding texts—the holy Quran and Hadiths.

Further, these leaders' significance encompasses knowledge production in law and jurisprudence, women's education, economics, politics, human behavior, and varying Islamic beliefs and movements. In addition, studies in Sufism (in Africa) and the life lessons and actions of Dan Fodio and Bamba are significant to the history of West Africa, particularly, and volumes of literature on them would contribute to the global study of religion, cultural influence, and understanding of Africa. Similarly, in the same fashion as African Traditional Religions, an expansive study of Sufism could also aid the development of African science and medicine. With Sufism boasting of branches of knowledge that involve herbal medicine as well as meditation for physical and mental healing, harnessing this knowledge with African Traditional Religions could prove revolutionary for African science and medicine.

Missionaries in Africa originally contributed to knowledge in and about Africa through their activities and documentation of those activities as well as what they witnessed on the continent. More importantly, indigenous missionaries' narratives about Africa are hugely significant in counterbalancing some of the misrepresentations of African cultural ethos by white missionary writers. Their significance is apparent in that their bodies of work and literature have contributed to the history of Africa, especially in the nineteenth century during the era of strife and warfare in West Africa. They contributed to not only the establishment and growth of the church in West Africa but also the political evolution of Nigeria within the aforementioned century via their documentation. However, it is apt to say their contribution to knowledge systems in Africa did not end there. Having established a foundation for the study of West African history, further research could investigate several aspects of African pasts for a holistic interpretation of the history of Africa while filling the existing lacuna in its history.

Pentecostalism, the penultimate chapter—like Chapter 3, Magic and Witchcraft—examines knowledge production through a comparative relationship between the introduction and practice of Pentecostalism in Africa and African Traditional Religions. The significance of this is that while it is common knowledge that Christianity, particularly Pentecostalism, abhors many African traditional practices, there were also practices that were embraced by Pentecostalism and allowed them to flourish. While this chapter explores the relationship between Pentecostalism and ATRs, further studies and research devoted to this relationship could contribute to the development of the production of knowledge in Africanized imported religions. It is also crucial to understanding the differing behavioral patterns between practitioners in Africa and in Pentecostal churches in other parts of the world.

The last chapter, African Spiritual Churches, is crucial to understanding the developing Africanized churches which embraced African cultural ethos, especially in liturgy. The chapter expansively defines, conceptualizes, and discusses the existence of African Christianity, different in practice from Western-originated and Western-introduced Christianity. The knowledge generated from this, like every preceding chapter, contributes to knowledge of churches in Africa and why they are different in both practice and doctrine from churches abroad. More study should be encouraged as well to examine in depth the origin, cultural values, and importance of these Africanized churches to fully comprehend the uniqueness of Africa as a deliberate culture and the practices not as absurd or discrete.

A continuous study of these churches would also show the creativity of Africans in developing churches that appeal to their cultural ethos and ideal liturgical practices, such that they did not miss what they were leaving behind. Furthermore, local instruments were developed to fit into their evolved liturgies. They also developed their own system of healing, through faith and belief, which they believe works for them. Indeed, African Christianity and African churches are deserving of more attention in African and global scholarship as a newly evolved, African-made religion, not simply derivative of Western-introduced Christianity.

In sum, knowledge production in Africa as chronicled in this book is not simply derivative of the past, and its contributions to African and global scholarship are limitless. A further academic investment in researching and investigating knowledge production of these three religions will contribute to significant knowledge exports through African literature to global academic communities and public spaces. It would also aid intellectual decolonization against Eurocentrism as this literature seeks to correct misinformation and deliberate mischaracterization of African religious practices. In addition, there are many practices (some identified above) that could be refined and developed to be more relevant and productive in contemporary Africa in the areas of entertainment, medicine, science, social sciences, and even humanities. Thus, these knowledges should be further researched, not just to comprehensively understand Africa but also to adapt the productive practices in contemporary Africa for global developmental purposes.

Notes

Introduction

1 See Preface.
2 Amanda Macias, "How Hitler's Populist Rhetoric Contributed to his Rise to Power," *Insider*. Available online: https://www.businessinsider.com/why-hitler-was-such-a-s uccessful-orator-2015-5?IR=T (accessed May 13, 2015).
3 Thomas Paine, "Common Sense" (Kindle edition), https://www.amazon.com/Common-Sense-Bestsellers-famous-Books-ebook/dp/B01M6WOBCS. Earlier in 1741, Jonathan Edward was credited to have used his speech to ignite a great revival. It is usually mentioned as one of most powerful sermons ever delivered in Christian history. People wept as they heard and it moved them to start the revival. (See Jonathan Edwards, "Sinners in the Hands of an Angry God," Blue Letter Bible, last modified May 1, 2014, https://www.blueletterbible.org/Comm/edwards_jonathan/Sermons/Sinners.cfm).
4 "Meaning of *Sacred* in English," Cambridge Dictionary, accessed November 18, 2020, https://dictionary.cambridge.org/dictionary/english/sacred.
5 Thomas W. Mann, *The Book of the Torah* (Oregon: Wipf and Stock Publishers, 2013). Many parts of the Bible are believed to be in oral forms for centuries and later set to words as written scriptures.
6 Shabbir Aktar, *The Quran and The Secular Mind: A Philosophy of Islam* (New York: Routledge, 2007).
7 Julius Lipner, *Hindus: Their Religious Beliefs and Practices* (New York: Routledge, 2012).
8 UNESCO, "Ifa Divination System," UNESCO. Available online: https://ich.unesco.org/en/RL/ifa-divination-system-00146 (accessed November 9, 2020).
9 Shawna Dolansky, "Gilgamesh and the Bible," Bible Odyssey. Available online: https://www.bibleodyssey.org/en/places/related-articles/gilgamesh-and-the-bible (accessed November 18, 2020,).
10 Michael T. Ndemanu, "Traditional African Religions and Their Influences on the Worldviews of Bangwa People of Cameroon: Expanding the Cultural Horizons of Study Abroad Students and Professionals," *Frontiers: The Interdisciplinary Journal of Study Abroad* 30, no. 1 (2018): 70–84.
11 André Lardinois, Josine Blok and Marc van der Poel, "Introduction," in *Sacred Words: Orality, Literacy and Religion*, ed. André Lardinois, Josine Blok and Marc van der Poel (Leiden: Brill, 2011), 1–14.
12 David Frankfurter, "Curses, Blessings, and Ritual Authority: Egyptian Magic in Comparative Perspective," *Journal of Ancient Near Eastern Religions* 5, no. 1 (2005): 157–85.
13 Ira Chernus, "Summary of Peter Berger, *The Sacred Canopy*." Available online: http://web.pdx.edu/~tothm/religion/Summary%20of%20Peter%20Berger,%20The%20Sacred%20Canopy.pdf (accessed November 18, 2020).

14 Kisilu Kombo, "Witchcraft: A Living Vice in Africa," *African Journal of Evangelical Theology* 22, no. 1 (2003): 73–86.

15 Ibid., 157. There is also division of labor: good angels may deliver blessings and bad angels and the angel of death deliver curses. So they are not necessarily the same all the time.

16 Frankfurter, "Curses, Blessings," 158. Also, Deut. 28 is classic in this respect; the first fourteen verses are blessings and the rest (15–68) are curses.

17 Passmore Hachalinga, "How Curses Impact People and Biblical Responses," *Journal of Adventist Mission Studies* 13, no. 1 (2017): 55–63.

18 John S. Mbiti, *African Religions and Philosophy* (Nairobi: East African Educational Publishers, 2002).

19 Hachalinga, "How Curses Impact People."

20 Ibid.

21 S. A. Oriloye, "Contents and Features of Yoruba Incantatory Poetry," *Journal of Communication and Culture* 1, no. 2 (2015): 32-44.

22 Walter Duru, "The Communicativeness of Incantations in the Traditional Igbo Society," *Journal of Media and Communication Studies* 8, no. 7 (2016): 63–70.

23 John S. Mbiti, *The Prayers of African Religion* (London: SPCK, 1975).

24 Mbiti, "The Prayers."

25 Peter F. Omonzejele, "African Concepts of Health, Disease and Treatment: An Ethical Enquiry," *Explore* 4, no. 2 (2008): 120–26.

26 Francis Mowang Ganyi and Atunka Patrick Ogar, "Orality and Medicine: The Efficacy of the Word in the Practice of Therapeutic Cures in Traditional African Medicine," *Studies in Sociology of Science* 3, no. 3 (2012): 31-5.

27 Ethel E. Thompson, "Primitive African Medical Lore and Witchcraft," *Bulletin of the Medical Library Association* 53, no. 1 (1965): 80–94.

28 Mikelle S. Omari-Obayemi, "An Indigenous Anatomy of Power and Art: A New Look at Yoruba Women in Society and Religion," *Dialectical Anthropology* 21, no. 1 (1996): 89–98.

29 Omari-Obayemi, "An Indigenous Anatomy."

30 See Prov. 18:21 KJV.

31 In some African societies, such as the Kalabari, every individual can potentially exhibit this power, but when it is misused, there is a ceremony to remove "from your mouth" the sacred power of words so that you can no longer use such power dangerously. If this rare ceremony is done, the person is essentially declared useless. Your words no longer mean anything to anybody.

32 Omari-Obayemi, "An Indigenous Anatomy."

33 See the recordings of S. A. Ọ̀ṣúnwọlé during his doctoral field research in Nigeria in the 1980s of a 65-year-old Mr. Ọlátìdoyè who was contracted to help alleviate a client's splitting headache, in Adeleke Adeeko, "Incantation, Ideophone, Reduplication, and Poetry," *The Savannah Review* 3 (2014): 73–98.

34 Adeeko, "Incantation," 79.

35 Hafizu Miko Yakasai, "Incantation in Hausa Culture: An Example of Syntactic Reduplication," *Studies of the Department of African Languages and Cultures* 44 (2010): 67–82.

36 Yakasai, "Incantation in Hausa Culture."

37 (Quran, 10:57); Qulsoom Inayat, "Islam, Divinity, and Spiritual Healing," in *Integrating Traditional Healing Practices into Counseling and Pyschotheraphy*, ed. Roy Moodley and William West (Thousand Oaks: Sage Publications, 2005), 159-169.

38 Inayat, "Islam, Divinity, and Spiritual Healing."
39 Ibid.
40 Ibid.
41 Frankfurter, "Curses, Blessings."
42 Luton Muslims Journal, "Dua: In the Name of Allah with Whose Name Nothing Can Harm (Laa Yadurru . . .)." Available online: https://lutonmuslimjournal.com/heart/laa yadduru (accessed November 18, 2020).
43 Luton Muslims Journal, "Dua: In the Name of Allah."
44 M. Mahmood Hammed and F. I. Haider, "Healing Secrets in Holy Quran," ResearchGate. Available online:https://www.researchgate.net/publication/333557344 (accessed November 18, 2020).
45 Anne Hege Grung, "Transformative Hermeneutics in the Making Through the Co-Reading of Biblical and Qur'anic Texts by Muslim and Christian Women," in *Transformative Readings of Sacred Scriptures: Christians and Muslims in Dialogue*, ed. Simone Sinn, Dina El Omari and Anne Hege Grung (Germany: The Lutheran World Federation, 2017), 29-37. It is worthy of addition that it is not the intention of the author or the book to endorse Grung's chapter. Even when contemporary beliefs, ideology, and civilization disavow this verse and its equivalent in the Bible, it has continually been used by perpetrators of domestic acts that subdues women's role to insignificance as their basis. Indeed, it is always a religious weapon in the hands of some.
46 Randall Holm, *A Paradigmatic Analysis of Authority within Pentecostalism* (Ottawa: National Library of Canada, 1996). This finds biblical reference in 2 Pet. 1:21 NIV: "For prophecy never had its origin in the human will, but prophets, though human, spoke from God as they were carried along by the Holy Spirit."
47 Holm, *A Paradigmatic Analysis.*
48 Ibid.
49 See the book of John 1:1 KJV.
50 See Gen. 1:3 and the entirety of the chapter for further explanation.
51 John Blofeld, *Mantras, Sacred Words of Power* (London: Unwin, 1977).
52 Gen. 1:1.
53 Corneliu Constantineanu and Christopher J. Scobie, "Introduction: Pentecostal Identity, Spirituality, and Theology," in *Pentecostals of the 21st Century: Identity, Belief and Praxis*, ed. Corneliu Constantineanu and Christopher J. Scobie (Eugene: Cascade Books, 2018), 4.
54 Constantineanu and Scobie, "Introduction: Pentecostal Spirituality."
55 Marius Nel, "An Attempt to Define the Constitutive Elements of a Pentecostal Spirituality," *In die Skriflig* 49, no. 1 (2015): 1–7. Also see Amos Yong, *Spirit, Word, Community: Theological Hermeneutics in Trinitarian Perspective* (Oregon: Wipf & Stock, 2006) to further see the interrelation between the spirit and the birth of the word which then translates to the community.
56 Nimi Wariboko, "West African Pentecostalism: A Survey of Everyday Theology," in *Global Renewal Christianity: Spirit-Empowered Movements, Past, Present and Future*, ed. Vinson Synan, Amos Yong, and Kwabena Asamoah-Gyadu (Florida: Charisma House Publishers, 2016), 1–18. For comparative study on the basis of the "linchpin," the central focus or engine of any gathering, he posited that Catholicism is Eucharist, Protestant is preaching the word, and Pentecostalism is prayer.
57 1 Pet 2:9 ESV.
58 Holm, *A Paradigmatic Analysis.*

59 Tom Boylston, "The Shade of the Divine: Approaching the Sacred in an Ethiopian Orthodox Christian Community," Ph. D. Thesis, Department of Anthropology London School of Economics (2012). It is also worthy of note that the Roman Catholic church had mystics who could relate directly to God; hence the famous tripartite system by Ernst Troeltsch: church, mystic, and sect. William R. Garrett, "Maligned Mysticism: The Maledicted Career of Troeltsch's Third Type," *Sociological Analysis* 36, no. 3 (1975): 205–23.

60 Marinus Iwuchukwu, "Pentecostalism, Islam, and Religious Fundamentalism in Africa," in *Pentecostalism and Politics in Africa: African Histories and Modernities,* ed. A. Afolayan, Olajumoke Yacob-Haliso and Toyin Falola (New York: Palgrave Macmillan, 2018), 43-63.

61 Holm, *A Paradigmatic Analysis.*

62 Oxford Dictionary, "Faith," Lexico. Available online: https://www.lexico.com/definition/faith (accessed on November 18, 2020).

63 Samuel Zalanga, "Pentecostalism as an Alternative Social Order in Africa," in *Pentecostalism and Politics in Africa: African Histories and Modernities,* ed. A. Afolayan, Olajumoke Yacob-Haliso and Toyin Falola (New York: Palgrave Macmillan, 2018), 277–302.

64 Zalanga, "Pentecostalism as an Alternative," 277.

65 Joseph Henrich, *The Secret of Our Success: How Culture is Driving Human Evolution, Domesticating Our Species, and Making us Smarter* (Princeton: Princeton University Press, 2017): 118.

66 Iwuchukwu, "Pentecostalism," 51.

67 Frankfurter, "Curses, Blessings."

68 Ibid.

69 See the biblical narrative of Esau and Jacob (Gen. 25; 27; 29–33; 35).

70 J. A. Motyer, "Curse," in *New Bible Dictionary,* ed. I. Howard Marshall, A. R Millard, J. I. Parker and D. J Wiseman (Illinois: Intervarsity Press, 1996), 248–9.

71 Mark 11:20–25 KJV.

72 Ps. 23.

73 Thomas Esposito and Stephen Gregg, *The Inspiration and Truth of Sacred Scripture: The Word that Comes from God and Speaks of God for the Salvation of the World* (Minnesota: Liturgical Press, 2014).

74 Isa. 55:10–11.

75 Isa. 55:10–11.

Chapter 1

1 E. J. Ozioma and O. A. N. Chinwe, "Herbal Medicines in African Traditional Medicine," *Herbal Medicine* 10 (2019): 191–214.

2 W. Bascom, *Ifa Divination: Communication Between Gods and Men in West Africa* (Bloomington: Indiana University Press, 1991).

3 F. O. Alamu, H. O. Aworinde and W. I. Isharufe, "A Comparative Study on Ifa Divination and Computer Science," *International Journal of Innovative Technology and Research* 1, no. 6 (2013): 524.

4 P. M. Peek, ed. *African Divination Systems: Ways of Knowing* (Bloomington: Indiana University Press, 1991), 193.

5 Peek, ed., "African Divination."
6 Ibid.
7 Awo Falokun Fatunmbi, *Inner Peace: Ifa Concept of Divination* (New York: Athelia Henrietta Press, 2005).
8 Evan M. Zuesse, "Divination and Deity in African Religions," *History of Religions* 15, no. 2 (1975): 158–82.
9 Zuesse, "Divination and Deity."
10 Peek, *African Divination Systems*, 3.
11 O. T. Òkéwándé, "A Semiotic Investigation of Philosophical Relations between Ifá and Ayò Olópòn among the Yorùbá People of Nigeria," *Nokoko Institute of African Studies* 6 (2017): 317–46.
12 Òkéwándé, "A Semiotic Investigation."
13 A. Adeeko, "Writing and 'Reference' in Ifa Divination Chants," *Oral Traditions* 25, no. 2 (2010): 283–303.
14 S. S. A. Odularu, "Ifa Divination in Yorùbáland 1851–1989: A Select Bibliography," *A Current Bibliography on African Affairs* 22, no. 3 (1990): 237–45.
15 Fatunmbi, *Inner Peace*, 6.
16 Oyekunle Oluyemisi Adegboyega, "The Metaphysical and Epistemological Relevance of Ifa Corpus," *International Journal of History and Philosophical Research* 5, no. 1 (2017): 28–40.
17 Practitioners and adherents believe Ifa is an oracle that derived its existence from Orunmila, the deity of knowledge. See Joseph O. Awolalu, *Yorùbá Beliefs and Sacrificial Rites* (Essex: Longman, 1979).
18 Gbenga Opasola, "Ifa as a Repository of Knowledge, Yorùbá Epistemology from Afrocentric Point of View," Academia. Available online: https://www.academia.edu/35393 902/IFA_AS_A_REPOSITORY_OF_KNOWLEDGE (accessed November 17, 2020).
19 Adegboyega, "The Metaphysical and Epistemological Relevance."
20 Ibid.
21 Oyekunle Oluyemisi Adegboyega, "Philosophical Issues in Yorùbá Proverbs," *International Journal of African Society, Cultures and Traditions* 5, no. 2 (2017): 21–30.
22 Peek, *African Divination Systems*, 38.
23 T. M. Ilesanmi, "The Traditional Theologians and the Practice of Orisa Religion in Yorùbáland," *Journal of Religion in Africa* 21, no. 3 (1991): 216–26.
24 Ilesanmi, "The Traditional Theologians," 217.
25 Peek, *African Divination Systems*, 3. It is also noteworthy to mention that the diviners, Onisegun and the Babalawo are devotees of Osanyin, the deity of herbs, leaves, and medicine.
26 D. D. O. Oyebola, "Traditional Medicine and Its Practitioners Among the Yorùbá of Nigeria: A Classification," *Social Science & Medicine. Part A: Medical Psychology & Medical Sociology* 14, no. 1 (1980): 23–9.
27 Oyebola, "Traditional Medicine and Its Practitioners."
28 Ibid., 25.
29 Ibid., 26.
30 Maria Natalia Ajayi, Gerisho Kirika, and Johnson Mavole, "Traditional Healing Practices and Holistic Health: The Implication for Christian Families in South West Region of Nigeria," *Journal of Family Medicine and Health Care* 5, no. 4 (2019): 50–8.
31 Oyebola, "Traditional Medicine and Its Practitioners," 27.
32 Ozioma and Chinwe, "Herbal Medicines," 193.
33 Ibid.

34 Ibid., 196.

35 Bascom, "Ifa Divination," 91.

36 Ibid., 95.

37 Ibid.

38 Oyebola, "Traditional Medicine and Its Practitioners," 28.

39 Wande Abimbola, *Àwọn Ojú Odù Mẹrèèrìndínlógún* (Ibadan: Ibadan University Press, 2004).

40 Tony Van Der Meer, "Spiritual Journeys: A Study of Ifa/Orisa Practitioners in the United States Initiated in Nigeria," (PhD Diss., Antioch University, 2017).

41 Fatunmbi, *Inner Peace*, 4.

42 Peek, *African Divination Systems*, 3.

43 A. R. Ogunleye, "IFA: An Epistle to the Indigenous Yorùbá Worshippers in Nigeria," *Journal of African Interdisciplinary Studies* 3, no. 1 (2019): 68–77.

44 M. J. Packer and S. T. Sierra, "A Concrete Psychological Investigation of Ifá Divination," *Revista Colombiana de Psicología* 21, no. 2 (2012): 355–71.

45 Ogunleye, "IFA: An Epistle," 71.

46 Bascom, "Ifa Divination," 84.

47 Ibid.

48 Ibid.

49 Ibid.

50 Ibid.

51 Abimbola, *Àwọn Ojú Odù Mẹrèèrìndínlógún*.

52 Ilesanmi, "The Traditional Theologians," 216.

53 Abimbola, *Àwọn Ojú Odù Mẹrèèrìndínlógún*.

54 Ibid.

55 Ilesanmi, "The Traditional Theologians," 220.

56 Agboola Odesanya, Sunday Oloruntola, and Kunle Akinjogbin, "Names as Message Vectors in Communication: Oduological Analysis of Traditional Yorùbá Personal Names from Ifa," *Journal of the Linguistic Association of Nigeria* 20, no. 1 (2017): 248–59.

57 Ibid.

58 Ibid.

59 Ibid.

60 Ogunleye, "IFA: An Epistle," 72.

61 Ibid.

62 Packer and Sierra, "A Concrete Psychological Investigation of Ifa Divination."

63 Ogunleye, "IFA: An Epistle," 73.

64 A. A. Oladiti and P. O. Oyewale, "The Yorùbá Concept of Ola in African Society: A Historical Overview," *World Scientific News* 80 (2017): 57–76.

65 Ibid., 72.

66 Eva-Marita Rinne, "Water and Healing—Experiences from the Traditional Healers in Ile-Ife, Nigeria," *Nordic Journal of African Studies* 10, no. 1 (2001): 41–65.

67 Ibid., 51.

68 Packer and Sierra, "A Concrete Psychological Investigation of Ifa Divination," 362.

69 Van der Meer, "Spiritual Journeys," 32.

70 Ibid., 33.

71 Ibid., 34–5.

72 Ibid., 35.

73 Peek, *African Divination Systems*, 2.

Chapter 2

1 Stanley Krippner, "Humanity's First Healers: Psychological and Psychiatric Stances on Shamans and Shamanism," *Archives of Clinical Psychiatry (São Paulo)* 34 (2007): 17–24.

2 Abby Wynne, "What is Shamanism?" Abby Wynne. Available online: https://abby-wynne.com/shamanic-healing-techniques/ (accessed June 27, 2021).

3 M. K. Franz, "A Gathering of Names: On the Categories and Collections of Siberian Shamanic Materials in Late Imperial Russian Museum 1880-1910" (PhD diss., University of Toronto, 2019), https://tspace.library.utoronto.ca/handle/1807/97429.

4 Zana Marovic and Mazvita M. Machinga, "African Shamanic Knowledge and Transpersonal Psychology: Spirits and Healing in Dialogue," *The Journal of Transpersonal Psychology* 49, no. 1 (2017): 21–44.

5 Marovic and Machinga, "African Shamanic Knowledge."

6 Nona J. T. Bock, "Shamanic Techniques: Their Use and Effectiveness in the Practice of Psychotherapy" (M.Sc. diss., University of Wisconsin-Stout, 2005). Available online: https://minds.wisconsin.edu/handle/1793/41567

7 Bock, "Shamanic Techniques," 34.

8 Ibid., 5.

9 Ibid.

10 Mayfair Yang, "Shamanism and Spirit Possession in Chinese Modernity: Some Preliminary Reflections on a Gendered Religiosity of the Body," *Review of Religion and Chinese Society* 2, no. 1 (2015): 52.

11 Mircea Eliade, "Recent Works on Shamanism: A Review," *History of Religions* 1, no. 1 (1961): 152–86.

12 Eliade, "Recent Works on Shamanism."

13 Manvir Singh, "The Cultural Evolution of Shamanism," *Behavioral and Brain Sciences* 41, no. 66 (2018): 1–17.

14 Krippner, "Humanity's First Healers," 16.

15 Ibid.

16 Ibid., 17.

17 Michael Witzel, "Shamanism in Northern and Southern Eurasia: Their Distinctive Methods of Change of Consciousness," *Social Science Information* 50, no. 1 (2011): 39–61.

18 Witzel, "Shamanism in Northern and Southern Eurasia."

19 There are several countries in Africa that still actively practice Shamanism such as South Africa, Kenya, Congo, and Togo. Indeed, Eric James Montgomery beliefs that "there very well may be more 'shamans' in sub-Saharan Africa than anywhere on earth." Eric James Montgomery, "Shamanism and Voodoo in Togo: The Life and Acts of Sofo Bisi," *Shaman: Journal of the International Society for Shamanistic Research* 24, no. 1–2 (2016): 65–92. Also, statistics has it that 4.7 percent of Congo citizens practice Ethnoreligions i.e., Animism and Shamanism. (See, The ARDA, "Congo, Republic of the," ARDA. Available online: https://www.thearda.com/internationalData/countries/Country_58_1.asp (accessed December 23, 2020)). In South Africa, it is referred to as "White Sangomas" in some sections of the population. (See, Ullrich Relebogilwe Kleinhempel, "White Sangomas: The Manifestation of Bantu Forms of Shamanic Calling among Whites in South Africa," *REVER-Revista de Estudos da Religião* 18, no. 1 (2018): 143–73.). Lastly as an example, there is the famous shaman,

Malidome Some, cited in Dick Russell, "How a West African Shaman Helped my
Schizophrenic Son in a Way Western Medicine Couldn't," *The Washington Post*.
Available online: https://www.washingtonpost.com/posteverything/wp/2015/03/24/
how-a-west-african-shaman-helped-my-schizophrenic-son-in-a-way-western-medi
cine-couldnt/ (accessed December 23, 2020).

20 Witzel, "Shamanism in Northern and Southern Eurasia," 33.
21 P. C. Joshi, "Psychotherapeutic Elements in Shamanistic Healing in the Context of
    Himalayan Traditions," *Delhi Psychiatry Journal* 13, no. 2 (2010): 254–7.
22 Marovic and Machinga, "African Shamanic Knowledge," 33.
23 Ibid.
24 Ibid., 11.
25 Joshi, "Psychotherapeutic Elements."
26 Ibid., 255.
27 Ibid.
28 Bock, "Shamanic Techniques," 11–12.
29 Krippner, "Humanity's First Healers," 17.
30 Ibid.
31 Ibid.
32 Bock, "Shamanic Techniques," 12.
33 Ibid., 13.
34 Mariko Namba Walter and Eva Jane Neumann Fridman, eds., *Shamanism: An
    Encyclopedia of World Beliefs, Practices, and Culture* (Oxford: ABC CLIO, 2004),
    206.
35 Bock, "Shamanic Techniques," 13–14.
36 Ibid., 14.
37 Krippner, "Humanity's First Healers."
38 Bock, "Shamanic Techniques."
39 Ibid., 15.
40 Ibid.
41 Walter and Fridman, *Shamanism*.
42 Joshi, "Psychotherapeutic Elements," 255.
43 Ibid.
44 Bock, "Shamanic Techniques," 28.
45 Ibid.
46 Ibid.
47 Ibid.
48 Ibid.
49 Ibid., 29.
50 Ibid.
51 Ibid.
52 Krippner, "Humanity's First Healers," 19.
53 Marovic and Machinga, "African Shamanic Knowledge."
54 Bock, "Shamanic Techniques," 34.
55 Ibid., 38.
56 Witzel, "Shamanism in Northern and Southern Eurasia," 5.
57 Diana Riboli, "Trance, Shamanism," in *Shamanism: An Encyclopedia of World Beliefs,
    Practices, and Culture*, ed. Mirako Namba Walter and Eva Jane Neumann Fridman
    (California: ABC-CLIO, 2004), 250–1.
58 Ibid., 252.

59 Ibid. 253.

60 Ibid.

61 James A. Overton, "Hypnosis and Shamanism," in *Shamanism: An Encyclopedia of World Beliefs, Practices, and Culture,* ed. Mirako Namba Walter and Eva Jane Neumann Fridman (California: ABC-CLIO, 2004), 149–52.

62 Overton, "Hypnosis and Shamanism."

63 Ibid.

64 Gregory G. Maskarinec, "Healing and Shamanism," in *Shamanism: An Encyclopedia of World Beliefs, Practices, and Culture,* ed. Mirako Namba Walter and Eva Jane Neumann Fridman (California: ABC-CLIO, 2004), 137–42.

65 Anne Schiller, "Offerings and Sacrifice in Shamanism," in *Shamanism: An Encyclopedia of World Beliefs, Practices, and Culture,* ed. Mirako Namba Walter and Eva Jane Neumann Fridman (California: ABC-CLIO, 2004), 197–200.

66 Bock, "Shamanic Techniques," 15.

67 Ibid., 16.

68 Ibid., 17.

69 Ibid.

70 Ibid., 19.

71 Ibid., 20.

72 Michael Winkelman, "Divination," in *Shamanism: An Encyclopedia of World Beliefs, Practices, and Culture,* ed. Mirako Namba Walter and Eva Jane Neumann Fridman (California: ABC-CLIO, 2004), 78–82.

73 Winkelman, "Divination."

74 Ibid., 78–9.

75 Marilyn Walker, "Music as Knowledge in Shamanism and Other Healing Traditions of Siberia," *Arctic Anthropology* 40, no. 2 (2003): 40–8.

76 Walker, "Music as Knowledge."

77 Ibid.

78 Ibid.

79 Ibid.

80 Stanley Krippner, "Shamans as Healers, Counselors, and Psychotherapists," *International Journal of Transpersonal Studies* 31, no. 2 (2012): 72–9.

81 L. N. Degarrod, "Dreams and Vision," in *Shamanism: An Encyclopedia of World Beliefs, Practices, and Culture,* ed. Mariko Walter and Eva Jane Neumann Fridman (California: ABC-CLIO, 2004), 89–95.

82 Degarrod, "Dreams and Vision," 90.

83 Ibid., 92.

84 Krippner, "Humanity's First Healers," 17.

85 Nancy H. Vuckovic, Christina M. Gullion, Louise A. Williams, Michelle Ramirez and Jennifer Schneider, "Feasibility and Short-term Outcomes of a Shamanic Treatment for Temporomandibular Joint Disorders," *Alternative Therapies* 13, no. 6 (2007): 18–29.

86 Vuckovic, et al., "Feasibility and Short-term Outcomes."

87 Ibid.

88 Ibid.

89 Ibid., 23.

90 Mihaly Hoppal, *Shamans and Symbols: Prehistory of Semiotics in Rock Art* (Budapest: International Society for Shamanistic Research, 2013), 41.

91 Hoppal, *Shamans and Symbols.*

92   Ibid., 52.

93   Ibid., 53.

94   Ingo Lambrecht, "A Psychological Study of Shamanic Trance States in South African Shamanism" (PhD diss., University of Witwatersrand, 1998), 4.

95   Ingo Lambrecht, "Shamans as Expert Voice Hearers." Available online: http://www .hearingvoices.org.nz/attachments/article/14/Shamans%20as%20Expert%20Voice% 20Hearers%20By%20Ingo%20Lambrecht.pdf (accessed June 27, 2020).

96   Lambrecht, "Shamans as Expert Voice Hearers," 9.

97   Krippner, "Shamans as Healers," 74.

98   Yang, "Shamanism and Spirit Possession," 55.

99   Daniel Kister, "Dramatic Performance in Shamanism," in *Shamanism: An Encyclopedia of World Beliefs, Practices, and Culture,* ed. Mariko Namba Walter and Eva Jane Neumann Fridman (California: ABC-CLIO, 2004), 82–9.

100 Kister, "Dramatic Performance in Shamanism."

Chapter 3

1   Dale Wallace, "Rethinking Religion, Magic and Witchcraft in South Africa: From Colonial Coherence to Postcolonial Conundrum," *Journal for the Study of Religion* 28, no. 1 (2015): 23–51.

2   Joseph Ki-Zerbo, *Methodology and African Prehistory* (London: James Currey, 1990).

3   James Kiernan, ed., *The Power of the Occult in Modern Africa: Continuity and Innovation in the Renewal of African Cosmologies* (Münster: LIT Verlag, 2006).

4   M. J. Wiener, "Magic Worlds Through Religion, Science and Magic," *Anthropological News* 45, no. 8 (2004): 10–11.

5   J. T. Mcneill, "Magic and Infant Science," *The Journal of Religion* 15, no. 3 (1935): 342–4.

6   J. Henry, "Magic and Science in the Sixteenth and Seventeenth Centuries," in *Companion to the History of Modern Science,* eds., R. C. Olby, G. N. Cantor, J. R. R. Christie, and M. J. S. Hodge (London: Routledge, 1996), 583–96.

7   Wiener, "Magic Worlds Through Religion."

8   P. K. Feyerabend, *Against Method: Outline of an Anarchist Theory of Knowledge* (London: NLB, 1978).

9   Martin Bernal, *Black Athena: The Afroasiatic Roots of Classical Civilization* (New Brunswick: Rutgers University Press, 1991).

10 Bernal, *Black Athena.*

11 Christian Emedolu, "From Magic to African Experimental Science: Toward a New Paradigm," *Filosofia Theoretica: Journal of African Philosophy, Culture and Religions* 4, no. 2 (2015): 68–88.

12 George James, *Stolen Legacy: The Greeks Were Not the Authors of Greek Philosophy, But the People of North Africa, Commonly Called the Egyptians* (New York: Philosophical Library, 1954).

13 Awolalu, *Yoruba Beliefs and Sacrificial Rites,* 75.

14 R. K. Popper, *Objective Knowledge: An Evolutionary Approach* (Oxford: Clarendon Press, 1972).

15 T. U. Nwala, "Summary Discourse on the Debate Concerning the Existence, Nature and Scope of African Philosophy (1970-90)," in *Critical Review of the Great Debate on*

African Philosophy 1970–1990, eds., T. U. Nwala and D. Opata (Enugu: Hillys Press, 1992), 1–60.

16 Thomas Aquinas, *Summa Theologiae*, ed. and trans. Timothy McDermott (Notre Dame: Ave Maria Press, 1989).

17 Aquinas, *Summa Theologiae*.

18 G. J. Frazer, *The Golden Bough: A Study of Magic and Religion* (London: Wordsworth, 1993).

19 Carol Nemeroff and Paul Rozin, "The Makings of the Magical Mind: The Nature and Function of Sympathetical Magical Thinking," in *Imagining the Impossible: Magical, Scientific, and Religious Thinking in Children,* eds. Karl Rosengren, Carl Johnson, and Paul Harris (Cambridge: Cambridge University Press, 2000), 1–34.

20 Nemeroff and Rozin, "The Makings of the Magical Mind."

21 Emedolu, "From Magic to African Experimental Science," 68–88.

22 Ibid.

23 Ibid.

24 Chukwueloka Uduagwu, "Understanding the Difference Between African Magic and African Science: A Conversation with Christian Emedolu," *Filosofia Theoretica: Journal of African Philosophy, Culture and Religions* 5, no. 2 (2016): 74–8.

25 Frazer, *The Golden Bough*.

26 Ibid.

27 Imre Lakatos, *Mathematics, Science and Epistemology*, eds. John Worrall and Gregory Currie (Cambridge: Cambridge University Press, 1978).

28 Merlin is a 2008–2012 British fantasy-adventure drama television program and Legend of the Seeker (also known as "Wizard's First Rule") is a 2008–2010 US television series based on novels, distributed in the United States by Disney-ABC Domestic Television. Both heavily depict a belief in wizardry, although in premodern times, with the former even linking up to modernity.

29 Monica Wilson, "Witch-beliefs and Social Structure," *American Journal of Sociology* 56 (1951): 307–13.

30 Elias K. Bongmba, *African Witchcraft and Otherness: A Philosophical and Theological Critique of Intersubjective Relations* (Albany: SUNY Press, 2001).

31 Bongmba, *African Witchcraft and Otherness*.

32 George Bond and Diane Ciekawy, eds., *Witchcraft Dialogues: Anthropological and Philosophical Exchanges* (Athens: Ohio University Center for International Studies, 2001).

33 Laurenti Magesa, *African Religion: The Moral Traditions of Abundant Life* (Toronto: Orbis Books, 2014).

34 Samuel Lumwe, "The Cosmology of Witchcraft in the African Context: Implications for Mission and Theology," *Journal of Adventist Mission Studies* 13, no. 1 (2017): 83–94.

35 Eric O. Ayisi, *An Introduction to the Study of African Culture* (Nairobi: East African Educational Publishers, 1979). See also: Jim Harries, "Witchcraft, Culture, and Theology in African Development," *African Nebula* 2 (2010): 138–53, and John S. Mbiti, *African Religions and Philosophy. Introduction to African Religions* (Nairobi: East African Educational Publishers, 2011).

36 Edward G. Parrinder, *African Traditional Religion* (London: SPCK, 1962).

37 Parrinder, *African Traditional Religion*.

38 Mbiti, "African Religions and Philosophy."

39 Ibid.

40 Matsobane J. Manala, "Witchcraft and its Impact on Black African Christians: A Lacuna in the Ministry of the Hervormde Kerk in Suidelike Afrika," *HTS Theological Studies* 60, no. 4 (2004): 1491–511.

41 Susan Drucker-Brown, "Mamprusi: Witchcraft, Subversion and Changing Gender Relations," *Africa: Journal of the International African Institute* 64, no. 4 (1993): 531–49.

42 Lumwe, "The Cosmology of Witchcraft."

43 E. E. Evans-Pritchard, "Witchcraft, Oracles and Magic among the Azande," in *Death, Mourning, and Burial: A Cross-Cultural Reader,* ed. Antonius Robben (Hoboken: Wiley-Blackwell, 1991), 83–8.

44 Evans-Pritchard, "Witchcraft, Oracles and Magic."

45 Leo Igwe, "The Witch is not a Witch: The Dynamics and Contestations of Witchcraft Accusations in Northern Ghana" (PhD diss., Universitaet Bayreuth, Germany, 2017).

46 M. Gluckman, *Custom and Conflict in Africa* (Oxford: Basil Blackwell, 1956).

47 Gluckman, *Custom and Conflict.*

48 Patrick Harries, "Exclusion, Classification and Internal Colonialism: The Emergence of Ethnicity among Tsonga-speakers of South Africa," in *The Creation of Tribalism in Southern Africa,* ed., Leroy Vail (Berkeley: University of California Press, 1989), 82–117.

49 NASA, NTC 828/308, V3586, Mr. F. McBribe, Land Agent, to Native Commissioner, Graskop, November 27, 1933.

50 Catherine Burns, "Censorship and Affection: South African Women's Letters During World War Two" presentation, History and African Studies Seminar, University of Natal, Durban, April 18, 2000).

51 Isak Niehaus, "Witchcraft and the South African Bantustans: Evidence from Bushbuckridge," *South African Historical Journal* 54, no. 1 (2012): 41–58.

52 Cameron Robert Mitchell, *African Primal Religions* (Niles: Argus Communications, 1977).

53 Larry A. Bellamy, "Witchcraft, Sorcery, Academic and Local Change in East Africa" (PhD diss., Miami University, 2004).

54 Magesa, *African Religion.*

55 Mbiti, *African Religions and Philosophy.*

56 Ibid.

57 Ibid.

58 N. Norman Miller, *Encounters with Witchcraft: Field Notes from Africa* (Albany: SUNY Press, 2012).

59 Bruce Bauer, "Cultural Foundations for Fear of Witchcraft in Africa," *Journal of Adventist Mission Studies* 13, no. 1 (2017): 1–12.

60 Miller, *Encounters with Witchcraft.*

61 Harries, "Exclusion, Classification and Internal Colonialism."

62 Lumwe, "The Cosmology of Witchcraft," 88.

63 Robert Priest, "On the Meaning of the Words 'Witch,' 'Witchcraft,' and 'Sorcery,'" HCTU. Available online: https://henrycenter.tiu.edu/2012/05/meaning-of-witch-witchcraft-and-sorcery/ (accessed November 24, 2020).

64 Dirk Kohnert, "Magic and Witchcraft: Implications for Democratization and Poverty-Alleviating Aid in Africa," *World Development: The Multi-Disciplinary International Journal Devoted to the Study and Promotion of World Development* 8, no. 24 (1996): 1347–55.

65 Kohnert, "Magic and Witchcraft."

66 Bauer, "Cultural Foundations."

67 Kisilu Kombo, "Witchcraft: A Living Vice in Africa," *Africa Journal of Evangelical Theology* 22, no. 1 (2003): 73–85.

68 Mbiti, *African Religions and Philosophy.*

69 Ibid., 41.

70 Francis Njoku, *Essays in African Philosophy, Thought & Theology* (Owerri: Claretian Institute of Philosophy, 2002).

71 Njoku, *Essays in African Philosophy.*

72 E. C. Ekeke and A. E. Chike, "God, Divinities and Spirits in African Traditional Religious Ontology," *American Journal of Social and Management Sciences* 1, no. 2 (2010): 209–18.

73 Laura S. Grillo, "African Rituals," in *The Wiley-Blackwell Companion to African Religions*, ed. Elias Bongmba (Malden: Wiley-Blackwell, 2012), 112–26.

74 Grillo, "African Rituals."

75 Ibid.

76 Ibid.

77 Ibid.

78 Ella Shohat and Robert Stam, *Unthinking Eurocentrism: Multiculturalism and the Media* (London: Routledge, 2013).

79 Walter Rodney, *How Europe Underdeveloped Africa* (Dar-Es-Salaam: Tanzanian Publishing House, 1972).

Chapter 4

1 Edward N. Zalta, ed., *The Stanford Encyclopedia of Philosophy* (Stanford: The Metaphysics Research Lab, Center for the Study of Language and Information, Stanford University, 2007).

2 Rudiger Seesemann, "Sufism in West Africa," *Religion Compass* 4, no. 10 (2010): 606–14.

3 M. A. Hanif, "Debating Sufism: The Tijāniyya and its Opponents" (PhD diss., Universität Bayreuth, Bayreuth International Graduate School of African Studies-BIGSAS, 2018), 19.

4 Karen Armstrong, *Islam: A Short History* (New York: Modern Library, 2007).

5 Sadia Dehlvi, *Sufism: The Heart of Islam* (India: Harper Collins, 2010).

6 Md Sablul Hoque, "Origin of Sufism," *EDULIGHT* 1, no. 2 (2012): 197.

7 Hoque, "Origin of Sufism."

8 Farida Khanam, "The Origin and Evolution of Sufism," *Al-Idah* 22, no. 1 (2011): 21–34.

9 Eric Geoffroy and Roger Gaetani, *Introduction to Sufism: The Inner Path of Islam* (Lanham: World Wisdom Inc., 2010).

10 Christopher Melchert, "Origins and Early Sufism," in *The Cambridge Companion to Sufism*, ed. Lloyd Ridgeon (New York: Cambridge University Press, 2015), 3–23.

11 Sara Nur Yıldız, "A Hanafi Law Manual in the Vernacular: Devletoğlu Yūsuf Balıkesrī's Turkish Verse Adaptation of the Hidāya-Wiqāya Textual Tradition for the Ottoman Sultan Murad II (824/1424)," *Bulletin of the School of Oriental and African Studies* 80, no. 2 (2017): 283–304.

12 John Glover, *Sufism and Jihad in Modern Senegal: The Murid Order* (Rochester: University of Rochester Press, 2007).

13 Malek Muhammad Towghi, "Foundations of Muslim Images and Treatment of the World Beyond Islam (Vols. I-IV)" (PhD diss., Michigan State University, 1991).

14 Melchert, "Origins and Early Sufism."

15 Deepshikha Shahi, "Introducing Sufism to International Relations Theory: A Preliminary Inquiry into Epistemological, Ontological, and Methodological Pathways," *European Journal of International Relations* 25, no. 1 (2019): 250–75.

16 Alexander Knysh, "'Th. Emil Homerin' (ed. and trans.): Ā 'ishah al-Bā ū' niyyah, The Principles of Sufism [Book review]," *Der Islam* 92, no. 1 (2015): 270–3.

17 Martin Lings, *What is Sufism?* (Berkeley: University of California Press, 1975).

18 Mohsen Tousi, "Education in Islam: Contemporary Issues and Challenges," *Journal of Educational and Social Research* 2, no. 4 (2012): 49.

19 Ali Asani, "'So That you may Know One Another': A Muslim American Reflects on Pluralism and Islam," *The Annals of the American Academy of Political and Social Science* 588, no. 1 (2003): 40–51.

20 William C. Chittick, *The Sufi Path of Knowledge: Ibn Al-Arabi's Metaphysics of Imagination* (Albany: SUNY Press, 2010).

21 Idries Shah, *The Way of the Sufi* (London: Octagon Press Ltd., 2004).

22 J. Spencer Trimingham, *The Sufi Orders in Islam* (Oxford: Oxford University Press, 1998).

23 Seán McLoughlin and Muzamil Khan, "Ambiguous Traditions and Modern Transformations of Islam: The Waxing and Waning of an 'Intoxicated' Sufi Cult in Mirpur," *Contemporary South Asia* 15, no. 3 (2006): 289–307.

24 Geoffroy and Gaetani, *Introduction to Sufism*.

25 Abdelaziz Mohamed and Mohamed Mosaad, "Ibn ʿAṭā ʾ Allāh al-Sakandarī: A Sufi, ʿĀlim and Faqīh," *Comparative Islamic Studies* 9, no. 1 (2015): 41–66.

26 Leonard Lewisohn, "Sufism and Ismāʿīlī Doctrine in the Persian Poetry of Nizārī Quhistānī (645–721/1247–1321)," *Iran* 41, no. 1 (2003): 229–51.

27 Olav Hammer, "Sufism for Westerners," in *Sufism in Europe and North America*, ed., David Westerlund (London: Routledge, 2004), 139–55.

28 Chittick, *The Sufi Path of Knowledge*.

29 Abu Nasr Al-Sarraj, "The Kitab al-Luma'fil Tasawwuf of Abu Nasr 'Abdallah B. 'Ali al-Sarraj al-Tusi," trans. Reynold Alleyne Nicholson, *Gibb Memorial Series* 22 (1914): 70–5. *Nicholson wrongly mentioned the ayah of Holy Quran as (3-182) instead of (3-185)*.

30 Robert Frager and Clifton Fadiman, *Essential Sufism* (San Francisco: HarperCollins Publishers, 1999).

31 Ǧawād Nūrbaḫš, *The Psychology of Sufism: (Del wa Nafs): A Discussion of the Stages of Progress and Development of the Sufi's Psyche while on the Sufi Path* (London: Khaniqahi-Nimatullahi, 1992).

32 Margaret Smith, *Studies in Early Mysticism in the Near and Middle East* (Bloomsbury: One World, 1995).

33 Dehlvi, *Sufism*.

34 Ahmad Dallal, "The Origins and Objectives of Islamic Revivalist Thought, 1750-1850," *Journal of the American Oriental Society* 113, no. 3 (1993): 341–59.

35 Julia Ann Clancy-Smith, *Rebel and Saint: Muslim Notables, Populist Protest, Colonial Encounters (Algeria and Tunisia, 1800-1904)* (Berkeley: University of California Press, 1994).

36 Ngala Chome, "The Political Role of Islam," in *The Oxford Handbook of Kenyan Politics*, eds., Nic Cheeseman, Karuti Kanyinga, and Gabrielle Lynch (Oxford: Oxford University Press, 2019), 150–61.

37 Paul L. Heck, "Sufism–What Is It Exactly?" *Religion Compass* 1, no. 1 (2007): 148–64.

38 Heck, "Sufism-What is it Exactly?"

39 Valerie J. Hoffman, *Sufism, Mystics, and Saints in Modern Egypt* (Columbia: University of South Carolina Press, 1995).

40 Miriam Hoexter, S. N. Eisentatdt and Nehemia Levtzion, *The Public Sphere in Muslim Societies* (Albany: SUNY Press, 2002), 109–18.

41 Heck, "Sufism–What Is It Exactly?"

42 Franklin D. Lewis, *Rumi-Past and Present, East and West: The Life, Teachings, and Poetry of Jalâl Al-Din Rumi* (Bloomsbury: Oneworld Publications, 2014).

43 Jawid Ahmad Mojaddedi, *The Biographical Tradition in Sufism: The Ṭabaqāt Genre from Al-Sulamī to Jāmī* (London: Psychology Press, 2001).

44 Jonathan G. Katz, "Dreams and their Interpretation in Sufi Thought and Practice," in *Dreams and Visions in Islamic Societies*, ed. Ozgen Felek and Alexander Knysh (Albany: SUNY Press, 2012), 190.

45 Geoffroy and Gaetani, *Introduction to Sufism*.

46 Ian Richard Netton, *Ṣūfī Ritual: The Parallel Universe* (London: Psychology Press, 2000).

47 Suha Taji-Farouki, *Beshara and Ibn'Arabi: A Movement of Sufi Spirituality in the Modern World* (Oxford: Anqa Publishing, 2007).

48 Muhannad Al-Tawil, "The Importance of Sufi Traditions to Jerzy Grotowski's Practice" (PhD diss., University of Kent, 2017).

49 Joseph Hill, "Sufism Between Past and Modernity," in *Handbook of Contemporary Islam and Muslim Lives*, ed. M. Woodward and R. Lukens-Bull (Cham: Springer, 2019), 1–26.

50 Aíshah al-Ba 'uniyyah, *The Principles of Sufism* (New York: NYU Press, 2014).

51 Rachida Chih, "What is a Sufi Order? Revisiting the Concept Through a Case Study of the Khalwatiyya in Contemporary Egypt," in *Sufism and the 'Modern' in Islam*, ed. Martin van Bruinessen and Julia Day Howell (London: Bloomsbury, 2007), 21–38.

52 Patrick J. Ryan, "The Mystical Theology of Tijānī Sufism and its Social Significance in West Africa," *Journal of Religion in Africa* 30, no. 2 (2000): 208–24.

53 Joseph Lumbard, "Al-Insan Al-Kamil Doctrine and Practice," *Islamic Quarterly* 38, no. 4 (1994): 261.

54 Idries Shah, *The Way of the Sufi* (London: Octagon Press Ltd., 1999).

55 Shah, *The Way of the Sufi*.

56 Etin Anwar, *Gender and Self in Islam* (London: Routledge, 2006).

57 Pavel V. Basharin, "The Problem of Free Will and Predestination in the Light of Satan's Justification in Early Sufism," *English Language Notes* 56, no. 1 (2018): 119–38.

58 William C. Chittick, *The Sufi Path of Love: The Spiritual Teachings of Rumi* (Albany: SUNY Press, 1984).

59 Elizabeth Sirriyeh, *Sufis and Anti-Sufis: The Defence, Rethinking and Rejection of Sufism in the Modern World* (London: Routledge, 2014).

60 Arthur John Arberry, *Sufism: An Account of the Mystics of Islam* (New York: Dover Publications, 2002).

61 William A. Graham, *Divine Word and Prophetic Word in Early Islam* (Berlin: de Gruyter, 1977).

62 Basharin, "The Problem of Free Will."

63 Arthur John Arberry, *The Doctrine of the Sufis* (Cambridge: Cambridge University Press, 1977).

64 Titus Burckhardt, *Introduction to Sufi Doctrine* (Bloomington: World Wisdom Inc., 2008).

65 Oludamini Ogunnaike, "Sufism and Ifa: Ways of Knowing in Two West African Intellectual Traditions." PhD diss., Harvard University, 2015).

66 Ogunnaike, "Sufism and Ifa."

67 Mizrap Polat, "Tasawwuf-Oriented Educational Philosophy and Its Relevance to the Formation of Religion and Ethics Course Curriculum," *Universal Journal of Educational Research* 5, no. 5 (2017): 806–14.

68 M. van Bruinessen, "Sufism and the 'Modern' in Islam," *ISIM Newsletter* 13, no. 1 (2003): 62.

69 Mark Woodward, Muhammad Sani Umar, Inayah Rohmaniyah and Mariani Yahya, "Salafi Violence and Sufi Tolerance? Rethinking Conventional Wisdom," *Perspectives on Terrorism* 7, no. 6 (2013): 58–78.

70 S. H. Nizamie, M. Z. Katshu and N. A. Uvais, "Sufism and Mental Health," *Indian Journal of Psychiatry* 55, no. 2 (2014): 215–23.

71 Mohammad Zarasi, "Interpretation of the Quran: A Comparative Study of the Methodologies of Abdolkarim Soroush and Mohammad Mojtahed Shabestari" (Phd diss., International Islamic University, 2018).

72 Titus Burckhardt, *Art of Islam: Language and Meaning* (Bloomington: World Wisdom Inc, 2009).

73 Burckhardt, *Art of Islam.*

74 Abdul Hamid El-Zein, "Beyond Ideology and Theology: The Search for the Anthropology of Islam," *Annual Review of Anthropology* 6, no. 1 (1977): 227–54.

75 Katherine Ewing, "The Politics of Sufism: Redefining the Saints of Pakistan," *The Journal of Asian Studies* 42, no. 2 (1983): 251–68.

76 Bruinessen, "Sufism and the 'Modern' in Islam."

77 Nile Green, *Sufism: A Global History* (Hoboken: Wiley-Blackwell, 2012).

78 Paul L. Heck, "Mysticism as Morality: The Case of Sufism," *Journal of Religious Ethics* 34, no. 2 (2006): 253–86.

79 Burckhardt, *Introduction to Sufi Doctrine.*

80 Idries Shah, *Learning How to Learn: Psychology and Spirituality in the Sufi Way* (London: Octagon Press Ltd., 1978.)

81 Charlene Tan, *Islamic Education and Indoctrination: The Case in Indonesia* (London: Routledge, 2012).

82 Shah, *The Way of the Sufi.*

83 Scott Kugle, *Sufis and Saints' Bodies: Mysticism, Corporeality, and Sacred Power in Islam* (Chapel Hill: University of North Carolina Press, 2011).

84 Kugle, *Sufis and Saints' Bodies.*

85 Sirriyeh, *Sufis and Anti-Sufis.*

86 Shahida Bilqies, "Understanding the Concept of Islamic Sufism," *Journal of Education & Social Policy* 1, no. 1 (2014): 55–72.

87 Shoaib Ul-Haq and F. R. Khan, "A Sufi View of Human Transformation and Its Organizational Implications," in *Handbook of Personal and Organizational Transformation*, ed. J. Neal (Cham: Springer International Publishing, 2018), 833–65.

88 Lamin O. Sanneh, *Beyond Jihad: The Pacifist Tradition in West African Islam* (Oxford: Oxford University Press, 2016).

89 Ernest Gellner, "The Great Patron: A Reinterpretation of Tribal Rebellions," *European Journal of Sociology/Archives Européennes de Sociologie/Europäisches Archiv für Soziologie* 10, no. 1 (1969): 61–9.

90 Saladdin Ahmed, "What is Sufism?" *Forum Philosophicum* 13, no. 2 (2008): 229–46.

91 Daisy Hilse Dwyer, "Women, Sufism, and Decision-Making in Moroccan Islam," in *Women in the Muslim World*, ed. Lois Beck and Nikki Keddie (Cambridge: Harvard University Press, 2013), 585–98.

92 Yalda Babaei, "Trends in Sufism: From The Beginning Until The Fifth Century AH," *Islamic Mysticism* 10, no. 37 (2013): 145–59.

93 Babaei, "Trends in Sufism."

94 Deepshikha Shahi, "The Entry of Sufism into Global International Relations: A Move Beyond the State of the Art," in *Sufism: A Theoretical Intervention in Global International Relations*, ed., Deepshika Shahi (London: Rowman & Littlefield International, 2020), 1–14.

95 Annemette Kirkegaard, "Music and Transcendence: Sufi Popular Performances in East Africa," *Temenos-Nordic Journal of Comparative Religion* 48, no. 1 (2012): 29–48.

96 Topp Fargion, Janet, Le Guennec-Coppens and Sophie Mery, "The Music of Zenj: Arab-African Crossovers in the music of Zanzibar," *Journal des africanistes* 72, no. 2 (2002): 203–12.

97 Abdul-Razzaq Solagberu, "The Impact of Sufism on the Culture of the People of Ilorin, Nigeria," *Journal of Muslim Minority Affairs* 32, no. 3 (2012): 400–10.

98 Solagberu, "The Impact of Sufism."

99 Ibid.

100 Anne Bang, *Sufis and Scholars of the Sea: Family Networks in East Africa, 1860-1925* (London: Routledge, 2004).

101 Bang, *Sufis and Scholars of the Sea.*

102 Solagberu, "The Impact of Sufism," 405–6.

103 Seesemann, "Sufism in West Africa."

104 Heck, "Sufism–What is it Exactly?"

105 Knut S. Vikør, "Sufi Brotherhoods in Africa," *The History of Islam in Africa*, eds. Nehemia Levtzion and Randall L. Pouwels (Oxford: James Currey, 2000), 441–76.

106 Zain Abdullah, *Black Mecca: The African Muslims of Harlem* (Oxford: Oxford University Press, 2010).

107 Aziz A. Batran, *The Qadiryya Brotherhood in West Africa and the Western Sahara: The Life and Times of Shaikh al-Mukhtar al-Kunti (1729-1811)* (Rabat: Publications de l'Institut des etudes Africaines, 2001).

108 Batran, *The Qadiryya Brotherhood.*

109 Lucy C. Behrman, *Muslim Brotherhoods and Politics in Senegal* (Cambridge: Harvard University Press, 2013).

110 Benjamin F. Soares, "Saint and Sufi in Contemporary Mali," in *Sufism and the 'Modern' in Islam*, eds. Martin Bruinessen and Julia Day Howell (London: IB Tauris, 2007), 76–91.

111 Jamil M. Abun-Nasr, *The Tijaniyya: A Sufi Order in the Modern World* (London: Oxford University, 1965).

112 Seesemann, "Sufism in West Africa."

113 Ryan, "The Mystical Theology of Tijānī Sufism."

114 Dinesh Bhugra, ed., *Psychiatry and Religion: Context, Consensus and Controversies* (London: Psychology Press, 1997).

115 Mohammad Iqbal, *The Reconstruction of Religious Thought in Islam* (Stanford: Stanford University Press, 2013).

116 Farid al-Din Attar, *Muslim Saints and Mystics: Episodes from the Tadhkirat Al-Auliya'* (London: Routledge, 2007).

117 Iqbal, *The Reconstruction of Religious Thought*.

118 Stephen Engstrom, "Kant's Conception of Practical Wisdom," *Kant-studien* 88, no. 1 (1997): 16.

119 Attar, *Muslim Saints and Mystics*.

120 K. W. M. Fulford and Mike Jackson, "Spiritual Experience and Psychopathology," *Philosophy, Psychiatry, & Psychology* 4, no. 1 (1997): 41–65.

121 World Health Organization, "The World Health Report 2001: Mental Health: New Understanding, New Hope," WHO. Available online: https://apps.who.int/iris/handle/10665/42390 (accessed September 30, 2020).

Chapter 5

1 Antony Black, *The History of Islamic Political Thought* (Edinburgh: Edinburgh University Press, 2002); and Bernard Lewis, *The Political Language of Islam* (Chicago: University of Chicago Press, 1988).

2 In the subsequent pages, it is mentioned that Dan Fodio sought to correct the erroneous practice of Islam in Hausaland.

3 The quest for change pursued by the Prophet was religious and not political, thus while what followed had great implications in defining the nature of politics and political system in the Muslim world, essentially, the Prophet's activities were strictly religious. This chapter shall focus on the political and intellectual aspect of the Sokoto Jihad rather than its religious prescriptions.

4 P. B. Clarke, *West Africa and Islam: A Study of Religious Development from the 8th to the 20th Century* (London: Edward Arnold, 1982), 60.

5 This term is not used here pejoratively, but rather to describe people who do not share a common religious practice with an intruding religion.

6 Murray Last, "The Book in the Sokoto Caliphate," in *The Meanings of Timbuktu*, ed. S. Jeppie, and S. B. Diagne (Cape Town: Human Sciences Research Council Press, 2008), 147–55.

7 Ibrahim Sulaiman, *A Revolution in History: The Jihad of Usman Dan Fodio* (London: Mansell, 1986), xvi–xviii.

8 A. Smith, "The Contemporary Significance of the Academic Ideals of the Sokoto Jihad," in *Studies in the History of Sokoto Caliphate: The Sokoto Seminar Papers*, ed. Y. B. Usman (Lagos: Third Press International, 1979), 245–6.

9 M. Hiskett, "Kitāb al-farq: A Work on the Habe Kingdoms Attributed to 'Uthmān dan Fodio," *Bulletin of the School of Oriental and African Studies* 23, no. 3 (1960): 558–79. Ismail Balogun, "The Life and Work of the Mujaddid of West Africa, "Uthmān B. Fūdī Popularly Known as Usumanu Ḍan Fodio," *Islamic Studies* 12, no. 4 (1973): 271–92. Available online: http://www.jstor.org/stable/20846894 (accessed November 27, 2020).

10 This piece is described by I. A. B. Balogun as Dan Fodio's magnum opus. See I. A. B. Balogun, *The Life and Works of Usman Dan Fodio: The Muslim Reformer of West Africa* (Lagos: Islamic Publications Bureau, 1981), 49.

11 Balogun, *The Life and Works of Usman Dan Fodio*.

12 John O. Hunwick, "A Region of the Mind: Medieval Arab Views of African Geography and Ethnography and their Legacy," *Sudanic Africa: A Journal of Historical Sources* 16 (2005): 103–36.

13 Y. B. Usman, *The Transformation of Katsina* (Zaria: ABU Press, 1981), 4. These arrangements were later transformed into an emirate system soon after the Usman Dan Fodio Jihad.

14 Saylor, "The Hausa Kingdoms," Saylor. Available online: http://www.saylor.org/site/wp-content/uploads/2012/10/HIST101-10.2.2-HausaKingdom-FINAL1.pdf (accessed November 27, 2020).

15 The Sarkin Gobir operated an oppressive political system that had no regard for Islamic principles of justice and equity. His subjects were aggrieved by social and economic exploitation, such as the imposition of uncanonical taxes. Dan Fodio's criticisms against such an oppressive system won the hearts of many Muslims and non-Muslims alike.

16 Hiskett, "Kitāb al-farq," 558–79.

17 Balogun, *The Life and Works of Usman Dan Fodio*, 27.

18 Sulaiman, *A Revolution in History*, 28–9.

19 Ibid., 10–11.

20 Ibn Khaldun, "The Muqaddimah (1377)," cited in Uthman ibn Muhammad ibn Fudi and Fathi Hasan al-Masri, *Bayan Wujub Al-hijra 'Ala 'L-'ibad* (Khartoum: Khartoum University Press, 1978), 14.

21 Ibn Khaldun, *The Muqaddimah*, 22.

22 Ibid., 24.

23 Aliyu Shehu Usman Shagari and J. Boyd, *Uthman Dan Fodio: The Theory and Practice of Leadership* (Lagos: Islamic Publication Bureau, 1978), 12.

24 Ibn Fudi and Masri, *Bayan Wujub Al-hijra Ala 'L-Ibad*, ed. and trans. F. H. E. Masri, 9.

25 Ibid., 10–11.

26 Ibid., 23.

27 Ibid.

28 Ibid.

29 Smith, "The Contemporary Significance," 245–6.

30 Masri discussed how the style and pattern of Dan Fodio are dictated by the way he begins and ends his writings in the introduction of the translated version of *Bayan Wujub Al-hijra Ala-l-Ibad* in 1978.

31 Alhaji Garba Saidu, "The Significance of Shehu's Sermon and Poems in Ajami," in *Studies in the History of Sokoto Caliphate: The Sokoto Seminar Papers*, ed. Y. B. Usman (Zaria: Department of History, Ahmadu Bello University, 1979), 195–216.

32 Balogun, *The Life and Works of Usman Dan Fodio*, 43–8.

33 Ibid., 49.

34 Ibn Fudi and Masri, *Bayan Wujub Al-hijra*.

35 Ibid.

36 Last, "The Book in the Sokoto Caliphate," 57.

37 Ibn Fudi and Masri, *Bayan Wujub Al-hijra*, 14.

38 Ibid.

39 For a specific definition of fiqh, see page 10.

40 Ibn Fudi and Masri, *Bayan Wujub Al-hijra*, 14.

41 Ibid., 135.

42 Ibid., 137.

43 Ibid.

44 Ibid.
45 Ibid., 61–2.
46 For details, see translations of some of his poems in Saidu, "The Significance of Shehu's Sermon," 197–216.
47 Shaykh Abdullahi Dan Fodio, *Taziyin Al-Waraqat*, ed. and trans. M. Hiskett (Ibadan: Ibadan University Press, 1963), 87.
48 Jean Boyd and Murray Last, "The Role of Women as 'Agents Religieux' in Sokoto," *Canadian Journal of African Studies* 19, no. 2 (1985).
49 Uthman ibn Fudi, *Kitab Nur-ul-Albab*, cited in Abdullah Hakim Quick, "Aspects of Islamic Social Intellectual History in Hausaland: 'Uthman ibn Fudi, 1774-1804 CE" (PhD diss. University of Toronto, 2002), 195.
50 Ibn Fudi, *Kitab Nar ul-Albab,* 195–6.
51 Ibid., 197.
52 Hiskett, "Kitāb Al-farq."
53 Ibid., 7–13.
54 Muhammad Bello, *Usul al-Siyasah*, cited in Mukhtar Umar Bunza, "The Application of Islamic Law and the Legacies of Good Governance in the Sokoto Caliphate, Nigeria (1804-1903): Lessons for the Contemporary Period," *Electronic Journal of Islamic and Middle Eastern Law (EJIMEL)* 1, no. 4 (2013): 84–101.
55 Ibn Fudi and Masri, *Bayan Wujub Al-hijra*, 74.
56 Ibid., 74–5.
57 Uthman ibn Fudi, *Manhai al-'Abidin*, cited in Quick, "Aspects of Islamic Social Intellectual History."
58 Sule Ahmed Gusau, "Economic Ideas of Shehu Usman Dan Fodio," *Journal of Muslim Minority Affairs* 10, no. 1 (1989): 151.
59 Gusau, "Economic Ideas of Shehu Usman Dan Fodio."
60 Mahdi Adamu, "Distribution of Trading Centres in the Central Sudan in the 18th and 19th Centuries," in *Studies in the History of Sokoto Caliphate: The Sokoto Seminar*, ed. Y. B. Usman (Lagos: Third Press International, 1979): 59–98.
61 Sa'ad Abubakar, "Survey of the Economy of the Eastern Emirates of the Sokoto Caliphate in the 19th Century," in *Studies in the History of Sokoto Caliphate: The Sokoto Seminar Papers*, ed. Y. B. Usman (Lagos: Third Press International, 1979): 105–24; and A. G. Na-Dama, "Urbanization in the Sokoto Caliphate: A Case Study of Kauran-Namoda," in *Studies in the History of Sokoto Caliphate: The Sokoto Seminar*, ed. Y. B. Usman (Lagos: Third Press International, 1979), 140–64.
62 When it became clear that Jihad was eminent, Dan Fodio wrote this text as an important handout on allegiance and the need to remain firm to the rules of engagement. To be able to conduct a successful war and establish a government, allegiance is required from those people who swore to take part. In *Bayan Wujub Al-hijra Ala-l-Ibad*, the sixteenth chapter was dedicated to the conditions that make Jihad obligatory.
63 Dan Fodio refers to the historical Joseph who later became leader in Egypt. His ascension to a position of authority was because he was found worthy and not because he requested it.
64 Ibn Fudi and Masri, *Bayan Wujub Al-hijra*, 64.
65 Ibid., 65.
66 Foduye, *Wathiqat al-ikhwaan*, 7.
67 Ibn Fudi and Masri, *Bayan Wujub Al-hijra*, 142.
68 Ibid..

69 Martin Z. Njuema, "Sokoto and her Provinces: Some Reflections on the Case of
    Adamawa," in *Studies in the History of Sokoto Caliphate: The Sokoto Seminar*, ed. Y. B.
    Usman (Lagos: Third Press International, 1979), 320.
70 The concept of state and politics in Western political thought does not envisage
    intimacy between the state and spirituality or matters of God. The Church and largely
    ceremonial monarchs are not essential to the development of politics and state.

Chapter 6

1   There are basically three most important Sufi orders in West Africa: the Qadiriyya,
    named after Abd al-Qadir al-Jilani (d. 1166 in Baghdad), the Tijaniyya, founded by
    Ahmad al-Tijani (d. 1815 in Fez, Morocco), and the Muridiyya, established in the late
    nineteenth century by the Senegalese Shaykh Amadou Bamba (1853–1927). K. S. Vikør,
    Sufi and Scholar on the Desert Edge: Muhammad b. ʿAlī al-Sānūsī and His Brotherhood
    (Evanston: Northwestern University Press, 1995); N. Levtzion and R. Pouwels, eds., *The
    History of Islam in Africa* (Athens: Ohio University Press, 2000), 441–76.
2   Farah Michelle Kimbal, "The Pen and the Cannon: Shaykh Ahmadou Bamba's Non-
    Violent Jihad."Available online: http://www.sacredweb.com/online_articles/SW24_ki
    mball.pdf (accessed November 25, 2020).
3   Ceddo is a Wolof culture that celebrates the court values of bravery, pride and
    leisurely life. For details, see Shaykh Anta Babou, "Educating the Murid: Theory and
    Practices of Education in Amadu Bamba's Thought," *Journal of Religion in Africa* 33,
    no. 3 (2003): 310–27.
4   *Wann* is a Wolof word which means to count. It was employed in the counting the
    sound of the drum and depicting the number of times a word appears in the Quran.
    Whoever that wins this contest is celebrated by friends and young girls in the village.
    Lawaan is a ceremony organized to celebrate young men who graduated from
    studying the Quran.
5   Donal Cruise O'Brien, *The Mourides of Senegal: The Political and Economic
    Organization of an Islamic Brotherhood* (London: Oxford University Press, 1971), 286.
6   Lucy E. Creevey, "Ahmad Bamba 1850–1927," in *Studies in West African Islamic
    History: The Cultivators of Islam*, ed. John Ralph Willis (London: Frank Cass, 1979),
    278–80.
7   Details about his nonviolent approach to peace will be discussed in subsequent sub-
    themes.
8   David Dickson, *Political Islam in Sub-Saharan Africa: The Need for a New Research
    and Diplomatic Agenda* (Washington, DC: United Institute of Peace, 2005), 1, 9.
9   This is not to undermine the impact of Qadiriyya as the oldest Sufi order in Senegal or
    even in Africa, but rather to further explain the influence and impact of Sufism in the
    formation of religious groups that in turn transformed the sociopolitical and cultural
    landscapes of their societies.
10 Babou, "Educating the Murid."
11 Fernand Dumont, "Amadou Bamba, apotre de la non-violence (1850-1927)," *Notes
    Africaines: Bulletin d'information et de Correspondance de l'Institut Français d'Afrique
    Noire Notes Africaines* 121 (1969): 20–4; Valentim Fernandes, Théodore Monod, and
    Raymond Mauny, *Description de la côte occidentale d'Afrique: (Sénégal du Cap de*

Monte, Archipels) Publicações do Centro de Estudos da Guiné Portuguesa 11 (Bissau: Centro de Estudos da Guiné Portuguesa, 1951).

12 Shaykhh Ahmadou Bamba, "Masālik-al-Jinān (The Ways of Paradise)," verses 80-82, trans. S. Sam Mbaye. Available online:https://www.kinti.se/mamediarra/downloads/f iles/Masalik_en_A5_aminta.pdf (accessed November 25, 2020)

13 The Tarbiyya School was highly populated compared to the conventional schools in Senegal. This is because adults who did not have previous Islamic education dominated the school. For details, see Fallou Ngom, "Amadu Bamba's Pedagogy and the Development of Ajam Literature," *African Studies Review* 52, no. 1 (2009): 99–123.

14 Amadu Bamba Mbacke, "Tazawudu Shubaan, 'Viatique des jeunes,'" in *Recueil de Poemes en Sciences Religieuses de Cheikh A. Bamba* 1 (Rabat: Dar El Kitab, 1988), quoted in Babou, "Educating the Murid," 314.

15 Babou, "Educating the Murid," 310–27.

16 Seesemann, "Sufism in West Africa," 588.

17 Ibid.

18 The practice of ascetic life (taming of the canal nature of man) ushers humans into the realm of the uncommon. Thus, the resort to such lifestyle was a common practice among the Qadiriyya and other Sufi order.

19 Saliou Mbacke, *The Mouride Order* (Berkeley: Berkley Center for Religion Peace and World Affairs, 2016), 4.

20 Babou, "Educating the Murid," 310–27.

21 Bamba Mbacke, "Tazawudu Shubaan, " quoted in Babou, "Educating the Murid," 314.

22 "*Nafs*" are the invincible creation in human that causes them to sin and which denies them the ultimate attainment of the total peace and communion with God. The battle to contain *nafs* is considered among Sufis as the greatest of all jihads.

23 John Renard, *Seven Doors to Islam: Spirituality and the Religious Life of Muslims* (Berkeley: University of California Press, 1944).

24 According to Shaykh Babou, the first village founded by Amadu Bamba is called *Daaru*. The establishment of the village attracted disciples. The village was completely out of sight of colonial administrators and offered a suitable environment for the cleric's mystical retreats and religious activities. Bamba spent two years in *Daaru*, thereafter he moved further north to found the village of *Tuba*. For details see, Shaykhh Anta Babou, "Contesting Space, Shaping Places: Making Room for the Muridiyya in Colonial Senegal, 1912-45," *The Journal of African History* 46, no. 3 (2005): 409.

25 Ngom Fallou, maintained that in Murid hagiographic sources, the death of Ahmadou Bamba's father was turning point in Bamba's rise as a reputable Islamic scholar. For details see Ngom Fallou, *Muslim Beyond the Arab World: The Odyssey of Ajami and Muridiyya* (Oxford: Oxford University Press, 2016), 58.

26 Mback, *The Mouride Order.*

27 Creevey, "Ahmad Bamba 1850-1927."

28 Babou, "Contesting Space," 410.

29 Ibid.

30 Global Nonviolent Action Database, "Sheikh Amadu Bàmba's Murid Resistance to French Colonial Oppression," Global Nonviolent Action Database. Available online: https://nvdatabase.swarthmore.edu/content/sheikh-amadu-b-mba-s-mur-d-resist ance-french-colonial-oppression (accessed November 25, 2020)

31 Ibid., David Robinson, for example, also mentioned that the French and the Murids governed the peanut basin in an arrangement that is similar to the indirect rule system as featured in Northern Nigeria, Morocco etc. This suggests a possible

arrangement by the Murids that denied total control of the peanut basin by the French colonialist. For details, see David Robinson, "Beyond Resistance and Collaboration: Amadu Bamba and the Murids of Senegal," *Journal of Religion in Africa* 21, no. 2 (1991): 149–71, https://www.jstor.org/stable/1580803.

32 Global Nonviolent Action Database, "Sheikh Amadu Bàmba's Murid Resistance."
33 Ibid., 219.
34 Ahmadou Bamba. "Masālik-al-Jinān (The Ways of Paradise)." Verses 80-2. Trans. Sam Mbaye. Available online: https://www.kinti.se/mamediarra/downloads/files/Masalik _en_A5_aminta.pdf (accessed November 25, 2020).53.
35 Ibid., 24.
36 Global Nonviolent Action Database, "Sheikh Amadu Bàmba's Murid Resistance."
37 Ngom, "Amadu Bamba's Pedagogy," 107.
38 Ibid., 322.
39 Ibid., 321.
40 Ibid., 108.
41 Fallou Ngom, "West African Manuscripts in Arabic and African Languages and Digital Preservation," in *Oxford Research Encyclopedia of African History* (Oxford: Oxford University Press, 2016), 1–28.
42 Kimbal, "Pen and the Cannon."
43 Ibid., 92.
44 Ibid.
45 Mouhammadou Lamine Diop, *Irwā al Nadeem* (Touba: Imprimérie Daray Borom Touba, 2006), 39.
46 David Robinson, *Paths of Accommodation: Muslim Societies and French Colonial Authorities in Senegal and Mauritania, 1880–1920* Western African Studies (Athens: Ohio University Press, 2000), 187.
47 Glover, *Sufism and Jihad in Modern Senegal*, 7.
48 Shaykhh Anta Babou, *Fighting the Greater Jihad: Amadou Bamba and the Founding of the Muridiyya* (Athens: Ohio University Press, 2007), 117–18.
49 Bamba had a very large following which was not restricted to those he had in eastern Bawol. He had a lot of followers in most part of Jolof and Cayor, which he had taught or met in the past. Following the demise of Lat Dior (Lat Dior was a Wolof king who resisted French conquest and occupation of his territory) in a battle with the French. Many saw Bamba as a rallying point. It was noted that when French political agents travelled through the Northern Cayor in 1889, he found in Bamba's followers, former weavers who had little Islamic instructions and were clearing new lands for cultivation, other came from important marabouts lineage in the region, while others were former slaves. Many were expelled from this region and Amadou Bamba was forced to leave for St. Louis where he was falsely charged with organizing jihad against the colonial state. For details see Robinson, "Beyond Resistance and Collaboration," 149–71. See also Babou, "Contesting Space," 405–26.
50 Touba is the Holy city of the Muridiyya Sufi order. Bamba was restricted to go to this city because the city has a significant population of Murids. Feared by the French, Bamba's presence could lead to insurrection of an unimaginable proportion which may affect colonial enterprise in the region. For more on the city of Touba, see Eric Ross Touba, "A Spiritual Metropolis in the Modern World," *Canadian Journal of African Studies / Revue Canadienne des Études Africaines* 29, no. 2 (1995): 222–59.
51 *Matlab ul Fawzayni*, cited in Babou, "Contesting Space," 405–26.
52 Babou, "Contesting Space," 412.

53 Robinson, *Paths of Accommodation*, 52–3.
54 Ed Van Hoven, "The Nation Turbaned? The Construction of Nationalist Muslim Identities in Senegal," *Journal of Religion in Africa* 30, no. 2 (2000): 225–48.
55 Archives Nationales Senegalaises G 13, vol. 7, no. 1, cited in Robinson, "Beyond Resistance," 164.
56 Robinson, "Beyond Resistance," 164.
57 Christopher Harrison, *France and Islam in West Africa, 1860-1960* (Cambridge: Cambridge University Press, 1988), 166.
58 Robinson, *Paths of Accommodation*, 224.
59 Paul Marty was an Arabist and ethnographer who de-rationalized the allegations and persecution of Bamba and his followers as a mere campaign of calumny and jealousy against Bamba and his followers. However, there are Murids who believe he was behind some of the plots against Bamba and convinced the colonial government of the dangers he posed.

Chapter 7

1 William Bascom, "African Culture and the Missionary," *Civilizations* 3, no. 4 (1953): 491–504, 493.
2 Bascom, "African Culture and the Missionary."
3 Heinz Hauser-Renner, "Examining Texts Sediments-Commending a Pioneer Historian as an 'African Herodotus,' On the making of the New Annotated Edition of C. C. Reindorf's *History of the Gold Coast and Asante*," *History in Africa* 35 (2008): 233.
4 Hauser-Renner, "Examining Texts Sediments."
5 Ibid., 233.
6 Heinz Hauser-Renner, "Tradition Meets Modernity: C. C. Reindorf and His 'History of the Gold Coast and Asante': A Late 19th Century Voice from Urban Accra," *Transactions of the Historical Society of Ghana* 8 (2004): 228.
7 Hauser-Renner, "'Tradition Meets Modernity."
8 Ibid., 229.
9 Ibid., 230.
10 Ibid., 232.
11 Ibid., 233.
12 Ibid., 235.
13 Ibid., 236.
14 Ibid., 237.
15 Paul Jenkins, *The Recovery of the West African Past: African Pastors and African History in the Nineteenth Century: C. C. Reindorf & Samuel Johnson* (Basel: Basler Afrika Bibliographien, 1998), 193.
16 M. R. Doortmont, *The Roots of Yoruba Historiography: Classicism, Traditionalism and Pragmatism* (Rijkuniversitetit: University of Groningen, 1993), 55.
17 Doortmont, *The Roots of Yoruba Historiography."
18 Harrison Adeniyi, "Language: Government and Mission Policies," in *Encyclopedia of the Yoruba*, ed. Toyin Falola and Akintunde Akinyemi (Bloomington: Indiana University Press, 2016), 192–3, 192.
19 Andrew F. Walls, "The Legacy of Samuel Ajayi Crowther," *International Bulletin of Missionary Research* 16, no. 1 (1992): 16.

20 Walls, "The Legacy of Samuel Ajayi Crowther."
21 Ibid.
22 Adeniyi Akangbe, "Crowther, Samuel Ajayi (1807-1891)," in *Encyclopedia of the Yoruba*, ed. Toyin Falola and Akintunde Akinyemi (Bloomington: Indiana University Press, 2016), 76–7, 77.
23 Adesola Oluseye, "Language: Standardization and Literacy," in *Encyclopedia of the Yoruba*, eds. Toyin Falola and Akintunde Akinyemi (Bloomington: Indiana University Press, 2016), 194.
24 Oluseye, "Language: Standardization and Literacy."
25 Ibid., 194.
26 Akintundé Akinyemi, "Translation Across Cultures: The Challenges of Rendering an African Oral Poetry in English," *Translation Review* 71, no. 1 (2006): 19–30.
27 Olufunke Adeboye, "Reading the Diary of Akinpelu Obisesan in Colonial Africa," *African Studies Review* 51, no. 2 (2008): 75–97.
28 Jacob Olupona, "The Study of Yoruba Religious Tradition in Historical Perspective," *Numen* 40, no. 3 (1993): 240–73, 244.
29 Mercy Akrofi Ansah, "Reminiscing on the Contribution of a Pioneer of the Development of the Twi Language; Clement Anderson Akrofi," *Ghana Journal of Linguistics* 7, no. 2 (2018): 244–7, 253.
30 Ansah, "Reminiscing on the Contribution of a Pioneer," 253.
31 Ibid., 256.
32 Ibid., 256–7.
33 Ibid., 258.
34 Toyin Falola, *Yoruba Gurus: Indigenous Production of Knowledge in Africa* (Eritrea: Africa World Press, 1999), 20.
35 Rina Okonkwo and Mojola Agbebi, "Apostle of the African Personality," *Presence Africaine* 114 (1980): 145.
36 Doortmont, *The Roots of Yoruba Historiography* 56.
37 Ibid.
38 Ibid.
39 Ibid.
40 Ibid., 57.
41 Ibid., 58.
42 Ibid.
43 Ibid.
44 Ibid.
45 Ibid.
46 J. D. Y. Peel, "The Pastor and the 'Babalawo,': The Interaction of Religions in Nineteenth-Century Yorubaland," *African Journal of the International African Institute* 60, no. 3 (1990): 228–369, 339.
47 Peel, "The Pastor and the Babalawo," 361.
48 Ibid.
49 Falola, *Yoruba Gurus*, 20.
50 Ibid.
51 Henry Mbaya and Ntozahke Simon Cezula, "Contribution of John S Mbiti to the Study of African Religions and African Theology and Philosophy," *STJ/Stellenbosch Theological Journal* 5, no. 3 (2019): 421–42, 427.
52 Eva Akosua Ebeli, "Atenteben: A Legacy of Ephraim Amu," *International Journal of Humanities Social Sciences and Education (IJHSSE)* 5, no. 8 (2018): 15–6.

53 Ebeli, "Atenteben: A Legacy of Ephraim Amu," 13.
54 Frieder Ludwig and Klaus Koschorke, eds. *Transcontinental Links in the History of Non-Western Christianity* (Wiesbaden: Otto Harrassowitz, 2002), 264.
55 Frieder Ludwig, "African Independent Churches in West Africa around 1900," in *Transcontinental Links in the History of Non-Western Christianity*, ed. Klaus Korchorke (Wiesbaden: Otto Harrassowitz, 2002), 264.
56 Ogbu U. Kalu, "Ethiopianism in African Christianity," in *African Christianity: An African Story*, ed. Ogbu Kalu (Pretoria: University of Pretoria, 2005), 227–43.
57 Olupona, "The Study of Yoruba Religious Tradition."
58 Ibid., 243–4.
59 Ibid., 245.
60 Ibid., 247.
61 Ibid., 249.

Chapter 8

1 Henri Gooren, "An Introduction to Pentecostalism: Global Charismatic Christianity," *Ars Disputandi* 4, no. 1 (2004): 206–9.
2 Marius Nel, "An Attempt to Define the Constitutive Elements of a Pentecostal Spirituality," *Die Skriflig* 49, no. 1(2015): 1–7.
3 Mookgo Solomon Kgatle, "African Pentecostalism: The Christianity of Elias Letwaba from Early Years Until his Death in 1959," *Scriptura* 116 (2017): 1–9.
4 Kgatle, "African Pentecostalism," 2.
5 Gooren, "An Introduction to Pentecostalism."
6 Olufunke Adeboye, "Explaining the Growth and Legitimation of the Pentecostal Movement in Africa," in *Pentecostalism and Politics in Africa*, ed. Adeshina Afolayan, Olajumoke Yacob-Haliso and Toyin Falola (Switzerland: Springer International Publishing, 2018), 25–39.
7 Adeboye, "Explaining the Growth."
8 Kwabena Asamoah-Gyadu, "Pentecostalism in Africa and the Changing Face of Christian Mission: Pentecostal/Charismatic Renewal Movements in Ghana," *Mission Studies* 19, no. 1–2 (2002): 14–38.
9 Ogbu U. Kalu, "Preserving a Worldview: Pentecostalism in the African Maps of the Universe," *PNEUMA: The Journal of the Society for Pentecostal Studies* 24, no. 2 (2002): 110–37.
10 Kalu, "Preserving a Worldview."
11 Todd M. Johnson, Gina A. Zurlo, Albert W. Hickman and Peter F. Crossing, "Christianity 2018: More African Christians and Counting Martyrs," *International Bulletin of Mission Research* 42, no.1 (2018): 20–8.
12 Gooren, "An Introduction to Pentecostalism."
13 Asamoah-Gyadu, "Pentecostalism in Africa," 16, 17.
14 Cedric Mayrargue, *The Paradoxes of Pentecostalism in South-Saharan Africa* (Paris: Institut Français des Relations Internationales, 2008).
15 Mayrargue, *The Paradoxes of Pentecostalism.*
16 Ibid., 4.
17 Asamoah-Gyadu, "Pentecostalism in Africa," 16.
18 Kalu, "Preserving a Worldview."

19 Asamoah-Gyadu, "Pentecostalism in Africa," 15, 16.
20 Derrick Mashau, "Ministering Effectively in the Context of Pentecostalism in Africa: A Reformed Missional Reflection," in *Die Skifilig/in Luce Verbi* 47, no. 1 (2013): 1–8.
21 Kalu, "Preserving a Worldview."
22 Allan Heaton Anderson, *Spirit-filled World: Religious Dis/continuity in African Pentecostalism* (Switzerland: Springer International Publishing AG, 2018).
23 Benjamin C. D. Diara and Nkechinyere G. Onah, "The Phenomenal Growth of Pentecostalism in the Contemporary Nigerian Society: A Challenge to Mainline Churches," *Mediterranean Journal of Social Sciences* 5, no. 6 (2014): 395–402.
24 John MacArthur, *Reckless Faith: When the Church Loses Its Will to Discern* (Illinois: Crossway Books, 1994), 40–1.
25 Nel, "Constitutive Elements of a Pentecostal Spirituality," 5.
26 Birgit Meyer, "Christianity in Africa: From African Independent to Pentecostal-charismatic Churches," *Annual Review Anthropology* 33, (2004): 447–74.
27 Mashau, "Ministering Effectively."
28 Ibid., 2.
29 Ibrahim Abraham, "Sincere Performance in Pentecostal Megachurch Music," *Religions* 9, no. 192 (2018): 1–21.
30 Abraham, "Sincere Performance," 1.
31 Asamoah-Gyadu, "Pentecostalism in Africa."
32 Patrick J. Ryan, "The Phenomenon of Independent Religious Movements in Ghana," *Catholic Standard* 15, no. 21 (1992): 22–8, 26.
33 James K. A. Smith, *Thinking in Tongues: Pentecostal Contributions to Christian Philosophy* (Michigan: William B Eerdmans Publishing Company, 2010).
34 Kwasi Wiredu, "Conceptual Decolonization as an Imperative in Contemporary African Philosophy: Some Personal Reflections," *Rue Descartes* 2, no. 36 (2002): 53–64, 53.
35 Nel, "Constitutive Elements of a Pentecostal Spirituality," 5.
36 Frederick L. Ware, "An Interim Assessment of the Pentecostal Manifesto Series," *The Journal of Religion* 94, no. 1 (2014): 97–107.
37 Nel, "Constitutive Elements of a Pentecostal Spirituality."
38 MacArthur, *Reckless Faith*.
39 Diara and Onah, "The Phenomenal Growth of Pentecostalism."
40 Adesina Afolayan, Olajumoke Yacob-Haliso and Toyin Falola, "Introduction: The Pentecostal and the Political in Africa," in *Pentecostalism and Politics in Africa*, eds. A. Afolayan, O. Yacob-Haliso, and Toyin Falola (Switzerland: Springer International Publishing, 2018), 3–23.
41 Nel, "Constitutive Elements of a Pentecostal Spirituality," 2.
42 MacArthur, *Reckless Faith*.
43 Mayrargue, "The Paradoxes of Pentecostalism."
44 Luke 6:38 (KJV).
45 Mayrargue, "The Paradoxes of Pentecostalism," 9.
46 Diara and Onah, "The Phenomenal Growth of Pentecostalism."
47 Anderson, *Spirit-Filled World*, 24.
48 Kalu, "Preserving a Worldview."
49 Stian Eriksen, "The Epistemology of Imagination and Religious Experience: A Global and Pentecostal Approach to the Study of Religion?" *Studia Theologica* 69, no. 1 (2015): 45–73.

50 Nel, "Constitutive Elements of a Pentecostal Spirituality."

51 Smith, *Thinking in Tongues*.

52 Peter Althouse, *Spirit of the Last Days: Pentecostal Eschatology in Conversation with Jürgen Moltmann* (London: T&T Clark International, 2003).

53 Stephen Land, *Pentecostal Spirituality: A Passion for the Kingdom* (Sheffield: Sheffield Academy Press, 1993).

54 Agrippa Goodman Khathide, *Hamba Vangeli Elisha: A Portrait of Rev Job Y Chiliza–Pioneer of the African Gospel Church* (Kempton Park: Acad SA, 2010).

55 Althouse, *Spirit of the Last Days*.

56 Louis T. Talbot, "Thousand Year's Reign of Christ Over the Earth: The Characteristics of that Reign," *Biola Radio Publications* 9 (2017): 3–13.

57 Talbot, "Thousand Year's Reign," 7.

58 Smith, *Thinking in Tongues*.

59 Ibid.

60 Anderson, *Spirit-Filled World*.

61 Ibid.

62 Smith, *Thinking in Tongues*.

63 Anderson, *Spirit-Filled World*, 5.

64 Adam Ashforth, "AIDS, Religious Enthusiasm and Spiritual Insecurity in Africa," *Global Public Health* 6, no. 2 (2011): 132–47.

65 John Mbiti, *African Religions and Philosophy* (London: Heinemann Publishers, 1989), 74.

66 Anderson, *Spirit-Filled World*; Kalu, "Preserving a Worldview," and Adeboye, "Explaining the Growth and Legitimation."

67 Anderson, *Spirit-Filled World*.

68 Ogbu U. Kalu, "Introduction: The Shape and Flow of African Church Historiography," *African Christianity: An African Story* (Trenton: Africa World Press, 2007), 6.

69 Anderson, *Spirit-Filled World*.

70 Kalu, "Preserving a Worldview," 132.

71 Ibid.

72 Ibid., 119.

73 Anderson, *Spirit-Filled World*, 102–3.

74 Ibid., 102–3.

75 Kalu, "Preserving a Worldview,"

76 Ibid.

77 Ibid.

78 Heb. 11:3b.

79 Ashforth, "AIDS, Religious Enthusiasm."

80 Ibid.

81 Jeffrey S. Hittenberger, "Toward a Pentecostal Philosophy of Education," *PNEUMA: The Journal of the Society for Pentecostal Studies* 23, no. 22 (2001): 217–44.

Chapter 9

1 David Chidester, "Christianity in South Africa," in *Christianity in South Africa: An Annotated Bibliography*, ed. David Chidester, Judy Tobler, and Darrel Wratten (London: Greenwood Press, 1997), 1–16.

2 Segun Gbadegesin, *African Philosophy: Traditional Yoruba Philosophy and Contemporary African Realities* (New York: Die Deutsche Bibliotek-CIP-Einheitsaufnahme, 1991), 87.

3 Amos Tutuola, *The Wild Hunter in the Bush of Ghosts* (Washington: Three Continents Press, [1948] 1989).

4 Hermione Harris, *Yoruba in Diaspora: An African Church in London* (New York: Palgrave Macmillan, 2006).

5 V. Y. Mudimbe, *The Invention of Africa: Gnosis, Philosophy and the Order of Knowledge* (Bloomington: Indiana University Press, 1988).

6 Bolaji Idowu, *Olodumare: God in Yoruba Belief* (Lagos: Longmans, 1962).

7 Olatunde Lawuyi, "No King as God: Toward the Understanding of Yoruba Slogan," *ODU: A Journal of West African Studies* 29, no. 2 (1986): 102–14.

8 Johnson Samuel, *The History of the Yoruba People* (Lagos: CMS Bookshop, 1921).

9 Clifford Geertz, *The Interpretation of Cultures* (New York: Basic Books, 1973).

10 N. A. Fadipe, *The Sociology of the Yoruba* (Ibadan: University of Ibadan, 1970).

11 John Mbiti, *African Religions and Philosophy* (Nairobi: East African Educational Publishers, 2002).

12 William Bascom, *The Yoruba of Southwestern Nigeria* (Prospect Heights: Waveland Press Inc., 1984).

13 Masondo Sibusiso, "The History of African Indigenous Churches in Scholarship," *Journal for the Study of Religion* 18, no. 2 (2005): 89–103.

14 Ivan Karp, "African Systems of Thought," in *Africa,* ed. Phyllis Martin and Patrick O'Meara (Bloomington: Indiana University Press, 1986), 199–211.

15 A. Anderson, "African Initiated Churches of the Spirit and Pneumatology," *Word on World* 23, no. 2 (2013): 178–86.

16 Harold Turner, *Modern African Religious Movements: An Introduction for the Christian Churches* (Nsukka: University of Nigeria, 1965).

17 J. O. Amasuomo, "Zion Brand Cherubim and Seraphim Churches in the Establishment of Primary Schools in Bayelsa State, Nigeria," *African Research Review* 8, no. 1 (2014): 53–61.

18 D. Ayegboyin and S. Ishola, *African Indigenous Churches: A Historical Perspective* (Lagos: Greater Heights Production, 1997).

19 E. W. Blyden, *Christianity, Islam and the Negro Race* (Edinburgh: Edinburgh University Press, 1967).

20 Nelson Geoffrey, *Spiritualism and Society* (London: Routledge & Kegan Paul, 1969).

21 P. Makhubu, *Who Are the Independent Churches?* (Johannesburg: Skotaville, 1988).

22 Pierre Verger, *The Yoruba High God: A Review of the Sources* (Ibadan: Institute of African Studies, University of Ibadan, 1964).

23 Verger, *The Yoruba High God.*

Conclusion

1 Oluwaseun O. Afolabi, "The Role of Religion in Nigerian Politics and Its Sustainability for Political Development," *Net Journal of Social Sciences* 3, no. 2 (2015): 42–9.

2 See the "Preface" above for context.

3 J. F. Sobiecki, "A Review of Plants Used in Divination in Southern Africa and Their Psychoactive Effects," *Southern African Humanities,* 20, no. 2 (2008): 333–51.

4 As quoted in Sobiecki, "A Review of Plants Used in Divination," 33.
5 Robert Thornton, "The Transmission of Knowledge in South African Traditional Healing," *Africa: Journal of the International African Institute* 79, no. 1 (2009): 17–34. doi:10.2307/29734388 (accessed December 15, 2020).
6 Thornton, "The Transmission of Knowledge."
7 T. Zuma, Daniel Wight, Tamsen Rochat and Mosa Moshabela, "The Role of Traditional Health Practitioners in Rural KwaZulu-Natal, South Africa: Generic or Mode Specific?" *BMC Complementary and Alternative Medicine* 16, no. 1 (2016): 304.
8 Zuma, et al., The Role of Traditional Health Pracitioners."
9 Ibid.

Bibliography

Abby, W. "What Is Shamanism?" Abby Wynne. Available online: https://abby-wynne.com/shamanic-healing-techniques/ (accessed June 27, 2021).

Abdullah, Z. *Black Mecca: The African Muslims of Harlem*. Oxford: Oxford University Press, 2010.

Abimbola, W. *Awon Oju Odu Mereerindinlogun*. Ibadan: Ibadan University Press, 2004.

Abraham, I. "Sincere Performance in Pentecostal Megachurch Music." *Religions* 9, no. 6 (2018): 192.

Abubakar, S. "Survey of the Economy of the Eastern Emirates of the Sokoto Caliphate in the 19th Century." In *Studies in the History of Sokoto Caliphate: The Sokoto Seminar Papers*, edited by Y. B. Usman, 105–124. Lagos: Third Press International, 1979.

Abun-Nasr, J. M. *The Tijaniyya: A Sufi Order in the Modern World*. London: Oxford University Press, 1965.

Adamu, M. "Distribution of Trading Centers in the Central Sudan in the 18th and 19th Centuries." In *Studies in the History of Sokoto Caliphate: The Sokoto Seminar Papers*, edited by Y. B. Usman, 59–104. Lagos: Third Press International, 1979.

Adeboye, O. "Reading the Diary of Akinpelu Obisesan in Colonial Africa." *African Studies Review* 51, no. 2 (2008): 75–97.

Adeboye, O. "Explaining the Growth and Legitimation of the Pentecostal Movement in Africa." In *Pentecostalism and Politics in Africa*, edited by Adeshina Afolayan, Olajumoke Yacob-Haliso and Toyin Falola, 25–39. Switzerland: Springer International Publishing, 2018.

Adedibu, B. A. "The Changing Faces of African Independent Churches as Development Actors Across Borders." *HTS Teologiese Studies/Theological Studies* 74, no. 1 (2018): 1–9.

Adeeko, A. "'Writing' and 'Reference' in Ifa Divination Chants." *Oral Traditions* 25, no. 2 (2010): 283–303.

Adeeko, A. "Incantation, Ideophone, Reduplication, and Poetry." *The Savannah Review* 3, no. 8 (2014): 73–98.

Adegboyega, O. O. "Philosophical Issues in Yoruba Proverbs." *International Journal of African Society, Cultures and Traditions* 5, no. 2 (2017): 21–30.

Adegboyega, O. O. "The Metaphysical and Epistemological Relevance of Ifa Corpus." *International Journal of History and Philosophical Research* 5, no. 1 (2017): 28–40.

Adeniyi, H. "Language: Government and Mission Policies." In *Encyclopedia of the Yoruba*, edited by Toyin Falola and Akintunde Akinyemi, 192–3. Bloomington: Indiana University Press, 2016.

Afolabi, O. "The Role of Religion in Nigerian Politics and Its Sustainability for Political Development." *Net Journal of Social Sciences* 3, no. 2 (2015): 42–9.

Afolayan, A., Olajumoke Yacob-Haliso and Toyin Falola. "Introduction: The Pentecostal and the Political in Africa." In *Pentecostalism and Politics in Africa*, edited by Adeshina Afolayan, Olajumoke Yacob-Haliso and Toyin Falola, 3–23. Switzerland: Springer International Publishing, 2018.

Ahmed, S. "What is Sufism?" *Forum Philosophicum* 13, no. 2 (2008): 229–46.

Ajayi, M. N., K. Gerisho and M. Johnson. "Traditional Healing Practices and Holistic Health: The Implication for Christian Families in South West Region of Nigeria." *Journal of Family Medicine and Health Care* 5, no. 4 (2019): 50–8.

Akangbe, A. "Crowther, Samuel Ajayi (1807–1891)." In *Encyclopedia of Yoruba*, edited by Toyin Falola and Akintunde Akinyemi, 76–7. Bloomington: Indiana University Press, 2016.

Akinyemi, A. "Translation Across Cultures: The Challenges of Rendering an African Oral Poetry in English." *Translation Review* 71, no. 1 (2006): 19–30.

Aktar, S. *The Quran and the Secular Mind: A Philosophy of Islam.* New York: Routledge, 2007.

Alamu, F. O., H. O. Aworinde and W. I. Isharufe. "A Comparative Study on Ifa Divination and Computer Science." *International Journal of Innovative Technology and Research* 1, no. 6 (2013): 524–8.

Al-Din Attar, F. *Muslim Saints and Mystics: Episodes from the Tadhkirat Al-Auliya'.* London: Routledge, 2007.

Al-Sarraj, A. N. *The Kitab Al-Luma Fi'l-Tasawwuf of Abu Nasr Abdallah B. Ali Al-Sarraj Al-Tusi*, transl. Reynold Alleyne Nicholson. London: E. J. Brill, 1914.

Al-Tawil, M. "The Importance of Sufi Traditions to Jerzy Grotowski's Practice." Ph.D. diss., University of Kent, 2017.

Althouse, P. *Spirit of the Last Days: Pentecostal Eschatology in Conversation with Jürgen Moltmann.* London: T&T. Clark, 2003.

Amad, H. "The Practice of Mysticism in Sufism." *Journal of Undergraduate Research* 6, no. 2 (2013): 1–8.

Amasuomo, J. O. M. "Zion Brand Cherubim and Seraphim Churches in the Establishment of Primary Schools in Bayelsa State, Nigeria." *African Research Review* 8, no. 1 (2014): 53–64.

Anderson, A. "African Initiated Churches of the Spirit and Pneumatology." *Word on World* 23, no. 2 (2013): 178–86.

Anderson, A. *Spirit-Filled World: Religious Dis/Continuity in African Pentecostalism.* Switzerland: Springer, 2018.

Ansah, M. A. "Reminiscing on the Contribution of a Pioneer on the Development of the Twi Language; Clement Anderson Akrofi." *Ghana Journal of Linguistics* 7, no. 2 (2018): 244–7.

Anwar, E. *Gender and Self in Islam.* New York: Routledge, 2006.

Aquinas, T. *Summa Theologiae*, trans. and edited by T. McDermott. Notre Dame: Ave Maria Press, 1989.

Arberry, A. J. *The Doctrine of the Sufis.* Cambridge: Cambridge University Press, 1977.

Arberry, A. J. *Sufism: An Account of the Mystics of Islam.* Massachusetts: Courier Corporation, 2002.

ARDA, The. "Congo, Republic of the." ARDA. Available online: https://www.thearda.com/internationalData/countries/Country_58_1.asp (accessed June 27, 2021).

Arif, S. "Sufi Epistemology: Ibn'Arabi on Knowledge ('Ilm)." *Jurnal Akidah & Pemikiran Islam* 3, no. 1 (2002): 81–94.

Armstrong, K. *Islam: A Short History.* New York: Modern Library, 2007.

Asamoah-Gyadu, K. "Pentecostalism in Africa and the Changing Face of Christian Mission: Pentecostal/Charismatic Renewal Movements in Ghana." *Mission Studies* 19, no. 2 (2002): 14–38.

Asani, A. "'So That you may Know One Another': A Muslim American Reflects on Pluralism and Islam." *The Annals of the American Academy of Political and Social Science* 588, no. 1 (2003): 40–51.

Ashforth, A. "AIDS, Religious Enthusiasm and Spiritual Insecurity in Africa." *Global Public Health* 6, no. 2 Supplement (2011): 132–47.

Awolalu, J. O. *Yoruba Beliefs and Sacrificial Rites.* Essex: Longman, 1979.

Ayandele, E. A. *The Missionary Impact of Modern Nigeria 1842–1914: A Political and Social Analysis.* London: Longmans, 1966.

Ayegboyin, D. and S. A. Ishola *African Indigenous Churches: An Historical Perspective.* Lagos: Greater Heights Publications, 1997.

Ayisi, O. E. *Introduction to the Study of African Culture.* Nairobi: East African Educational Publishers, 1979.

Aziabah, M. A. "Amu Ephraim Koku." In *Dictionary of African Biography*, edited by E. K. Akyeampong and H. L. Gates, 225–6. New York: Oxford University Press. 2012.

Babaei, Y. "Trends in Sufism: From The Beginning Until The Fifth Century AH." *Islamic Mysticism* 10, no. 37 (2015): 145–59.

Babou, C. A. "Educating the Murid: Theory and Practices of Education in Amadu Bamba's Thought." *Journal of Religion in Africa* 33, no. 3 (2003): 310–27.

Babou, S. A. "Contesting Space, Shaping Places: Making Room for the Muridiyya in Colonial Senegal, 1912–45." *The Journal of African History* 46, no. 3 (2005): 405–26.

Babou, C. A. *Fighting the Greater Jihad: Amadu Bamba and the Founding of the Muridiyya of Senegal.* Athens: Ohio University Press, 2007.

Balogun, I. A. B. "The Life and Work of the Mujaddid of West Africa, "Uthmān B. Fūdī Popularly Known as Usumanu Ḍan Fodio." *Islamic Studies* 12, no. 4 (1973): 271–92. Available online: http://www.jstor.org/stable/20846894 (accessed November 27, 2020).

Balogun, I. A. B. *The Life and Works of Usman Ḍan Fodio: The Muslim Reformer of West Africa.* Lagos: Islamic Publications Bureau, 1981.

Bamba, A. "Masālik-al-Jinān (The Ways of Paradise)." Verses 80–2. Translated by S. Sam Mbaye. Available online: https://www.kinti.se/mamediarra/downloads/files/Masalik _en_A5_aminta.pdf (accessed November 25, 2020).

Bang, A. *Sufis and Scholars of the Sea: Family Networks in East Africa, 1860–1925.* London: Routledge, 2004.

Barrett, D. B. *Schism and Renewal in Africa: An Analysis of Six Thousand Contemporary Religious Movements.* London: Oxford University Press, 1970.

Bascom, W. "African Culture and the Missionary." *Civilizations* 3, no. 4 (1953): 491–504, 493.

Bascom, W. *The Yoruba of Southwestern Nigeria.* Prospect Heights: Waveland Press, Inc., 1984.

Bascom, W. *Ifa Divination: Communication between Gods and Men in West Africa.* Bloomington: Indiana University Press, 1991.

Basharin, P. V. "The Problem of Free Will and Predestination in the Light of Satan's Justification in Early Sufism." *English Language Notes* 56, no. 1 (2018): 119–38.

Batran, A. A. *The Qadiryya Brotherhood in West Africa and the Western Sahara: The Life and times of Shaykh al-Mukhtar al-Kunti (1729–1811).* Rabat: Publications de l'Institut des etudes Africaines, 2001.

Bauer, B. "Cultural Foundations for Fear of Witchcraft in Africa." *Journal of Adventist Mission Studies* 13, no. 1 (2017): 1–12.

Behrman, C. L. *Muslim Brotherhoods and Politics in Senegal.* Cambridge: Havard University Press, 2013.

Bellamy, L. A. "Witchcraft, Sorcery, Academic and Local Change in East Africa." PhD diss., Miami University, 2004.

Bernal, M. *Black Athena: The Afro-Asiatic Roots of Classical Civilization.* New Jersey: Rutgers University Press, 1991.

Bhugra, D. ed. *Psychiatry and Religion: Context, Consensus and Controversies.* London: Psychology Press, 1997.

Biagi, E. *Plunging into the Wave's Ebb: Sufi Words, Biographies of Humanity.* Altre *Modernità* 16 (2016): 161–76.

Bilqies, S. "Understanding the Concept of Islamic Sufism." *Journal of Education and Social Policy* 1, no. 1 (2014): 55–72.

Black, A. *The History of Islamic Political Thought.* Edinburgh: Edinburgh University Press, 2002.

Blofeld, J. *Mantras, Sacred Words of Power.* London: Unwin, 1977.

Blyden, E. W. *Christianity, Islam and the Negro Race.* Edinburgh: Edinburgh University Press, 1967.

Bock, N. J. "Shamanic Techniques: Their Use and Effectiveness in the Practice of Psychotherapy." M.Sc. diss., University of Wisconsin-Stout, 2005.

Bond, G. and D. Ciekawy, eds. *Witchcraft Dialogues: Anthropological and Philosophical Exchanges.* Athens: Ohio University Center for International Studies, 2001.

Bongmba, E. K. *African Witchcraft and Otherness: A Philosophical and Theological Critique of Intersubjective Relations.* Albany: SUNY Press, 2001.

Born, J. B. "A Personal Look at African Spiritual Churches—Reflections, Challenges, Hopes." *Mission Focus: Annual Review* 12 (2004): 46–55.

Boyd, J. and M. L. "The Role of Women as 'Agents Religieux' in Sokoto." *Canadian Journal of African Studies/La Revue Canadienne des études Africaines* 19, no. 2 (1985): 283–300.

Boylston, T. "The Shade of the Divine: Approaching the Sacred in an Ethiopian Orthodox Christian Community." PhD diss., London School of Economics and Political Science (LSE), 2012.

Bretton, H. L. *The Rise and Fall of Kwame Nkrumah: A Study of Personal Rule in Africa.* London: Pall Mall, 1966.

Bruinessen, M. van. "Sufism and the 'Modern' in Islam." *ISIM Newsletter* 13, no. 1 (2003): 62.

Bunza, M. U. "The North African Factor in Tajdeed Tradition in Hausaland, Northern Nigeria." *The Journal of North African Studies* 10, no. 3–4 (2005): 325–38.

Bunza, M. U. "The Application of Islamic Law and the Legacies of Good Governance in the Sokoto Caliphate, Nigeria (1804–1903): Lessons for the Contemporary Period." *Electronic Journal of Islamic and Middle Eastern Law (EJIMEL)* 1, no. 4 (2013): 84–101.

Burckhardt, T. *Introduction to Sufi Doctrine.* Bloomington: World Wisdom Inc., 2008.

Burckhardt, T. *Art of Islam: Language and Meaning.* Bloomington: World Wisdom Inc., 2009.

Burns, C. *Censorship and Affection: South African Women's Letters during World War Two.* Durban: University of Natal Durban, 2000.

Callaway, H. *The Religious System of the Amazulu in the Zulu Language with Translation into English and Notes in Four Parts.* London: Trubner and Co., 1870.

Cambridge Dictionary. "Meaning of 'Sacred' in English." Cambridge Dictionary. Accessed November 18, 2020. https://dictionary.cambridge.org/dictionary/english/sacred.

Chernus, I. "Summary of Peter Berger, *The Sacred Canopy*." Available online: http://web
.pdx.edu/~tothm/religion/Summary%20of%20Peter%20Berger,%20The%20Sacred
%20Canopy.pdf (accessed November 18, 2020).

Chidester, D. "Christianity in South Africa." In *Christianity in South Africa: An Annotated
Bibliography*, edited by David Chidester, Judy Tobler, and Darrel Wratten, 1–16.
London: Greenwood Press, 1997.

Chih, R. "What Is a Sufi Order? Revisiting the Concept Through a Case Study of the
Khalwatiyya in Contemporary Egypt." In *Sufism and the 'Modern' in Islam*, edited by
Martin Van Bruinessen and Julia Day, 21–38. London: Bloomsbury, 2007.

Chittick, W. C. *The Sufi Path of Love: The Spiritual Teachings of Rumi*. Albany: SUNY
Press, 1984.

Chittick, W. C. *The Sufi Path of Knowledge: Ibn al-Arabi's Metaphysics of Imagination*.
Albany: SUNY Press, 2010.

Chome, N. "The Political Role of Islam." In *The Oxford Handbook of Kenyan Politics*,
edited by Nic Cheeseman, Karuti Kanyinga, and Gabrielle Lynch, 150–561. Oxford:
Oxford University Press, 2019.

Clancy-Smith, J. A. *Rebel and Saint: Muslim Notables, Populist Protest, Colonial Encounters
(Algeria and Tunisia, 1800–1904)*. Berkeley: University of California Press, 1997.

Clarke, P. B. *West Africa and Islam: A Study of Religious Development from the 8th to the
20th Century*. London: Edward Arnold, 1982.

Constantineanu, C. and C. J. Scobie "Introduction: Pentecostal Identity, Spirituality, and
Theology." In *Pentecostals in the 21st Century: Identity, Belief and Praxis*, edited by
Corneliu Constantineanu and Christopher J. Scobie, 1–13. Oregon: Cascade Books,
2018.

Creevey, L. E. "Ahmad Bamba 1850–1927." In *Studies in West African Islamic History: The
Cultivators of Islam*, edited by John Ralph Willis, 278–80. London: Frank Cass, 1979.

Dallal, A. "The Origins and Objectives of Islamic Revivalist Thought, 1750–1850." *Journal
of the American Oriental Society* 113, no. 3 (1993): 341–59.

Daneel, L. *Old and New in Southern Shona Independent Churches*. Netherlands: Mouton &
Co., 1971.

Degarrod, L. N. "Dreams and Vision." In *Shamanism: An Encyclopedia of World Beliefs,
Practices, and Culture*, edited by Mariko Walter and Eva Jane Fridman, 89–95.
California: ABC-CLIO, 2004).

Dehlvi, S. *Sufism: The Heart of Islam*. India: HarperCollins Publishing, 2009.

Diara, B. C. and N. G. Onah. "The Phenomenal Growth of Pentecostalism in the
Contemporary Nigerian Society: A Challenge to Mainline Churches." *Mediterranean
Journal of Social Sciences* 5, no. 6 (2014): 395–402.

Dickson, D. A. *Political Islam in Sub-Saharan Africa: The Need for a New Research and
Diplomatic Agenda*. Washington, DC: United Institute of Peace, 2005.

Dilley, R. "Specialist Knowledge Practices of Craftsmen and Clerics in Senegal." *Africa:
Journal of the International African Institute* 79 (2009): 53–70.

Diop, M. L. *Irwā al Nadeem*. Touba: Imprimérie Daray Borom Touba, 2006.

Dolansky, S. "Gilgamesh and the Bible." Bible Odyssey. Available online: https://www.bib
leodyssey.org/en/places/related-articles/gilgamesh-and-the-bible (accessed November
18, 2020).

Doortmont, M. R. *The Roots of Yoruba Historiography: Classicism, Traditionalism and
Pragmatism*. Rijksuniversiteit: University of Groningen, 1993.

Drucker-Brown, S. "Mamprusi: Witchcraft, Subversion and Changing Gender Relations."
Africa: Journal of the International African Institute 64, no. 4 (1993): 531–49.

Du Toit, W. and N. H. Ngada. *Hearing the AIC-voice: Proceedings of a Conference held by the Research Institute for Theology and Religion at Unisa*. Pretoria: Research Institute for Theology and Religion, 1999.

Dumont, F. "Amadou Bamba, Apotre de la Non-violence (1850–1927)." *Notes Africaines: Bulletin d'information et de Correspondance de l'Institut Français d'Afrique Noire Notes Africaines* 121 (1969): 20–4

Duru, W. "The Communicativeness of Incantations in the Traditional Igbo Society." *Journal of Media and Communication Studies* 8, no. 7 (2016): 63–70.

Dwyer, D. H. "Women, Sufism, and Decision-Making in Moroccan Islam." In *Women in the Muslim World*, edited by Lois Beck and Nikki Keddie, 585–98. Cambridge: Harvard University Press, 2013.

Ebeli, E. A. "Atenben: A Legacy of Ephraim Amu." *International Journal of Humanities Social Sciences and Education (IJHSSE)* 5, no. 8 (2018): 12–8.

Edwards, J. "Sinners in the Hands of an Angry God," Blue Letter Bible, last modified May 1, 2014, https://www.blueletterbible.org/Comm/edwards_jonathan/Sermons/Sinners.cfm.

Ekeke, E. C. and A. E. Chike. "God, Divinities and Spirits in African Traditional Religious Ontology." *American Journal of Social and Management Sciences* 1, no. 2 (2010): 209–18.

Eliade, M. "Recent Works on Shamanism: A Review." *History of Religions* 1, no. 1 (1961): 152–86.

El-Zein, A. H. "Beyond Ideology and Theology: The Search for the Anthropology of Islam." *Annual Review of Anthropology* 6, no. 1 (1977): 227–54.

Emedolu, C. C. "From Magic to African Experimental Science: Toward a New Paradigm." *Filosofia Theoretica: Journal of African Philosophy, Culture and Religions* 4, no. 2 (2015): 68–88.

Engstrom, S. "Kant's Conception of Practical Wisdom." *Kant-studien* 88, no. 1 (1997): 16.

Eriksen, S. "The Epistemology of Imagination and Religious Experience: A Global and Pentecostal Approach to the Study of Religion?" *Studia Theologica* 69, no. 1 (2015): 45–73.

Esposito, J. L., ed. *The Oxford Dictionary of Islam*. Oxford: Oxford University Press, 2004.

Esposito, T. and S. Gregg. *The Inspiration and Truth of Sacred Scripture: The Word that Comes from God Speaks of God for the Salvation of the World*. Minnesota: Liturgical Press, 2014.

Evans-Pritchard, E. E. "Witchcraft, Oracles and Magic among the Azande." In *Death, Mourning, and Burial: A Cross-Cultural Reader*, edited by Antonius Robben, 83–8. New Jersey: Wiley-Blackwell, 1991.

Ewing, K. "The Politics of Sufism: Redefining the Saints of Pakistan." *The Journal of Asian Studies* 42, no. 2 (1983): 251–68.

Fadipe, N. A. *The Sociology of the Yoruba*. Ibadan: University of Ibadan, 1970.

Falaye, T. A. and O. A. Babalola. "The Relevance of African Independent Churches to the Yoruba of South-Western Nigeria." *Contemporary Humanities* 5, no. 45 (2012): 10–15.

Fallou, N. "Aḥmadu Bamba's Pedagogy and the Development of Ajamī Literature." *African Studies Review* 52, no. 1 (2009): 99–123.

Fallou, N. *Muslim Beyond the Arab World: The Odyssey of Ajami and Muridiyya*. Oxford: Oxford University Press, 2016.

Fallou, N. "West African Manuscripts in Arabic and African Languages and Digital Preservation." *Oxford Research Encyclopedia of African History*. Oxford: Oxford University Press, 2016.

Falola, T. *Yoruba Gurus: Indigenous Production of Knowledge in Africa*. Eritrea: Africa World Press, 1999.

Fatunmbi, F. A. *Inner Peace: The Yoruba Concept of Ori*. New York: Athelia Henrietta Press, 2005.

Fernandes, V. T. Monod, A. Teixeira da Mota, S. Rodrigues and R. Mauny. *Description de la côte occidentale d'Afrique: (Sénégal du Cap de Monte, Archipels)*. Publicações de Centro de Estudos da Guiné Portuguesa 11. Bissau: Centro de Estudos da Guine Portuguesa, 1951).

Feyerabend, P. K. *Against Method: Outline of an Anarchist Theory of Knowledge*. London: NLB, 1978.

Fincher, W. "Logocentrism." *The Blackwell Encyclopedia of Sociology*, edited by G. Ritzer. https://doi.org/10.1002/9781405165518.wbeosl055.

Fodio, A. D. *Taziyin Al-Waraqat*. Edited and trans. M. Hisket. Ibadan: Ibadan University Press, 1963.

Frager, R. and C. Fadiman. *Essential Sufism*. San Francisco: Harper Collins, 1999.

Frankfurter, D. "Curses, Blessings, and Ritual Authority: Egyptian Magic in Comparative Perspective." *Journal of Ancient Near Eastern Religions* 5, no. 1 (2005): 157–85.

Franz, M. K. "A Gathering of Names: On the Categories and Collections of Siberian Shamanic Materials in Late Imperial Russian Museum, 1880–1910." PhD diss., University of Toronto, 2019.

Frazer, G. J. *The Golden Bough: A Study in Magic and Religion*. London: Wordsworth, 1993.

Fudi, U. I. F. *Bayan Wujub Al-hijra Ala 'L-Ibad*, trans. F. H. El Masri. Khartoum: Khartoum University Press, 1978.

Fulford, K. W. M. and M. Jackson. "Spiritual Experience and Psychopathology." *Philosophy, Psychiatry, & Psychology* 4, no. 1 (1997): 41–65.

Gaiya, A. B. *The Pentecostal Revolution in Nigeria*. Occasional Paper of the Centre of African Studies, University of Copenhagen. Copenhagen: Centre of African Studies, University of Copenhagen, 2002.

Ganyi, F. M. and A. P. Ogar. "Orality and Medicine: The Efficacy of the Word in the Practice of Therapeutic Cures in Traditional African Medicine." *Studies in Sociology of Science* 3, no. 3 (2012): 31–5.

Garrett, W. R. "Maligned Mysticism: The Maledicted Career of Troeltsch's Third Type." *Sociological Analysis* 36, no. 3 (1975): 205–23.

Gbadegesin, S. *African Philosophy: Traditional Yoruba Philosophy and Contemporary African Realities*. New York: Die Deutsche Bibliotek-CIP-Einheitsaufnahme, 1991.

Geertz, C. *The Interpretation of Cultures*. New York: Basic Books, 1973.

Gellner, E. "The Great Patron: A Reinterpretation of Tribal Rebellions." *European Journal of Sociology/Archives Européennes de Sociologie/Europäisches Archiv für Soziologie* 10, no. 1 (1969): 61–9.

Geoffrey, N. *Spiritualism and Society*. London: Routledge & Kegan Paul, 1969.

Geoffroy, E. and R. Gaetani. *Introduction to Sufism: The Inner Path of Islam*. Lanham: World Wisdom, Inc., 2010.

Giddens, A. *Sociology*. Cambridge: Polity Press, 1998.

Global Nonviolent Action Database. "Sheikh Amadu Bàmba's Murid Resistance to French Colonial Oppression." Global Nonviolent Action Database. Available online: https://nvdatabase.swarthmore.edu/content/sheikh-amadu-b-mba-s-mur-d-resistance-french-colonial-oppression (accessed November 25, 2020).

Glover, J. *Sufism and Jihad in Modern Senegal: The Murid Order*. Rochester: University of
    Rochester Press, 2007.
Gluckman, M. *Custom and Conflict in Africa*. Oxford: Blackwell, 1956.
Gooren, H. "An Introduction to Pentecostalism: Global Charismatic Christianity." *Ars
    Disputandi* 4, no. 1 (2004): 206–9.
Graham, W. A. *Divine Word and Prophetic Word in Early Islam*. New York: De Gruyter,
    1977.
Green, N. *Sufism: A Global History*. Hoboken: Wiley-Blackwell, 2012.
Grillo, L. S. "African Rituals." In *The Wiley-Blackwell Companion to African Religions*,
    edited by Elias Bongmba, 112–26. Malden: Wiley-Blackwell, 2012.
Grung, A. H. "Transformative Hermeneutics in the Making Through the Co-reading
    of Biblical and Qur'anic texts by Muslim and Christian Women." In *Transformative
    Readings of Sacred Scriptures: Christians and Muslims in Dialogue*, edited by Simone
    Sinn, Dina El Omari and Anne Hege Grung, 29–37. Germany: The Lutheran World
    Federation, 2017.
Gusau, S. A. "Economic Ideas of Shehu Usman Dan Fodio." *Journal of Muslim Minority
    Affairs* 10, no. 1 (1989): 139–51.
Hachalinga, P. "How Curses Impact People and Biblical Responses." *Journal of Adventist
    Mission Studies* 13, no. 1 (2017): 55–63.
Hammed, M. M. and F. I. Haider. "Healing Secrets in Holy Quran," ResearchGate.
    Available online: https://www.researchgate.net/publication/333557344 (accessed
    November 18, 2020).
Hammer, O. "Sufism for Westerners." In *Sufism in Europe and North America*. London:
    Routledge, 2004.
Hanif, M. A. "Debating Sufism: The Tijāniyya and Its Opponents." PhD diss., Universität
    Bayreuth, Bayreuth International Graduate School of African Studies-BIGSAS, 2018.
Harries, P. "Exclusion, Classification and Internal Colonialism: The Emergence of Ethnicity
    among the Tsonga-speakers of South Africa." In *The Creation of Tribalism in Southern
    Africa*, edited by Leroy Vail, 82–227. Berkeley: University of California Press, 1989.
Harries, J. "Witchcraft, Culture, and Theology in African Development." *African Nebula* 2
    (2010): 138–53.
Harris, H. *Yoruba in Diaspora: An African Church in London*. New York: Palgrave
    Macmillan, 2006.
Harrison, C. *France and Islam in West Africa, 1860–1960*. Cambridge: Cambridge
    University Press, 1988.
Hauser-Renner, H. "Tradition Meets Modernity: C. C. Reindorf and his History of the
    Gold Coast and Asante: A Late 19th Century Voice from Urban Accra." *Transactions of
    the Historical Society of Ghana* 8 (2004): 227–55.
Hauser-Renner, H. "Examining Texts Sediments-Commending a Pioneer Historian as an
    'African Herodotus': On the Making of the New Annotated Edition of C.C. Reindorf's
    History of the Gold Coast and Asante." *History in Africa* 35 (2008): 231–99.
Hazen, J. "Contemporary Islamic Sufism in America: The Philosophy and Practices of the
    Alami Tariqa in Waterport, New York." PhD diss., SOAS, University of London (2012).
Heck, P. L. "Mysticism as Morality: The Case of Sufism." *Journal of Religious Ethics* 34, no.
    2 (2006): 253–86.
Heck, P. L. "Sufism–What Is It Exactly?" *Religion Compass* 1, no. 1 (2006): 148–64.
Henrich, J. *The Secret of Our Success: How Culture is Driving Human Evolution,
    Domesticating Our Species, and Making us Smarter*. Princeton: Princeton University
    Press, 2017.

Henry, J. "Magic and Science in the Sixteenth and Seventeenth Centuries." In *Companion to the History of Modern Science*, edited by R. C. Olby, G. N. Cantor, J. R. R. Christie and M. J. S. Hodge, 583–96. New York: Routledge, 1990.

Hill, J. "Sufism Between Past and Modernity." In *Handbook of Contemporary Islam and Muslim Lives*, edited by M. Woodward and R. Lukens-Bull, 1–26. Cham: Springer, 2019.

Hiskett, M. "Kitāb al-farq: A Work on the Habe Kingdoms Attributed to Uthman dan Fodio." *Bulletin of the School of Oriental and African Studies, University of London* 23, no. 3 (1960): 558–79.

Hittenberger, J. S. "Toward a Pentecostal Philosophy of Education." *PNEUMA: The Journal of the Society for Pentecostal Studies* 23, no. 22 (2001): 217–44.

Hoexter, M., S. N. Eisentatdt and N. Levtzion, *The Public Sphere in Muslim Societies*. Albany: SUNY Press, 2002.

Hoffman, V. J. *Sufism, Mystics, and Saints in Modern Egypt*. Columbia: University of South Carolina Press, 1995.

Holm, R. "A Paradigmatic Analysis of Authority within Pentecostalism. Unpublished Ph.D. diss., Laval University, Canada (1996).

Hoppál, M. *Shamans and Symbols: Prehistory of Semiotics in Rock Art*. Budapest: International Society for Shamanistic Research, 2013.

Hoque, M. S. "Origin of Sufism." *EDULIGHT* 1, no. 2 (2012): 197.

Hoven, E. V. "The Nation Turbaned? The Construction of Nationalist Muslim Identities in Senegal." *Journal of Religion in Africa* 30, no. 2 (2000): 225–48.

Hunwick, J. O. "A Region of the Mind: Medieval Arab Views of African Geography and Ethnography and Their Legacy." *Sudanic Africa: A Journal of Historical Sources* 16 (2005): 103–36.

Hussain, F. *Chishtis During the Delhi Sultanate: A Balance Between Ideal and Practice*. New Delhi: Centre for Historical Studies. Ph.D. Thesis, Jawaharlal Nehru University (2002).

Idowu, B. *Olodumare: God in Yoruba Belief*. Lagos: Longmans, 1962.

Idowu, B. *African Traditional Religion: A Definition*. London: SCM Press Ltd., 1973.

Igwe, L. "The Witch is not a Witch: The Dynamics and Contestations of Witchcraft Accusations in Northern Ghana." Ph.D. diss., Universitaet Bayreuth, Germany (2017).

Ilesanmi, T. M. "The Traditional Theologians and the Practice of Orisa Religion in Yorubaland." *Journal of Religion in Africa* 21, no. 3 (1991): 216–26.

Inayat, Q. "Islam, Divinity, and Spiritual Healing." In *Integrating Traditional Healing Practices into Counseling and Psychotherapy*, edited by Roy Moodley and William West, 159–69. California: Sage Publications, 2015.

Islahi, A. A. "Shehu Usman Dan Fodio and His Economic Ideas." In *Munich Personal Respect Archive*. Jeddah: Islamic Economics Institute, King AbduAziz University, 2015.

Iqbal, M. *The Reconstruction of Religious Thought in Islam*. Stanford: Stanford University Press, 2013.

Iwuchukwu, M. "Pentecostalism, Islam, and Religious Fundamentalism in Africa." In *Pentecostalism and Politics in Africa: African Histories and Modernities*, eds. A. Afolayan, Olajumoke Yacob-Haliso and Toyin Falola, 43–63. New York: Palgrave Macmillan, 2018.

James, G. *Stolen Legacy: The Greeks Were Not the Authors of Greek Philosophy, But the People of North Africa, Commonly Called the Egyptians*. New York: Philosophical Library, 1954.

Jenkins, P. *The Recovery of the West African Past: African Pastors and African History in the Nineteenth Century: C. C. Reindorf & Samuel Johnson*. Basel: Basler Afrika Biliogrphien, 1998.

Johnson, T. M., G. A. Zurlo, A. W. Hickman and P. F. Crossing. "Christianity 2018: More African Christians and Counting Martyrs." *International Bulletin of Mission Research* 42, no. 1 (2018): 20–8.

Joshi, P. C. "Psychotherapeutic Elements in Shamanistic Healing in the Context of Himalayan Traditions." *Delhi Psychiatry Journal* 13, no. 2 (2010): 254–7.

Kalu, O. "Preserving a Worldview: Pentecostalism in the African Maps of the Universe." *PNEUMA: The Journal of the Society for Pentecostal Studies* 24, no. 2 (2002): 110–37.

Kalu, O. "Ethiopianism in African Christianity." In *African Christianity: An African Story*, edited by Ogbu Kalu, 227–43. Pretoria: University of Pretoria, 2005.

Kalu, O. "Introduction: The Shape and Flow of African Church Historiography." In *African Christianity: An African Story*. Trenton: Africa World Press, 2007.

Karp, I. "African Systems of Thought." In *Africa*, edited by Phyllis Martin and Patrick O'Meara, 199–211. Bloomington: Indiana University Press, 1986.

Katz, J. G. "Dreams and their Interpretation in Sufi Thought and Practice." In *Dreams and Visions in Islamic Societies*, edited by Özgen Felek and Alexander D. Knysh, 181–97. Albany: SUNY Press, 2012.

Kealotswe, O. N. "Acceptance and Rejection: The Traditional-healer Prophet and His Integration of Healing Methods." *BOLESWA Journal of Theology, Religion and Philosophy (BJTRP)* I, no. 1 (2005): 109–22.

Kealotswe, O. N. "The Nature and Character of the African Independent Churches (AICs) in the 21st Century: Their Theological and Social Agenda." *Studia Historiae Eccleiasticae* 40, no. 2 (2014): 227–42.

Kgatle, M. S. "African Pentecostalism: The Christianity of Elias Letwaba From Early Years Until his Death in 1959." *Scriptura* 116 (2017): 1–9.

Khaldun, I. "The Muqaddimah (1377)," cited in Uthman ibn Muhammad ibn Fudi and Fathi Hasan al-Masri, *Bayan Wujub Al-hijra 'Ala 'L-'ibad*, 14. Khartoum: Khartoum University Press, 1978.

Khanam, F. "The Origin and Evolution of Sufism." *Al-Idah* 22, no. 1 (2011): 21–34.

Khathide, A. G. *Hamba Vangeli Elisha: A Portrait of Rev Job Y Chiliza–Pioneer of the African Gospel Church*. Kempton Park: Acad SA, 2010.

Kiernan, J., ed. *The Power of the Occult in Modern Africa: Continuity and Innovation in the Renewal of African Cosmologies. Modernity and Belonging*, Vol 4. Berlin: Münster Lit, 2006.

Kimbal, F. M. "The Pen and the Cannon: Shaykh Ahmadou Bamba's Non-violent Jihad." Available online: http://www.sacredweb.com/online_articles/SW24_kimball.pdf (accessed November 25, 2020).

Kirkegaard, A. "Music and Transcendence: Sufi Popular Performances in East Africa. The Finnish Society for the Study of Religion." *Temenos* 48, no. 1 (2012): 29–48.

Kister, D. "Dramatic Performance in Shamanism." In *Shamanism: An Encyclopedia of World Beliefs, Practices, and Culture*, edited by Mariko Namba Walter and Eva Jane Neumann Fridman, 82–9. California: ABC-CLIO, 2004.

Ki-Zerbo, J. *Methodology and African Prehistory*. London: James Currey, 1990.

Kleinhempel, U. R. "White Sangomas: The Manifestation of Bantu Forms of Shamanic Calling among Whites in South Africa." *REVER-Revista de Estudos da Religião* 18, no. 1 (2018): 143–73.

Knysh, A. "Th. Emil Homerin (ed. and trans.): Āʿishah al-Bāʿūniyyah, The Principles of Sufism [Book Review]." *Der Islam* 92, no. 1 (2015): 270–3.

Kohnert, D. "Magic and Witchcraft: Implications for Democratization and Poverty-Alleviating Aid in Africa." *World Development: The Multi-Disciplinary International*

Journal Devoted to the Study and Promotion of World Development 8, no. 24 (1996): 1347–55.

Kombo, K. "Witchcraft: A Living Vice in Africa." *African Journal of Evangelical Theology* 22, no. 1 (2013): 73–86.

Krippner, S. "Humanity's First Healers: Psychological and Psychiatric Stances on Shamans and Shamanism." *Archives of Clinical Psychiatry (São Paulo)* 34, (2007): 17–24.

Krippner, S. "Shamans as Healers, Counselors, and Psychotherapists." *International Journal of Transpersonal Studies* 31, no. 2 (2012): 72–9.

Kugle, S. *Sufis and Saints' Bodies: Mysticism, Corporeality, and Sacred Power in Islam.* Chapel Hill: University of North Carolina Press, 2011.

Lakatos, I. *Mathematics, Science and Epistemology. Philosophical Papers Vol 2*, edited by John Worrall and Gregory Currie, 247–53. Cambridge: Cambridge University Press, 1980.

Lambrecht, I. "A Psychological Study of Shamanic Trance States in South African Shamanism." Ph.D. diss., University of the Witwatersrand, Johannesburg (1998).

Lambrecht, I. "Shamans as Expert Voice Hearers." Available online: http://www.hearingvo ices.org.nz/attachments/article/14/Shamans%20as%20Expert%20Voice%20Hearers% 20By%20Ingo%20Lambrecht.pdf (accessed June 27, 2020).

Land, S. J. *Pentecostal Spirituality: A Passion for the Kingdom.* Sheffield: Sheffield Academy Press, 1993.

Lardinois, A., J. Blok and M. van der Poel. "Introduction." In *Sacred Words: Orality, Literacy and Religion*, edited by André Lardinois, Josine Blok and Marc van der Poel, 1–14. Leiden: Brill, 2011.

Last, M. "The Book in the Sokoto Caliphate." In *The Meanings of Timbuktu*, edited by S. Jeppie and S. B. Diagne, 135–63. Cape Town: Human Sciences Research Council Press, 2008.

Lawuyi, O. "No King as God: Toward the Understanding of Yoruba Slogan." *ODU: A Journal of West African Studies* 29, no. 2 (1986): 102–14.

Levtzion, N. and R. Pouwels, eds. *The History of Islam in Africa.* Athens: Ohio University Press, 2000.

Levtzion, N. "The Dynamics of Sufi Brotherhoods." In *The Public Sphere in Muslim Societies*, edited by Miriam Hoexter, Shmuel N. Eisenstadt and Nehemia Levtzion, 109–18. Albany: SUNY Press, 2002.

Lewis, B. *The Political Language of Islam.* Chicago: University of Chicago Press, 1988.

Lewis, F. D. *Rumi - Past and Present, East and West: The Life, Teachings, and Poetry of Jalâl Al-Din Rumi.* Bloomsbury: One World Publications, 2014.

Lewisohn, L. "Sufism and Ismāʿīlī Doctrine in the Persian Poetry of Nizārī Quhistānī (645–721/1247–1321)." *Iran* 41, no. 1 (2003): 229–51.

Lings, M. *What is Sufism?* Berkeley: University of California Press, 1975.

Lipner, J. *Hindus: Their Religious Beliefs and Practices.* New York: Routledge, 2012.

Ludwig, F. "African Independent Churches in West Africa around 1900." In *Transcontinental Links in the History of Non-Western Christianity*, edited by Klaus Korchorke, 264–72. Wiesbaden: Otto Harrassowitz Verlag, 2002.

Ludwig, F. and K. Koschorke. *Transcontinental Links in the History of Non-Western Christianity.* Wiesbaden: Otto Harrassowitz Verlag, 2002.

Lumbard, J. "Al-Insan Al-Kamil Doctrine and Practice." *Islamic Quarterly* 38, no. 4 (1994): 261.

Lumwe, S. "The Cosmology of Witchcraft in the African Context: Implications for Mission and Theology." *Journal of Adventist Mission Studies* 13, no. 1 (2017): 83–94.

Luton Muslims Journal. "Dua: In the Name of Allah with whose Name Nothing can Harm." https://lutonmuslimjournal.com/heart/laayadduru (accessed October 15, 2017).

MacArthur, J. *Reckless Faith: When the Church Loses Its Will to Discern*. Illinois: Crossway Books, 1994.

Macias, A. "How Hitler's Populist Rhetoric Contributed to his Rise to Power," Insider. Available online: https://www.businessinsider.com/why-hitler-was-such-a-successful-orator-2015-5?IR=T (accessed May 13, 2015).

Magesa, L. *African Religion: The Moral Traditions of Abundant Life*. Toronto: Orbis Books, 2014.

Makhubu, P. *Who Are the Independent Churches?* Johannesburg: Skotaville, 1988.

Manala, M. J. "Witchcraft and Its Impact on Black African Christians: A Lacuna in the Ministry of the Hervormde Kerk in Suidelike Afrika." *HTS Theological Studies* 60, no. 4 (2004): 1491–511.

Mann, T. W. *The Book of the Torah*. Oregon: Wipf and Stock Publishers, 2013.

Mark, W., M. Sani Umar, I. Rohmaniyah and M. Yahya. "Salafi Violence and Sufi Tolerance? Rethinking Conventional Wisdom." *Perspectives on Terrorism* 7, no. 6 (2013): 58–78.

Marovic, Z. and M. Machinga. "African Shamanic Knowledge and Transpersonal Psychology: Spirits and Healing in Dialogue." *The Journal of Transpersonal Psychology* 49, no. 1 (2017): 31–44.

Mashau, D. "Ministering Effectively in the Context of Pentecostalism in Africa: A Reformed Missional Reflection." *In Die Skiflig/in Luce Verbi* 47, no. 1 (2013): 1–8.

Maskarinec, G. G. "Healing and Shamanism." In *Shamanism: An Encyclopedia of World Beliefs, Practices, and Culture*, edited by Walter, M. N. and Fridman, E. J., 137–42. California: Library of Congress Cataloging-in-Publication Data, 2004. Available online: http://www.abc-clio.com.

Mayrargue, C. *The Paradoxes of Pentecostalism in South-Saharan Africa*. Paris: Institut Français des Relations Internationales. 2008.

Mbacke, B. A. "Tazawudu Shubaan, 'Viatique des jeunes.'" In *Recueil de Poemes en Sciences Religieuses de Cheikh A. Bamba* 1. Rabat: Dar El Kitab, 1988.

Mbacke, S. *The Mouride Order*. Washington, DC: : Berkley Center for Religion Peace and World Affairs, 2016.

Mbaya, H. and N. S. Cezula. "Contributions of John S. Mbiti to the Study of African Religions and African Theology and Philosophy." *STJ/Stellenbosch Theological Journal* 5, no. 3 (2019): 421–42.

Mbiti, J. *Introduction to African Religion*. London: Heinemann Educational Books, 1975.

Mbiti, J. *The Prayers of African Religion*. London: SPCK, 1975.

Mbiti, J. *African Religions and Philosophy*. Nairobi: East African Educational Publishers, 2002.

McLoughlin, S. and M. Khan. "Ambiguous Traditions and Modern Transformations of Islam: The Waxing and Waning of an 'Intoxicated' Sufi Cult in Mirpur." *Contemporary South Asia* 15, no. 3 (2006): 289–307.

Mcneill, J. T. "Magic and Infant Science." *The Journal of Religion* 15, no. 3 (1935): 342–4.

Melchert, C. "Origins and Early Sufism." In *The Cambridge*, edited by Lloyd Ridgeon, 3–23. New York: Cambridge University Press, 2015.

Meyer, B. "Christianity in Africa: From African Independent to Pentecostal-charismatic Churches." *Annual Review Anthropology* 33 (2004): 447–74.

Michon, J.-L. and R. Gaetani, eds. *Sufi Doctrine and Method in Sufism: Love and Wisdom*. Indiana: World Wisdom, 2006.

Miller, N. N. *Encounters with Witchcraft: Field Notes from Africa*. Albany: SUNY Press, 2012.

Mitchell, C. R. *African Primal Religions*. Niles: Argus Communications, 1977.

Mohamed, A. and M. Mohamed. "Ibn ʿAṭāʾ Allāh al-Sakandarī: A Sufi, ʿĀlim and Faqīh." *Comparative Islamic Studies* 9, no. 1 (2013): 41–66.

Mohammad, A. H. "Debating Sufism: The Tijaniyya and Its Opponents." Ph.D. diss., Bayreuth University, Graduate School of African Studies, Germany (2018).

Mojaddedi, J. A. *The Biographical Tradition in Sufism: The Onentsica Pentecostal-charismatic Ch.* London: Psychology Press, 2001.

Montgomery, J. E. "Shamanism and Voodoo in Togo: The Life and Acts of Sofo Bisi." *Shaman: Journal of the International Society for Shamanistic Research* 24, 1–2 (2016): 65–92.

Motyer, J. A. "Curse." In *New Bible Dictionary*, edited by I. Howard Marshall, A. R Millard, J. I. Parker and D. J. Wiseman, 248–9. Illinois: Intervarsity Press, 1996.

Mudimbe, V. Y. *The Invention of Africa: Gnosis, Philosophy and the Order of Knowledge*. Bloomington: Indiana University Press, 1988.

Na-Dama, G. "Urbanization in the Sokoto Caliphate: A Case Study of Gusau and Kaura-Namoda." In *Studies in the History of the Sokoto Caliphate: The Sokoto Semina Papers*, edited by Y. B. Usman, 140–64. Sokoto: History Bureau, 1979.

NASA, NTC 828/308, V3586, Mr. F. McBribe, Land Agent, to Native Commissioner, Graskop, November 27, 1933.

Ndemanu, M. T. "Traditional African Religions and Their Influences on the World Views of the Bangwa People of Cameroon: Expanding the Cultural Horizons of Study Abroad Students and Professionals." *The Interdisciplinary Journal of Study Abroad* 30, no. 1 (2018): 70–84.

Nel, M. "An Attempt to Define the Constitutive Elements of a Pentecostal Spirituality." *Die Skriflig* 49, no.1 (2015): 1–7.

Nemeroff, C. and P. Rozin. "The Makings of the Magical mind: The Nature and Function of Sympathetic Magical Thinking." In *Imagining the Impossible: Magical, Scientific, and Religious Thinking in Children*, edited by K. S. Rosengren, C. N. Johnson and P. L. Harris, 1–34. New York: Cambridge University Press, 2000.

Netton, I. R. *Ṣūfī Ritual: The Parallel Universe*. London: Psychology Press, 2000.

Niehaus, I., E. Mohlala, K. Shokane and F. Bernault. "Witchcraft, Power and Politics: Exploring the Occult in the South African Lowveld." *Journal of Modern African Studies* 41, no. 1 (2003): 155–6.

Niehaus, I. "Witchcraft and the South African Bantustans: Evidence from Bushbuckridge." *South African Historical Journal* 64, no. 1 (2012): 41–58.

Nizamie, S. H., M. Zia Ul Haq Katshu, and N. A. Uvais. "Sufism and Mental Health." *Indian Journal of Psychiatry* 55, no. 2 (2013): 215–23.

Njoku, F. *Essays in African Philosophy, Thought & Theology*. Owerri: Claretian Institute of Philosophy, 2002.

Njuema, Z. M. "Sokoto and her Provinces: Some Reflections on the Case of Adamawa." In *Studies in the History of Sokoto Caliphate: The Sokoto Seminar*, edited by Y. B. Usman, 320. Lagos: Third Press International, 1979.

Nmah, P. E. "The Rise of Independent African Churches, 1890–1930: An Ethical-genesis of Nigerian Nationalism." *African Research Review* 4, no. 4 (2010): 482–93.

Nūrbaẖš, Ǧ. *The Psychology of Sufism: (Del Wa Nafs); A Discussion of the Stages of Progress and Development of the Sufi's Psyche While on the Sufi Path*. London: Khaniqahi-Nimatullahi, 1992.

Nwala, T. U. "Summary Discourse on the Debate Concerning the Existence, Nature and Scope of African Philosophy (1970–90)." In *Critical Review of the Great Debate on African Philosophy 1970–1990*, edited by T. U. Nwala and D. Opata, 1–60. Enugu: Hillys Press, 1992.

Obasola, K. E. "A Cultural Perspective on Environmental Preservation." *Ogun Journal of Arts* 11 (2006): 101–10.

O'Brien, D. C. *The Mourides of Senegal: The Political and Economic Organization of an Islamic Brotherhood*. London: Oxford University Press, 1971.

Odesanya, S. A. O. and K. Akinjogbin. "Names as Message Vectors in Communication: Oduological Analysis of Traditional Yoruba Names from Ifa." *Journal of the Linguistic Association of Nigeria* 20, no. 1 (2017): 248–59.

Odularu, S. S. A. "Ifa Divination in Yorubaland 1851–1989: A Selected Bibliography." *A Current Bibliography on African Affairs* 22, no. 3 (1990): 237–45.

Ogunewu, M. and D. Adegboyin. "The Stories of Christianah Abiodun Akinsowon, Timothy Oluwole Obadare, Emmanuel Adeleke Adejobi, and Alexander Abiodun Bada: Successors to the Aladura Trailblazers of Nigeria." *Journal of African Christian Biography* 3, no. 3 (2018): 13–35.

Ogunleye, A. R. "Ifa: An Epistle to the Indigenous Yoruba Worshippers in Nigeria." *Journal of African Interdisciplinary Studies* 3, no. 1 (2019): 68–77.

Ogunnaike, O. "Sufism and Ifa: Ways of Knowing in Two West African Intellectual Traditions." Ph.D. diss., Harvard University, Graduate School of Arts and Sciences (2015).

Öhlmann, P. M. F. and W. Gräb. "African Initiated Churches' Potential as Development Actors." *HTS Teologiese Studies/Theological Studies*, 72 (2016): 1–12.

Okewande, O. T. "A Semiotic Investigation of Philosophical Relations between Ifa and Ayo Olopon Among the Yoruba People of Nigeria." *Nokoko Institute of African Studies* 6 (2017): 317–46.

Okonkwo, R. and M. Agbebi. "Apostle of the African Personality." *Presence Africaine* 114 (1980): 144–59.

Oladiti, A. A. and P. Oluwaseun Oyewale. "The Yoruba Concept of Ola in African Society: A Historical Overview." *World Scientific News* 80 (2017): 57–76.

Olupona, J. K. "The Study of Yoruba Religious Tradition in Historical Perspective." *Numen* 40, no. 3 (1993): 240–73.

Oluseye, A. "Language: Standardization and Literacy." In *Encyclopedia of Yoruba*, edited by Toyin Falola and Akintunde Akinyemi, 194–5. Bloomington: Indiana University Press, 2016.

Omari-Obayemi, M. S. "An Indigenous Anatomy of Power and Art: A New Look at Yoruba Women in Society and Religion." *Dialectical Anthropology* 21, no. 1 (1996): 89–98.

Omonzejele, P. F. "African Concepts of Health, Disease and Treatment: An Ethical Enquiry." *Explore* 4, no. 2 (2008): 120–6.

Oosthuizen, G. C., ed. *Religion Alive: Studies in the New Movements and Indigenous Churches in Southern Africa*. Johannesburg: Hodder and Stoughton, 1986.

Opasola, G. "Ifa as a Repository of Knowledge, Yoruba Epistemology from Afrocentric Point of View." Academia. Available online: , https://www.academia.edu/35393902/IFA_AS_A_REPOSITORY_OF_KNOWLEDGE (accessed November 17, 2020).

Oriloye, S. A. "Contents and Features of Yoruba Incantatory Poetry." *Journal of Communication and Culture* 1, no. 2 (2015): 32–44.

Oshitelu, G. A. *History of the Aladura (Independent) Churches 1918–1940: An Interpretation*. Ibadan: Hope Publications, 2007.

Overton, J. A. "Hypnosis and Shamanism." In *Shamanism: An Encyclopedia of World Beliefs, Practices, and Culture*, edited by M. N. Walter and E. J. Fridman, 149–52. California: Library of Congress Cataloging-in-Publication Data, 2004.

Oxford Dictionary. "Faith," Lexico. Available online: https://www.lexico.com/definition/faith (accessed on November 18, 2020).

Oyebola, D. D. O. "Traditional Medicine and its Practitioners Among the Yoruba of Nigeria: A Classification." *Social Science and Medicine. Part A: Medical Psychology & Medical Sociology* 14, no. 1 (1980): 23–9.

Ozioma, E.-O. J. and O. A. Nwamaka Chinwe. "Herbal Medicines in African Traditional Medicine." *Herbal Medicine* 10 (2019): 191–214.

Packer, M. J. and S. Tibaduiza Sierra. "A Concrete Psychological Investigation of Ifa Divination." *Revista Colombiana De Psicologia* 21, no. 2 (2012): 355–71.

Paine, T. "Common Sense" (Kindle edition), https://www.amazon.com/Common-Sense -Bestsellers-famous-Books-ebook/dp/B01M6WOBCS.

Parrinder, E. G. *African Traditional Religion*. London: SPCK, 1962.

Parrinder, E. G. *Religion in Africa*. Harmondsworth: Penguin Books, 1969.

Pauw, B. A. *Religion in a Tswana Kingdom*. Oxford: Oxford University Press, 1964.

Peek, P. M., ed. *African Divination Systems: Ways of Knowing*. Bloomington: Indiana University Press, 1991.

Peel, J. D. Y. "The Pastor and the 'Babalawo,' The Interaction of Religions in Nineteenth-Century Yorubaland." *African Journal of the International African Institute* 60, no. 3 (1980): 228–369.

Polat, M. "Tasawwuf-oriented Educational Philosophy and its Relevance to the Formation of Religion and Ethics Course Curriculum." *Universal Journal of Educational Research* 5, no. 5 (2017): 806–14.

Popper, R. K. *Objective Knowledge: An Evolutionary Approach*. Oxford: Clarendon Press, 1972.

Priest, R. "On the Meaning of the Words 'Witch,' 'Witchcraft,' and 'Sorcery.'" HCTU. Available online: https://henrycenter.tiu.edu/2012/05/meaning-of-witch-witchcraft-and-sorcery/ (accessed November 24, 2020).

Quick, A. H. *Aspects of Islamic Social Intellectual History in Hausaland,' Uthman Ibn Fudi, 1774–1804 CE*. Ph.D. diss., National Library of Canada= Bibliothèque nationale du Canada. Available online: http://www.collectionscanada.ca/obj/s4/f2/dsk3/ftp04/NQ 28150.pdf.

Razali, Q., W. Akmal, S. Radiman, Z. Fakhru-razi, M. Ahmad and A. L. Samian. "A Brief Review: Light Cosmology in Sufism and Modern Science Perspective." 10th International Symposium on Islam, Civilization & Science (ISICAS), 2019.

Renard, J. *Seven Doors to Islam: Spirituality and the Religious Life of Muslims*. Berkeley: University of California Press, 1944.

Riboli, D. "Trance, Shamanism." In *Shamanism: An Encyclopedia of World Beliefs, Practices, and Culture*, edited by M. N. Walter and E. J. Fridman, 250–5. California: Library of Congress Cataloging-in-Publication Data. Available online: http://www.abc-clio.com.

Rinne, E.-M. "Water and Healing – Experiences from the Traditional Healers in Ile-Ife, Nigeria." *Nordic Journal of African Studies* 10, no. 1 (2001): 41–65.

Robinson, D. "Beyond Resistance and Collaboration: Amadu Bamba and the Murids of Senegal." *Journal of Religion in Africa* 21, no. 2, (1991): 149–71.

Robinson, D. *Paths of Accommodation: Muslim Societies and French Colonial Authorities in Senegal and Mauritania, 1880–1920*. Western African Studies. Athens: Ohio University Press, 2000.

Rodney, W. *How Europe Underdeveloped Africa*. Dar-Es-Salaam: Tanzanian Publishing House, 1972.

Ross, E. "Touba: A Spiritual Metropolis in the Modern World." *Canadian Journal of African Studies/La Revue Canadienne des Études Africaines* 29, no. 2 (1995): 222–59.

Russell, D. "How a West African Shaman Helped my Schizophrenic Son in a Way Western Medicine Couldn't." *The Washington Post*. Available online: https://www.washingtonpost .com/posteverything/wp/2015/03/24/how-a-west-african-shaman-helped-my-schizophr enic-son-in-a-way-western-medicine-couldnt/ (accessed December 23, 2020).

Ryan, P. J. "The Phenomenon of Independent Religious Movements in Ghana." *Catholic Standard* 15, no. 21 (1992): 22–8.

Ryan, P. J. "The Mystical Theology of Tijānī Sufism and its Social Significance in West Africa." *Journal of Religion in Africa* 30, no. 2 (2000): 208–24.

Saidu, A. G. "The Significance of Shehu's Sermons and Poems in Ajami." In *Studies in the History of the Sokoto Caliphate: The Sokoto Seminar Papers*, edited by Y. B. Usman, 195–216. Zaria: Department of History, Ahmadu Bello University for the Sokoto State History Bureau, 1979.

Samuel, J. *The History of the Yoruba People*. Lagos: CMS Bookshop, 1921.

Sanneh, L. O. *Beyond Jihad: The Pacifist Tradition in West African Islam*. Oxford: Oxford University Press, 2016.

Saylor. "The Hausa Kingdoms." Available online: http://www.saylor.org/site/wp-content/ uploads/2012/10/HIST101-10.2.2-HausaKingdom-FINAL1.pdf (accessed November 27, 2020).

Schiller, A. "Offerings and Sacrifice in Shamanism." In *Shamanism: An Encyclopedia of World Beliefs, Practices, and Culture*, edited by M. N. Walter and E. J. Fridman, 197–200. California: Library of Congress Cataloging-in-Publication Data, Available online: http://www.abc-clio.com.

Schimmel, A. *Mystical Dimensions of Islam*. Chapel Hill: University of North Carolina Press, 1975.

Seesemann, R. "Sufism in West Africa." *Religion Compass* 4, no. 10 (2010): 606–14.

Setiloane, G. M. *The Image of God among the Sotho-Tswana*. Rotterdam: Balkema, 1976.

Shagari, S. U. A. and J. Boyd. *Uthman dan Fodio: The Theory and Practice of His Leadership*. Lagos: Islamic Publications Bureau, 1978.

Shah, I. *Learning how to Learn: Psychology and Spirituality in the Sufi Way*. London: Octagon Press Ltd., 1978.

Shah, I. *The Way of the Sufi*. London: Octagon Press Ltd., 2004.

Shah-Kazemi, R. "The Notion and Significance of Ma 'Rifa in Sufism." *Journal of Islamic Studies* 13, no. 2 (2002): 155–81.

Shahi, D. "Introducing Sufism to International Relations Theory: A Preliminary Inquiry into Epistemological, Ontological, and Methodological Pathways." *European Journal of International Relations* 25, no. 1 (2019): 250–75.

Shahi, D. "The Entry of Sufism into Global International Relations: A Move Beyond the State of the Art." In *Sufism: A Theoretical Intervention in Global International Relations*, edited by Deepshika Shahi, 1–14. London: Rowman & Littlefield Publishers, 2020.

Shohat, E. and R. Stam. *Unthinking Eurocentrism: Multiculturalism and the Media*. London: Routledge, 2013.

Sibusiso, M. "The History of African Indigenous Churches in Scholarship." *Journal for the Study of Religion* 18, no. 2 (2005): 89–103.

Singh, M. "The Cultural Evolution of Shamanism." *Behavioral and Brain Sciences* 41, no. 66 (2018): 1–17.

Sirriyeh, E. *Sufis and Anti-Sufis: The Defence, Rethinking and Rejection of Sufism in the Modern World*. London: Routledge, 2014.

Smith, E. W. *Knowing the African*. Cambridge: United Society for Christian Literature, 1946.

Smith, A. "The Contemporary Significance of the Academic Ideals of the Sokoto Jihad." In *Studies in the History of Sokoto Caliphate: The Sokoto Seminar Papers*, edited by Y. B. Usman, 245–6. Lagos: Third Press International, 1979.

Smith, M. *Studies in Early Mysticism in the Near and Middle East*. Bloomsbury: One World Publications, 1995.

Smith, Jr. and L. James. "Sufism: Islamic Mysticism." *Verbum* 3, no. 1 (2005).

Smith, J. K. A. *Thinking in Tongues: Pentecostal Contributions to Christian Philosophy*, Vol. 1. Michigan: William B Eerdmans Publishing Company, 2010.

Soares, B. F., M. Bruinessen and J. D. Howell. "Saint and Sufi in Contemporary Mali." In *Sufism and the 'Modern' in Islam*, edited by Martin van Bruinessen and Julia Day Howell, 76–91. London: IB Tauris, 2007.

Sobiecki, J. "A Review of Plants Used in Divination in Southern Africa and Their Psychoactive Effects." *Southern African Humanities* 20, no. 2 (2008): 333–51.

Solagberu, A.-R. "The Impact of Sufism on the Culture of the People of Ilorin, Nigeria." *Journal of Muslim Minority Affairs* 32, no. 3 (2012): 400–10.

Sorgenfrei, S. "Hidden or Forbidden, Elected or Rejected: Sufism as 'Islamic Esotericism.'" *Islam and Christian–Muslim Relations* 29, no. 2 (2018): 145–65.

Strassberg, B. A. "Magic, Religion, Science, Technology, and Ethics in the Postmodern World." *Zygon* 40, no. 2 (2005): 307–22.

Sulaiman, I. *A Revolution in History: The Jihad of Usman Dan Fodio*. London: Mansell, 1986.

Sundkler, B. G. M. *Bantu Prophets in South Africa*. Oxford: Oxford University Press, 1961.

Taji-Farouki, S. *Beshara and Ibn'Arabi: A Movement of Sufi Spirituality in the Modern World*. Oxford: Anqa Publishing, 2007.

Talbot, L. T. "Thousand Year's Reign of Christ over the Earth: The Characteristics of that Reign." *Biola Radio Publications* 9 (2017): 3-13.

Tan, C. *Islamic Education and Indoctrination: The Case in Indonesia*. London: Routledge, 2012.

Thompson, E. E. "Primitive African Medical Lore and Witchcraft." *Bulletin of the Medical Library Association* 53, no. 1 (1965): 80–94.

Thornton, R. "The Transmission of Knowledge in South African Traditional Healing." *Africa: Journal of the International African Institute* 79, no. 1 (2009): 17–34.

Topp Fargion, J., F. Le Guennec-Coppens and S. Mery. "The Music of Zenj: Arab-African Crossovers in the Music of Zanzibar." *Journal des Africanistes* 72, no. 2 (2002): 203–12.

Tousi, M. "Education in Islam: Contemporary Issues and Challenges." *Journal of Educational and Social Research* 2, no. 4 (2012): 49.

Towghi, M. M. "Foundations of Muslim Images and Treatment of the World Beyond Islam (Vols. I-IV)." Ph.D. diss., Michigan State University (1991).

Trimingham, J. S. *The Sufi Orders in Islam*. Oxford: Oxford University Press, 1998.

Turner, H. *Modern African Religious Movements: An Introduction for the Christian Churches*. Nsukka: University of Nigeria, 1965.

Turner, H. *History of an African Independent Church: The Church of the Lord (Aladura)*. Nsukka: Oxford: Oxford University Press, 1967.

Tutuola, A. *The Wild Hunter in the Bush of Ghosts*. Washington, DC: Three Continents Press, 1948.

Uduagwu, C. "Understanding the Difference between African Magic and African Science: A Conversation with Christian Emedolu." *Filosofia Theoretica: Journal of African Philosophy, Culture and Religions* 5, no. 2 (2016): 74–8.

Ul-Haq, S. and F. R. Khan. "A Sufi View of Transformation and Its Organizational Implications." In *Handbook of Personal Organizational Transformation*, edited by J. Neal, 833–65. Cham: Springer International Publishing.

UNESCO. "Ifa Divination System." UNESCO. Available online: https://ich.unesco.org/en/RL/ifa-divination-system-00146. Accessed November 9, 2020.

Uniyyah, A. al-Ba. *The Principles of Sufism*. Library of Arabic Literature 23. New York: New York University Press, 2014.

Usman, A. S. S. and J. Boyd. *Uthman Dan Fodio: The Theory and Practice of Leadership*. Lagos: Islamic Publication Bureau, 1978.

Usman, Y. B. *The Transformation of Katsina*. Zaria: ABU Press, 1981.

Van Der Meer, T. "Spiritual Journeys: A Study of Ifa/Orisa Practitioners in the United States Initiated by Nigeria." Ph.D. Thesis, Antioch University (2017).

Van Hoven, ED. "The Nation Turbaned? The Construction of Nationalist Muslim Identities in Senegal." *Journal of Religion in Africa* 30, no. 2 (2000): 225–48.

Verger, P. *The Yoruba High God: A Review of the Sources*. Ibadan: Institute of African Studies, University of Ibadan, 1964.

Vikør, K. S. *Sufi and Scholar on the Desert Edge: Muḥammad B. 'Alī Al-Sanūsī and His Brotherhood*. Evanston: Northwestern University Press, 1995.

Vikør, K. S. "Sufi Brotherhoods in Africa." *The History of Islam in Africa*, edited by Nehemia Levtzion and Randall L. Pouwels, 441–76. Oxford: James Currey, 2000.

Vilakazi, A. et al. *Shembe: The Revitalization of African Society*. Johannesburg: Skotaville Publishers, 1986.

Vuckovic, N. H., C. M. Gullion, L. A. Williams, M. Ramirez and J. Schneider. "Feasibility and Short-term Outcomes of a Shamanic Treatment for Temporomandibular Joint Disorders." *Alternative Therapies* 13, no. 6 (2007): 18–29.

Walker, M. "Music in Shamanism and Other Healing Traditions of Siberia." *Arctic Anthropology* 40, no. 2 (2003): 40–8.

Wallace, D. "Rethinking Religion, Magic and Witchcraft in South Africa: From Colonial Coherence to Postcolonial Conundrum." *Journal for the Study of Religion* 28, no. 1 (2015): 3–4.

Walls, A. F. "The Legacy of Samuel Ajayi Crowther." *International Bulletin of Missionary Research* 16, no. 1 (1992): 15–21.

Walter, M. N. and E. N. Fridman, eds., *Shamanism: An Encyclopedia of World Beliefs, Practices, and Culture*. Oxford: ABC CLIO, 2004.

Ware, F. L. "An Interim Assessment of the Pentecostal Manifesto Series." *The Journal of Religion* 94, no. 1 (2014): 97–107.

Wariboko, N. "West African Pentecostalism: A Survey of Everyday Theology." In *Global Renewal Christianity: Spirit-Empowered Movements, Past, Present and Future*, edited by Vinson Synan, Amos Yong, and Kwabena Asamoah-Gyadu, 1–18. Florida: Charisma House Publishers, 2016.

Welbourn, F. B. and B. A. Ogot. *A Place to Feel at Home: A Study of Two Independent Churches in Western Kenya*. London: Oxford University Press, 1966.

Werbner, P. "Powerful Knowledge in a Global Sufi Cult: Reflections on the Poetics of Travelling Theories." In *The Pursuit of Certainty: Religious and Cultural Formulations*, edited by Wendy James, 134–160. London and New York: Routledge, 1995.

West, M. E. *Bishops and Prophets in a Black City: African Independent Churches in Soweto, Johannesburg. Journal of Religion in Africa.* London: R. Collins, 1975.

Wiener, M. J. "Magic Worlds Through Religion, Science and Magic." *Anthropological News* 45, no. 8 (2004): 10–11.

Wilson, M. "Witch-beliefs and Social Structure." *American Journal of Sociology* 56 (1951): 307–13.

Winkelman, M. "Divination." In *Shamanism: An Encyclopedia of World Beliefs, Practices, and Culture,* edited by M. N. Walter and E. J. Fridman, 78–82. California: Library of Congress Cataloging-in-Publication Data. Available online: http://www.abc-clio.com.

Wiredu, K. "Conceptual Decolonization as an Imperative in Contemporary African Philosophy: Some Personal Reflections." *Rue Descartes* 2, no. 36 (2002): 53–64.

Witzel, M. "Shamanism in Northern and Southern Eurasia: Their Distinct Methods of Change of Consciousness." *Social Science Information* 50, no. 1 (2011): 39–61.

Woodward, M., M. Sani Umar, I. Rohmaniyah, and M. Yahya. "Salafi Violence and Sufi Tolerance? Rethinking Conventional Wisdom." *Perspectives on Terrorism* 7, no. 6 (2013): 58–78.

World Health Organization, "The World Health Report 2001: Mental Health: New Understanding, New Hope." WHO. Available online: https://apps.who.int/iris/handle/10665/42390 (accessed September 30, 2020).

Yakasai, H. M. "Incantation in Hausa Culture: An Example of Syntactic Reduplication." *Studies of the Department of African Languages and Cultures* 44 (2010): 67–82.

Yang, M. "Shamanism and Spirit Possession in Chinese Modernity: Some Preliminary Reflections on a Gendered Religiosity of the Body." *Review of Religion and Chinese Society* 2, no.1 (2015): 51–86.

Yıldız, S. N. "A Hanafi Law Manual in The Vernacular: Devletoğlu Yūsuf Balıreliminary Reflections on a Gendered Religiosity of the Bodydological Pathways the Aladura Trailblazers (824/1424)." *Bulletin of the School of Oriental and African Studies* 80, no. 2 (2017): 283–304.

Zalanga, S. "Pentecostalism as an Alternative Social Order in Africa." In *Pentecostalism and politics in Africa,* edited by Adeshina Afolayan, Olajumoke Yacob-Haliso and Toyin Falola, 277–302. Switzerland: Springer International Publishing, 2018.

Zalta, E., ed. *The Stanford Encyclopedia of Philosophy.* Stanford: The Metaphysics Research Lab, Center for the Study of Language and Information, Stanford University, 2007.

Zarasi, M. "Interpretation of the Quran: A Comparative Study of the Methodologies of Abdolkarim Soroush and Mohammad Mojtahed Shabestari." Ph.D. diss., International Islamic University, Malaysia (2018).

Zuesse, E. M. "Divination and Deity in African Religions." *History of Religions* 15, no. 2 (1975): 158–82.

Zuma, T., D. Wight, T. Rochat and M. Moshabela. "The Role of Traditional Health Practitioners in Rural KwaZulu-Natal, South Africa: Generic or Mode Specific?" *BMC Complementary and Alternative Medicine* 16, no. 1 (2016): 304.

Index

www.ingramcontent.com/pod-product-compliance
Lightning Source LLC
Chambersburg PA
CBHW060152280326
41932CB00012B/1733